D0309299

Aphasia in
Atypical Populations

Aphasia in Atypical Populations

Edited by

Patrick Coppens
Moorhead State University
Moorhead, Minnesota

Yvan Lebrun
Vrije Universiteit Brussel
Brussels, Belgium

Anna Basso
Institute of Clinical Neurology,
Milan University
Milan, Italy

LEA LAWRENCE ERLBAUM ASSOCIATES, PUBLISHERS
1998   Mahwah, New Jersey   London

Lawrence Erlbaum Associates, Inc., Publishers
10 Industrial Avenue
Mahwah, New Jersey 07430

Cover design by Kathryn Houghtaling Lacey

Library of Congress Cataloging-in-Publication Data

Aphasia in atypical populations / edited by Patrick Coppens, Yvan
    Lebrun, Anna Basso.
        p.   cm.
    Includes bibliographical references and index.
    ISBN 0-8058-1738-7 (alk. paper).
        1. Aphasia.   2. Brain—Localization of functions.   3. Laterality.
    I. Coppens, Patrick.   II. Lebrun, Yvan.   III. Basso, Anna.
    RC425.A637   1998
    616.85′52—dc21   97-41461
                                                                       CIP

Books published by Lawrence Erlbaum Associates are printed on acid-free paper,
and their bindings are chosen for strength and durability.

Printed in the United States of America
10 9 8 7 6 5 4 3 2 1

Contributors

ANNA BASSO, Institute of Clinical Neurology, Milan University, Milan, Italy

PATRICK COPPENS, Speech-Language-Hearing Sciences, Moorhead State University, Moorhead, Minnesota

DAVID CORINA, Department of Psychology, University of Washington, Seattle, Washington

JACK GANDOUR, Department of Audiology and Speech Sciences, Purdue University, West Lafayette, Indiana

SUZANNE HUNGERFORD, Speech-Language-Hearing Sciences, Moorhead State University, Moorhead, Minnesota

YVAN LEBRUN, Department of Neurolinguistics, Vrije Universiteit Brussel, Brussels, Belgium

ANDRÉ ROCH LECOURS, Centre de Recherche du Centre Hospitalier Côte des Neiges, Montréal, Québec, Canada

PHILIPPE F. PAQUIER, Deparment of Neurology, Hospital Universitaire Erasme, Free University of Brussels, and Division of Applied Neurolinguistics, School of Medicine, University of Antwerp, Antwerp, Belgium

MICHEL PARADIS, Department of Linguistics, McGill University, Montréal, Québec, Canada

MARIA ALICE DE MATTOS PIMENTA PARENTE, Universidade de São Paolo, São Paolo, Brazil

MARIA LUISA RUSCONI, Department of General Psychology, Padua University, Padua, Italy

HUGO R. VAN DONGEN, Department of Pediatric Neurology, University Hospital Rotterdam, Sophia Children's Hospital, Rotterdam, The Netherlands

ATSUSHI YAMADORI, Section of Neuropsychology, Division of Disability Science, Tohoku University Graduate School of Medicine, Sendai, Japan

Contents

Preface

The genesis of this project was the realization that the correlation between symptoms and anatomy in aphasiology has been derived from a very limited sample of the world population. Or as Lecours (1980) put it, "the anatomo-clinical correlation includes . . . adults or adolescents, right-handed, monolinguals, speaking a nontonal and alphabetic or syllabic language. . . . In relative numbers, this represents a little more than a quarter of the world population" (p. 604, our translation).

The corollary to this statement is that specific patient populations (e.g., children, left-handers, bilinguals, tonal or ideographic language users, etc.) have been excluded because they were considered "atypical." This atypicality likely refers to the perception that language lateralization and/or localization in these patient populations somehow must be different than in the "typical" aphasic subjects. For example, ideographic languages are intuitively more visual than alphabetic languages and hence must involve the right hemisphere. The purpose of this review is to establish the validity of these conclusions.

The impetus for this volume and its timeliness were reinforced by recent statements recognizing the need to broaden our definition of aphasia to include some of these different populations. In his recent book, Goodglass (1993) stated that the cases of aphasia in polyglots "pose a major conundrum that should be addressed in any model of language representation in the brain" (p. 11). Regarding aphasia in American Sign Language users, Goodglass further remarked that "whatever is lateralized in language dominance, it must be defined in terms broad enough to encompass at least these two modes of communication" (p. 12). This is precisely the aim of this endeavor.

The specific purpose of each chapter in this volume is to review the literature pertinent to each population and to try to deduce whether (and potentially how) these "atypical" populations are indeed different from something defined as the "typical" aphasic population as it regards language organization. The ultimate goal of this volume is then to understand better whether the language representation model used in aphasiology can be extended to these "atypical" populations, or conversely, whether significant differences merit the development of a new model.

In chapter 1, Basso and Rusconi tackle the thorny issue of language lateralization in left-handed individuals. The authors argue that the perceived differences between right- and left-handed aphasic patients regarding incidence of aphasia, aphasia type, and recovery rates have been overestimated. They maintain that left-handed aphasics with left-hemisphere lesions have a very similar clinical symptomatology to that of right-handed aphasics. They present data on an original comparison between left-handed aphasic patients with a right-hemisphere lesion and right-handed aphasics with a comparable left-hemisphere lesion. They conclude that the symptomatology is remarkably similar. Finally, they acknowledge that comparing left-handed aphasics to "typical" aphasics is rendered difficult by our lack of detailed understanding of that "typicality."

In chapter 2, Paradis first reminds us that bilingualism is the rule rather than the exception in the world population and thus that bilingual aphasia is hardly "atypical" in terms of sheer numbers. Based on an impressive body of literature and a critical review of past and current theories and hypotheses, Paradis posits that language is lateralized and organized similarly in bilingual aphasics and in monolingual speakers. However, the author does not champion the view of an inactive right hemisphere in bilingual speakers, but rather maintains that the abilities located in the right hemisphere, known to contribute to specific aspects of language generation, are similar to what can be expected in monolingual speakers. In other words, Paradis suggests that the cerebral organization underlying communication abilities is specific to language in general rather than to one language in particular.

In chapter 3, Paquier and van Dongen review the available literature on acquired aphasia in children. They provide us with an excellent historical perspective of that population by focusing on how the issues, theories, and definitions were modified over time. Recently, more stringent control over etiology, more refined measurements, and more precise lesion localization through modern imaging techniques have brought about a revision in the previously supported theories. The authors argue compellingly that acquired aphasia in children is similar to that in adults in terms of frequency, prognosis, symptomatology, and clinical–anatomical correlations.

In chapter 4, Gandour focuses on tone language speakers. The reader will perhaps find it surprising that there are more tone than nontone languages in the world. Again, as was the case for bilingualism, the perceived "atypical" character of this population is definitely not confirmed by the numbers. Gandour critically analyzes the competing hypotheses about lateralization of linguistic and nonlinguistic prosodic features in tone and nontone language speakers. His in-depth review of the literature prompts Gandour to conclude that language lateralization is the same in tone language users as in nontone language users, and that linguistic and affective prosody lateralization is also comparable in the two populations.

In chapter 5, Yamadori introduces the reader to the subtleties of one ideographic language, namely, Japanese. The author describes in detail the rhythmic nature of the Japanese language and the differences between Kana, Kanji, and alphabetic languages. Yamadori uses case studies of aphasic patients to further illustrate how these specific features of the Japanese language impact on the aphasic symptomatology. The author argues that the available literature clearly shows the same language lateralization, localization, and symptomatology in Japanese aphasic patients as in aphasic patients speaking an alphabetically based language. However, Yamadori maintains that although the brain structures responsible for language processing are the same, the fashion in which the information is processed depends on the characteristics of the specific language in use.

In chapter 6, Coppens, Parente, and Lecours examine the influence of literacy on language and cognition. The authors first argue that a true comparison between literate and illiterate subjects is extremely difficult to obtain because of the presence of confounding factors, such as socioeconomic status, cultural differences, or schooling. Their broad review of the literature indeed reveals significant differences between literate and illiterate normal subjects, but these discrepancies (e.g., naming, visuospatial skills) are attributable to the influence of schooling on cognitive processing rather than to literacy differences between the populations. Hence, the group differences between literate and illiterate aphasics mostly reflect the discrepancy found in nonaphasic subjects. Metaphonological skills are the only variable clearly linked with literacy training specifically. However, one interesting difference involves a greater participation of the right hemisphere of illiterate aphasics in naming tasks. Several hypotheses are presented to explain this phenomenon. The authors conclude that language representation and localization in illiterate aphasics is the same as in literate subjects, and that the few discrepancies observed reflect a language processing variant.

In chapter 7, Coppens and Hungerford present an extensive review of the crossed aphasia cases reported in the literature. They first argue for the need to broaden the definition of crossed aphasia. The strict exclusion criteria applied in recent studies did not seem to yield a better understanding of this language lateralization variant. From their review, Coppens and Hungerford conclude that crossed aphasia does not appear to resolve more quickly than "typical" aphasia following a left-hemisphere lesion in right-handed patients. Furthermore, they maintain that the majority of crossed aphasia patients have their language strongly lateralized to the right hemisphere and organized similarly to "typical" aphasic patients. Still, there is a significant number of exceptions to this rule, which may be manifested by various unexpected symptoms. However, these exceptions also occur in "typical" aphasia to an extent that is yet unknown; thus, comparisons between the two populations must be drawn very cautiously. This observation suggests, however, that the possible differences between crossed aphasia and "typical" aphasia would be quantitative rather than qualitative.

In chapter 8, Corina discusses aphasia in users of sign language. He offers an excellent description of the linguistic aspects of sign language and how they compare to oral languages, and then offers a neurolinguistic analysis of the symptoms observed in sign language aphasia. Corina argues that lateralization of verbal and nonverbal skills is the same for sign language users as for oral language speakers. Similarly, both populations also share the anterior/posterior dichotomy in language organization in the left hemisphere. However, some subtle differences recently uncovered between the two populations seem to point to slight differences in language organization. For example, the right hemisphere may be more active in sign language users during language tasks, but it is unclear whether this difference is due to linguistic or visuospatial processing factors. More research is needed before definite conclusions can be confidently drawn.

In a short concluding chapter, we (the editors) identify common threads between chapters, reconcile some positions, and compare various hypotheses and conclusions, all in an attempt to create a more homogeneous picture combining all these "atypical" populations. First, most authors are in agreement that their "atypical" population is instead highly "typical"; thus, these conclusions reinforce each other. Therefore, we implicitly tend to agree with Goodglass that a coherent model must and could include these "atypical" populations instead of systematically ignoring them. Second, some or all of the minor differences between the populations identified by some authors in this volume could potentially be related. This possible common explanatory mechanism can only come to light by comparing the various authors' conjectures, hypotheses, and conclusions. It is the hope of the editors that these theoretical reflections will trigger some reactions and in turn spur needed research.

Patrick Coppens
Yvan Lebrun
Anna Basso

REFERENCES

Goodglass, H. (1993). *Understanding aphasia*. Orlando, FL: Academic Press.

Lecours, A. R. (1980). Corrélations anatomo-cliniques de l'aphasie. La zone du langage. *Revue Neurologique, 136,* 591–608.

CHAPTER ONE

Aphasia in Left-Handers

Anna Basso
Institute of Clinical Neurology, Milan University

Maria Luisa Rusconi
Department of General Psychology, Padua University

For many years, the belief has dominated that the association between hemisphere dominance for language and for handedness is not random and that these two dominance factors are two aspects of the same function, with structural asymmetries being sought (and found!) to explain functional asymmetries. For approximately 80 years, from Broca (1865) to Brain (1945), the view that "the cerebral hemisphere in which are situated the neural pathways of speech is the left hemisphere in right-handed persons, and conversely" (Brain, 1945, p. 839) has been well entrenched. However, it rapidly became apparent that the simple rule of right-handedness = left-hemisphere language dominance, left-handedness = right-hemisphere language dominance, did not hold true because many left-handers developed aphasia after left-hemisphere lesions, as did some right-handers after right-hemisphere lesions. When a patient did not conform to the rule, various explanations were offered that did not put the rule itself into question. For right-handers who had become aphasics after a right-hemisphere lesion, it was either supposed that they were natural left-handers who had been obliged to use their right hand or that they came from left-handed stock (see chapter 7, Crossed Aphasia, this volume). For left-handed (LH) aphasics with left-hemisphere damage, left-hemisphere dominance for language was considered due to right-hand training for writing, which conferred dominance for language to the left hemisphere. Incidentally, hand training was also suggested as a rehabilitation technique: If an aphasic acquired skilled movements with the hand ipsilateral to the lesion, this was supposed to help the relocation of language to the opposite side of the brain (Buzzard, 1882, cited in Goodglass & Quadfasel, 1954).

Only during the second half of the 20th century was this principle challenged. Meanwhile, classification of handedness has proven to be more
complicated than initially thought. The original system of classification into
two types of handedness (right or left) quickly gave way to a threefold
classification, right, left, and mixed, but it was soon recognized that hand
dominance is not a discrete but a continuous variable.

It is also difficult to define the precise age at which a child becomes
fixedly right-handed (RH) or LH, and different researchers have divergent
opinions. The first evidence of the preferential use of one hand occurs at
approximately 7 months of age according to Quadfasel (1955; quoted by
Subirana, 1969) or as late as the fifth year according to Gloning, Gloning,
and Hoff (1954). According to Subirana (1969), hand preference will be
stronger the more precociously it appears. Gesell and Ames (1947) observed
that it was possible to predict the future left-handedness on the basis of a
stronger tonic neck reflex on the left side. Throughout the chapter we use
the terms *left-handed* (LH) and *left-handers* to refer to all non-right-handers,
that is, both left-handers and ambidextrous.

In this chapter we describe Annett's and Geschwind and Galaburda's
models of left-handedness and review literature on left-handers and aphasia,
apraxia, and visuospatial abilities; we then report the results of an experimental study on LH aphasic patients with right-hemisphere lesions.

ANNETT'S MODEL

In 1964, Annett argued that some of the problems concerning the relationships between hand and cerebral dominance for language were caused by
inadequate classification of handedness. Failure to isolate mixed handers
from consistent left- and right-handers could explain the anomalous behavior
of a certain number of LH patients. She therefore proposed a classic Men-
delian model of the inheritance of handedness and cerebral dominance.
Handedness was assumed to be determined by two alleles (R for right-handedness and L for left-handedness): R is usually dominant and L usually
recessive. RR (dominant homozygotes) are right-handers with speech lateralized to the left hemisphere and LL (recessive homozygotes) are left-handers
with right-hemisphere speech. RL (heterozygotes) may use either hand and
develop speech in either hemisphere. In these mixed handers, hemispheric
language dominance is independent of hemisphere hand dominance, and
this can explain why mixed-handers respond in a more random way than
left- and right-handers to cerebral damage.

In 1967, Annett tested this model in seven samples of normal subjects.
The numbers of right-, left-, and mixed-handers found in these samples
agreed closely with those expected by her monofactorial model of the genetic
basis of handedness. The random combination of right and left tendencies

predicted by the model and confirmed in these samples, however, did not hold true when more than one generation was considered.

According to Annett's latest model (1985), handedness is determined by three main factors:

1. In humans (and in animals) differences between efficiency and skill of the two hands are approximately normally distributed, with the majority of people having equal efficiency in both sides: 25% of right-handers, 50% of mixed-handers, and 25% of left-handers.

2. The normal distribution is shifted to the right in humans by a "human right shift factor" or gene, probably linked with the human capacity for speech, which depends (in most people) on the left hemisphere. The consequent proportions of left-, mixed-, and right-handedness in humans are 4, 30, and 66.

3. The third factor is social pressure, which generally induces dextral writing in people with equal skill in both hands.

Annett did not posit a necessary connection between handedness and language dominance. When the left-hemisphere factor is absent, language dominance and handedness arise by chance, independently of each other. Therefore, no more than 50% of left-handers will have right-hemispheric dominance for language.

To support the concept that laterality can be randomly determined, Annett cited the well-documented case of hereditary situs inversus in mice (Layton, 1976). Parents, homozygous for the disorder, give birth both to offspring with situs inversus (with heart, e.g., located to the right of the midline rather than to the left) and to apparently normal offspring, which, however, will in turn generate as many abnormal offspring as their normal litter-mates.

GESCHWIND AND GALABURDA'S MODEL

In a special article on cerebral lateralization, Geschwind and Galaburda (1985) recapitulated their hypotheses about the biological mechanisms of lateralization. The most important consideration is that cerebral dominance is generally based on structural asymmetries. The relevant anatomical findings are:

1. The sylvian fissures are asymmetric at the posterior end (Cunningham, 1892; Eberstaller, 1884). The pattern of asymmetry varies with handedness: A higher right sylvian fissure is more frequent in right-handers than in left-handers (Hochberg & Le May, 1975).

2. Asymmetry of the planum temporale, located on the upper surface of the temporal lobe and posterior to the anterior transverse gyrus of Heschl. This

was originally shown by Pfeiffer (1936) and confirmed later by other observations (Geschwind & Levitsky, 1968). Several postmortem studies have
demonstrated that the planum temporale (particularly, the temporo-parietal
cytoarchitectonic area) in the left hemisphere was larger than that in the
right (Galaburda, Le May, Kemper, & Geschwind, 1978). The asymmetry of
the planum temporale is already present at birth; in fact, it appears in the human
fetus at about the 30th week of gestation (Chi, Dooling, & Gilles, 1977).

More recently, Steinmetz, Volkman, Jancke, and Freund (1991) showed,
with magnetic resonance in vivo, the anatomical asymmetry of language-related temporal cortex in left-handers. Familial sinistrality has been shown
to influence the anatomical pattern and to produce a shift of language
representation to the right hemisphere in left-handers.

3. The left frontal opercular region (which makes up part of Broca's area)
is more infolded (therefore, wider) than the right (Falzi, Perrone, & Vignolo,
1982).

4. Certain subcortical regions, in the posterior thalamus (in particular, the
lateralis posterior nucleus), are larger on the left (Eidelberg & Galaburda, 1982).

5. Left-handers and subjects with right-hemisphere speech have a larger
corpus callosum (O'Kusky et al., 1988; Witelson, 1989).

6. Computed tomography (CT) scan studies showed the left occipital-pa-
rietal region to be typically wider than the right (Le May & Kido, 1978). In
about 70% of right-handers, both aphasics and controls, the left occipital
length and width are increased while in left-handed controls this finding is
confirmed by some studies (Chui & Damasio, 1980; Koff, Naeser, Pieniadz,
Foundas, & Levine, 1986) but not by others (Le May, 1977).

In a retrospective study of LH chronic aphasics with left or right lesions,
Naeser and Borod (1986) found a left occipital asymmetry (increased left
occipital length compared to right occipital length) in 59% of their subjects
and confirmed the observation that the left occipital asymmetry is the most
common CT asymmetry in both left- and right-handers. This, however, does
not appear to be useful in predicting handedness or which hemisphere, if
damaged, will produce aphasia.

Geschwind and Galaburda, as did Annett, postulated an innate bias toward left-hemisphere dominance for both language and handedness in humans. However, many nongenetic factors can alter the pattern of lateralization. Among these factors the most powerful are variations in the chemical
environment, and the authors suggested a relationship between non-right-
handedness, immune disorders, and developmental learning disabilities.

The right hemisphere develops earlier than the left and is therefore less
subject to disrupting influences than the left hemisphere. If the left-hemisphere growth is delayed by changing levels of sex hormones, growth of
cortical regions on the opposite side should be favored. The normal asym-

metries in these regions will be diminished, giving rise to a group of people with symmetric brains. Dominance for language and handedness in this group is random, as suggested by Annett.

Both Annett and Geschwind and Galaburda stressed the importance of random dominance, but its supposed cause differs in the two models. According to Annett, in subjects without the right-shift gene, lateralization of language and handedness is determined by accidental factors such as, for instance, social pressure. By contrast, Geschwind and Galaburda postulated a left-hemisphere dominance for speech and handedness; various factors, with testosterone playing a central role, diminish the left-hemisphere dominance and create random dominance. According to these authors, handedness develops earlier and over a shorter period of time than language; there are then less chances of a shift of handedness from left-hemisphere to right-hemisphere dominance, and random dominance should be more frequent for language.

Partial support for Geschwind and Galaburda's theory comes from a study by Crawford, Kaplan, and Kinsbourne (1994). They used questionnaire data to examine immune disorders and left-handedness in families with learning-disabled children and in control families with normal children. As predicted by the theory, they found evidence in support of an association between learning difficulties and certain immune disorders, but not with left-handedness. (For a critical review, see Bryden, McManus, & Bulman-Fleming, 1994.)

SIGN LANGUAGE

The relation between language and handedness can usefully be studied in sign language, which uses both hands as articulators. Some interesting data about speech lateralization have been produced by studies on deaf signers who have been found to depend on the left hemisphere for language, as do hearing and speaking subjects: In deaf-signers left-hemisphere lesions cause aphasia, whereas right-hemisphere lesions cause visuospatial impairments as in normal hearing patients (Poizner, Klima, & Bellugi, 1987; Vaid, Bellugi, & Poizner, 1989; chapter 8, Aphasia in Users of Signed Languages, this volume). The observation of these patients supports the idea that oral speech is not necessary for the development of left-hemisphere language dominance. Furthermore, Corina, Vaid, and Bellugi (1992) compared results between native users of American Sign Language and normal hearing subjects in three experimental tasks using the concurrent activities procedure to determine the underlying basis of the left-hemisphere specialization for language. The question was whether this specialization is due to the linguistic, motoric, or symbolic properties of language. Their results confirmed the linguistic basis of left-hemisphere specialization for sign and spoken language in deaf and hearing individuals.

Vaid, Bellugi, and Poizner (1989) examined the signing speed of the right and left hand in RH and LH native deaf signers. As is the case in normal hearing individuals, in right-handers the only difference was an inferior signing speed of the left hand. Left-handers showed a higher flexibility in signing with their nonpreferred hand than did right-handers. This result was interpreted as an indication that, in left-handers, language can be bilaterally represented whereas skilled movements are unilaterally controlled by the right hemisphere.

EVALUATION OF HANDEDNESS
AND HEMISPHERE DOMINANCE

In clinical practice the most common way of determining handedness consists of the use of questionnaires and tests. A review of the literature has shown that different criteria were used to establish handedness: writing (Chamberlain, 1928); a series of questions about how one carries out certain acts, such as writing, use of knife, spoon, scissors, and so forth. (Falek, 1959; Rife, 1940); and a battery of uni- and bimanual motor actions, for hand, foot, eye, and ear (Subirana, 1951, cited in Subirana, 1969). More recently, Oldfield (1971) proposed a handedness battery (the Edinburgh Inventory), which is commonly used in clinical practice. Although the use of these questionnaires and tests has been criticized by some authors and their use with aphasic people requires that verbal instructions be easily understood and supported by gestures, these instruments are simple and provide a quantitative measure of handedness.

It is also possible to assess directly hemisphere dominance for language, but these procedures are distinctly more cumbersome and there is no evidence that they identify hemispheric dominance more accurately than questionnaires. The Wada test consists of an injection of sodium amytal into a carotid artery, which produces transient contralateral hemiplegia and aphasia when the hemisphere is dominant for language, or contralateral hemiplegia without aphasia if it is not. Milner, Branch, and Rasmussen (1964) used this technique to study normal subjects. Forty-four non-right-handers without early neurological damage were submitted to the Wada test: Language disorders were evident in 64% of the subjects after injection in the left carotid artery, in 20% after injection in the right carotid artery, and in 16% after injection in either side, demonstrating that hemispheric language dominance is more heterogeneous in left- than in right-handers. A more recent review (Milner, 1974) essentially confirmed their previous conclusions: In 96% of right-handers and 70% of left-handers the left hemisphere is dominant for language. If, however, a lesion occurred at an early age, 81% of right-handers and 30% of left-handers had left-hemisphere representation of language.

Another technique to investigate cerebral lateralization is the dichotic listening test (Kimura, 1964), consisting of the simultaneous stimulation of both ears with competing stimuli. In right-handers, the superiority of the right ear on the simultaneous presentation of verbal stimuli to both ears has been demonstrated, whereas presentation of nonverbal competing stimuli has produced left ear superiority. RH subjects have smaller perceptual asymmetries than LH subjects, particularly those with a family history of left-handedness (Satz, Fenelle, & Jones, 1969). According to Satz et al., this result suggests that in LH subjects with familial sinistrality the cerebral representation of language is on the same side as the dominant hand. Later, Satz (1979) suggested the existence of three different types of cerebral language organization: 70% of left-handers demonstrated a bilateral representation of language, 15% a unilateral left-sided, and 15% a unilateral right-sided localization of language function. Familial sinistrality, as well as left-handedness, seems to correlate with an increased representation of language in the right hemisphere in left-handers.

The combination of the results from two studies of speech lateralization using the Wada test and the dichotic test with the same subjects (Strauss, Gaddes, & Wada, 1987; Zatorre, 1989) showed that 89% of subjects with left-hemisphere dominance for language on the Wada test had right-ear advantage (REA). A left-ear advantage (LEA), however, was found in only 65% of subjects with right-hemisphere dominance for language on the Wada test and, finally, in subjects with bilateral language representation an LEA or an REA was equally probable (44% vs. 56%).

More recently, Jancke, Steinmetz, and Volkmann (1992) compared auditory lateralization in 26 RH and 26 LH subjects in seven different dichotic tasks. Different patterns of ear preference were found for the different dichotic tasks. All in all, it can be concluded that REA has only statistical value: Significantly more subjects with left-hemisphere dominance for language will show an REA than subjects with right-hemisphere dominance for language. However, it is not possible to predict hemispheric language dominance in a single subject from dichotic tasks.

APHASIA IN LEFT-HANDERS

Three questions often recur in the literature on aphasia in left-handers. The first concerns the frequency of occurrence of aphasia after left- or right-hemisphere lesion; the second concerns types of aphasia, whether they differ from types of aphasia in RH patients. Finally, recovery from aphasia in left-handers has been compared to recovery from aphasia in right-handers.

Incidence of Aphasia

Goodglass and Quafasel (1954) compared the presence of aphasia in 110 published cases and in 13 personal cases of left-handers with a left- or right-hemisphere lesion. Of these, 61 patients had lesions of the left hemisphere and 62 of the right hemisphere; 87% of the left-damaged patients and 81% of the right-damaged patients showed aphasia (such a high percentage of right-hemisphere damage and aphasia has never been reported in subsequent studies). According to Hécaen and Ajuriaguerra (1963), 50% of left-handers with right-hemisphere lesion have aphasia, but this percentage falls to 6.7% according to Penfield and Roberts (1959). However, patients in this last series were epileptic and those in the other series were generally trauma patients; the two populations are not directly comparable. The general conclusions are that a left-hemisphere lesion in left-handers gives rise to aphasia in approximately the same percentage of subjects as a left-hemisphere lesion in right-handers; a right-hemisphere lesion causes aphasia in a lesser number of subjects than a left-hemisphere lesion but it does so more frequently in left- than in right-handers. According to Hécaen and Sauguet (1971), aphasia from right-hemisphere lesion is almost exclusively seen in left-handers with familial sinistrality. However, patients with right-hemisphere lesion and aphasia have been reported in the literature who do not have familial sinistrality (Basso, Farabola, Grassi, Laiacona, & Zanobio, 1990; Naeser & Borod, 1986).

The greater vulnerability to aphasia of left-handers has been explained by the hypothesis that in a certain number of left-handers language is represented bilaterally. This hypothesis is supported by the results we reported previously by Milner, Branch, and Rasmussen (1964). This conclusion, however, has been challenged by Kimura (1983). According to this author, a careful consideration of the sampling characteristics of many previous studies reporting a higher incidence of aphasia in LH subjects demonstrates that the claim that the series were unselected is not tenable. The only unequivocal data from the literature that support a more bilateral organization of language in a small number of LH subjects come from studies using the Wada technique. In this paper, Kimura reported results from a consecutive series of 520 patients only selected for unilateral damage. Incidence of aphasia was not higher in the 48 LH patients than in the 472 RH patients. Based on these findings, Kimura suggested "a negligible role of the right hemisphere in speech function in most left handers who do not have early left hemisphere damage" (p. 147). However, the number of patients studied was still comparatively small.

Aphasia Profiles

Another interesting aspect developed in the literature regards the different profiles of aphasic disturbances in RH versus LH patients. Qualitative differences are difficult to study; one of the many reasons is that, besides comparison of left- and right-handers, left- and right-hemispheric lesions must also be compared among left-handers.

Gloning, Gloning, Haub, and Quatember (1969) paired 57 RH patients and 57 LH patients for various linguistic tasks—confrontation naming, reading, writing, comprehension. They then compared the number of cases in which the RH or the LH patients fared better. No difference was found for patients with left-hemisphere lesions, whereas among right-hemisphere-damaged patients more LH patients fared worse in numerous tasks. Hécaen and Ajuriaguerra (1963) and Hécaen and Sauguet (1971) reached a similar conclusion for left-hemisphere-damaged patients: With two exceptions, aphasia profiles did not differ in RH and LH patients. LH aphasics were less frequently impaired in comprehension and writing; however, they had spatial reading disorders more frequently than RH aphasics. Among left-handers the comparison of right- and left-hemispheric disorders revealed fewer (non-linguistic) differences than did the comparison in right-handers. These results would be consistent with the hypothesis that in left-handers the two hemispheres are less specialized than in right-handers.

One of the limitations of these studies is that they did not consider certain factors supposed to affect aphasia type, such as age or etiology. These factors were considered by Basso et al. (1990), who conducted a retrospective analysis of clinical aspects of and recovery from aphasia in RH and non-right-handed patients. From 1,200 brain-damaged patients, they selected 24 non-right-handers (19 with left-hemisphere lesion and 5 with right-hemisphere lesion) and matched 14 of them with 14 RH patients, similar for lesion and other anamnestic and neuropsychological data. Clinically, they did not observe (with only one exception) relevant differences in the type of aphasia. Their data on the frequency of some disturbances confirmed the results obtained by Hécaen and Sauguet (1971); that is, dyscalculia was equally frequent in non-right-handed and RH patients with left-side lesion, ideomotor apraxia was less frequent, and constructive apraxia was more frequent in non-right-handers than in right-handers.

Recovery

It has been frequently suggested that aphasia is transient in left-handers but it is difficult to find sound experimental data on recovery in the literature. Subirana (1958) found more right-handers (80%) in a group of nonrecovered aphasic patients than in a group of recovered aphasic patients (20%). In a subsequent study, he found (Subirana, 1969) that only 6% of strong RH aphasics recovered, against 59% of preferential right-handers and 100% of left-handers. These percentages of recovered patients are corroborated in the series studied by Luria (1970), who also emphasized the importance of familial sinistrality for recovery. Basso et al. (1990) compared recovery in a group of rehabilitated RH and a group of rehabilitated LH patients with left-hemisphere lesion. Despite the small number of left-handed patients

(12), their results clearly indicated that recovery from aphasia does not differ between non-right-handers and right-handers with left-hemisphere lesion. They concluded that the previously reported differences in type of aphasia and recovery between right-handers and non-right-handers have probably been overemphasized and must be reconsidered.

APRAXIA IN LEFT-HANDERS

According to Liepmann (1908), handedness reflects the greater capacity of one side of the brain to acquire the programs for particular motor skills. Thus, in a right-hander the left hemisphere is superior at acquiring certain unimanual skilled movements whereas in a left-hander the right hemisphere is dominant. The relationship between handedness and eupraxis is in fact very strong, but a few cases of dissociation have been recorded.

Cases of RH patients with clinically evident limb apraxia and a right-hemisphere lesion are very few and the clinical documentation is not completely satisfactory (Hécaen & Gimeno Alava, 1960). Cases of LH patients with limb apraxia and left-sided lesions are relatively more frequent, although still rare (for a review, see Signoret & North, 1979). These cases, however few, seriously challenge the notion of a causal relationship between handedness and praxis.

A few authors advanced the hypothesis that praxis and speech are two expressions of the same basic mechanisms, which also utilize the same anatomical structures (Kimura, 1976, 1982; Mateer & Kimura, 1977; Ojemann, 1984). However, a pattern of alternated dominance has been reported both in right-handers (Heilman, Gonyea, & Geschwind, 1974; Selnes, Pestronk, Hart, & Gordon, 1991; Selnes, Rubens, Risse, & Levy, 1982) and in left-handers (for a review, see Faglioni & Basso, 1985). The independence of language and praxis is also supported by cases of crossed aphasia in right-handers (see chapter 7, Crossed Aphasia, this volume). The observation that many of these patients are not apraxic is consistent with a left-hemisphere dominance for skilled motor functions and a right-hemisphere dominance for language functions.

Once the most current views have been excluded, that is, that dominance for praxis is determined either by manual preference or speech dominance, it can be speculated that the basis is anatomical. Some cortical areas, crucial for eupraxis, are more developed in the left hemisphere in most right-handers and in the right hemisphere in the majority of left-handers.

VISUOSPATIAL ABILITIES

Many studies reported in literature have investigated the possible distinct cerebral organization of nonverbal functions (visuospatial and constructional abilities) in left-handers compared to right-handers.

Snyder and Harris (1993) documented differences in visuospatial ability in normal RH and LH subjects. They have studied right-handers and two subgroups of left-handers (with "consistent" and "inconsistent" use of the left hand) on two spatial tasks, one visuoperceptual and one visuoconstructional. The results indicated no overall handedness effect, although consistent left-handers performed significantly worse than right-handers in the visuoperceptual task. This was a mental rotation task requiring the subjects to choose one of five drawings representing a target figure drawn from different angles. Snyder and Harris suggested that some controversial findings about the correlation between left-handedness and some cognitive abilities previously reported in the literature can partly be explained by the fact that in many studies LH subjects were pooled together, without consideration of the consistency of use of the preferred hand.

In brain-damaged patients, left-handers with left-hemispheric lesion are frequently compromised in functions typically related to the right hemisphere, such as visuospatial, perceptual, and constructional abilities. In some studies of brain-damaged patients, however, most of the variables (neurological, linguistic, and demographic) that affect performance on nonverbal tasks are not equivalent among the groups of patients. Borod, Carper, Naeser, and Goodglass (1985) examined the performance on nonverbal tasks of 21 LH and 57 RH aphasic patients (with unilateral left lesion), matched for the variables just mentioned. They found an important impairment of left-handers in visuospatial and constructional capacities, and they interpreted their data as supporting the hypothesis that LH aphasics with left-hemisphere lesion may have more left-hemispheric representation of some typically right-hemisphere functions than RH aphasics.

Little information is available regarding attention disorders in LH patients. Recently, Maeshima, Shigeno, Dohi, Kajiwara, and Komai (1992) investigated the correlation between handedness and unilateral spatial neglect in RH and LH patients who suffered from a left-hemispheric stroke. They selected all patients (20) with unilateral neglect and left-hemisphere lesions; most of the patients also had aphasia, which was more severe in the right-handers. In the RH patients, Gerstmann's syndrome, agraphia, and apraxia were also observed. The authors pointed out the qualitative differences in unilateral neglect in the two groups. Hemineglect was more severe and more persistent in left-handers. The observation that three of their LH patients showed unilateral neglect but no aphasia or apraxia led to the assumption that in these patients the nondominant hemisphere functions (visuospatial) were to be located in the left hemisphere whereas the functions normally belonging to the dominant hemisphere were to be assigned to the right hemisphere. In six other LH patients, unilateral neglect, aphasia, and bucco-facial apraxia co-occurred. This suggests that the left hemisphere plays a role in the control not only of the language function but also of some cognitive abilities related to the nondominant hemisphere (visuospatial perception). On the basis of these observations, it does not seem unreasonable to maintain a reversed lateralization of some higher cortical functions such as visuospatial perception in LH patients or an overlapping of some cortical areas.

Delis, Knight, and Simpson (1983) described the case of an LH patient with a right temporo-parietal lesion who developed Wernicke's aphasia and some visuospatial disturbances. This suggests the possibility that the cerebral organization of this patient is reversed compared to that of a right-hander; that is, the language function would be lateralized in the right hemisphere and the spatial in the left. The absence of a typical right-hemisphere syndrome (unilateral neglect, constructional disabilities, amusia, and dressing apraxia) suggests that these functions may be subserved by his left hemisphere.

The literature reports a few cases of right-hemisphere syndrome observed in left-handers. An interesting contribution is that of Dronkers and Knight (1989), who had the opportunity of studying a LH patient with an acute left frontal stroke, showing hemineglect, anosognosia, aprosodia, and visuospatial constructive deficits (i.e., a typical right-hemisphere syndrome observed in right-handers) but no aphasia. The case of this patient (in particular, the severity and persistence of his neglect) suggests the hypothesis that attention and visuospatial abilities may sometimes be reversed in left-handers. Another possibility that has generally been overlooked in these cases is that both hemispheres are needed for visuospatial skills.

We can conclude by saying that data on hemispheric dominance for nonverbal functions in left-handers are sparse and strong conclusions cannot be drawn.

EXPERIMENTAL STUDY

From data in the literature it seems safe to conclude that LH aphasics with left-hemisphere lesions do not differ in important ways from standard RH aphasics. However, the same cannot be said for LH aphasics with right hemisphere lesions, mainly due to the paucity of case studies. Table 1.1 reports all the cases in literature (of which we are aware) of LH aphasic patients with right-hemisphere lesions. The patients studied by Gloning et al. (1969) were all very severely impaired neurologically; they were seen within the first week following admission and all died within 3 months. For each task the authors computed the number of LH patients who were more severely impaired than their RH matched controls. The comparison between the 32 LH and the 32 RH patients with comparable right-hemisphere lesions has shown, as expected, that a higher percentage of LH patients was more severely impaired in all the verbal behaviors studied (comprehension, expressive language, confrontation naming, writing, and reading).

Hécaen and Sauguet (1971) compared 26 LH patients with right-hemisphere lesions to 47 LH patients with left-hemisphere lesions and two groups

TABLE 1.1
Cases Reported in Literature of Left-Handed (LH) Aphasic Patients With Right-Hemisphere Lesion

Gloning et al. (1969)	The authors compared 32 LH patients and 32 RH patients with almost identical (anatomically verified) right lesion.
Hécaen & Sauget (1971)	The authors compared 26 LH patients and three groups of patients: LH patients with left lesion, RH patients with left or right lesion.
Poeck & Kerschesteiner (1971)	One LH patient with ideomotor apraxia and aphasia. Both symptoms cleared in 2 weeks.
Signoret & North (1979)	Case 2 (very briefly described).
Poeck & Lehmkul (1980)	One LH patient (very apractic), but aphasia cleared in a few days.
Delis et al. (1983)	One LH patient with aphasia and visual-spatial functioning typical of a right-hander with left-hemisphere lesion.
Naeser & Borod (1986)	The authors examined language behavior in LH patients with left- (= 27) and right- (= 4) hemisphere lesions.
Archibald (1987)	Two LH patients with aphasia and apraxia. According to the author the data are consistent with those for right-handers with left-hemisphere lesions.
Basso et al. (1990)	Four LH patients (only one matched to an RH patient with left lesion), all included in the present study.

of RH patients with left- or right-hemisphere lesions. Among LH patients, disturbances of calculation, reading of textual material, and writing complex sentences were more frequent in the left-hemisphere-damaged group and constructional apraxia and unilateral spatial agnosia in the right-hemisphere-damaged group. Poeck and co-workers (Poeck & Kerschesteiner, 1971; Poeck & Lehmkhul, 1980) described two LH patients with right-hemisphere lesions and apraxia, ideomotor in the first patient and ideational in the second; both patients showed signs of aphasia for a few days. Apraxia was also the focus of interest in the LH aphasic patients described by Signoret and North (1979) and Archibald (1987). Speech and language were evaluated in sufficient detail in Archibald's cases, and the conclusion reached by the author, as well as by Delis, Knight, and Simpson (1983), who presented a similar case, is that the language disorders corresponded to the aphasia type following a similarly located left-hemisphere lesion in RH aphasics. This apparently is not true for Naeser and Borod's patients 28 and 29 with large right fronto-temporo-parietal lesions that damaged both Broca's and Wernicke's areas. Both patients had nonfluent output but moderate to good comprehension. The authors suggested that these patients had hand and speech output dominance in the right hemisphere, and comprehension dominance in the left. Case 30 is only briefly mentioned, and case 31 had a long-lasting global aphasia similar to what is expected in an RH patient with left-hemisphere lesions.

No direct comparison has ever been made between LH aphasic patients with right-hemisphere lesions and standard RH patients with left-hemisphere lesions. In a previous study (Basso et al., 1990), LH aphasic patients were matched to RH aphasic patients with comparable lesions, but out of four LH patients with right-hemisphere lesion only one could be matched to an RH left-hemisphere-damaged patient. In that case, the aphasia profiles were similar, though the LH aphasic was less severely impaired.

The following retrospective study follows the same lines of our previous study (Basso et al., 1990), but here we report on the clinical aspects of aphasia in LH patients with right-hemisphere lesions. These are compared to clinical aspects of aphasia in standard left-hemisphere-damaged aphasics. Recovery of oral and written confrontation naming and of Token Test results are compared in the four pairs of matched patients who had a second evaluation.

Materials and Methods

Subjects. From a continuous series of 1,900 subjects seen at the Aphasia Unit of the Neurological Clinic of Milan University between 1979 and 1994, we selected all patients conforming to the following criteria:

1. Left-handedness according to the Edinburgh Inventory (Oldfield, 1971) (maximum score: 6 of 10 items executed with the right hand).
2. No previous lesion of the central nervous system.
3. A single right-hemisphere vascular lesion ascertained by CT scan.
4. A full neuropsychological examination performed at least 15 days postonset.
5. Clear evidence of aphasia.

Based on these criteria, nine subjects were included. To match these patients, we then selected, from the whole sample, all those RH patients with comparable CT lesions; among these subjects we selected patients matched for etiology, sex, length of illness, and, as far as possible, for education and age. We did not find a matchable subject for one patient and the sample was then reduced to eight pairs, one LH aphasic with right-hemisphere lesion and a matched standard left-hemisphere-damaged aphasic. Four of these patients were included in the previous study (Basso et al., 1990), but only one matched RH subject could be found at the time (LH patient 3036 and the matched RH 2835, corresponding to NRH3 and RH 3 of Basso et al., 1990). In this study, these patients' scores for the Token Test are slightly different because the raw scores are reported whereas in the previous study they were corrected for education. Mappings of the lesions (Figs. 1.1–1.8), performed according to the method described by Damasio and Damasio (1989), are shown in the Appendix.

Tests and Procedures. All subjects were examined using the following tests:

Aphasia Testing. A Standard Language Examination (Basso, Capitani, & Vignolo, 1979) currently used in our Aphasia Unit.

Token Test. A shortened version of the Token Test was administered (De Renzi & Faglioni, 1978) with 36 items and a cutoff score for normals of 29 correct responses.

Raven's Coloured Progressive Matrices (RCPM) were administered with a time limit of 10 min (Basso, De Renzi, Faglioni, Scotti, & Spinnler, 1973).

Oral apraxia (OA) was evaluated with a 10-item test requiring the execution of buccofacial movements (De Renzi, Pieczuro, & Vignolo, 1966). Cutoff score: 16/20.

Ideomotor apraxia (IMA) was evaluated with a 24-item test (De Renzi, Motti, & Nichelli, 1980) requiring the patient to imitate, with the hand ipsilateral to the lesion, movements of the whole arm or fingers, single or in sequences, meaningful or meaningless. Cutoff score: 53/72.

Ideational Apraxia (IA) was evaluated with a 7-item test (De Renzi, Pieczuro, & Vignolo, 1968) requiring the patient to show how to use different objects. Cutoff score: 14/14.

Acalculia. Patients were asked to perform written additions, subtractions, divisions, and multiplications (Basso & Capitani, 1979). Cutoff score: 74/101.

Results

Table 1.2 reports the data for the eight pairs of patients. In pair 1, the difference in severity of language disorders was important. Both patients had Wernicke's aphasia. In the LH patient (2623), speech output was fluent and abundant but of low informative value because of frequent verbal paraphasias and generic words. He could, however, sustain a simple conversation on familiar subjects. He also had oral apraxia, mild ideomotor apraxia, and acalculia. The RH patient (4083) was more severely impaired. Comprehension was nil (he could not pass the Token Test because he did not understand what he was asked to do); speech output was fluent and abundant but incomprehensible because of frequent phonemic errors. He too had oral apraxia (but no ideomotor apraxia) and moderate acalculia.

In pair 2, the LH patient (2827) had mild anomic aphasia with slightly better written than oral confrontation naming; she had no apraxia (oral or ideomotor) and very mild acalculia. The RH patient was slightly more impaired; she was suffering from Broca's aphasia with verbal apraxia. Writing was more severely impaired than oral production. She too had oral apraxia and acalculia.

TABLE 1.2
Anamnestic and Neuropsychological Data of the Eight NRH and the Eight Paired RH Patients

Patient Number	Sex	Age (years)	School	Ed. Inv.	Fam. Sin.	I/H	On-Ex (days)
2623[a]	M	64	13	3	-	I	43
4083	M	76	13	10	-	I	34
2827[a]	F	47	8	3	+	H	34
2941	F	29	13	10	-	H	16
2934	M	71	5	6	+	I	74
2488	M	64	7	10	-	I	64
3026[a]	M	38	17	2	+	I	253
2835	M	48	12	10	-	I	235
3030[a]	M	47	5	2	-	H	172
3049	M	48	7	10	-	H	227
4062	M	70	5	2	+	I	72
3426	M	58	5	10	-	I	97
4254	F	69	11	6	-	I	29
2640	F	49	8	10	-	I	28
4459	F	69	8	6	-	H	282
3568	F	53	8	10	+	H	297

Aphasia Type (maximum score)	OCN (40)	WCN (40)	TT (36)	OA (20)	IMA (72)	IA (14)	RV (36)	AC (101)
Wernicke (verbal paraphasias).	28	22	9	12	44	14	17♦	15
Severe Wernicke (phonemic errors)	10	6	unt.	14	56	14	30♦	51
Mild anomic aphasia (WFD, verbal paraphasias).	22	32	26	18	63	14	17♦	72
Broca (verbal apraxia)	28	18	19	14	71	14	16	44
Broca (mild verbal apraxia).	32	26	25	18	61	14	16	27
Severe global	0	0	5	2	21	8	14	13
Broca (mild agrammatism, verbal apraxia).	30	38	26	12	64	14	35	72
Broca (verbal apraxia)	18	22	20	4	57	14	26	88
Unclassified aphasia (WFD, dysgraphia).	22	6	23	12	24	6	11♦	40
Mixed non fluent (WFD)	0	0	13	11	40	9	4	unt.
Dyslexia, dysgraphia	30	8	23	10	61	14	17	59
Wernicke (phonemic errors)	14	18	20	10	64	14	26	47
Mixed transcortical	30	10	10	14	55	12	11	25
Mixed nonfluent (echolalia, WFD, verbal apraxia)	2	10	11	3	35	8	27	30
Wernicke	8	4	7	11	64	12	13	27
Global (severe verbal apraxia).	0	14	8	4	59	14	31	45

Note: M = male; F = female; + = present; - = absent; School = years of schooling; Ed. In. = Edinburgh Inventory; Fam. Sin. = familial sinistrality; I = Ischemic; H = hemorrhagic; On-Ex.= onset exam; OCN = oral confrontation naming; WCN = written confrontation naming; TT = token test; OA = oral apraxia; IMA = ideomotor apraxia; IA = ideative apraxia; Rv = Raven Progressive Matrices (47); AC = acalculia; unt = untestable; WFD = word finding difficulty, ♦ = position preference; a = cases published in Basso et al.(1990).

In pair 3, the difference in severity of aphasia was striking. The LH patient (2934) had mild Broca's aphasia with mild verbal apraxia and moderate word-finding difficulties (WFD); he also omitted some verbs. Comprehension was only mildly impaired and he had no oral or ideomotor apraxia. Acalculia was severe. His RH matched patient (2488), on the contrary, had a severe global aphasia and all language tasks were severely impaired. He also had severe apraxia (oral, ideomotor, and of use) and acalculia.

Pair 4's patients (3026 [LH] and 2835 [RH]) have already been described (Basso et al., 1990). Briefly, they both suffered from Broca's aphasia, overall slightly less severe in patient 3026, who, however, was the only one to omit some verbs; both had oral apraxia and the LH patient also had very mild acalculia.

In pair 5's patients (3030 [LH] and 3049 [RH]), the difference in severity of language disorder was impressive. Patient 3030's speech was scarce, emitted in very short runs, but fluent with few content words; confrontation naming was only moderately impaired and oral comprehension was adequate; writing was only slightly more impaired than oral production. His language disorders were not easily classifiable into any of the classical language syndromes. He had severe oral, ideomotor, and ideational apraxia, and acalculia. The RH patient was severely aphasic with effortful and scanty speech; he had severely impaired comprehension, agraphia, and alexia. He was diagnosed as a mixed nonfluent because his comprehension, although severely impaired, was adequate for single words and short sentences. He also had severe apraxia.

The main difference between the patients of pair 6 was in the quality of speech output, which was fluent and informative in patient 4062 (LH) without obvious aphasic errors. His comprehension was adequate but reading and writing were impaired, and he was diagnosed as dyslexic and dysgraphic. His RH matched control (3426) had moderate Wernicke's aphasia; his speech was fluent with frequent phonemic errors. Both patients had oral apraxia and acalculia.

The LH patient (4254) of pair 7 had fluent but very sparse speech. She did not initiate speech spontaneously; when interrogated she repeated part of the question and could not go further. Oral confrontation naming and reading aloud were only moderately impaired; repetition was good. Comprehension, however, was severely impaired and she was diagnosed as a mixed transcortical aphasic. She also had oral apraxia and acalculia. Her RH partner (patient 2640), with mixed nonfluent aphasia, was slightly more impaired; she had sparse and effortful speech; oral and written confrontation naming were severely impaired, as were comprehension and reading. She could, however, write under dictation and repeat words and short sentences. Echolalia was also present in this patient, as well as severe apraxia (oral, ideomotor, and ideational) and acalculia.

Both patients in the last pair were severely impaired, with the LH patient slightly better. The aphasia type in the two patients was dramatically different. The LH patient (4459) had severe Wernicke's aphasia with fluent but empty speech with frequent semantic paraphasias and a few neologisms. She could, however, name a few pictures; comprehension of oral and written words and short sentences was possible, and repetition and reading aloud were well preserved. The RH patient (3568) had global aphasia; her speech consisted of a single phoneme (/n/) although it was sometimes possible to elicit YES and NO as answers to simple questions; comprehension did not differ from that of patient 4459, but she could not read or repeat. Both patients had oral apraxia and acalculia.

Perusal of individual results on the Aphasia Examination shows that language disorders are more severe in the RH patients. We compared mean scores of LH and RH patients in a number of language tasks. The scores for the oral confrontation naming task are higher in seven LH patients; the difference is noteworthy and significant (mean score 25.2 vs. 9.0; $df = 14$, $t = 3.5$, $p = .003$). The mean score for the written confrontation naming task, too, is higher for the LH patients (18.2 vs. 11.0), but the difference is not significant and does not consistently point in the same direction. Besides the LH patient with dysgraphia, another LH patient had lower score than his matched control, and in another case the score was the same for the two patients. In comprehension, six LH patients scored higher than their RH controls on the Token Test; for 2 pairs the reverse is true, but in both cases there is only one point difference. The difference between mean scores for the LH and RH patients (18.6 vs. 12.0) is not significant.

Results for the RCPM go in the opposite direction: LH patients have a lower score than RH patients (mean scores: 18.2 vs. 21.7) but the difference is not significant. The lower score by LH patients may be due to spatial neglect: two patients (2827 and 3030) showed position preference. They indicated significantly more frequently the right-hand choice versus the left-hand choice (9 vs. 18, 1 vs. 14; chi square 5.07, $p < .05$; 16.4, $p < .001$); one of the RH patients (2941) indicated more frequently the left in preference to the right, but the difference was not statistically significant (15 vs. 8; chi square 3.12, $p < .10$).

If we now turn to the other neuropsychological disorders, we see that disorders of written calculation were present in all patients but one RH (2835). Oral apraxia, too, was a very frequent finding; only two LH patients did not show it. IMA and IA were both present in three RH patients and in one LH patient; moreover, one LH patient had IMA only and another one had IA only.

Table 1.3 reports the results for oral and written confrontation naming, the Token Test, the RCPM, the type of aphasia at first and second examinations, and the interval between the two testing sessions for the four pairs of patients with a control evaluation. With the exception of patient 2941 (an RH patient), all patients were rehabilitated between the two evaluations.

TABLE 1.3
Neuropsychological Data at First and Second Examination of the Four Pairs (NRH, RH) of Reexamined Patients

Patient Number	OCN	WCN	TT	Rv	Aphasia	$1°$ - $2°$ Ex (days)	Reha- bilit.	OCN	WCN	TT	Rv	Aphasia
2623	28	22	9	17	Wernicke	380	+	32	30	11	20	Wernicke
4083	10	6	unt[a]	30	Wernicke	278	+	18	18	2	25	Wernicke
2827	22	32	26	17	Anomic	184	+	36	40	29	29	Anomic
2941	28	18	19	16	Broca	193	-	40	40	34	26	Nonaphasic
4254	30	10	10	11	Mixed Transcort.	184	+	31	38	19	24	Transcortical motor
2640	2	10	11	27	Mixed nonfluent	212	+	28	38	27	31	Very mild Broca
4459	8	4	7	13	Wernicke	283	+	22	10	15	13	Wernicke
3568	0	14	8	31	Global	258	+	0	26	15	28	Broca, verbal apraxia

Note. OCN = oral confrontation naming; WCN = written confrotation naming; TT = Token test; Rv = Raven Progressive Matrices (47); $1°$, - $2°$ Ex = first, second exam (days); Rehabilit. = language rehabilitation; + = yes; - = no; [a] = patient was affected by a difficulty in color recognition.

Recovery was most marked in patient 2941, who was no longer diagnosed as aphasic at the second examination. His LH matched patient, less severely impaired at the first examination, was still diagnosed as an anomic aphasic at the second examination, although scores at the Standard Language Examination were good. He, however, had frequent word-finding difficulties in spontaneous speech and in confrontation naming tasks with infrequent words.

In a second RH patient (2640) recovery was remarkable; at the second examination she only had very mild apraxia of speech and a Token Test score (27) that was just under the cutoff for normals (29). Her LH matched patient recovered less, although her language disorders at the first examination were less severe.

Table 1.3 shows recovery of patient 4083 (RH) as slightly superior to the recovery of his matched LH patient, but inspection of the results in all the language tasks shows that recovery was in fact better for the LH patient, who did not have clear aphasic errors at the second examination, whereas patient 4083 still had many phonemic paraphasias in spontaneous speech. In the last pair of patients, recovery was distinctly better for the LH patient.

If we consider the LH patients together and compare their results to those of the RH patients as a group, we see that in all the language tasks considered the LH group has a higher score, except for the Token Test at the second examination. The difference, however, is always smaller at the second examination, meaning that recovery was less marked for the LH patients. For RCPM, RH patients had a higher score at the first examination, the LH patients recovered better than the RH patients, and the difference is less marked at the second examination.

Discussion

The main objective of our study was to explore whether aphasia from right-hemisphere lesions in LH patients constitutes a mirror image of the aphasia linked to left-hemisphere lesion in RH patients, or if it has distinguishing features suggestive of a different organization of language function in this subgroup of left-handers.

Obviously, we do not have a conclusive answer. First, the number of LH subjects with right-hemisphere lesions is small, indirectly confirming once more, if necessary, that most LH subjects have left-hemisphere dominance for speech. Another important reason is that, notwithstanding the great number of RH patients with left-hemisphere lesions with whom we compared the LH patients, it is almost impossible to find an exactly similar lesion and it cannot be excluded that differences in behavior are to be explained by differences in lesion locations.

Notwithstanding these limitations and contrary to the findings of our previous study (Basso et al., 1990) with LH patients with left-hemisphere lesions, our results indicate that language disorders are less severe in LH patients with right-hemisphere lesions. The difference is not large but all LH patients had milder disorders, with the possible exception of patient 4062. Reading and writing were more impaired in this patient than in his RH control, but the reverse was true for oral language, in which he was free of aphasic errors while his RH control made frequent phonological errors.

The consistency of the pattern is striking and compelling. However, in 1979 a 74-year-old woman with a right-hemisphere lesion was examined at our Aphasia Unit 20 days postonset. She had severe global aphasia with severe apraxia and a score of 1 on the RCPM. No reliable data are reported for handedness in this patient, except for a casual notation of ambidexterity. We found a corresponding left-hemisphere lesion in a RH patient. In this case, the RH patient was much less severely impaired; she had no comprehension disorders (she scored 31 on the Token Test), her speech output was sufficiently informative although effortful, and she made frequent orthographic errors in all writing tasks. It is, however, difficult to assess the utility of this observation due to the absence of any reliable data on hand preference in the supposedly LH patient.

If we now turn to the qualitative aspects of the language disorders, we see that despite differences in severity, the language disorders were similar in patients of pairs 1, 4, and 7. The differences are more marked in patients of pairs 2 and 3 but in both cases this could be a direct result of the difference in severity. In pair 2, patient 2827 had anomic aphasia and LH patient 2941 had Broca's aphasia, which can evolve into an amnestic aphasia (Kertesz, 1979). At the second evaluation patient 2941 was no longer aphasic and her LH partner still had WFD. The same type of reasoning can explain differences between the patients of pair 3. The LH patient suffered from Broca's aphasia and the RH aphasic had global aphasia, which can sometimes ameliorate to a point where it can be classified as Broca's aphasia.

For two pairs, however, the differences between the two patients do not seem to be so easily explained. Let us consider the patients of pair 8, who showed the most striking difference. The LH patient had a severe Wernicke's aphasia with fluent and very abundant speech output, devoid of any informative value; she was also anosognosic with a very low RCPM score (13). Her RH control had global aphasia with very reduced speech output, slightly better writing, and a very good RCPM score (31). When seen 6/7 months later, both patients had improved but qualitatively, and the aphasic symptoms had not changed.

In our previous study of LH patients with left hemisphere lesion (Basso et al., 1990) we also found that 1 of 14 pairs of patients with comparable CT-scan lesions had very different aphasic disorders. There are, however, no sufficiently compelling reasons to ascribe the heterogeneity of the language disorders to handedness. Although it is true that in standard right-handers lesion of, say, Wernicke's area gives rise to Wernicke's aphasia in the majority of patients, there are now on record well-documented cases of "incongruent" aphasic disorders as compared to what can be expected on the basis of the location of the lesion (Basso, Lecours, Moraschini, & Vanier, 1985). If handedness were the cause of such differences, one would expect them to be more evident in strong left-handers. This, however, is not true for our sample. Patients 2827, 3026, and 4062 were strong left-handers with familial sinistrality but they do not differ greatly from their RH controls. Of the strong left-handers, only patient 3030, who has no familial sinistrality, markedly differs from his RH control. The most striking difference has been found in pair 8 where the two patients do not differ significantly for the handedness factor: the LH patient is in fact ambidextrous without familial sinistrality, and the RH patient, although totally RH, has an LH sister.

Recovery has not been studied because of the theoretical difficulty in finding the correct control group. Relationships between size and location of lesion and aphasia type in LH patients with right-hemisphere lesions were the topic of this study, and therefore we could not know a priori what the correct control group should be because both size and location of lesion and aphasia type affect recovery. However, in the four pairs of patients matched for lesion location who had a follow-up, there are indications that recovery was better in the RH patients notwithstanding a more severe initial language disorder.

In summary, our data indicate that aphasia in LH patients with right-hemisphere damage is less severe than in standard RH patients and there are indications that recovery can be less. As for the qualitative differences found, these are rare in our sample and there is no strong evidence that they are to be ascribed to handedness. These conclusions are tentative and based only on a very small number of patients. They must be confirmed on larger samples of LH patients.

CONCLUSIONS

In this chapter, we tried to elucidate the concept of left-handedness and we have reported some of the tentative explanations given as to its causes. Throughout, we spoke of left-handers and right-handers as if they were two clearly distinct populations. It should be clear that this is not the case. Right-handers generally show greater consistency of hand preference across a variety of tasks compared to left-handers, and they are more likely to constitute a single group. The consistency of hand preference corresponds to consistency of hemisphere dominance for language and other cognitive functions, although there are no indications of a causal relationship between hand and language dominance. Left-handers are a highly heterogeneous group that would be better defined as non-strong-right-handers. Not only is there high variability of hand preference among left-handers, but there also is less consistency of hand preference across tasks in individual LH subjects. A higher variability of hemisphere dominance for language and praxis, and possibly also for visuospatial capacities, corresponds to this variability of hand preference. As for right-handers, there is no indication of a causal link between hand preference and hemisphere preference for language.

In the second part of the chapter, we considered the literature on aphasia in left-handers and we reported our own data. We compared language disorders in LH and RH patients and we came to the conclusion that, in the past, differences among left-handers and right-handers probably have been overestimated.

This conclusion is reinforced by recent studies on aphasia. Many researchers have argued that aphasia syndromes are not real entities in the sense that there is not an invariant pattern shared by all members of the category (for discussion see Vallar, 1993); in fact, an in-depth study of single cases has stressed the fact that differences are more common than similarities between individual aphasic patients. When studying aphasia in left-handers we are therefore left without a frame of reference because aphasia in right-handers is not clearly and uncontrovertedly delineated. Aphasia in left-handers may be considered a nonexistent problem because they do not constitute a homogeneous group and also because no comparison is possible, because "aphasia in right-handers" is too vague a concept.

REFERENCES

Annett, M. (1964). A model of the inheritance of handedness and cerebral dominance. *Nature (London), 204*, 59–60.

Annett, M. (1967). The binomial distribution of right, mixed and left handedness. *Quarterly Journal of Experimental Psychology, 29*, 327–333.

Annett, M. (1985). *Left, right, hand and brain: The right shift theory.* London: Lawrence Erlbaum Associates.

Archibald, Y. M. (1987). Persisting apraxia in two left-handed, aphasic patients with right hemisphere lesion. *Brain and Cognition, 6*, 412–428.

Basso, A., & Capitani, E. (1979). Un test standardizzato per la diagnosi di acalculia. Descrizione e valori normativi. *AP-Rivista di applicazioni psicologiche, 1*, 551–564.

Basso, A., Capitani, E., & Vignolo, L. A. (1979). Influence of rehabilitation on language skills in aphasic patients. A controlled study. *Archives of Neurology, 36*, 190–196.

Basso, A., De Renzi, E., Faglioni, P., Scotti, G., & Spinnler, H. (1973). Neuropsychological evidence for the existence of cerebral areas critical to the performance of intelligence tasks. *Brain, 96*, 715–728.

Basso, A., Farabola, M., Grassi, M. P., Laiacona, M., & Zanobio, M. E. (1990). Aphasia in left-handers: Comparison of aphasia profiles and language recovery in non-right-handed and matched right-handed patients. *Brain and Language, 38*, 373–393.

Basso, A., Lecours, A. R., Moraschini, S., & Vanier, M. (1985). Anatomoclinical correlations of the aphasias as defined through computerized tomography: Exceptions. *Brain and Language, 26*, 201–229.

Borod, J. C., Carper, M., Naeser, M., & Goodglass, H. (1985). Left-handed and right-handed aphasics with left hemisphere lesions compared on nonverbal performance measures. *Cortex, 21*, 81–90.

Brain, W. R. (1945). Speech and handedness. *Lancet, 2,* 837–842.

Broca, P. P. (1865). Du siège de la faculté du langage articulé. *Bulletin de la Société d'Anthropologie, 6,* 373–393.

Bryden, M. P., McManus, I. C., & Bulman-Fleming, M. B. (1994). Evaluating the empirical support for the Geschwind–Behan–Galaburda model of cerebral lateralization. *Brain and Cognition, 26,* 103–167.

Chamberlain, H. D. (1928). The inheritance of left-handedness. *Journal of Heredity, 19,* 557–559.

Chi, J. G., Dooling, E. C., & Gilles, F. H. (1977). Left-right asymmetries of the temporal speech area of the human fetus. *Archives of Neurology, 34,* 346–348.

Chui, H. C., & Damasio, A. R. (1980). Human cerebral asymmetries evaluated by computerized tomography. *Journal of Neurology, Neurosurgery and Psichiatry, 43,* 873–878.

Corina, D. P., Vaid, J., & Bellugi, U. (1992). The linguistic basis of left hemisphere specialization. *Science, 255,* 1258–1260.

Crawford, S. G., Kaplan, B. J., & Kinsbourne, M. (1994). Are families of children with reading difficulties at risk for immune disorders and nonrighthandedness? *Cortex, 30,* 281–292.

Cunningham, D. J. (1892). *Contribution to the surface anatomy of the cerebral hemispheres.* Dublin: Royal Irish Academy.

Damasio, H., & Damasio A. R. (1989). *Lesion analysis in neuropsychology.* New York: Oxford University Press.

Delis, D., Knight, R. T., & Simpson, G. (1983). Reversed hemispheric organization in a left-hander. *Neuropsychologia, 21,* 13–24.

De Renzi, E., & Faglioni, P. (1978). Normative data and the screening power of a shortened version of the Token test. *Cortex, 14,* 41–49.

De Renzi, E., Motti, F., & Nichelli, P. (1980). Imitating gestures: A quantitative approach to ideomotor apraxia. *Archives of Neurology, 37,* 6–10.

De Renzi, E., Pieczuro, A., & Vignolo, L. A. (1966). Oral apraxia and aphasia. *Cortex, 2,* 50–73.

De Renzi, E., Pieczuro A., & Vignolo, L. A. (1968). Ideational apraxia: A quantitative study. *Neuropsychologia, 6,* 41–52.

Dronkers, N. F., & Knight, R. T. (1989). Right-sided neglect in a left-hander: Evidence for reversed hemispheric specialization of attention capacity. *Neuropsychologia, 5,* 729–735.

Eberstaller, O. (1884). Zur oberflachen Anatomie des Grosshirn Hemispharen. *Wien Med Blatt, 7,* 479, 642, 644.

Eidelberg, D., & Galaburda, A. M. (1982). Symmetry and asymmetry in the human posterior thalamus. I. Cytoarchitectonic analysis in normal persons. *Archives of Neurology, 39,* 325–332.

Faglioni, P., & Basso, A. (1985). Historical perspectives on neuroanatomical correlates of limb apraxia. In E. A. Roy (Ed.), *Neuropsychological studies of apraxia and related disorders* (pp. 3–44). Amsterdam: Elsevier.

Falek, A. (1959). Handedness: A family study. *American Journal of Human Genetics, 11,* 52–62.

Falzi, G., Perrone, P., & Vignolo, L. A. (1982). Right-left asymmetry in anterior speech region. *Archives of Neurology, 39,* 239–240.

Galaburda, A. M., Le May, M., Kemper, T. C., & Geschwind, N. (1978). Right-left asymmetries in the brain. *Science, 199,* 852–856.

Geschwind, N., & Galaburda A. M. (1985). Cerebral lateralization. Biological mechanisms, associations, and pathology: A hypothesis and a program for research. *Archives of Neurology, 42,* 428–459.

Geschwind, N., & Levitsky, W. (1968). Human brain: Left-right asymmetries in temporal speech region. *Science, 161,* 186–187.

Gesell, A., & Ames, L. B. (1947). Development of handedness. *Journal of Genetic Psychology, 70,* 155–175.

Gloning, I., Gloning, H., Haub, G., & Quatember, R. (1969). Comparison of verbal behavior in right-handed patients with anatomically verified lesion of one hemisphere. *Cortex, 5,* 43–52.

Gloning, I., Gloning, H., & Hoff, H. (1954). Die Dominanz einer Hemisphare. *Nervenartz, 25,* 49–55.

Goodglass, H., & Quadfasel, F. A. (1954). Language laterality in left-handed aphasics. *Brain, 77,* 521–548.

Hécaen, H., & de Ajuriaguerra, J. (1963). *Les gauchers, prévalence manuelle et dominance cérébrale.* Paris: Presse Universitaire de France.

Hécaen, H., & Gimeno Alava, A. (1960). L'apraxie idéomotrice unilatérale gauche. *Revue Neurologique, 102,* 648–653.

Hécaen, H., & Sauguet, J. (1971). Cerebral dominance in left-handed subjects. *Cortex, 7,* 19–48.

Heilman, K. M., Gonyea, E. F., & Geschwind, N. (1974). Apraxia and agraphia in a right-hander. *Cortex, 10,* 284–288.

Hochberg, F. M., & Le May, M. (1975). Arteriographic correlates of handedness. *Neurology, 25,* 218–222.

Jancke, L., Steinmetz, H., & Volkmann, J. (1992). Dichotic listening: What does it measure? *Neuropsychologia, 30,* 941–950.

Kimura, D. (1964). Left-right differences in the perception of melodies. *Quarterly Journal of Experimental Psychology, 16,* 355–358.

Kimura, D. (1976). The neural basis of language qua gesture. In H. Whitaker & N. A. Whitaker (Eds.), *Studies in neurolinguistics* (pp. 145–176). New York: Academic Press.

Kimura, D. (1982). Left hemisphere control of oral and brachial movements and their relation to communication. *Philosophical Transactions of the Royal Society of London,* B298 (pp. 135–149).

Kimura, D. (1983). Speech representation in an unbiased sample of left-handers. *Human Neurolobiology, 2,* 147–154.

Koff, E., Naeser, M. A., Picniadz, J. M., Foundas, A. R., & Levine, H. (1986). CT scan hemispheric asymmetries in right- and left-handed males and females. *Archivies of Neurology, 43,* 487–491.

Layton, W. M. Jr. (1976). Random determination of a developmental process. *Journal of Heredity, 67,* 336–338.

Le May, M. (1977). Asymmetries of the skull and handedness: phrenology revisited. *Journal of Neurological Science, 32,* 243–253.

Le May, M., & Kido, D. K. (1978). Asymmetries of the cerebral hemispheres on computed tomograms. *Journal of Computer Assissted Tomography, 2,* 471–476.

Liepmann, H. (1908). *Drei Aufsatze aus dem Apraxiegebiet.* Berlin: S. Karger.

Luria, A. R. (1970). *Traumatic aphasia.* The Hague: Mouton.

Maeshima, S., Shigeno, K., Dohi, N., Kajiwara, T., & Komai, N. (1992). A study of right unilateral spatial neglect in left hemispheric lesions: The difference between right-handed and non-right-handed post-stroke patients. *Acta Neurologica Scandinavica, 85,* 418–424.

Mateer, C., & Kimura, D. (1977). Impairment of nonverbal oral movement in aphasia. *Brain and Language, 4,* 262–276.

Milner, B. (1974). Functional recovery after lesions of the nervous system. 3. Developmental processes in neural plasticity. Sparing of language functions after early unilateral brain damage. *Neuroscience Research Program Bulletin, 12,* 213–217.

Milner, B., Branch, G., & Rasmussen, T. (1964). Observations on cerebral dominance. In A. V. S. Reuck and M. O'Connor (Eds.), *Disorders of language* (pp. 200–214). London: Churchill.

Naeser, M. A., & Borod, J. C. (1986). Aphasia in left-handers: Lesion site, lesion side, and hemispheric asymmetries on CT. *Neurology, 36,* 471–488.

Ojemann, G. A. (1984). Common cortical and thalamic mechanisms for language and motor functions. *American Journal of Psychology, 246,* R901–R906.

O'Kusky, J., Strauss, E., Kosaka, B., Wada, J., Li, D., Druhan, M., & Petrie, J. (1988). The corpus callosum is larger with right hemisphere cerebral speech dominance. *Annals of Neurology, 24,* 379–383.

Oldfield, R. C. (1971). The assessment and analysis of handedness: The Edinburgh Inventory. *Neuropsychologia, 9*, 97–113.

Penfield, W., & Roberts, L. (1959). *Speech and brain mechanisms*. Princeton, NJ: Princeton University Press.

Pfeiffer, R. A. (1936). Pathologie der Horstrahlung und der corticaler Horsphare. In O. Bumke & O.Forster (Eds.), *Handbuch der Neurologie*, Vol. 6 (pp. 534–626). Berlin: Springer-Verlag.

Poeck, K., & Kerschensteiner, M. (1971). Ideomotor apraxia following right-sided cerebral lesion in a left-handed subject. *Neuropsychologia, 9*, 359–361.

Poeck, K., & Lehmkuhl, G. (1980). Ideatory apraxia in a left-handed patient with a right-sided brain lesion. *Cortex, 16*, 273–284.

Poizner, H., Klima, E. S., & Bellugi, U. (1987). *What the hands reveal about the brain*. Cambridge, MA: MIT Press.

Rife, D. C. (1940). Handedness, with special reference to twins. *Genetics, 25*, 178–186.

Satz, P. (1979). A test of some models of hemispheric speech organization in the left- and right-handed. *Science, 203*, 1131–1133.

Satz, P., Fennelle, E., & Jones, M. B. (1969). Comments on a model of the inheritance of handedness and cerebral dominance. *Neuropsychologia, 7*, 101–103.

Selnes, O. A., Pestronk, A., Hart, J., & Gordon, B. (1991). Limb apraxia without aphasia from a left sided lesion in a right handed patient. *Journal of Neurology, Neurosurgery and Psychiatry, 54*, 734–737.

Selnes, O. A., Rubens, A. B., Risse, G. L., & Levy, R. S. (1982). Transient aphasia with persistent apraxia. Uncommon sequela of massive left hemisphere stroke. *Archives of Neurology, 39*, 122–126.

Signoret, J. L., & North, P. (1979). *Les apraxies gestuelles*. Paris: Masson.

Snyder, P. J., & Harris, L. J. (1993). Handedness, sex, and familial sinistrality. Effects on spatial tasks. *Cortex, 29*, 115–134.

Steinmetz, H., Volkmann, J., Jancke, L., & Freund, H. J. (1991). Anatomical left-right asymmetry of language-related temporal cortex is different in left- and right-handers. *Annals of Neurology, 29*, 315–319.

Strauss, E., Gaddes, W. H., & Wada, J. (1987). Performance on a free-recall dichotic listening task and cerebral dominance determined by the carotid amytal test. *Neuropsychologia, 25*, 747–753.

Subirana, A. (1958). The prognosis in aphasia in relation to cerebral dominance and handedness. *Brain, 81*, 415–425.

Subirana, A. (1969). Handedness and cerebral dominance. In P. J. Vinken & G. W. Bruyn (Eds.), *Handbook of clinical neurology* Vol. 4 (pp. 248–272). Amsterdam: North-Holland.

Vaid, J., Bellugi, U., & Poizner, H. (1989). Hand dominance for signing: clues to brain lateralization of language. *Neuropsychologia, 27*, 949–960.

Vallar, G. (1993). Neuropsychological issues in human neuropsychology. In J. Grafman & F. Boller (Eds), *Handbook of neuropsychology* (Vol. 5, pp. 343–378). Amsterdam: Elsevier.

Witelson, S. F. (1989). Hand and sex differences in the isthmus and genu of the human corpus callosum. *Brain, 112*, 799–835.

Zatorre, R. (1989). Perceptual asymmetry on the dichotic fused words test and cerebral speech lateralization determined by the carotid sodium amytal test. *Neuropsychologia, 27*, 1207–1219.

APPENDIX

Lesion maps of eight pairs of patients with cortico-subcortical right- and left-hemispheric lesions are shown in Figs. 1.1–1.8.

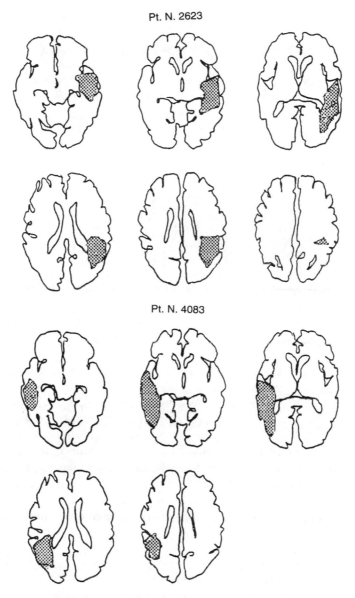

Pt. N. 2623

Pt. N. 4083

FIG. 1.1. Patient 2623: middle and inferior temporal gyri, auditory region (A.42), anterior and posterior to auditory region (A.22), inferior and superior parietal lobules, paraventricular occipital area. Patient 4083: middle and inferior temporal gyri, auditory region (A.42), anterior and posterior to auditory region (A.22), inferior and superior parietal lobules, paraventricular occipital area.

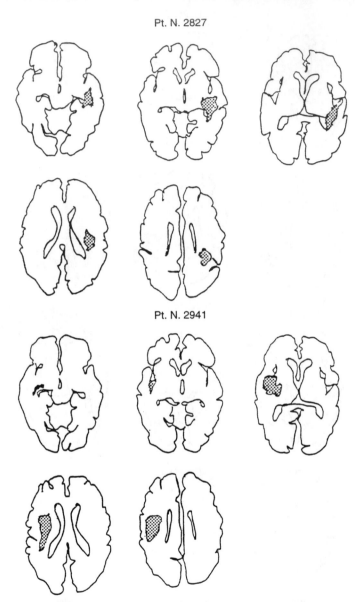

FIG. 1.2. Patient 2827: anterior to auditory region (A.22), auditory region (A.42), middle temporal gyrus, superior parietal lobule, paraventricular occipital region. Patient 2941: premotor and rolandic regions, paraventricular frontal area, anterior to auditory region (A.22), auditory region (A.42), paraventricular parietal area.

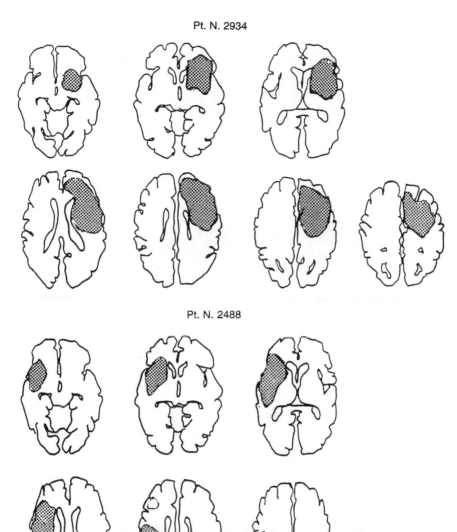

FIG. 1.3. Patient 2934: supplementary motor area, prefrontal region, frontal operculum, supraventricular and paraventricular frontal areas, superior parietal lobule, internal capsule, caudate nucleus. Patient 2488: frontal operculum, premotor and rolandic regions, paraventricular frontal area, auditory region (A.42), supramarginal gyrus, superior parietal lobule, internal capsule, caudate nucleus.

29

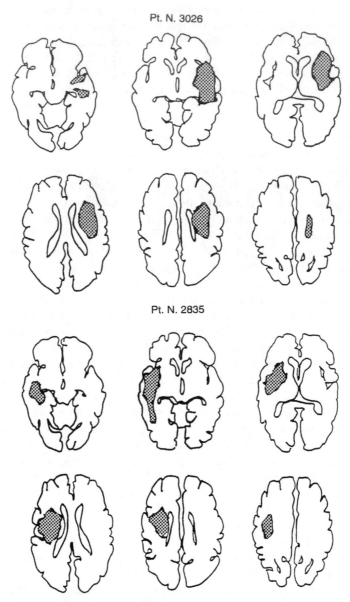

Pt. N. 3026

Pt. N. 2835

FIG. 1.4. Patient 3026: premotor and rolandic regions, paraventricular frontal area, anterior to auditory region (A.22), superior parietal lobule, insula. Patient 2835: premotor and rolandic regions, paraventricular frontal area, middle and inferior temporal gyri, anterior to auditory region (A.22), auditory region (A.42), supramarginal gyrus, paraventricular occipital area.

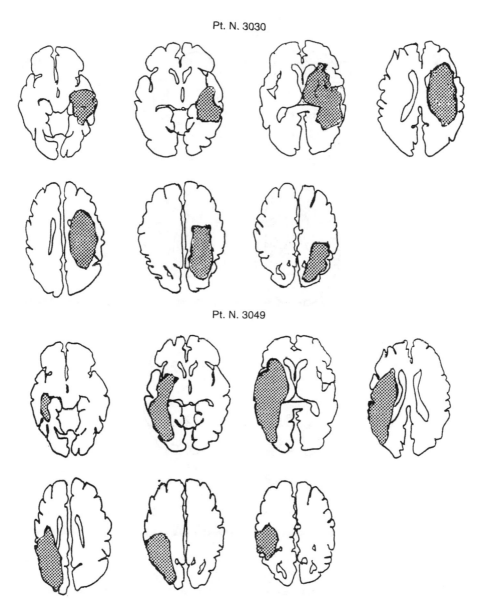

FIG. 1.5. Patient 3030: cingulate gyrus, premotor and rolandic regions, paraventricular frontal area, middle and inferior temporal gyri, anterior and posterior to auditory region (A.22), auditory region (A.42), angular gyrus, paraventricular parietal area, supracalcarine area, paraventricular occipital area. Patient 3049: premotor and rolandic regions, middle and inferior temporal gyri, auditory region (A.42), supramarginal gyrus, angular gyrus, paraventricular parietal area, supracalcarine area, paraventricular occipital area.

Pt. N. 4062

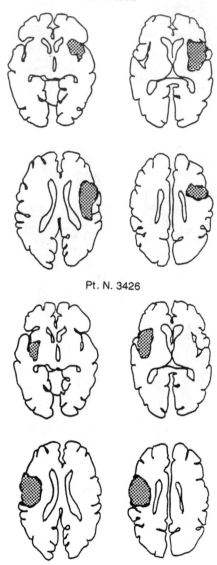

Pt. N. 3426

FIG. 1.6. Patient 4062: frontal operculum, premotor and rolandic regions, anterior to auditory region (A.22), auditory region (A.42), paraventricular parietal area, internal capsule. Patient 3426: paraventricular frontal area, premotor and rolandic regions, anterior to auditory region (A.22), auditory region (A.42), paraventricular parietal area, external capsule, insula.

32

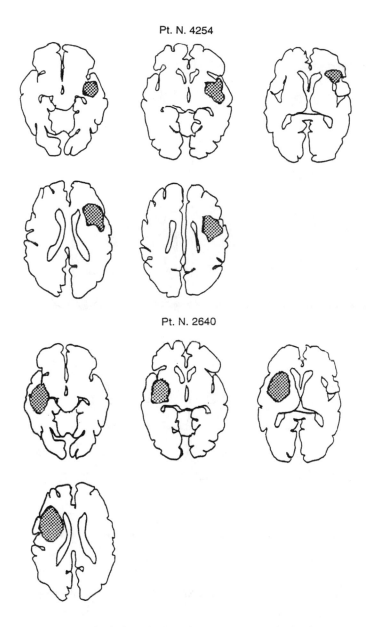

FIG. 1.7. Patient 4254: frontal operculum, premotor and rolandic regions, paraventricular frontal area, anterior to auditory region (A.22), paraventricular parietal area. Patient 2640: frontal operculum, premotor and rolandic regions, paraventricular frontal area, anterior to auditory region (A.22), middle temporal gyrus, paraventricular parietal area, paraventricular occipital area.

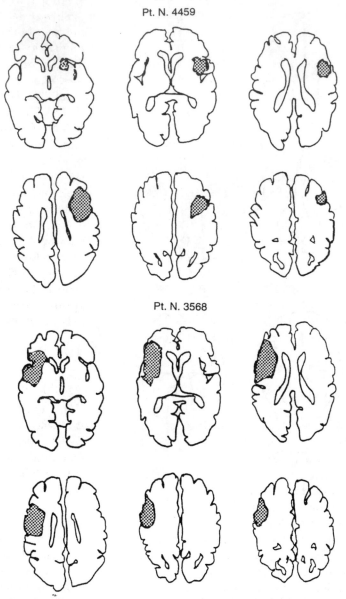

Pt. N. 4459

Pt. N. 3568

FIG. 1.8. Patient 4459: premotor and rolandic regions, paraventricular frontal area, anterior to auditory region (A.22), caudate nucleus. Patient 3568: frontal operculum, premotor and rolandic regions, paraventricular frontal area, anterior to auditory region (A.22), auditory region (42).

CHAPTER TWO

Aphasia in Bilinguals:
How Atypical Is It?

Michel Paradis
McGill University

What makes bilinguals atypical for the purpose of this volume is the fact that they are generally not included—and sometimes are explicitly excluded—from current aphasiology models. The reason for their exclusion is that they are often suspected of not fitting these models (Habib, Joanette, Ali-Chérif, & Poncet, 1983; Henderson, 1983; Lecours, 1980; Lecours, Branchereau, & Joanette, 1984). Yet it will be argued here that there is nothing atypical about bilingual aphasics on two counts: (a) Bilinguals represent the majority of the world population and (b) there is no cognitive or neural mechanism that is specific to bilingualism. Ever since Albert and Obler (1978) speculated that bilinguals may differ from unilinguals with regard to their patterns of cerebral organization, research has concentrated on identifying differences; nevertheless, no valid clinical or experimental evidence for any qualitative difference between people who speak one language and people who speak more than one language has been identified. Hence, bilinguals do fit into any model of the cerebral representation of language and of aphasiology. In fact, it will be shown that, ironically enough, models developed to account for certain aspects of bilingual aphasia may be fruitfully extended to the study of the unilingual brain.

PERVASIVENESS OF BILINGUALISM

Until rather recently, because of a long-standing habit, most hospital staff involved in the assessment and treatment of aphasia did not take into consideration the fact that patients spoke more than one language. Patients were routinely assessed in the hospital language. In the best of cases, the fact that the patient also spoke another language was simply recorded in his or her file, but no further action was taken. This behavior is typical of most hospitals in countries that have traditionally been considered unilingual. But even in bilingual cities such as Montreal, patients were seen either in a French- or English-language hospital and no attempt was made to ascertain whether other languages were available to the aphasic patient.

The general belief in most aphasia wards in cosmopolitan cities is that bilinguals are rare. When one asks neurologists in a British or French hospital if they see bilingual patients, the answer is generally that they do not, or extremely rarely. The following anecdote is quite representative of the general situation. The first time I visited the aphasia ward of a large Paris hospital, the head of the Language Pathology unit expressed a keen interest in the phenomenon of bilingual aphasia but declared that bilingual patients were rarely seen in his ward. After a few seconds, and with the help of his staff, he realized that, yes, it so happened that just at that moment there was this Frenchman who had lived in England for a long time and had married an Englishwoman . . . and come to think of it, Mrs. B was a Rumanian who had lived in France for over 20 years, and yes, there was also Mrs. C who was an Alsatian who spoke both French and German. Before two minutes were up, he and his co-workers had identified five bilingual patients with whom the staff had been quite familiar, without being explicitly aware that they were bilingual. This attitude is also reflected in the literature where a "normal language background" refers to a unilingual as opposed to bilingual background (Sewell & Panou, 1983, p. 516). Yet in France, there are more than 1 million Maghrebian Arabic–French bilinguals, 120,000 Basque speakers, 200,000 Catalan speakers, not to mention the numerous Portuguese, Spanish, Italian, and Vietnamese immigrants who speak French in addition to their native language and raise their children bilingually. Similarly Gujarati– and Punjabi–English bilinguals number in the hundreds of thousands in Great Britain. As Grosjean (1994) put it, "Bilingualism is present in practically every country of the world, in all classes of society, and in all age groups." It is therefore not the case that bilingual aphasic patients are rare. They probably represent the majority worldwide and at least a sizable proportion anywhere, a fact that psycholinguists and neurolinguists are beginning to acknowledge. Aitchison (1994, p. 236), for example, considered the unilingual situation "somewhat unusual in the world at large, where it is common for humans to use more than one language." Much of the world's verbal communication takes place by means of languages that are not the user's mother tongue (Ferguson, 1983). According to Harris and McGhee Nelson (1992), on a worldwide basis, bilingualism is very common and much more the rule than the exception in most places. Porch and de Berkeley-Wykes (1985) even estimated that approximately 80% of the world is bilingual. This situation is not limited to exotic places in Asia or Africa. Palij and Aaronson (1992) reported that the number of bilinguals in American college subject pools and in the general population is increasing. In fact, experimental psychologists are finding it increasingly difficult to come up with unilingual subjects.

Given that in the United States there are over 1 million persons with acquired aphasia (*National Aphasia Association Newsletter*, fall 1989) and that there are over 300,000 new cases of aphasia every year—100,000 caused by stroke and at least twice that many by head injury (Damasio, 1992)—and given that 15% of the total American population grew up in a minority language household, a very conservative estimate would predict that there are over 150,000 bilingual aphasic patients in the United States today, with 45,000 new cases each year. These figures represent only those individuals who grew up bilingually. To the 30% of the people living in the United States who are members of ethnic minorities must be added all those native English speakers who have learned a foreign language and all the individuals who have learned English after having immigrated fairly recently. Similarly, in a demographic study of Australia, Rowland (1991) predicted that almost 25% of Australians aged 65 or over will be from non-English-speaking backgrounds within the next 5 years. This means that today bilinguals already represent well over a quarter of the overall population of Australia (Baker, 1993). In the capital cities of Australia, between 16% and 22% of aphasic patients are bilingual or multilingual (Whitworth & Sjardin, 1993). In a survey taken in New South Wales between January and June 1993, 43.75% of the patients were bi- or multilingual (Sjardin, 1993).

Fortunately, more and more aphasiologists, logopedists, and neurolinguists are becoming aware of the increasing number of patients who speak more than one language, and many of them are beginning to do something about it. As mentioned earlier, until recently (and still in too many hospitals and clinics today), aphasic patients were diagnosed and treated only in the language of the hospital. Yet we know that patients do not necessarily recover the language that they spoke most fluently before the accident better or faster than other languages, nor does their native language or the language of the environment necessarily recover better. The situation in hospitals is rapidly changing. For instance, the American Speech-Language Hearing Association has mandated that, as of 1993, all training programs in speech-language pathology and audiology must incorporate bilingualism issues in the curriculum. In Great Britain, too, most speech-language curricula have modules or courses dealing with bilingualism. It has been realized that it is essential to examine all the languages of a given patient in order to ascertain which language is best available for communicative purposes, as well as to discover symptoms that might be observable in only one of the patient's languages and that would go forever unnoticed were the patient assessed in only one language.

WHAT IS A BILINGUAL?

One of the reasons for the belief that one rarely encounters bilingual patients might stem from the problems inherent in the very definition of bilingualism. Because there is no such thing as complete knowledge of a language in all its varieties and in all its full lexical range (Martinet, 1960, pp. 172–173), *a fortiori*, no speaker has complete knowledge of two languages. However, as long as individuals speak each of their languages in the same way as unilingual speakers do, with the same automaticity and accuracy with respect to the norm, they are considered to be "perfect" bilinguals (or ambilinguals). As long as they speak both languages with equal proficiency (irrespective of degree of mastery or accuracy), they are considered to be balanced (or equilingual). If neither of their languages is native-like and both languages together are necessary to express their thoughts, they are considered to be semilingual. A dominant bilingual is a person who speaks one language better (more fluently or accurately) than the other, and hence is not an equilingual. An equilingual, on the other hand, can be either ambilingual if both languages are equally native-like or semilingual if both are mastered equally poorly. Most definitions of bilingualism refer to the ability to speak two languages. Some then go on to specify that the use must be habitual, regular, constant, or customary; that the languages must be accent-free and spoken fluently, easily, correctly, each with equal ease (see Baetens Beardsmore, 1986, chapter 1, for an extensive discussion of definitions and Paradis, 1987, for a discussion of dimensions of bilingualism). Obviously, one is not either bilingual or not bilingual—one is bilingual to some degree.

According to the minimalist definition, to the extent that a person can use a single expression in a foreign language, that person is bilingual. According to the maximalist definition, to the extent that a person uses elements deviant with respect to the norm in one of the languages, that person is not bilingual. Once the relativity of bilingualism is acknowledged, the minimalist and maximalist definitions are but opposite poles of a continuum. For the practical purpose of assessing a bilingual aphasic patient, one would expect some degree of premorbid mastery, not just the ability to use a few phrases. However, that degree of mastery need not be extensive, as illustrated by the 18-year-old French salesman reported by Hegler (1931), who recovered only what little German he had managed to learn over the preceding 6 months and could not express himself in French at all, not even in the presence of his brother who did not understand German.

Bilinguals also differ with respect to the context of acquisition, manner of acquisition, context and frequency of use, and degree of mastery of each language. Context of acquisition may affect the contents of the grammar. Context and frequency of use may affect the availability of certain items. Manner of acquisition—whether the second language was acquired incidentally and hence stored implicitly and used automatically, like the first, or learned consciously and hence stored in declarative memory and used in a controlled manner—will determine the (procedural/declarative) cerebral memory system involved (Paradis, 1994a).

RESEARCH INTO THE BILINGUAL BRAIN

Aphasiologists and neuropsychologists have mainly focused their attention on two issues: since 1895, on patterns of recovery (Paradis, 1977, 1983, 1989, 1993a), and for the past 20 years, on the participation of the right hemisphere in the language functions of bilinguals (Mendelsohn, 1988; Paradis, 1990, 1992, 1995; Vaid, 1983; Vaid & Genesee, 1980). In addition, for the past decade, the localization of the cerebral representation of two languages in the left hemisphere (Berthier, Starkstein, Lylyk, & Leiguarda, 1990; Ojemann & Whitaker, 1978; Rapport, Tan, & Whitaker, 1983) has also been investigated, as have, more recently, the types of memory (procedural and declarative) that subserve implicit linguistic competence and metalinguistic knowledge (Paradis, 1993d, 1994a).

Bilingual Aphasia

When bilingual persons exhibit dysphasia, one would expect that all of their languages should be equally affected and that they would recover them in proportion to their premorbid relative fluency. Some, indeed, do undergo such a parallel recovery. Others, however, exhibit a differential pattern whereby one language is recovered much better than another even though they were both spoken with equal fluency before insult, or speak both languages equally well, even though one was decidedly more fluent premorbidly. Sometimes the better recovered language is the one that the patient spoke the least well. In some cases, one of the languages is never recovered (selective recovery). In that case, the patient may or may not retain comprehension of the language that remains inaccessible for production. In some cases, one of the languages recovers spontaneously only weeks or months after the other (successive recovery). On some occasions, when the inaccessible language begins to be regained, the first recovered language regresses proportionately (antagonistic recovery), possibly to the point of disappearance. This pattern may recur over successive days, weeks, or months (alternating antagonistic or see-saw recovery). Patients during this period have also been reported to exhibit paradoxical translation behavior, being able to translate into the language that is not available for spontaneous speech or confrontation naming, but not able to do the reverse, namely, to translate from a language they do understand into a language that is also available for spontaneous speech and naming. Some patients are unable to speak only one language at a time and mix items of both languages within the same sentence or even within monomorphemic words (blending recovery). They may also speak one of their languages with the accent of the other, even though both languages were spoken with native-like pronunciation before the cerebral accident. These patterns of recovery are not mutually exclusive either between languages or over time. Two languages may show antagonistic recovery whereas a third is recovered successively; two languages may show parallel recovery with a third remaining differentially impaired; or an antagonistic recovery may eventually develop into a parallel recovery.

One case of selective aphasia has been reported, in which one of three languages was never found to be measurably impaired, while the other two underwent antagonistic recovery, with one of them starting out unimpaired, but deteriorating as the other improved (Paradis & Goldblum, 1989). Two authors have also reported cases of differential aphasia, namely, one type of aphasia in one language, and a different type in the other (Albert & Obler, 1978; Silverberg & Gordon, 1979). However, one of the languages of those patients was Hebrew, and it is therefore not unlikely that the patients actually exhibited the same deficit, agrammatism, in both their languages, and that it manifested itself as the omission of grammatical morphemes in their native language and the substitution of same in Hebrew. At that time, substitutions were interpreted as being symptomatic of paragrammatism. Given what we now know about the surface manifestation of agrammatism in languages like Hebrew, the authors would probably interpret their cases differently today.

The language preferentially recovered is not necessarily the native language, the most familiar or the most useful to the patient, or the language of the environment. No general principle seems to be compatible with all cases of recovery. Neither site nor size of lesion, context of acquisition, nor any other factor correlates better than chance with nonparallel types of recovery. It was suggested at one point that a lesion in the parietal-temporal-occipital junction (PTO) might be responsible for problems of switching from one language to another and hence for selective or blending recoveries, depending on whether the hypothesized switch mechanism was stuck in one position or loose (Leischner, 1948; Pötzl, 1930). However, cases with PTO involvement have been reported without switching difficulty (Gloning & Gloning, 1965; L'Hermitte, Hécaen, Dubois, Culioli, & Tabouret-Keller, 1966; Schulze, 1968), as well as switching problems subsequent to frontal lesions without PTO involvement (Gloning & Gloning, 1965; L'Hermitte et al., 1966; Minkowski, 1927; Stengel & Zelmanowicz, 1933). Similarly, it has been hypothesized that languages acquired in different contexts would be more neurofunctionally separated than languages acquired in the same context and hence more susceptible of nonparallel recovery (Lambert & Fillenbaum, 1959). That hypothesis too failed to be supported by the evidence (Paradis, 1977). Reflecting on cases of subjects who learn one language through reading, Lebrun (1971, 1976) suggested that languages that are learned differently may rest on different neural organizations or be subserved by different cerebral circuits. One possible difference lies in the availability of additional written language representations, another in the availability of metalinguistic knowledge, even when implicit linguistic competence is inaccessible, as discussed later.

In some cases, it would be possible to explain the better recovery of one language over another because of some particular peripheral circumstance. For example, Minkowski (1927) explained some cases of recovery of a standard language over an exclusively spoken dialect by hypothesizing that the patients were able to "visualize" in their mind the written forms, thus facilitating retrieval of the items, whereas this strategy was not available for unwritten dialects. Halpern (1949) concluded that, in some cases, the recovery of a language may be facilitated by the fact that it had been acquired through the written form. A lesion in the temporal lobe will damage that part of the cortex that subserves acoustic engrams but will not interfere with the visual engrams of words. Hinshelwood (1902) described the case of an English scholar who differentially recovered Greek, Latin, French, and English, in that order. The two classical languages, which had been learned through reading and writing, were less affected than French, which had been learned from both the written text and the spoken words, and which was itself less affected than English, his native language, which had been acquired by hearing and speaking long before it was mastered in written form. Halpern (1941) also remarked that patients with right hemianopia could more easily read languages written from right to left than languages written from left to right since in the latter case patients move their gaze toward their blind field. The reverse may be true for patients with left hemifield neglect.

Right-Hemisphere Participation in Unilinguals and in Bilinguals

One of the suspected differences between bilinguals' and unilinguals' cerebral language representation has been the extent of involvement of the right hemisphere (RH). Based on a small sample of published cases and a misreading of the paper by Nair and Virmani (1973), Albert and Obler (1978, pp. 205, 239) thought that there was evidence that language is less lateralized in bilingual adults than in unilingual adults and suggested that bilinguals and unilinguals may have different cerebral organization patterns for language. They argued forcefully in favor of the notions of cerebral ambilaterality of language representation in bilinguals, asymmetrical dominance for each language, and greater right-hemisphere participation in general. But before we can speak of greater participation of the RH in bilingual than in unilingual speakers, we ought to establish the nature of this increased participation. A number of possibilities come to mind (Paradis, 1987, pp. 3–4).

Initially, it was believed that the RH had no language capacity. Only when the left hemisphere (LH) was incapacitated early in life could the RH acquire some language to a limited extent. This plasticity would diminish with age. A lesion in the RH sustained in adulthood would therefore have no consequences for language. This is still by and large believed to be the case, if by *language* one means the grammar or implicit linguistic competence (i.e., that which allows speakers to generate any well-formed sentence in the language with respect to phonology, morphology, syntax, and the lexicon). This statement must be qualified by the fact that a RH lesion in some right-handers has been shown to cause subtle deficits observable through sophisticated testing (Bryan, 1988; Joanette, 1980; Joanette, Lecours, Lepage, & Lamoureux, 1983), but as a rule these deficits are negligible and for the most part go unnoticed.

In addition to the already mentioned Nil Participation Hypothesis, a number of other hypotheses have been considered over the years. For instance, both hemispheres might process information in identical ways, though the participation of the LH might be quantitatively greater. Either the processing in the RH would be redundant and lesions there would be of little consequence for language (the Redundant Participation Hypothesis), or there would be a mass effect and the whole bilaterally represented language area would be necessary for normal language processing (the Quantitatively Complementary Participation Hypothesis). Lesions to homologous parts of either hemisphere would cause qualitatively identical deficits proportional to the extent of language subserved by that hemisphere. Joanette's data tend to support such an interpretation, given that mild deficits have been demonstrated in some individuals consequent upon unilateral RH lesions.

It is also conceivable that the same information (e.g., linguistic prosody) may be processed in a qualitatively different manner in each hemisphere, for example, analytic processing in the LH and gestaltist in the RH (the Qualitatively Complementary Hypothesis). Or, as seems to be confirmed by increasing evidence from reports of deficits subsequent to RH lesions, different information is processed in each hemisphere (e.g., linguistic prosody in the LH, affective prosody in the RH). In this case, lesions cause selective impairments in those aspects subserved by the affected hemisphere (the Qualitatively Selective Participation Hypothesis).

In fact, it appears that both right and left cerebral hemispheres supply their own specific contributions to the microgenetic processing of utterances. The LH is known to be involved in the decoding and encoding of phonological, morphological, syntactic, and lexical properties, whereas there is rapidly increasing converging evidence that the RH is involved in the interpretation of what is implicitly meant, although not explicitly said, such as inferences from general knowledge and situational context, affective prosody, and other paralinguistic features.

Generative grammars, through their successive mutations (e.g., from the transformational grammar of the 1960s to government-binding and principles and parameters of the 1980s, to the recent minimalist program for the 1990s), have been concerned with (context-independent) sentence grammar. Linguistic competence, as described by Chomsky (1965), is the implicit knowledge of the speaker-hearer's (sentence) grammar. The automatic, unconscious use of this linguistic competence is what allows speaker-hearers to produce and understand sentences. In the normal use of language, various additional cognitive entities have been recognized as either necessary (e.g., conceptual and episodic memory, the speaker's "encyclopedia," i.e., that which the speaker speaks about) or as placing constraints on the use of linguistic competence (e.g., short-term memory constraints, attention-span limitations, etc.). These RII deficits may be grouped under the term *dyshyponoia.*

In the normal use of language, in addition to the interpretation of the literal meaning of sentences, a discourse grammar, including rules of pre-supposition and inference, and in general any extrasentential, context-dependent phenomenon, is required. Sociolinguistic rules, which determine the appropriate choice among the various possible structures available in linguistic competence, are equally necessary. Paralinguistic competence, comprising the use of affective prosody, facial expressions, gestures, and anything that serves to specify the meaning of the sentence, such as whether it is meant as a sarcastic remark or an indirect speech act, or whether it is to be given a figurative, metaphoric, or idiomatic meaning, is likewise required.

Damage in specific areas of the left cerebral hemisphere has been reported to disrupt the comprehension and/or production of various aspects of phonology, morphology, syntax, and the lexicon to varying degrees. These deficits are grouped under the term *aphasia.* It is therefore well established that these aspects of language (as they pertain to sentence grammar) are subserved by areas of the LH.

In addition to occasional mild symptoms of aphasia subsequent to RH lesions in sites homologous to the classical LH language areas in some patients, as mentioned earlier, clear deficits of a different nature, affecting the comprehension and production of indirect speech acts, humor, affect, and various aspects of nonliteral interpretation of utterances, have been reported (Bihrle, Brownell, & Gardner, 1988; Bihrle, Brownell, Powelson, & Gardner, 1986; Brookshire & Nicholas, 1984; Brownell, 1988; Brownell, Gardner, Prather, & Martino, 1995; Brownell, Michel, Powelson, & Gardner, 1983; Brownell, Potter, Bihrle, & Gardner, 1986; Dwyer & Rinn, 1981; Foldi, 1987; Foldi, Cicone, & Gardner, 1983; Gardner, Brownell, Wapner, & Michelow, 1983; Heilman, Bowers, Speedie, & Costlett, 1984; Hier & Kaplan,

1980; Hirst, LeDoux, & Stein, 1984; Joanette, Goulet, & Hannequin, 1990; Kaplan, Brownell, Jacobs, & Gardner, 1990; Kawashima et al., 1993; McDonald & Wales, 1986; Molloy, Brownell, & Gardner, 1990; Ross, 1981, 1984; Tompkins & Mateer, 1985; Weylman, Brownell, Roman, & Gardner, 1989). Deficits secondary to RH damage thus typically involve those aspects of language use other than the literal interpretation of (context-independent) sentences and requiring some form of inference from the situational or discursive context and/or general knowledge.

Based on the available evidence, the following hypothesis can be formulated (Paradis, 1994b): Context-independent sentence grammar is separable from other aspects of sentence interpretation (discourse context-dependent rules and nonliteral meanings) and is indeed separated neurofunctionally; that is, although LH damage causes context-independent sentence grammar (phonological, morphological, syntactic and lexical) deficits, RH damage causes deficits in context-dependent interpretations, nonliteral interpretations, and affect-related aspects of language processing (in comprehension and production).

It is proposed that (context-independent) sentence grammar (linguistic competence as narrowly defined in theoretical linguistics) is subserved by specific areas of the LH and that, consequently, damage to those areas results in language structure deficits (i.e., deficits in the use of phonology, morphology, syntax, and the lexicon in comprehension and production). It is further proposed that pragmatic aspects of language are subserved by the RH and that consequently, damage to specific areas of the RH results in context-dependent language deficits (e.g., deficits in the use of presupposition, inference, cross-sentential anaphora and cataphora, sarcasm, indirect speech acts, idioms, metaphors, and any aspect of the nonliteral interpretation of sentences, in comprehension and production, including recognition and production of affective prosody). Communicative competence necessarily includes linguistic competence (as narrowly defined). In addition, and independently, it contains implicit pragmatic competence. Each is necessary but neither is sufficient for the normal use of language.

Studies of language laterality in bilinguals have suffered from a lack of specification of what the authors mean by *language*, although in the earlier studies it seems apparent that authors were referring to the language system (the grammar, or implicit linguistic competence).

It all began with suggestions that the RH of bilinguals might be specialized to a certain degree for foreign languages (Vildomec, 1963). Tachistoscopic tests had shown a greater right visual field effect for English than for Hebrew or Yiddish words in native speakers of English (Mishkin & Forgays, 1952; Orbach, 1953, 1967). In the face of studies that did not demonstrate any difference in asymmetry between unilinguals and bilinguals, the population suspected of showing greater RH participation was consequently restricted to those individuals who had learned their second language *after* puberty (Albanèse, 1985; Sussman, Franklin, & Simon, 1982). Then again, in the face of failure to replicate, the population was further reduced to those who had learned their second language after puberty *informally*. Then it was reduced to only people at the beginning stages of the informal acquisition of a second language after puberty (Galloway & Krashen, 1980). Although studies that showed no difference continued to appear (Barton, Goodglass, & Shai, 1965; Carroll, 1980; Galloway & Scarcella, 1982; Gordon, 1980; Hall & Lambert, 1988; Hoosain, 1992; Hoosain & Shiu, 1989; Hynd, Teeter, & Stewart, 1980; Kershner & Jeng, 1972; Kotik, 1975; McKeever & Hunt, 1984; Obrzut, Conrad, Bryden, & Boliek, 1988; Piazza Gordon & Zatorre, 1981; Schönle, 1978; Soares, 1982, 1984; Soares & Grosjean, 1981; Walters & Zatorre, 1978), those that did find a difference showed contradictory results with respect to the appropriate subpopulation: greater RH participation in late learners as a function of increased proficiency (Bergh, 1986), as well as greater LH lateralization than unilinguals in early bilinguals (Ben Amar & Gaillard, 1984; Starck, Genesee, Lambert, & Seitz, 1977). The least one can say is that results from experimental studies are far from compelling. Even a recent meta-analysis (Vaid & Hall, 1991) has failed to come up with a difference. In addition, the clinical evidence from the incidence of crossed aphasia (Chary, 1986; Karanth & Rangamani, 1988; Rangamani, 1989), Wada testing (Berthier, Starkstein, Lylyk, & Leiguarda, 1990; Rapport, Tan, & Whitaker, 1983), and all the patients seen at the Montreal Neurological Institute over the past 25 years (Brenda Milner, personal communication, October 1994) points to language being subserved by areas of the LH in bilinguals in the same proportion as in unilinguals. Not only is there no evidence of greater incidence of crossed aphasia in bilinguals, but all the evidence there is points in the opposite direction.

The evidence to date is compatible with the hypothesis that the LH subserves the grammar and the RH subserves the pragmatic aspects of language use. There is no evidence that the RH participates in any significant way in the processing of the grammar of either language in bilingual individuals. The dichotic listening, finger tapping, and tachistoscopic procedures have yielded contradictory results, which, together with the overwhelming clinical evidence, have led to serious doubts about the validity of the experimental procedures (Paradis, 1990, 1992, 1995), and most researchers have finally abandoned this fruitless search for a differential cerebral asymmetry for language. On the other hand, it is not unlikely that, in order to compensate for the lacunae in their implicit linguistic competence, speakers rely to a greater extent on RH-based pragmatic aspects when using their weaker language, in the same way that children do during the acquisition of their native language.

For a long time it was taken for granted that both hemispheres are more or less equipotential at birth and that children use both hemispheres at the beginning of language acquisition (language being understood as implicit linguistic competence). It was assumed that both hemispheres were active in the first stages of language acquisition and that language gradually lateralized to the left. The age at which this operation was completed was a matter of controversy, with some researchers claiming completion before the age of 5 (Krashen, 1973, 1975a, 1975b), and others by puberty (Lenneberg, 1967). Goodglass (1978) attempted to explain the phenomenon by conjecturing that, because the neurons recruited in the RH in the early stages of language acquisition are slower and less efficient, they would eventually drop out of the processing of language altogether. An alternative explanation might be that the RH was never involved in the processing of language (*qua* grammar, that which gets lateralized to the LH) in the first place, but that during the first stages of language acquisition the child uses pragmatic competence and processes verbal information not through a not-yet-existent linguistic competence, but through inference from situational context, general knowledge, and possibly from an understanding of a few isolated words. Thus, it is not necessarily the case that bilinguals, duplicating the first language acquisition stages, should process any grammar in their RH, even at the earliest stages of acquisition.

Language Organization in the Left Hemisphere

Whatever the participation of the RH might be, the question remains as to how two languages are represented in the same brain, whether they are subserved by a common neural substrate or whether each language is stored and processed in distinct neural substrates. At least four hypotheses can be formulated (Paradis, 1981, 1987).

The first is the Extended System Hypothesis, according to which the various languages are represented in an undifferentiated way in the cortical language areas. The bilingual language system then simply contains more elements (those from two languages instead of just one), that is, contains more phonemes, more morphemes, more possible syntactic constructions, and more lexical items. These are treated as allo-elements within the language system, namely, elements used only in specific contexts—those of L1 in L1 contexts and those of L2 in L2 contexts. Parallel recovery is compatible with such a hypothesis.

Then there is the Dual System Hypothesis, according to which elements of each language are stored separately, each in an independent system. The two languages are thus separately stored in the brain with two independent sets of phonemes, morphemes, syntactic constructions, and lexical items. This hypothesis is compatible with selective and any other type of nonparallel recovery.

The Tripartite System Hypothesis posits that those items that are identical in both languages are represented in one common underlying neural substrate, whereas items that differ between languages are stored separately, each in its independent neural substrate. Thus whatever the languages have in common is represented only once, and what is specific to each is represented independently. Evidence from electrical stimulation provided by Ojemann and Whitaker (1978) and Rapport et al. (1983) is compatible with this hypothesis because both languages are reported to have been affected at some stimulation sites and only one at other sites. The authors concluded that there are cortical sites common to both languages and sites specific to one of them. Berthier, Starkstein, Lylyk, and Leiguarda (1990) reported similar findings with respect to the resorption of the effects of amytal on language functions. However, the data do not unambiguously support such an interpretation.

The areas of stimulation reported by Ojemann and Whitaker (1978) were much too extensive and imprecise for one to ascertain whether the same system of neurons had been disrupted on two separate occasions. Bipolar stimulation with electrodes 5 mm apart, given the dispersion of current at the end of each electrode, would affect an area of close to 1 cm². It is therefore not surprising that, at the periphery of the language area, naming was sometimes interfered with, and sometimes not. If identical sites had been stimulated on each trial it would be difficult to explain why at some sites a given language would be affected only some of the time. Either the language in question is assumed to be subserved by neurons at that locus, in which case it should be affected every time, without exception, or not at all, or we must assume that a particular language occupies different loci at different times, in which case we need a theory of migrating language representation. At some sites, Dutch was disturbed more often than English, and at other sites English was disturbed more than Dutch. To paraphrase Scoresby-Jackson (1867): "Where was that gentleman's Dutch deposited the two times out of five that it was not disturbed?" (The very rationale for electrical stimulation of the brain is that language is represented in some specific loci and not in others.)

Finally, we have the Subset Hypothesis, according to which each language constitutes a subsystem of the larger cognitive system known as language, in the same way that various registers constitute subsystems of the overall language competence of an individual, or even that phonology and syntax, for example, constitute separate modules within the language system. Each subsystem can be selectively impaired by pathology; however, each subsystem is nevertheless part of the overall language system, as distinguished from other higher cognitive systems. This hypothesis at least has the merit of being compatible with all the patterns of recovery reported so far, as well as with unilingual phenomena.

Note that all of these various hypotheses are compatible with unilingual systems—whether a (single) language is represented as a whole, with all stylistic and sociolinguistic registers confounded; whether each register is represented as an independent system; whether elements of one register shared by another would be represented in a common system, whereas whatever is specific to each register would be represented in its own respective separate system; or whether they are represented as subsystems of language.

Implicit Linguistic Competence
Versus Metalinguistic Knowledge

Another important distinction to bear in mind when discussing bilingual aphasia is that between implicit linguistic competence and metalinguistic knowledge. The former is acquired incidentally, is stored in the form of procedural know-how without conscious knowledge of its contents, and is used automatically (i.e., without conscious control). The latter is learned consciously (possibly, but not necessarily, effortfully), is available for conscious recall, and is applied to the production (and comprehension) of language in a controlled manner. Implicit linguistic competence is acquired through interaction with speakers of the particular language in situational contexts. Metalinguistic knowledge is usually learned in school (Paradis, 1994a). The extent of metalinguistic knowledge of one's native language is therefore generally proportional to one's degree of schooling. Very often a foreign language is learned almost exclusively through metalinguistic knowledge, and whatever implicit linguistic competence develops subsequently does so through practice of the language in communicative situations. Considering that implicit linguistic competence is what is affected by aphasia, and that explicit knowledge, being subserved by entirely different cerebral structures, is generally not impaired in aphasic patients, it is not unreasonable to expect that metalinguistic knowledge, together with all other items of episodic and encyclopedic declarative memory, remains available to aphasic patients. It is likewise not unlikely that some patients were exposed to much more explicit metalinguistic knowledge during the learning of a foreign language than during the acquisition of their native language, especially if their native language is a spoken dialect not used in school. Some patients may even have had their entire schooling in a second language, while continuing to use the first language in the home, a language in which they remain illiterate (whether or not it has a written form) and about which they may have little metalinguistic knowledge.

In such individuals, metalinguistic knowledge about their second and possibly weaker language may be much more extensive than about their native language. Consequent upon aphasia, they may lose access to their implicit linguistic competence equally in both languages but retain access to their metalinguistic knowledge, which, being more extensive in their nonnative language, may give the impression of preferential recovery of the language that was the least fluent before insult. Even though implicit competence may be equally impaired in both languages, the patient has more metalinguistic knowledge to fall back on in his or her weaker language. And because these patients are aphasic, the fact that they speak slowly and control their production consciously and ask their interlocutor to slow down and/or to repeat may go unnoticed, because it would be masked by the fact that the patients, being aphasic, are expected to speak more effortfully anyhow. This might explain the paradoxical recovery of some of the patients mentioned earlier (e.g., Hegler, 1931; Hinshelwood, 1902; Minkowski, 1927). This hypothesis is also compatible with the suggestion that educated patients tend to have a better prognosis (Baruzzi, 1985).

BILINGUALS DO NOT DIFFER FUNCTIONALLY FROM UNILINGUALS

Psycholinguists have come to realize that "most or all processes encountered in bilingualism have a monolingual parallel" (Kirsner, 1986) and that bilingualism is actually "an extreme example of register difference" (Smith & Wilson, 1980). Whatever behavior is generally associated with bilingualism is available to the unilingual as well, albeit possibly to different extents. For every bilingual function, there is a unilingual homologue. Unilingual and bilingual speakers alike switch, mix, borrow, suffer interference (Baetens Beardsmore, 1980), and are able to translate.

There are two types of interference: competence interference, when an item from one language is systematically (albeit erroneously) used when speaking another language (a component of implicit linguistic competence deviant with respect to the norm), and performance interference, which refers to the inadvertent use of an item (word, syntactic construction) from one language when speaking another. The first has its parallel in the systematic use of an item from one register in another (a component of linguistic competence deviant with respect to the prescriptive norm); the second, in the occasional intrusion of items from a different register (inadvertent use of a word from one register when speaking in another, in a context where register switching/mixing is not appropriate).

Language switching, the change from one language to another, has its counterpart in what sociolinguists have called code switching, namely, style shift, register shift (where several variants may be available for selection), the alternate use of two speech styles (sociolinguistic registers) within one language (baby talk, familiar, formal registers) or between two dialects (sociolects or topolects) as well as between two closely related or unrelated languages (Hymes, 1966; Labov, 1972). In either case, the shift is determined by social and other contextual constraints. Switching from baby talk to colloquial and from colloquial to formal speech, like switching between languages, results in differences at the phonological, morphosyntactic, and lexical levels.

Code mixing refers to the use of elements of more than one language within the same utterance. This corresponds to sociolinguistic register code mixing, such as mixing within an utterance elements of different registers. Nonce borrowing refers to the occasional borrowing of a word from another language. Nonce borrowing can also occur between registers, either unwittingly, as when avoiding a temporary word-finding difficulty in a context where strict adhesion to the register is not necessary, or deliberately in order to produce a certain effect. Translation, or saying in one language a close approximation of what has been said or written in another, has its analogy in paraphrasing, either between registers (involving phonology as well as morphosyntax and the lexicon) or even within the same register (involving only morphosyntax and the lexicon).

Sometimes, in a bilingual environment, people may read words from one language as though they belonged to the other until further context reveals their delusion. For example, in Montreal, TV guides give descriptions of programs from English-language stations in English and programs from French-language stations in French; thus, paragraphs will randomly appear in English or in French, depending on the order of the stations listed for that time slot. Because many written words are ambiguous with respect to membership in these two languages, it very often happens that a reader, having started reading a text as though it were in French, realizes by the third word or so that it is actually in English, or vice versa. This type of experience is not unique to bilingualism. Cognates, faux-amis, and other cross-language ambiguities are resolved in the same way as ambiguity (homophony/homography) between two words or phrases in the same language. Newspaper headlines in English often result in the same delusion: A verb mistaken for a noun may lead the reader up the garden path. Context generally disambiguates the meaning of a word, phrase, or sentence. A sentence such as *The boy found a bat in the attic* may have to be reinterpreted if the next sentence refers to the boy's wanting to play baseball.

It has been reported that bilinguals and trilinguals have longer reaction times (RT) for naming than unilinguals (Mägiste, 1986). The extra time may be accounted for by the fact that the combined vocabularies of the two or three languages contain more entries than the vocabulary of the average unilingual. However, the published data show that there is considerable variation in RTs among unilinguals and that the curves of unilinguals and bilinguals overlap. Hence it appears that what is responsible for the difference in RT is not the fact that there are two languages per se, but the fact that the number of choices is generally larger in bilinguals and larger still in trilinguals. Those unilinguals whose RTs overlap with those of bilinguals are likely to be those individuals with extensive vocabularies. The relevant variable here is the number of lexical items, irrespective of the number of languages.

If we accept the metaphor that words are "tagged" for language membership, then not only must words also be tagged for register membership, but for grammatical properties as well, so that they may be selected only in the appropriate contexts. In other words, the language tag is just another feature of the word's lemma. Whatever is responsible for the selection of an English word in a given context must also be responsible for the selection of a verb, and a transitive one at that. A word is set apart as "English" in the same way that it is set apart as "baby talk" or "count noun."

BILINGUALS DO NOT DIFFER NEUROANATOMICALLY OR NEUROPHYSIOLOGICALLY FROM UNILINGUALS

It has often been mistakenly assumed that the organization of the neural substrate is in some way modified as a consequence of the differential organization of language structure. It has thus been assumed that a compound organization of the grammars (a linguistic construct) in certain individuals would cause them to have a cerebral organization (a neurolinguistic construct) different from that of individuals with a coordinate organization of their language systems (Albert & Obler, 1978). Yet, although the contents of the grammar differ from language to language and from one bilingual individual to another (depending on the degree and kind of deviance from the unilingual norm in each language), there is no necessary effect on *how* the grammar is subserved. In other words, the internal structure of the grammar may differ but it is subserved by the brain as a grammar, irrespective of its specific contents, and hence irrespective of the number of illicit borrowings.

One linguistic consequence of early bilingualism in some individuals may be a systematic deviance with respect to the unilingual norm at some or all levels of language representation (e.g., some degree of compoundness in voice onset time, vowel quality, the idiosyncratic use of a particular preposition in some contexts, the use of some expressions) without any consequences for the way in which (i.e., the mechanisms according to which) the grammar is subserved by neural substrates. A grammar rule (or whatever implicit process results in the systematic verbal behavior of the speaker) is processed as a grammar rule (or whatever), and a phoneme or a syllable is processed as a phoneme or a syllable, whether it is a legitimate element or one that properly belongs to another language and is thus improperly incorporated. There is no reason to assume that there should be one way for the brain to process legitimate elements and another to process illegitimate ones. Improper borrowings are processed as if they were legitimate. It is often an historical accident that such features are not in fact legitimate. The actual number of shared elements between English and French, for example, is contingent upon such historical accidents—it is not necessary and could easily be different. In fact, the shared elements continue to change over time.

The accuracy (with respect to the unilingual norm) of the languages spoken by an individual is independent of the manner in which they are processed by the brain. An early bilingual may possess closed class words in the same way as unilingual native speakers, even though the use of some of these words may be deviant with respect to the norm (e.g., the systematic use of the preposition *to* instead of the preposition *of* in some contexts), whereas a late bilingual may use each language with native-like accuracy, although processing closed class words in a manner that differs from unilinguals' and early bilinguals', as evidenced by event-related potentials (see Weber-Fox & Neville, 1994, 1996). Thus the contents of implicit linguistic competence, as inferred from the observed performance, may be independent of the various cerebral processes that subserve them. Different processes may yield the same linguistic output. The same cerebral process may yield linguistic output that differs from the norm (and from one individual to another).

In a recent study applying positron emission tomography (PET) techniques in the context of a cognitive neuroscience approach, Klein, Zatorre, Milner, Meyer, and Evans (1995) showed that the storage of translation equivalents is essentially identical to the storage of synonyms in the same language for bilingual subjects, even though all their subjects had learned their second language after age 5. Nor was any right-hemisphere cortical activity observed for either the first or the second language. The Klein et al. results also strongly suggest that word generation in the two languages makes demands on overlapping neural substrates and that the same neural processes subserve both first- and second-language performance. They found no evidence that a fluent second language, even one learned later in life, is represented differently from the native language.

Differential Use of the Same Cerebral Mechanisms

To use a metaphor, one may type French and German with the same typewriter. In either case, the typewriter functions in the same way, letters being printed on a page as a result of keys being pressed and the pressure being relayed by a system of springs and pulleys. Only the outcome, the text, is different, depending on the sequence of keystrokes. Thus the system (here, how a typewriter operates) works in identical ways whether one uses it to type French or German, although the use one makes of it, such as a much more extensive use of the dieresis (umlaut) key in German, differs. Note that the difference is only quantitative. Maybe some possibilities of the typewriter are activated only when typing one of the two languages (say, acute accents when typing French). But the principles of functioning of the typewriter do not change with the language that one chooses to type. Perhaps the metaphor of a personal computer with different fonts comes even closer. Texts in several languages may be typed, using the same system, possibly using different programs compatible with that system. The point is that the type of operation is the same, even though the operations themselves differ between languages, as in fact they differ within the same language when producing different texts.

A distinction is thus to be made between the way in which a system works and the way it is used. The same system may be used differently (e.g., different parts of the system may be used to differing extents) by different populations, depending on their experiential needs (unilinguals vs. bilinguals; bilinguals who commonly mix vs. bilinguals who do not mix; professional simultaneous interpreters vs. average bilinguals; bilinguals who have acquired both their languages from the crib vs. those who have learned a second language formally, etc.). These experiential circumstances may determine the extent to which metalinguistic knowledge is put to use, right-hemisphere-based pragmatic strategies are substituted for linguistic process-ing of verbal information, or the activation threshold baseline is raised or lowered, as is examined in further detail later.

Nor is it necessary to assume that the extent to which the bilingual speaker has command of the two systems has consequences for the organization within the brain and the way in which the neurofunctional systems subserv-ing language work (only the way in which the systems are used). A neuro-functional system for comprehension and production in the bilingual does not need any additional component that is not already present in the uni-lingual speaker-hearer. Nor is there a need for a component in a neurofunc-tional system that is different for fluent and nonfluent bilinguals. The only difference is the extent to which they make use of parts of the system. Different types of bilinguals will make differential use of various parts of the system, depending on the extent to which they rely on pragmatic cues and/or metalinguistic knowledge.

In the same vein, structural differences between the bilingual's languages should be irrelevant for the working of the neurofunctional system. There is no evidence to suggest that the neurofunctional system is not the same for all bilinguals (and, in fact, unilinguals). To the extent that the speaker uses implicit linguistic competence, he or she will rely on areas of the left hemisphere subserving implicit grammar. Hence, the more implicit linguistic competence is used in verbal communication for understanding and pro-ducing utterances, the more procedural memory for linguistic competence is used. The less implicit linguistic competence is used, the less the left-hemisphere areas subserving implicit grammar are used (i.e., the more prag-matic aspects are relied on and hence the more areas of the RH are used and/or the more metalinguistic knowledge is used and hence the more the neural substrates underlying declarative memory are used). The neural substrates of verbal communication are thus the same for all speakers, irrespective of the language(s) spoken, and the only dissimilarity is in the degree of use of the various components of the system and the relative activation threshold of its various parts—not a difference in nature or in kind.

The same neurofunctional system can thus account for all possibilities. The brain is not organized differently for any language pair. The verbal communicative system does not work differently for different language pairs. But the extent to which this or that aspect of the system is used depends on the languages' typology, the extent of switching and mixing, the extent of relative use, and any other relevant feature. Therefore, the structural differences between the bilingual's languages (as well as any other aspect) is irrelevant 'to the structure of the system but relevant to the degree to which any part of the system is put to use (or how high the activation threshold will be for a given item or a given function). In other words, in different types of bilinguals, what changes is not the mechanism but the individual's grammar; not *the way* in which the two languages are represented but *what* is represented; not the makeup of the underlying cerebral system but its contents.

By the same token, sociolinguistic considerations will not affect the system, only the use of it. Just as sociolinguistic competence in a unilingual dictates whether to select *Du* or *Sie* when addressing a particular person in German, both *Du* and *Sie* being available in the speaker's linguistic competence (or language system), sociolinguistic factors will determine which of the two languages is used, although this will have no impact on the design of the underlying neural system, only on its use.

There is abundant experimental (Grosjean, 1994) and clinical evidence (Lecours & Joanette, 1980) to the effect that conceptual mental representations are phylogenetically and ontogenetically prior to implicit linguistic competence, and that linguistic competence, once acquired, remains independent of conceptual representation (Hécaen, 1968; Rosenberger, 1978). Not being *langage*-specific, mental representations are not *langue*-specific (i.e., not English- or Japanese-specific). The message to be communicated is elaborated before being encoded either in English or in Japanese. The end product of the linguistic decoding of an utterance (the message conveyed by the utterance) is likewise a nonlinguistic mental representation. There is only one such mental representational system (fractionable into various components, to be sure), irrespective of the number of language systems represented in the brain, be it one, two, or more. Each language system may impose constraints on how various mental representations can be verbalized, but the process of verbalization (i.e., matching concepts with words) is the same for unilinguals and bilinguals. There is no reason to assume that the system involved in selecting the language to be used to encode any given utterance is not the same as the one that is involved in selecting the register to be used. The basis on which such a choice is made is the same whether it is between languages or registers, namely, the appropriateness of the situation, given the interlocutors. The same is the case with aphasic patients, who use whichever item is more readily accessible.

The study of bilingualism has thus drawn attention to the fact that the linguistic competence of a unilingual speaker actually contains several subsets (registers) that must be accounted for in a model of cerebral language representation. Their representation can be accounted for in the same way as the representation of different languages has been. For example, Riese (1948) relates the case of a patient who, for a few months, in the course of a postoperative transient aphasia, expressed his thoughts using only the formal register with very long, technical, and Shakespearean words, and never used simple words. This was absolutely involuntary and surprised the patient himself.

All of the clinical evidence suggests that there is no structural difference between bilingual and unilingual brains and that there is no need to postulate any neurofunctional mechanism specific to bilingualism. Intrasubject variability on tasks over short periods of time as exhibited in antagonistic or seesaw recovery patterns is of the same nature as intrasubject variability in unilingual aphasic patients. Performance in unilingual aphasic patients is indeed far from uniform. They too exhibit variability on the same task from day to day. Problems of inhibition/disinhibition are called upon to account for both unilingual and bilingual phenomena.

Cases of aphasia in polyglots may "pose a major conundrum that should be addressed in any model of language representation in the brain" (Goodglass, 1993, p. 11), but the models of the unilingual and the bilingual brain need not differ qualitatively, that is, with respect to the various mechanisms involved. Only the relative use of each of these various mechanisms, a quantitative attribute, varies. There is no evidence to suggest that the bilingual brain should present a different cerebral organization, that is, a way of processing information that differs from that of unilingual brains. The difference may be considered simply a question of emphasis on one or the other function, on the quantitative use of the various mechanisms available to both. Because unilinguals are able to do in kind whatever bilinguals do, there is no reason to suppose that the languages are represented in a way radically different from that of the different registers of unilinguals. Researchers have come to agree that "bilingualism can be explained without reference to unique processes" (Kirsner, Lalor, & Hird, 1993, p. 244). Since there is no qualitative difference, there is no need to postulate additional mechanisms specific to bilingualism.

The Activation Threshold

A neurofunctional system is activated when the sum of positive (activating) impulses exceeds that of negative (inhibitory) impulses to an extent sufficient to allow it to reach its activation threshold, and when all competitors have been sufficiently inhibited (i.e., when they have received enough inhibitory impulses not to reach their activation threshold). Inhibition is thus a matter of degree. It may be overridden by a superior influx of activating impulses or a reduction of inhibitory impulses. The higher the activation threshold of an item, the greater the amount of activating impulses necessary to cause it to reach activation. Different items will thus require varying amounts of impulses to reach activation. Hence it will be easier to recall some items than others.

To different degrees of activation correspond various states reflected in the capacities of the system: Self-activation requires a lower threshold than reconstruction, which in turn requires a lower threshold than recognition. In terms of language, it is easier to comprehend (to activate the mental representation corresponding to the item) than to reconstruct the representation on the basis of a partial or degraded stimulus (e.g., for a word, its initial sound, the number of syllables, intonation pattern, any habitual context, etc.), or to produce the item in the absence of external sensory stimulation (self-activation).

Various states of the system, reflected in its various capacities, require different degrees of inhibition, depending on their activation thresholds. Each item requires more or less activation to reach the threshold, depending on the frequency and recency of its use. Every time an item is used, its activation threshold is lowered, making it easier to activate again with fewer impulses. When an item is not activated, its activation threshold will gradually rise again. This may be true of an item within a system (a word, a syntactic construction, or a morphological derivation), a system as a whole (Spanish or Japanese), or parts of a system (a register or a domain of discourse). PET studies that show decreased activity after priming (Schacter, 1994) suggest that priming—and in general the previous encounter of a particular stimulus—decreases the amount of energy needed to activate circuits subserving the item in question. In other words, after activation, a trace is easier to activate again or, in our terms, its activation threshold has been lowered.

The activation threshold is thus influenced by experience. Hence, different patterns of use will lead to different threshold baselines. In most bilinguals the activation threshold of the language other than the one currently being used is raised sufficiently to avoid interference (though never sufficiently to prevent comprehension of the other language). In the case of frequent mixers, in communities where mixing is the norm, however, the activation threshold of the other language is not raised as high as in the case of those bilinguals who habitually speak only one language to any specific group of interlocutors. In the case of professional simultaneous interpreters, the threshold of both languages must be still lower so as to allow their concurrent processing (Paradis, 1994b).

The partial activation (lowering of the activation threshold, though not sufficiently to reach activation) of the nonselected lexicon (in particular the translation equivalent item) must be comparable to the partial activation of synonyms or ambiguous representations in unilinguals. For example, *bug* lowers the activation threshold of both *spy* and *ant*—although only one reaches threshold, as facilitated by context (Swinney, 1979). Similarly, *dent* will prime *fender* as well as *carie*—though only *fender* reaches threshold in the context of an English linguistic and/or situational environment, only *carie* in a French-biasing context. As in unilingual processing, several related items (including translation equivalents) get some amount of activation and the various influences of context, if successful, activate the selected item enough for it to reach threshold.

Pitres's (1895) first conclusion, that patients recover the language that was premorbidly the most familiar, subsequently known as "Pitres's rule," has been abundantly referred to ever since, and researchers, to this day, continue to report whether their findings are consistent or inconsistent with it (e.g., Junqué, Vendrell, & Vendrell, 1995). Pitres's other two conclusions have drawn much less attention, yet they are still very relevant. He suggested that the neural substrates of the languages that are not available to the patient have not been destroyed by the lesions that brought on the aphasia, but rather, the aphasia is caused by more or less complete and more or less persistent "functional inertia" of the cortical language centers, that is, by partial or total inhibition of "the motor and sensory images used to under-stand and to utter words." In terms of the Activation Threshold Hypothesis, this means that the threshold is raised to the point that both languages are inaccessible, at first. But as the system recovers, the threshold is gradually lowered to the point that first comprehension, then production, are possible in one language and, eventually, in the other languages that the patient knew premorbidly. Pitres himself made the parallel with unilingual aphasia, where comprehension is recovered before production.

CONCLUSION

No difference has been reported between unilingual and bilingual aphasic patients with respect to localization, frequency of occurrence, or any other parameter. Lesions in the same classical language areas in the left hemisphere are responsible for aphasia. There is no greater incidence of aphasia—crossed or otherwise—in bilinguals than in unilinguals. Bilinguals exhibit the same aphasia types as unilinguals. Their aphasias do not evolve differently. However, because two languages differ structurally in less subtle ways than two registers, and because the quantitative differences in the use of various phenomena (activation threshold levels, relative use of implicit linguistic competence vs. explicit metalinguistic knowledge, and pragmatic vs. grammatical aspects of language) are greater, the nonparallel recovery of languages is more striking. In other words, there is no difference in the way the grammar (implicit linguistic competence) is represented (even though contents may be radically different) but, to the extent that the second language is weaker than the native language, we may expect (a) greater reliance on pragmatic aspects of language use (affective prosody, facial expressions, gestures, situational context, inference from general knowledge) and hence greater reliance on the right hemisphere to compensate for the lack of full-blown morphosyntax, as well as (b) greater reliance on metalinguistic knowledge, which, inasmuch as it relies on declarative memory, is subserved by cerebral structures different from those underlying the first language (hippocampal–amygdalar–diffuse tertiary cortex vs. striatal–basal ganglia–focal cortical systems). These systems do exist in unilinguals; they are simply not used as much.

The degree of implicit linguistic competence lateralization for any individual will depend on several interrelated genetic and environmental factors (Joanette, Lecours, Lepage, & Lamoureux, 1983). So will the degree of reliance on implicit linguistic competence versus metalinguistic knowledge, pragmatics versus grammar, in language use. This is also true of the degree of integration of the language system within the limbically based communicative system (Lamendella, 1977). These are dimensions that vary among unilingual individuals but are more obvious among bilinguals as well as between unilinguals and bilinguals because of the more diverse and extreme environmental factors connected with bilingualism. Indeed, there are several possible contexts for the acquisition/learning of a second language, from acquiring two languages simultaneously from the crib, where each may be spoken with a different group of interlocutors or indiscriminately with everybody, with or without mixing, to learning a foreign language in school, using various methods (Paradis, 1987). Each of these contexts involves one or the other cerebral system to varying degrees: for example, the extent of limbic system participation during the acquisition of L2 and consequently of integration within the communicative system; the degree of procedural memory involvement, depending on the extent of practice in authentic communicative situations (Paradis, 1993d).

In conclusion, bilinguals are not atypical: "Many people live in multilingual societies and we all live in a multidialectal society" (Davies, 1991, p. 16). Moreover, the processes underlying language use (and aphasia) in unilinguals and bilinguals are of the same kind. Only their relative contribution to the process and, trivially, the represented grammar may differ. Although the grammars may indeed differ with respect to their contents, there is no reason to believe that the English and the Japanese of an English–Japanese bilingual speaker are processed through underlying cerebral structures and physiological mechanisms that differ from those that underlie English and Japanese in unilingual speakers of those languages. Only to the extent that the second language is weaker than the first will there be quantitative differences in the extent of reliance on compensatory strategies involving pragmatic competence and/or metalinguistic knowledge. Many of the constructs that were developed to account for bilingual aphasia phenomena can be fruitfully applied to unilingual aphasia and, by implication, to the representation and processing of language in the brain.

If a model works for unilingual speakers (i.e., accounts for all comprehension and production phenomena), then there is no reason for it not to also work—without structural changes—for bilinguals. The use of certain components may be extended, but there is no need for additional components. Conversely, everything in a model of bilingual production should have a unilingual counterpart. When a language is added (or coexists from the start), it is as though one or more registers are added. Whatever allows registers within the same language to be kept separate most of the time (although switching, borrowing, and paraphrasing may take place between them) also allows the new language with its additional registers (when applicable, i.e., when the second language does contain more than one register) to be kept separate from each other and from those of the other language(s).

REFERENCES

Aitchison, J. (1994). *Words in the mind: An introduction to the mental lexicon* (2nd ed.). Oxford: Basil Blackwell.

Albanèse, J. F. (1985). Language lateralization in English-French bilinguals. *Brain and Language, 24*, 284–296.

Albert, M., & Obler, L. (1978). *The bilingual brain.* New York: Academic Press.

Baetens Beardsmore, H. (1980). On the similarities between bilingualism and unilingualism. *Zeitschrift für Dialektologie und Linguistik Beihefte, 32*, 11–17.

Baetens Beardsmore, H. (1986). *Bilingualism: Basic principles* (2nd ed.). Clevedon, Avon: Multilingual Matters.

Baker, R. (1993). The assessment of language impairment in elderly bilinguals and second language speakers in Australia. *Language Testing, 10*, 255–276.

Barton, M., Goodglass, H., & Shai, A. (1985). Differential recognition of tachistoscopically presented English and Hebrew words in right and left visual fields. *Perceptual and Motor Skills, 21*, 431–437.

Baruzzi, A. (1985). *Effects of degree of literacy on syntactic comprehension in normal and aphasic populations.* Unpublished master's thesis, McGill University.

Ben Amar, M., & Gaillard, F. (1984). Langage et dominance cérébrale chez les monolingues et les bilingues au seuil de l'école. *Les Sciences de l'éducation pour l'ère nouvelle, 1–2*, 93–111.

Berg, T., & Schade, U. (1992). The role of inhibition in a spreading-activation model of language production. I. The psycholinguistic perspective. *Journal of Psycholinguistic Research, 21,* 405–434.

Bergh, G. (1986). *The neuropsychological status of Swedish-English subsidiary bilinguals.* Göteborg: Acta Universitatis Gothoburgensis.

Berthier, M., Starkstein, S., Lylyk, P., & Leiguarda, R. (1990). Differential recovery of languages in a bilingual patient: A case study using selective amytal test. *Brain and Language, 38,* 449–453.

Bihrle, A. M., Brownell, H. H., & Gardner, H. (1988). Humor and the right hemisphere: A narrative perspective. In H. A. Whitaker (Ed.), *Contemporary reviews in neuropsychology* (pp. 109–126). New York: Springer-Verlag.

Bihrle, A. M., Brownell, H. H., Powelson, J. A., & Gardner, H. (1986). Comprehension of humorous and non-humorous materials by left and right brain-damaged patients. *Brain and Cognition, 5,* 399–411.

Brookshire, R. H., & Nicholas, L. E. (1984). Comprehension of directly and indirectly stated main ideas and details in discourse by brain-damaged and non-brain-damaged listeners. *Brain and Language, 21,* 21–36.

Brownell, H. H. (1988). Appreciation of metaphoric and connotative word meaning by brain-damaged patients. In C. Chiarello (Ed.), *Right hemisphere contributions to lexical semantics* (pp. 19–32). New York: Springer-Verlag.

Brownell, H., Gardner, H., Prather, P., & Martino, G. (1995). Language, communication, and the right hemisphere. In H. S. Kirshner (Ed.), *Handbook of neurological speech and language disorders* (pp. 325–349). New York: Marcel Dekker.

Brownell, H. H., Michel, D., Powelson, J., & Gardner, H. (1983). Surprise but not coherence: Sensitivity to verbal humor in right-hemisphere patients. *Brain and Language, 18,* 20–27.

Brownell, H. H., Potter, H. H., Bihrle, A. M., & Gardner, H. (1986). Inference deficits in right brain-damaged patients. *Brain and Language, 27,* 310–321.

Bryan, K. L. (1988). Assessment of language disorders after right hemisphere damage. *British Journal of Disorders of Communication, 23,* 111–125.

Carroll, F. (1980). Neurolinguistic processing in bilingualism and second language. In R. Scarcella & S. Krashen (Eds.), *Research in second language acquisition* (pp. 81–86). Rowley, MA: Newbury House.

Chary, P. (1986). Aphasia in a multilingual society: A preliminary study. In J. Vaid (Ed.), *Language processing in bilinguals: Psycholinguistic and neuropsychological perspectives* (pp. 183–197). Hillsdale, NJ: Lawrence Erlbaum Associates.

Chomsky, N. (1965). *Aspects of the theory of syntax.* Cambridge, MA: MIT Press.

Damasio, A. R. (1992). Aphasia. *New England Journal of Medicine, 326,* 531–539.

Davies, A. (1991). *The native speaker in applied linguistics.* Edinburgh: Edinburgh University Press.

Dwyer, J., & Rinn, W. (1981). The role of the right hemisphere in contextual inference. *Neuropsychologia, 19,* 479–482.

Ferguson, C. (1983). Language planning and language change. In J. Cobarrubias & J. Fishman (Eds.), *Progress in language planning* (pp. 29–40). Berlin: Mouton.

Foldi, N. S. (1987). Appreciation of pragmatic interpretations of indirect commands: Comparison of right and left hemisphere brain-damaged patients. *Brain and Language, 31,* 88–108.

Foldi, N. S., Cicone, M., & Gardner, H. (1983). Pragmatic aspects of communication in brain-damaged patients. In S. J. Segalowitz (Ed.), *Language functions and brain organization* (pp. 51–86). New York: Academic Press.

Galloway, L., & Krashen, S. (1980). Cerebral organization in bilingualism and second language. In R. Scarcella & S. Krashen (Eds.), *Research in second language acquisition* (pp. 74–80). Rowley, MA: Newbury House.

Galloway, L., & Scarcella, R. (1982). Cerebral organization in adult second language acquisition: Is the right hemisphere more involved? *Brain and Language, 16,* 56–60.

Gardner, H., Brownell, H., Wapner, W., & Michelow, D. (1983). Missing the point: The role of the right hemisphere in the processing of complex linguistic materials. In E. Perecman (Ed.), *Cognitive processing in the right hemisphere* (pp. 169–191). Orlando, FL: Academic Press.

Gloning, I., & Gloning, K. (1965). Aphasien bei Polyglotten. Beitrag zur Dynamik des Sprachabbaus sowie zur Lokalisationsfrage dieser Störungen. *Wiener Zeitschrift für Nervenheilkunde, 22,* 362–397. [Translated in Paradis (1983), pp. 681–716.]

Goodglass, H. (1978). Acquisition and dissolution of language. In A. Caramazza & E. B. Zurif (Eds.), *Language acquisition and language breakdown* (pp. 101–108). Baltimore, MD: Johns Hopkins University Press.

Goodglass, H. (1993). *Understanding aphasia.* San Diego: Academic Press.

Gordon, H. W. (1980). Cerebral organization in bilinguals. I. Lateralization. *Brain and Language, 9,* 255–268.

Grosjean, F. (1994). Individual bilingualism. In *The encyclopedia of language and linguistics* (pp. 1656–1660). Oxford: Pergamon Press.

Habib, M., Joanette, Y., Ali-Chérif, A., & Poncet, M. (1983). Crossed aphasia in dextrals: A case report with special reference to site of lesion. *Neuropsychologia, 21,* 413–418.

Hall, G., & Lambert, W. E. (1988). French immersion and hemispheric language processing. A dual-task study. *Canadian Journal of Behavioural Science, 20,* 1–14.

Halpern, L. (1941). Beitrag zur Restitution der Aphasie bei Polyglotten im Hinblick auf das Hebräische. *Schweizer Archiv für Neurologie und Psychiatrie, 47,* 150–154. [Translated in Paradis (1983), pp. 418–422.]

Halpern, L. (1949). La langue hébraïque dans la restitution de l'aphasie sensorielle chez les polyglottes. *Semaine des Hôpitaux de Paris, 58,* 2473–2476. [Translated in Paradis (1983), pp. 517–523.]

Harris, R., & McGhee Nelson, M. (1992). Bilingualism: not the exception any more. In R. J. Harris (Ed.), *Cognitive processes in bilinguals* (pp. 3–14). Amsterdam: North Holland.

Hécaen, H. (1968). L'aphasie. In A. Martinet (Ed.), *Le Langage* (pp. 390–414). Paris: Gallimard.

Hegler, C. (1931). Zur Aphasie bei Polyglotten. *Deutsche Zeitschrift für Nervenheilkunde, 117,* 236–239. [Translated in Paradis (1983), pp. 317–319.]

Heilman, K. M., Bowers, D., Speedie, L., & Costlett, H. B. (1984). Comprehension of affective and nonaffective prosody. *Neurology, 34,* 917–921.

Henderson, V. W. (1983). Speech fluency in crossed aphasia. *Brain, 106,* 837–857.

Hier, D. B., & Kaplan, J. (1980). Verbal comprehension deficits after right hemisphere damage. *Applied Psycholinguistics, 1,* 279–294.

Hinshelwood, J. (1902). Four cases of word-blindness. *Lancet, 1,* 358–363.

Hirst, W., LeDoux, J., & Stein, S. (1984). Constraints on the processing of indirect speech acts: Evidence from aphasiaology. *Brain and Language, 23,* 26–33.

Hoosain, R. (1992). Differential cerebral lateralization of Chinese-English bilingual functions? In R. J. Harris (Ed.), *Cognitive processing in bilinguals* (pp. 561–571). Amsterdam: Elsevier.

Hoosain, R., & Shiu, L.-P. (1989). Cerebral lateralization of Chinese-English bilingual functions. *Neuropsychologia, 27,* 705–712.

Hymes, D. H. (1966). *On communicative competence.* Paper presented at the Research Planning Conference on Language Development Among Disadvantaged Children, Yeshiva University, 7–8 June. [A revised version was published in *On communicative competence.* Philadelphia: University of Pennsylvania Press (1971).]

Hynd, G. W., Teeter, A., & Stewart, J. (1980). Acculturation and lateralization of speech in the bilingual native American. *International Journal of Neuroscience, 11,* 1–7.

Joanette, Y. (1980). *Contribution à l'étude anatomoclinique des troubles du langage dans les lésions cérébrales droites du droitier.* Unpublished doctoral dissertation, Université de Montréal.

Joanette, Y., Goulet, P., & Hannequin, D. (1990). *Right hemisphere and verbal communication.* New York: Springer Verlag.

Joanette, Y., Lecours, A. R., Lepage, Y., & Lamoureux, M. (1983). Language in right-handers with right-hemisphere lesions: A preliminary study including anatomical, genetic and social factors. *Brain and Language, 20,* 217–248.

Junqué, C., Vendrell, P., & Vendrell, J. (1995). Differential impairment and specific phenomena in 50 Catalan-Spanish bilingual aphasic patients. In M. Paradis (Ed.), *Aspects of bilingual aphasia* (pp. 177–209). Oxford: Pergamon Press.

Kaplan, J. A., Brownell, H. H., Jacobs, J. R., & Gardner, H. (1990). The effects of right hemisphere damage on the pragmatic interpretation of conversational remarks. *Brain and Language, 38,* 315–333.

Karanth, P., & Rangamani, G. N. (1988). Crossed aphasia in multilinguals. *Brain and Language, 34,* 169–180.

Kawashima, R., Itoh, M., Hatazawa, J., Miyazawa, H., Yamada, K., Matsuzawa, T., & Fukuda, H. (1993). Changes of regional cerebral blood flow during listening to an unfamiliar spoken language. *Neuroscience Letters, 161,* 69–72.

Kershner, J., & Jeng, A. (1972). Dual functional hemispheric asymmetry in visual perception: Effects of ocular dominance and post-exposural processes. *Neuropsychologia, 10,* 437–445.

Kirsner, K. (1986). Lexical function: Is a bilingual account necessary? In J. Vaid (Ed.), *Language processing in bilinguals* (pp. 21–45). Hillsdale, NJ: Lawrence Erlbaum Associates.

Kirsner, K., Lalor, E., & Hird, K. (1993). The bilingual lexicon: Exercise, meaning and morphology. In R. Schreuder & B. Weltens (Eds.), *The bilingual lexicon* (pp. 215–248). Amsterdam: John Benjamins.

Klein, D., Zatorre, R. J., Milner, B., Meyer, E., & Evans, A. C. (1995). The neural substrates of bilingual language processing: Evidence from positron emission tomography. In M. Paradis (Ed.), *Aspects of bilingual aphasia* (pp. 23–36). Oxford: Pergamon Press.

Kotik, B. (1975). *Lateralization in multilinguals.* Thesis, Moscow State University, USSR.

Krashen, S. (1973). Lateralization, language learning, and the critical period: Some new evidence. *Language Learning, 23,* 63–74.

Krashen, S. D. (1975a). The critical period for language acquisition and its possible bases. In D. Aaronson & R. W. Rieber (Eds.), *Developmental psycholinguistics and communication disorders* (pp. 211–222). New York: Annals of the New York Academy of Sciences.

Krashen, S. D. (1975b). The development of cerebral dominance and language learning: More new evidence. In D. P. Dato (Ed.), *Georgetown University Round Table* (pp. 179–192). Washington, DC: Georgetown University Press.

Labov, W. (1972). *Sociolinguistic patterns.* Philadelphia: University of Pennsylvania Press.

Lamendella, J. (1977). General principles of neurofunctional organization and their manifestation in primary and secondary language acquisition. *Language Learning, 27,* 155–196.

Lambert, W., & Fillenbaum, S. (1959). A pilot study of aphasia among bilinguals. *Canadian Journal of Psychology, 13,* 28–34.

Lebrun, Y. (1971). The neurology of bilingualism. *Word, 27,* 179–186.

Lebrun, Y. (1976). Recovery in polyglot aphasics. In Y. Lebrun & R. Hoops (Eds.), *Recovery in aphasics* (pp. 96–108). Amsterdam: Swetz & Zeitlinger.

Lecours, A. R. (1980). Correlations anatomo-cliniques de l'aphasie. La zone du langage. *Revue neurologique, 136,* 591–605.

Lecours, A. R., Branchereau, L., & Joanette, Y. (1984). La zone du langage et l'aphasie: Enseignement standard et cas particuliers. *Μετα, Translators' Journal, 29,* 10–26.

Lecours, A. R., & Joanette, Y. (1980). Linguistic and other psychological aspects of paroxysmal aphasia. *Brain and Language, 10,* 1–23.

Leischner, A. (1948). Über die Aphasie der Mehrsprachigen. *Archiv für Psychiatrie und Nervenkrankheiten, 180,* 731–775. [Translated in Paradis (1983), pp. 456–502.]

Lenneberg, E. (1967). *Biological foundations of language.* New York: Wiley & Sons.

L'Hermitte, R., Hécaen, H., Dubois, J., Culioli, A., & Tabouret-Keller, A. (1966). Le problème de l'aphasie des polyglottes: Remarques sur quelques observations. *Neuropsychologia, 4,* 315–329. [Translated in Paradis (1983), pp. 727–743.]

Magiste, E. (1986). Selected issues in second and third language learning. In J. Vaid (Ed.), *Language processing in bilinguals* (pp. 97–122). Hillsdale, NJ: Lawrence Erlbaum Associates.

Martinet, A. (1960). *Eléments de linguistique générale.* Paris: Armand Colin.

McDonald, S., & Wales, R. (1986). An investigation of the ability to process inferences in language following right hemisphere brain damage. *Brain and Language, 29,* 68–80.

McKeever, W. F., & Hunt, L. (1984). Failure to replicate the Scott *et al.* findings of reversed ear dominance in the Native American Navaho. *Neuropsychologia, 22,* 539–541.

Mendelsohn, S. (1988). Language lateralization in bilinguals. Facts and fantasy. *Journal of Neurolinguistics, 3,* 261–292.

Minkowski, M. (1927). Klinischer Beitrag zur Aphasie bei Polyglotten, speziell im Hinblick aufs Schweizerdeutsche. *Schweizer Archiv für Neurologie und Psychiatrie, 21,* 43–72. [Translated in Paradis (1983), pp. 205–232.]

Mishkin, M., & Forgays, D. (1952). Word recognition as a function of retinal focus. *Journal of Experimental Psychology, 43,* 43–48.

Molloy, R., Brownell, H. H., & Gardner, H. (1990). Discourse comprehension by right hemisphere stroke patients: Deficits of prediction and revision. In Y. Joanette & H. Brownell (Eds.), *Discourse ability and brain damage: Theoretical and empirical perspectives* (pp. 113–130). New York: Springer Verlag.

Nair, K., & Virmani, V. (1973). Speech and language disturbances in hemiplegics. *Indian Journal of Medical Research, 61,* 1131–1138.

National Aphasia Association Newsletter. (1989). *1*(2), 2.

Obrzut, J., Conrad, P., Bryden, M., & Boliek, C. (1988). Cued dichotic listening with right-handed, left-handed, bilingual and learning-disabled children. *Neuropsychologia, 26,* 119–131.

Ojemann, G. A., & Whitaker, H. A. (1978). The bilingual brain. *Archives of Neurology, 35,* 409–412.

Orbach, J. (1953). Retinal locus as a factor in the recognition of visually perceived words. *American Journal of Psychology, 65,* 555–562.

Orbach, J. (1967). Differential recognition of Hebrew and English words in right and left visual fields as a function of cerebral dominance and reading habits. *Neuropsychologia, 5,* 127–134.

Palij, M., & Aaronson, D. (1992). The role of language background in cognitive processing. In R. J. Harris (Ed.), *Cognitive processes in bilinguals* (pp. 63–87). Amsterdam: North Holland.

Paradis, M. (1977). Bilingualism and aphasia. In H. A. Whitaker & H. Whitaker (Eds.), *Studies in neurolinguistics* (Vol. 3, pp. 65–121). New York: Academic Press.

Paradis, M. (1979). Review of *The bilingual brain* by M. L. Albert and L. K. Obler. *Neuropsychologia, 17,* 550–551.

Paradis, M. (1981). Neurolinguistic organization of a bilingual's two languages. In J. E. Copeland & P. W. Davis (Eds.), *The seventh LACUS forum* (pp. 486–494). Columbia, SC: Hornbeam Press.

Paradis, M. (Ed.). (1983). *Readings on aphasia in bilinguals and polyglots.* Montreal: Marcel Didier.

Paradis, M. (1987). Neurolinguistic perspectives in bilingualism. In M. Paradis & G. Libben, *The assessment of bilingual aphasia* (chapter 1). Hillsdale, NJ: Lawrence Erlbaum Associates.

Paradis, M. (1989). Bilingual and polyglot aphasia. In F. Boller & J. Grafman (Eds.), *Handbook of neuropsychology* (Vol. 2, pp. 117–140). Amsterdam: Elsevier.

Paradis, M. (1990). Language lateralization in bilinguals: Enough already! *Brain and Language, 39,* 576–588.

Paradis, M. (1992). The Loch Ness Monster approach to lateralization in bilingual aphasia: A response to Berquier & Ashton. *Brain and Language, 43,* 534–537.

Paradis, M. (1993a). Multilingualism and aphasia. In J. C. Marshall (Ed.), *Handbooks of linguistics and communication sciences* (Vol. 9, pp. 278–288). New York: Walter de Gruyter.

Paradis, M. (1993b). Bilingual aphasia rehabilitation. In M. Paradis (Ed.), *Foundations of aphasia rehabilitation* (pp. 413–420). Oxford: Pergamon Press.

Paradis, M. (1993c). Linguistic, psycholinguistic, and neurolinguistic aspects of "interference" in bilingual speakers: The Activation Threshold Hypothesis. *International Journal of Psycholinguistics, 9*, 133–145.

Paradis, M. (1993d). Implication de mécanismes mnésiques cérébraux différents selon les méthodes d'apprentissage. In J. Chapelle & M.-T. Claes (Eds.), *Proceedings of the 1st International Congress on Memory and Memorization in Acquiring and Learning Languages* (pp. 205–223). Louvain-la-Neuve: C.L.L.

Paradis, M. (1994a). Neurolinguistic aspects of implicit and explicit memory: Implications for bilingualism. In N. Ellis (Ed.), *Implicit and explicit learning of second languages* (pp. 393–419). London: Academic Press.

Paradis, M. (1994b). Toward a neurolinguistic theory of simultaneous translation: The framework. *International Journal of Psycholinguistics, 10*, 319–335.

Paradis, M. (1995). Another sighting of differential language laterality in multilinguals, this time in Loch Tok Pisin: Comments on Wuillemin, Richardson and Lynch (1994). *Brain and Language, 49*.

Paradis, M., & Goldblum, M.-C. (1989). Selective crossed aphasia in one of a trilingual's languages followed by antagonistic recovery. *Brain and Language, 36*, 62–75.

Piazza Gordon, D., & Zatorre, R. J. (1981). A right-ear advantage for dichotic listening in bilingual children. *Brain and Language, 13*, 389–396.

Pitres, A. (1895). Etude sur l'aphasie chez les polyglottes. *Revue de Médecine, 15*, 873–899. [Translated in Paradis (1983), pp. 26–49.]

Pötzl, O. (1930). Aphasie und Mehrsprachigkeit. *Zeitschrift für die gesamte Neurologie und Psychiatrie, 124*, 145–162. [Translated in Paradis (1983), pp. 301–316.]

Porch, B., & de Berkeley-Wykes, J. (1985). Bilingual aphasia and its implications for cerebral organization and recovery. *Clinical Aphasiology, 15*, 107–112.

Rangamani, G. N. (1989). *Aphasia and multilingualism: Clinical evidence towards the cerebral organization of language.* Unpublished doctoral dissertation, University of Mysore.

Rapport, R. L., Tan, C. T., & Whitaker, H. A. (1983). Language function and dysfunction among Chinese- and English-speaking polyglots: Cortical stimulation, Wada testing, and clinical studies. *Brain and Language, 18*, 342–366.

Riese, W. (1948). Type, evolution and localization of aphasia following neuro-surgical relief in a 60-year-old scientist, affected by paralysis agitens. *Confina Neurologica, 9*, 216–225.

Rosenberger, P. B. (1978). Neurological processes. In R. L. Schiefelbusch (Ed.), *Bases of language intervention* (pp. 13–41). Baltimore, MD: University Park Press.

Ross, E. D. (1981). The aprosodias: Functional-anatomical organization of the affective components of language in the right hemisphere. *Archives of Neurology, 38*, 561–569.

Ross, E. D. (1984). Right hemisphere's role in language, affective behavior and emotion. *Trends in Neurosciences, 7*, 342–346.

Rowland, D. T. (1991). *Pioneers again: Immigrants and ageing in Australia.* Canberra: AGPS.

Schacter, D. (1994). *Implicit memory: Cognitive and neuropsychological perspectives.* Paper presented as part of the Donald Hebb Lecture Series, McGill University, 4 February.

Schönle, P. (1978). *Otität versus Lingualität: Dichotische Untersuchungen zur Prävalenz der Ohrigkeit und Sprachigkeit bei deutschen und russischen Studenten.* Unpublished doctoral dissertation, Tübingen, Germany.

Schulze, H. A. F. (1968). Unterschiedliche Rückbildung einer sensorischer und einer ideokinetischen motorischen Aphasie bei einem Polyglotten. *Psychiatrie, Neurologie und medizinische Psychologie, 20*, 441–445. [Translated in Paradis (1983), pp. 753–760.]

Scoresby Jackson, R. (1867). Case of aphasia with right hemiplegia. *Edinburgh Medical Journal,* *12,* 696–706.

Sewell, D. F., & Panou, L. (1983). Visual field asymmetries for verbal and dot localization tasks in monolingual and bilingual subjects. *Brain and Language, 18,* 28–34.

Silverberg, R., & Gordon, H. W. (1979). Differential aphasia in two bilingual individuals. *Neurology, 29,* 51–55.

Sjardin, H. (1993). *Is there equal opportunity for a person with non-English-speaking background following stroke?* Poster presented at the National Conference "Health for Multicultural Australia," University of Sydney, Australia, November 1993.

Smith, N., & Wilson, D. (1980). *Modern linguistics: The Chomskyan revolution.* New York: Penguin Books.

Soares, C. (1982). Converging evidence for left hemisphere language lateralization in bilinguals. *Neuropsychologia, 20,* 653–660.

Soares, C. (1984). Left hemisphere language lateralization in bilinguals: Use of the concurrent activities paradigm. *Brain and Language, 23,* 86–96.

Soares, C., & Grosjean, F. (1981). Left hemisphere language lateralization in bilinguals and monolinguals. *Perception and Psychophysics, 29,* 599–604.

Solin, D. (1989). The systematic misrepresentation of bilingual crossed aphasia data and its consequences. *Brain and Language, 36,* 92–116.

Starck, R., Genesee, F., Lambert, W., & Seitz, M. (1977). Multiple language experience and the development of cerebral dominance. In S. Segalowitz & F. Gruber (Eds.), *Language development and neurological theory* (pp. 48–55). New York: Academic Press.

Stengel, E., & Zelmanowicz, J. (1933). Über polyglotte motorische Aphasie. *Zeitschrift für die gesamte Neurologie und Psychiatrie, 149,* 292–311.

Sussman, H. M. (1989). A reassessment of the time-sharing paradigm with ANCOVA. *Brain and Language, 37,* 514–520.

Sussman, H., Franklin, P., & Simon, T. (1982). Bilingual speech: Bilateral control? *Brain and Language, 15,* 125–142.

Swinney, D. (1979). Lexical access during sentence comprehension: (Re)consideration of context effects. *Journal of Verbal Learning and Verbal Behavior, 18,* 523–534.

Tompkins, C. A., & Mateer, C. A. (1985). Right hemisphere appreciation of prosodic and linguistic indication of implicit attitude. *Brain and Language, 24,* 185–203.

Vaid, J. (1983). Bilingualism and brain lateralization. In S. Segalowitz (Ed.), *Language function and brain organization* (pp. 315–339). New York: Academic Press.

Vaid, J., & Genesee, F. (1980). Neuropsychological approaches to bilingualism: A critical review. *Canadian Journal of Psychology, 34,* 417–445.

Vaid, J., & Hall, D. G. (1991). Neuropsychological perspectives on bilingualism: Right, left, and center. In A. Reynolds (Ed.), *Bilingualism, multiculturalism and second language learning* (pp. 81–113). Hillsdale, NJ: Lawrence Erlbaum Associates.

Vaid, J., & Lambert, W. E. (1979). Differential cerebral envolvement in the cognitive functioning of bilinguals. *Brain and Language, 8,* 92–110.

Vildomec, V. (1963). *Multilingualism.* Leijden: A. W. Sythoff.

Walters, J., & Zatorre, R. J. (1978). Laterality differences for word identification in bilinguals. *Brain and Language, 6,* 158–167.

Weber-Fox, C. M., & Neville, H. J. (1994). *Sensitive periods differentiate neural systems for grammatical and semantic processing: ERP evidence in bilingual speakers.* Paper presented at the Cognitive Neuroscience Society inaugural meeting, San Francisco, 28 March.

Weber-Fox, C. M., & Neville, H. J. (1996). Maturational constraints on functional specializations for language processing: ERP and behavioral evidence in bilingual speakers. *Journal of Cognitive Neuropsychology, 8,* 231–256.

Weylman, S. T., Brownell, H. H., Roman, M., & Gardner, H. (1989). Appreciation of indirect requests by left and right brain-damaged patients: The effects of verbal context and conventionality of wording. *Brain and Language, 36,* 580–591.

Whitworth, A., & Sjardin, H. (1993). The bilingual person—The Australian context. In D. Lafond, Y. Joanette, J. Ponzio, R. Di Giovanni, & M. Taylor Sarno (Eds.), *Living with aphasia. Psychosocial issues* (pp. 131–149). Beverly Hills, CA: Singular Publishing.

CHAPTER THREE

Is Acquired Childhood
Aphasia Atypical?

Philippe F. Paquier
University of Antwerp (UIA) and University Hospital of Brussels
(Erasme, ULB)

Hugo R. van Dongen
University Hospital Rotterdam, Sophia Children's Hospital

In adults, *aphasia* denotes the loss or impairment of language subsequent to cerebral damage. Consequently, the term implies that language had already been acquired prior to lesion onset. In children, on the contrary, the term has been used in reference to a number of language disorders attributable to both developmental and acquired factors. Thus, congenital, developmental, and acquired aphasia have been distinguished.

According to Vargha-Khadem, Watters, and O'Gorman (1985), *congenital aphasia* "is a consequence of early and extensive lesions in the thalamocortical projection system" (p. 168). Due to such demonstrable structural lesions, children with congenital aphasia fail to develop normal language functions (Landau, Goldstein, & Kleffner, 1960).

Following Woods (1985a), *developmental aphasia* (also called *developmental dysphasia*) refers to

> a level of language function that is significantly below age norms, has always been so (i.e. it has not been arrested at, nor has it declined from an earlier level) and is not adequately accounted for by general mental retardation, peripheral sensory or motor defects, severe emotional disturbance, or major environmental deprivation. (p. 139)

In addition, we would like to stress, in line with Aram (1991), that "a frank neurological basis is not apparent" (p. 426).

In agreement with Hécaen (1976), we consider *acquired childhood aphasia* (ACA) to refer "only to disturbances of language due to cerebral lesions which have occurred after language acquisition" (p. 115). Because Woods and Carey (1979) showed that lesions incurred after 1 year of age leave more severe language sequelae than those sustained prior to age 1, the somewhat arbitrary demarcation for the onset of language was fixed at that age (Aram, 1991). The upper limit of language development conventionally corresponds to early adolescence (Woods, 1985b). We must keep in mind, however, that these boundaries are artificial, and one could—quite rightly—argue that language already begins to develop in the preverbal period before age 1 (Marchman, Miller, & Bates, 1991), and further evolves throughout the entire life span (enrichment of vocabulary has no age limitation whatever).

Having subscribed to these definitions and agreed with the arbitrary limits proposed for delimitating the field of ACA, we now focus our attention on the study of children who acquired aphasia following brain lesions sustained after onset of language development.[1] This chapter consists of two main parts, the boundary between them being formed by Woods and Teuber's (1978) landmark paper on changing patterns of ACA, in which the authors formulated several conclusions that were at variance with the traditional teaching on ACA. The first part attempts to give an impression of the genesis and the slow evolution of the commonly held views, or "standard doctrine," on ACA. By presenting the different studies in a chronological perspective, we intend to demonstrate that for a century, the clinical description has barely known any significant progress. Since 1978, however, critical reviews of previous studies and case reports of "deviant" clinical pictures have considerably changed our insights in ACA. Thus, the second part addresses recent advances in the study of ACA by proceeding thematically. It illustrates the contribution of the study of ACA to our understanding of cerebral language representation.

Because of its specific presentation, the syndrome of acquired childhood aphasia with convulsive disorder, also known as Landau–Kleffner syndrome (Landau & Kleffner, 1957), is not considered in this chapter. As a matter of fact, several reviews (Deonna, 1991; Gordon, 1990; Paquier, Van Dongen, & Loonen, 1992) have recently concentrated on this intriguing syndrome.

HISTORICAL BACKGROUND

Genesis of the Standard Doctrine on Acquired Childhood Aphasia

The publication as early as 1760 of the history of a case of childhood hemiplegia with aphasia following scarlet fever has been attributed to De

---

[1]Reference to congenital aphasia is exclusively made when necessary for our understanding of theories on cerebral language organization and for our insights into their development, or when earlier studies discussed in the first part of this chapter include both children with congenital and acquired aphasia.

Haen by Imbert-Goubeyre (1863, cited in Ford & Schaffer, 1927). Scattered case studies were subsequently published. However, the earliest elaborated study on childhood aphasia (Cotard, 1868) appeared soon after Broca's (1861) observation that a loss of speech follows damage to a localized small area in the third convolution of the left frontal lobe. Cotard (1868) analyzed the autopsy reports of 42 patients, of whom 25 were adults who had been hemiplegic since childhood. He found that the brains of seven subjects with a right-sided hemiplegia who had had a normal language and intelligence development showed damage to either the left frontal lobe or the entire left hemisphere. He assumed that normal language functions had unfolded in the right hemisphere, and postulated that when either hemisphere has been destroyed in early infancy, the other one can take over its functions. In this way, he might be considered to have prepared an ideal breeding ground for the ulterior development of what would later on be termed the *hypothesis of equipotentiality* (Basser, 1962; Lenneberg, 1967). Cotard (1868) also concluded that aphasia never occurred in childhood:

> Il est extrêmement remarquable que, quel que soit le côté de la lésion cérébrale, les individus hémiplégiques depuis leur enfance ne présentent *jamais* d'aphasie, c'est-à-dire d'abolition de la faculté du langage avec conservation plus ou moins complète de l'intelligence . . . l'intelligence n'est jamais mieux développée que la faculté du langage, on n'observe jamais cette impossibilité d'exprimer les idées, ce contraste singulier entre les facultés intellectuelles et les facultés d'expression qui donnent aux aphasiques une physionomie si originale . . . dans tous les cas où les facultés intellectuelles ont acquis quelque développement, nous voyons que les malades parlaient facilement, même lorsque le lobe frontal gauche ou l'hémisphère gauche tout entier étaient profondément altérés. (pp. 89–90)[2]

This conclusion gave rise to the widely held idea that ACA is a rare disorder. Despite the emergence of some contradictory studies a few years later, the notion of rarity anyhow received a tacit acceptance because, Guttmann (1942) assumed, "few neurologists were able to collect large experience in this particular field" (p. 205). In turn, Satz and Bullard-Bates (1981) explained the shortage of criticism by stating that the early reports on ACA, "although equally meritorious, have been overshadowed by Broca's and Wernicke's

---

[2]It seems that this original quotation has been altered in the course of time. Apparently, Guttmann (1942) took some liberties when interpreting Bernhardt's (1885) German translation of Cotard's (1868) words. Bernhardt (1885) in turn had used a quotation found in Jendrassik and Marie (1885). Since Guttmann (1942), the passage in major reviews reads as follows: "Il est extrêmement remarquable que, quel que soit le côté de la lésion cérébrale, les individus hémiplégiques depuis leur enfance ne présentent jamais d'aphasie et cela même quand tout l'hémisphère gauche est atrophié" (Guttmann, 1942, p. 205; Satz & Bullard-Bates, 1981, p. 400).

reports because of the disproportionate interest directed to the adult aphasias, especially in the twentieth century" (p. 399).

The same year Carl Wernicke published his monograph on aphasia symptom complexes, Clarus (1874) contradicted Cotard's (1868) statement that
aphasia did not occur in childhood by analyzing reports of 50 cases of
childhood aphasia, including 3 congenital ones. Based on this review of the
literature, he concluded that (a) childhood aphasia is not rare; (b) the prognosis is not unequivocally favorable, but partially depends on both the
etiology and the severity of the cerebral lesion; and (c) the right hemisphere
is able to take over language functions when the left hemisphere is lesioned.
Seeligmüller (1879) subsequently followed Clarus (1874) in noticing that
children who sustained a hemiplegia at an age when they had already
developed language skills often presented a concomitant aphasia.

One year later, Förster (1880) reported on several cases of childhood
paralyses of different etiologies he had come across in the newly built
children's hospital in Dresden. Without dwelling upon the communication
disorders of those children who had acquired a hemiplegia of central origin,
he nevertheless mentioned aphasic disturbances in the two patients with a
right-sided and in one out of the two children with a left-sided hemiplegia
he described. Thus, he tacitly indicated that Clarus (1874) was right in concluding that childhood aphasia is not rare. A few years later, Strümpell (1884)
believed that language disorders in hemiplegic children could be related to
the presence of an affection of the right hemicorpus, whereas no specific
language impairment seemed to be associated with the presence of a left-
sided hemiplegia. However, he was of the opinion that the language disorder
generally evolved favorably.

Jendrassik and Marie (1885) did not share these previous views. On the
contrary, they adhered to Cotard's (1868) opinion by stating that (a) children
who had acquired a right-sided hemiplegia early in life did not present with
any aphasia, and (b) when a language impairment did occur anyhow, it
always appeared in the context of a global intellectual disability.

Although a controversy seemed to have emerged from these contradictory
statements, in a well-known publication Bernhardt (1885) listed a number
of cardinal features of childhood aphasia that remained essentially unchallenged until recent years:

1. Aphasia in childhood is not rare.
2. The prognosis is favorable.
3. The duration is brief.
4. Childhood aphasia is predominantly of the motor (expressive) type.
5. The right hemisphere can take over language functions in case of a
   left hemisphere lesion.

Furthermore, Bernhardt (1885) noted the possible occurrence of childhood aphasia with either a left- or right-sided hemiplegia, although the latter seemed to be more frequently associated with aphasia. As our further review will show, few authors ulteriorly paid attention to this co-occurrence.

The same year, Steffen (1885) published a study on childhood aphasia that, strange as it may be, never received much attention in any major review on ACA published ulteriorly.[3] After having summarized Clarus's (1874) findings, he completed his overview by adding 25 new cases of ACA (aged between 3 and 12) reviewed in the literature. He confirmed the good outcome of ACA (18 out of 25 cases "completely" recovered), although some reservations had to be expressed (two cases had not recovered at 2 years postonset). The most frequent etiology was an infectious one. Aphasia was more frequently associated with a right-sided (82%) than with a left-sided hemiplegia (18%). The latter findings, together with a quoted analysis of two studies on the laterality of the hemiplegia and of the brain lesion in aphasic patients,[4] led Steffen (1885) to conclude that, even at an early age, the left hemisphere plays a major role in the development of language skills. However, in agreement with Clarus (1874) and Bernhardt (1885), he also assumed that the right hemisphere was able to take over language functions when the left one was severed. This process would show better prospects in children than in adults because of the still ongoing maturation of the brain.

The rarity of ACA was further contradicted by McNutt (1885), who, in her study on infantile spastic hemiplegia, reported aphasia to occur in three out of seven cases. Describing her case V, who was 3½ years old when she developed a right-sided hemiplegia, McNutt wrote: "She had complete aphasia lasting five or six weeks, and when she recommenced she had to learn to talk as at first" (p. 25). In a study on childhood hemiplegia published 1 year later, Ranke (1886) touched briefly upon the field of childhood aphasia by taking a completely opposite stand to the one of Jendrassik and Marie (1885). He was of the opinion that aphasia was associated with a right-sided hemiplegia, and was not necessarily embedded in a more general intellectual impairment.

Wallenberg (1886) reported on two cases of acquired childhood hemiplegia. A 9-year-old girl, who had presented with scarlet fever complicated by nephritis and convulsions at the age of 3, showed a left-sided hemiplegia without language disorders ever since. The second child, an 8½-year-old

---

[3]This finding is all the more striking as the reference to Steffen (1885) is to be found in Bernhardt's (1885) so frequently cited study on infantile spastic hemiplegia and childhood aphasia.

[4]According to a reference to William A. Hammond (*A Treatise on the Diseases of the Nervous System*, 1876), who cited the findings of two of Seguin's studies, aphasia was found in 143/160 (89%) right hemiplegics and 17/160 (11%) left hemiplegics, whereas in 514/545 (94%) cases of autopsied aphasic patients, the lesion resided in the left frontal lobe (Steffen, 1885, p. 141).

girl, presented with a right-sided hemiplegia and aphasia following scarlatina with a progress similar to the previous patient. Without drawing any conclusion as to the presence or absence of a concomitant language disorder in the two children reported, Wallenberg (1886) summarized his ideas about childhood aphasia as follows:

1. Childhood aphasia is not rare, as it is seen in almost every case of acquired childhood hemiplegia.
2. Injury to either the left or right third frontal gyrus can cause aphasia.
3. Aphasia is transitory.
4. Recovery from language disorder is favorable as long as intelligence is preserved.
5. Childhood aphasia is of the motor type.

Apparently, Wallenberg (1886) did not stop at Bernhardt's (1885) and Steffen's (1885) findings that childhood aphasia seemed to be more frequently associated with a right-sided hemiplegia. In contrast with Cotard (1868) and Jendrassik and Marie (1885), who even denied the existence of aphasia in children, he explicitly stated that either left- or right-hemispheric lesions could be associated with childhood aphasia.

A few years later, Wallenberg's (1886) claim was supported by Sachs and Peterson (1890), who put down one of the first outlines of what would later on be called the *hypotheses of equipotentiality and progressive lateralization* (Basser, 1962; Lenneberg, 1967). Sachs and Peterson (1890) observed that the relatively large proportion of childhood aphasia in cases of left-sided hemiplegia was rather striking when compared with the adult cases. They concluded that "in earlier years both hemispheres are equally entrusted, so it seems, with this highest faculty of speech" (p. 311), and that "as we grow older we appear to become more and more left-brained" (p. 311).

A few years later, Freud (1897) published a monograph on infantile cerebral paralysis. He confirmed Sachs and Peterson's (1890) opinion by stating that aphasia in children occurs relatively frequently with lesions of the right hemisphere, as opposed to its infrequency in adults. In this way, he significantly contributed to the generally accepted view that crossed aphasia, that is, aphasia with right-hemisphere injury in dextrals, is far more frequent in children than in adults, and that consequently, in early years both the left and right hemisphere play an active role in language production. Furthermore, Freud (1897) clearly distinguished between acquired aphasia and developmental language delay, because he had noticed that most authors up to then (Bernhardt, 1885; Clarus, 1874; Förster, 1880; Lovett, 1888; McNutt, 1885; Wallenberg, 1886) had drawn their conclusions as to the occurrence of language impairments from data collected in patient populations and in reviews of the literature that both included cerebral lesions sustained perinatally as well as brain injuries acquired later in childhood. Without stating so explicitly, Sachs and Peterson (1890) had previously made the same distinction in their discussion on aphasia by excluding from their sample of 105 hemiplegic children all cases of hemiplegia that occurred before the age of 2, because, they stated, "aphasia can only be said to be present if the hemiplegia comes on in an individual who had already acquired articulate speech" (p. 311). Moreover, Freud (1897) very properly observed that the term *aphasia* had been used by several authors in a rather questionable manner because, he conjectured, in their studies or reviews they had often included patients who might be dysarthric.[5] Finally, he confirmed the motor type of childhood aphasia by calling it "die rein motorische Aphasie (Broca's)" (p. 71).

In summary, by the end of the 19th century, a description of ACA had thus originated from the observations reported since Cotard (1868). This "standard doctrine," which remained roughly unchallenged throughout the first half of the 20th century, can be summarized as follows:

1. Auditory comprehension remains relatively preserved.
2. Expressive language is markedly reduced, ranging from mutism to articulatory difficulties.
3. Recovery of language disorders is rapid and complete.
4. Acquired aphasia after right cerebral lesion is common.

Although several authors (Bernhardt, 1885; Clarus, 1874; Freud, 1897; Steffen, 1885) had explicitly pointed out that childhood aphasia was by no means a rare disorder (even though a transient one), the idea that hemiplegic children never or seldom presented with aphasia, whatever the side of the lesion, was further advocated by some authors through the first half of the 20th century.

The 1900–1941 Period

The key features of ACA, for the greater part listed in the late 1800s, were left uncriticized in the beginning of the 20th century. Thus, Taylor (1905) and Sachs and Hausman (1926) confirmed Freud's (1897) observations that ACA was transient, and common with lesions of the right hemisphere. But in a review of the literature on hemiplegia as a complication in typhoid fever, Smithies (1907) found no clinical evidence of right hemispheric involvement in the aphasic children recorded. Unfortunately, the children's handedness was not mentioned. Of the 11 children, aged 5 to 15, 8 were

---

[5]For example, Clarus (1874), Förster (1880), Strümpell (1884), McNutt (1885), Wallenberg (1886), Lovett (1888), Osler (1888), Wulff (1890).

aphasic. Seven had a right-sided hemiplegia (the side was not stated in the remaining case). Two nonaphasic children also had a right-sided hemiplegia. In one case neither the side of hemiplegia nor the language status were indicated. However, the author did not engage in discussion on the relationship between childhood aphasia and lesion laterality.

In accordance with Cotard (1868) and Jendrassik and Marie (1885), Marie (1922) emphasized the absence of aphasia in children having acquired a right-sided hemiplegia early in life. He subsequently expressed the view that the inborn anatomical centers known at that time were bilateral and clearly symmetrical, and that, consequently, far from possessing a language center at birth, each individual had to create one by his own effort. This occurred in the left hemisphere because, he felt, the nerve elements on that side develop a little before those of the right hemisphere. In this way, Marie (1922) also contributed to the later elaboration of the progressive lateralization hypothesis (Basser, 1962; Lenneberg, 1967).

Mingazzini (1925) also interpreted the rapid and complete recovery from ACA as evidence that in early life both hemispheres play an active role in language activity. He also supported the view, previously sketched out by Sachs and Peterson (1890), that as one gets older, the right hemisphere becomes decreasingly involved in language.

In a study on the etiologies and morbid anatomy of infantile acquired hemiplegia, Ford and Schaffer (1927) incidentally mentioned "speech defect" and "loss of speech" in 6 out of the 43 cases they recorded. In 4 children, aged between 1 and 3, this speech defect was associated with a right-sided hemiplegia. This seems to indicate that, in contradistinction to Marie's (1922) view, there is some reason to believe that in their series a communication impairment such as aphasia can be associated with a right-sided hemiplegia acquired in early childhood. However, a further interpretation based on their findings is extremely hazardous, because of the lack of precision in their use of the term *loss of speech*.

Comparing three nonhemiplegic patients who had suffered an encephalopathy early in childhood, Roussy and Levy (1933) contradicted Marie's (1922) view, and concluded that cerebral lesions sustained in early years could bring forth aphasic disorders without a concomitant intellectual impairment.

As to the clinical picture, in the 1920s and 1930s the prevailing impression that ACA was invariably of the motor (expressive) type was slightly modified by a few scattered studies reporting cases of children with acquired sensory (receptive) aphasia. In a detailed description of a 7-year-old boy who presented with an aphasia of unclear origin, Pötzl (1926) argued soundly that the clinical features of the child's language impairment did not fit the usually described symptomatology of ACA, but rather presented characteristics of both a sensory aphasia and a pure word deafness. However, Pötzl (1926) insisted on the point that although the child's verbal output was apparently fluent, it differed from the one encountered in many adult sensory aphasics by lacking the typical logorrhea.

A few years later, Brunner and Stengel (1932) carefully studied a 4-year-old girl presenting with a peculiar type of sensory aphasia consequent upon the extirpation of a left temporal brain abscess. Besides the extremely reduced verbal output, which, to be sure, fits into the standard doctrine, the girl displayed severe auditory comprehension disorders that stood in contrast with the classical belief that auditory comprehension remained relatively spared in ACA. The child had but little insight into her language difficulties. Regarding the good outcome of ACA, Brunner and Stengel (1932) supported Pötzl's (1926) assumption that in cases of acquired sensory aphasia in children, the recovery of language skills did not appear to be as favorable as in cases of motor aphasia.

Thereupon, Wagner and Mayer (1933) extensively reported on a 12-year-old girl who became aphasic subsequently to an infectious process. She developed a mild right-sided paresis of the upper limb 2 days after a bilateral paracentesis.[6] The girl showed no signs of any auditory comprehension ability, and could only say "ja, mia, mia, ja." She could not repeat spoken language. Reading and writing were globally affected. At follow-up 1 year postonset, auditory comprehension was considered accurate. Spontaneous speech had become agrammatic, and contained numerous phonemic paraphasias. Repetition was less severely disordered. Reading and writing were disturbed. The authors noted the reduced impulse to speak, "der geringe Antrieb zum Spontansprechen" (p. 112). Wagner and Mayer (1933) considered the clinical presentation to resemble that of Brunner and Stengel's (1932) case in many points, and put forward the diagnosis "temporale Wortstummheit" (*temporal word muteness*), that is, a specific type of sensory aphasia, in the acute stage of the illness. They confirmed the lack of logorrhea in such cases, and agreed with Pötzl (1926) that childhood sensory aphasia is characterized by a decreased spontaneous output.

Of a particular interest are de Girardier's (1938) and de Girardier and Jeannin's (1939) reports, which unfortunately remained unnoticed in subsequent (mostly English-speaking) studies. They recorded the case of a 7-year-old girl who had sustained a left temporal depressed skull fracture without any loss of consciousness following a fall from a step. Three days later, she developed aphasia as sole neurological symptom. It was characterized by severe word-finding difficulties, alexia, and agraphia, in the ab-

---

[6]*Paracentesis* is the insertion, for either diagnostic or therapeutic reasons, of a fine hollow needle into a body cavity for the purpose of aspirating fluid. Before the advent of antibiotics, it was the obligatory treatment for acute suppurative otitis media with a bulging drumhead (*paracentesis tympani*).

sence of significant auditory comprehension disorders. The girl had not been mute for one moment, nor had she ever presented with apraxia of speech. Although she had always been able to speak fluently, the authors never mentioned paraphasic jargon. There was no word deafness. The girl was operated upon 10 days after the fall. Bone splinters and subdural blood clots located up to the level of the second temporal gyrus were removed. Because of the late onset of the language disorder and the rapid postoperative disappearance of all aphasic difficulties, the authors concluded that the aphasia had resulted from the progressive cerebral compression caused by the subdural hematoma. By stating that the type of aphasia did not fit the Broca-like symptomatology, but corresponded with an anomic aphasia ("aphasie amnésique de Pitres") with alexia and agraphia, as seen in Wernicke's aphasia, de Girardier and Jeannin (1939) can be considered predecessors of the subsequent "discovery" that ACA was more heterogeneous than had previously been thought.

A few remaining case reports added only little to the study of ACA. Their mere existence toned down in some degree the generally accepted notion of the rarity of the disorder. However, they mainly confirmed its traditional description. For instance, Grossi and Famiglietti (1934) presented the case of a 22-month-old boy who showed a postpneumonic motor aphasia that lasted 3 weeks. They concluded that the prognosis of ACA is always favorable. Moschini (1935) reported on the occurrence of a postscarlatinal hemiplegia complicated by motor aphasia in a 5-year-old boy in whom recovery was rapid and complete. The four cases of postinfectious motor aphasia recorded by Prandi (1935) were congruous with the notion of rapid recovery: The language disorder lasted from 10 to 26 days. Describing a case of motor aphasia in a 6-year-old boy who had sustained a left fronto-parieto-temporal skull fracture in a traffic accident, André-Thomas, Sorrel, and Sorrel-Dejerine (1935) also concluded that recovery from aphasia is favorable and more rapid in children than in adults. In a report of three cases of ACA, Taillens (1937) subsequently confirmed the main traditional features of ACA: its rarity, its motor type, and its good outcome. Minkowski (1930), however, had previously contradicted these optimistic statements, and had suggested that children with ACA displayed residual but unequivocal symptoms that could prejudice further language, scholastic, and social development. In the case of an 8-year-old boy who had acquired a motor aphasia (of the Broca type, the author specified) subsequent to a severe closed head injury, he estimated the sequelae (lexical impoverishment, agrammatism, attentional difficulties, emotional lability) to cause a lasting disability of 33%.

Thus, on the eve of World War II, the standard doctrine on ACA seemed to stand firm. The scattered case reports published between 1900 and 1940 apparently were not open to every author, and they barely succeeded in changing the idea, or should we say the "fixed idea," that ACA is rare or perhaps altogether absent (André-Thomas et al., 1935; Marie, 1922; Taillens, 1937). Pötzl's (1926), Minkowski's (1930), and Brunner and Stengel's (1932) observations that in some aphasic children the favorable outcome had to be toned down apparently was not considered in later studies (André-Thomas et al., 1935; Grossi & Famiglietti, 1934; Taillens, 1937). It would take another few years before more cautious statements as to the good prognosis of ACA would appear.

The most significant addition to the traditional description of ACA was introduced by Pötzl (1926), Brunner and Stengel (1932), Wagner and Mayer (1933), and de Girardier and Jeannin (1939), who demonstrated that the clinical picture of ACA was not restricted to the motor type, but could also include types of sensory aphasia. Moreover, Pötzl (1926), Wagner and Mayer (1933), and Brunner and Stengel (1932) showed that phonemic and verbal paraphasias could be observed in the verbal output of aphasic children. However, these conclusions were barely withheld in subsequent studies. True enough, as shown later in this chapter, attention was paid to the observation that logorrhea, frequently reported in adults with left temporal lesions, does not occur in aphasic children. This finding confirmed the apparently atypical character of ACA.

The 1942–1977 Period

The 1940s and 1950s. The first major 20th century study that addressed in detail the incidence, the clinical picture, and the prognosis of ACA in a larger series of children came from Guttmann (1942). He collected data from 30 cases of primary unilateral cerebral hemisphere affections of different etiologies (trauma, neoplasm, abscess, thrombosis), aged 2–14 years, of whom 16 were aphasic (handedness not stated). Regarding the incidence, he remarked that aphasia in left-hemisphere lesions in childhood is not at all rare (14/16 cases), and stated that it is just as regular a symptom in children as in adults. As to the clinical picture, he concluded that in all cases under 10 years of age it was uniformly that of reduced spontaneous speech, varying in degree from complete mutism to dysarthria and telegraphic style in the recovery period, and that this was "equally true of cases with frontal and temporal lesions" (p. 218). Aphasic children with posterior lesions, however, also displayed receptive disorders besides the expressive ones. The author supported Pötzl's (1926) view that logorrhea does not occur in children with temporal lobe lesions. Finally, Guttmann (1942) noted that, in considering the prognosis, one had to keep in mind the severity of the lesion. However, this was difficult to express in comparable figures, because of the various etiologies. Of the original 16 cases of aphasia (14 with left- and 2 with right-hemisphere lesions), only 10 were available at follow-up, which ranged from 4 months to 10 years. The etiologies comprised trauma (6 cases), abscess (3 cases), and thrombosis (1 case). A dramatic improvement of language skills was observed in 5 of the 6 trauma cases, of which each had an initial nonfluent type of aphasia. One abscess case completely recovered, whereas recovery was less marked in the 2 remaining cases. Little improvement was noticed in the vascular case, which displayed an expressive as well as receptive aphasia. Thus the author concluded that (a) motor and sensory aphasia combined has a worse prognosis than motor aphasia alone, (b) the recovery from aphasia of the motor type is surprisingly rapid, and (c) the prognosis is guarded when aphasic signs are still present after 4 weeks. We see later in this chapter that the notion of rapid recovery would especially be propagated.

In presenting these results, Guttmann (1942) refined on the description of ACA by adding that (a) logorrhea is absent and (b) the clinical picture is uniformly that of diminished speech production with dysarthria and telegraphic style in all cases under 10 years of age, wherever the anatomical lesion.[7] However, Guttmann (1942) did not provide information on the relationship between age at lesion onset and recovery, nor on subsequent scholastic achievements.

A few years later, Stengel (1950) supported Guttmann's (1942) conclusions, and, referring to a previous publication of his (Brunner & Stengel, 1932), emphasized that "left-sided temporal lesions which in adults would produce receptive aphasia usually associated with logorrhea, would in young children cause loss of speech impulses in addition to loss of understanding of spoken language" (p. 10). He also pointed to the poor prognosis of the "temporal aphasia" in children, in contrast to the rapid disappearance of aphasia due to pre-central lesions. This feature was implicitly confirmed by Creak (1950), who, in an 8-year-old boy admitted in comatose state with meningitis, still observed traces of his earlier sensory aphasia more than 10 months after admission.

In line with Guttmann's (1942) observation that aphasic children often speak in a telegraphic manner, Heuyer, Lebovici, Dubois, and Diatkine (1948) reported a 13-year-old girl who had acquired a severe motor aphasia and a right-sided hemiplegia after a generalized epileptic insult followed by unconsciousness lasting for 3 days. The girl was severely agrammatic. Of interest is the description of the child's reading impairment: She could read practically no letters, and was quite unable to read syllables and single words. When attempting to decode words and sentences, she made semantic errors (e.g., *mois* instead of *février*, *je regarde par la fenêtre* instead of *il fait beau dehors*). The Heuyer et al. (1948) case study may thus well represent the first—incidental—report of deep dyslexia in a child.

---

[7]Pötzl's (1926), Brunner and Stengel's (1932), Wagner and Mayer's (1933), and de Girardier and Jeannin's (1939) observations had clearly not been taken into consideration in the "updating" of the standard doctrine.

After the study of Guttmann (1942), one could notice a gradual and discrete change in the idea that ACA was a rare disorder. In a review of the mostly French- and Italian-speaking literature, Launay, Borel-Maisonny, Duchene, and Diatkine (1949) contested the notion of rarity, and stated that an appreciable number of aphasic children could be observed after brain lesions sustained as early as 2 or 3 years of age. However, they immediately added that vascular etiologies common in adulthood were barely encountered in children. In support of the classical description of ACA the authors also emphasized the relative shortness of the language disorder.

This view was indeed also advocated by Critchley (1950), who stated that in children, "focal, non-progressive lesions of the brain are rarely followed by a permanent speech-defect" (p. 6). In the same discussion, he turned away from the subject of ACA to expatiate on that of congenital aphasia. In line with Marie (1922), he also questioned the existence of aphasia after early hemispheric lesions: "How often do we see a patient with a congenital or infantile hemiplegia who is also aphasic?" (p. 6), he rhetorically asked. He had clearly not taken notice of the studies of Hécaen and Anglade (1944), Heuyer, Duchene, and Roumajon (1945), and Heuyer and Lebovici (1947), who in the meantime had reported several instances of persistent language impairment in children having acquired a right-sided hemiplegia early in life. What is more, a few years later, de Ajuriaguerra (1958) reported a new case of congenital (right-sided) hemiplegia with concomitant language disorder. By the middle of the 20th century, these studies and some additional reports (Miller, 1950; Palmer, 1952; Van Gelder, Kennedy, & Laguaite, 1952) had thus contested Cotard's (1868), Marie's (1922), and Critchley's (1950) statements concerning the absence of childhood aphasia subsequent to hemispheric lesions sustained early in life. These studies, however, did not succeed in influencing the commonly accepted notion that congenital aphasia is rare or altogether absent (Subirana, 1960).

After this short digression on the occurrence of congenital aphasia, let us return to the main subject of this review, namely ACA. A few years after the Guttmann (1942) and Heuyer et al. (1948) studies, Branco-Lefèvre (1950) published his findings collected in a study on five children with ACA, 3–14 years of age. He agreed with the rarity of the disorder, as opposed to Guttmann (1942). In accordance with the traditional description of ACA, he also pointed to the motor type of aphasia, with initial mutism followed by a reduced initiative for speech and hesitations. He further noted the rarity of auditory comprehension disorders and the absence of logorrhea. However, he tempered the notion of good prognosis by stating that in his series, "the duration of the disturbance was long and the recovery slow and difficult" (p. 390). Finally, he was one of the first to direct attention to the occurrence of writing disturbances in aphasic children.

de Ajuriaguerra (1958), in turn, contradicted the view that ACA is rare, and presented a 7-year-old and a 12-year-old boy with acquired aphasia. A few months after the neurosurgical removal of a left temporal necrotic mass resulting from a meningitis, the first boy still displayed severe syntactic disturbances in spontaneous speech, whereas auditory comprehension appeared normal. Three and a half years after a traffic accident, the second patient was still severely aphasic and totally alexic. In line with Guttmann (1942), Branco-Lefèvre (1950), and Stengel (1950), the author confirmed the absence of logorrhea in ACA, and expressed his doubts about the claim that recovery from ACA is always rapid and complete.

On the threshold of the 1960s, Subirana (1960) summarized the main topics in the study of (acquired) childhood aphasia. He confirmed Freud's (1897) dichotomy differentiating congenital from acquired aphasia in children, but emphasized the extreme rarity of aphasia associated with congenital hemiplegia. He subsequently insisted on the rarity of aphasia associated with postnatal cerebral lesions. He suggested that in early childhood both hemispheres possess the potential of taking over language functions that do not develop on the contralateral side. He derived his assumption from the observation that aphasia following hemispherectomy or other unilateral hemispheric lesions is absent or extremely brief. So if ACA does occur, this viewpoint also implies that it has a good prognosis.

Before discussing one of the most widely quoted studies on childhood aphasia (Basser, 1962), let us recapitulate the past period, and summarize the current description of ACA at that time. The most comprehensive study undoubtedly was that of Guttmann (1942). He emphasized the nonfluent pattern of ACA in young children, ranging from mutism to dysarthria and telegraphic style, and denied the presence of logorrhea in the clinical picture. Branco-Lefèvre's (1950) findings also supported this clinical pattern. Guttmann (1942) threw some doubt upon the idea that the prognosis of ACA was favorable in all cases, and stated that the presence of auditory comprehension difficulties impeded the recovery from ACA. However, he confirmed the good prognosis of "purely" motor aphasia.

Guttmann's (1942) observation that ACA is by no means a rare disorder was supported by the publication of several case reports. However, the scattered reports that incidentally mentioned the presence of a sensory type of aphasia in children (Creak, 1950) did not succeed in tempering the view that ACA is invariably nonfluent.[8] Unlike Guttmann (1942), Branco-Lefèvre (1950), Stengel (1950), and de Ajuriaguerra (1958), prominent authors such as Critchley (1950) and Subirana (1960) kept on doubting the existence of persisting language disorders in children with ACA. In this way, they also

---

[8]In 1957, Landau and Kleffner described a singular type of acquired childhood aphasia associated with epilepsy that appeared to escape any description of ACA known at that time. Some children even displayed a fluent jargon-like aphasia with severe comprehension disorders, thus presenting with a clinical picture the existence of which has explicitly been denied by many authors.

contributed to the elaboration of the hypotheses of equipotentiality and progressive lateralization.

One could have hoped that the new, albeit discrete, insights in the clinical picture and the prognosis of ACA would subsequently have been included in the description of ACA. As later publications illustrate, these slowly growing ideas hardly managed to leave their mark on the views on ACA. Thus, some 20 years later, the standard doctrine would still be propagated. For instance, Denckla (1979) stated that:

> Besides general agreement about acute nonfluency in acquired aphasia of childhood, there is also virtually universal agreement that children recover useful conversational language more completely and rapidly than do adults: weeks or few months for children as opposed to many months or years for adults. (p. 539)

One year later, Ludlow (1980) claimed that "Acquired lesions in the left hemisphere of normally developing children produce a period of aphasia followed by rapid and close to complete recovery" (p. 502). She continued, "Injury to the left hemisphere in childhood produces language symptoms similar to Broca's aphasia. Such children have primarily expressive difficulties; they are nonfluent, have speech articulation problems, make syntactic errors, and speak in a telegraphic style" (p. 504).

The 1960s and 1970s. In the early 1960s, Basser (1962) confirmed the widely admitted nonfluent clinical picture with preserved auditory comprehension abilities, as well as the favorable outcome of ACA. In a well-known study of 102 cases of acquired childhood hemiplegia, he recorded 30 cases in which language had already developed before the occurrence of the cerebral lesion (15 left- and 15 right-sided lesions). Language was disturbed as a result of the lesion, producing hemiplegia in 13 children with left- and 7 with right-hemisphere lesions. The author, however, did not mention the patients' handedness. At follow-up, Basser (1962) reported that:

> There was complete loss of speech for a time in 19 cases, 13 with left and 6 with right hemisphere lesions. . . . It seems certain that understanding was intact in spite of complete loss of verbal expression. . . . The speech loss was not permanent in any case, recovery always taking place after varying periods with subsequent improvement. (p. 435)

According to his observations, the duration of the aphasia was not related to the severity of the hemiplegia. He noted that the outcome of the aphasia was associated with the age at onset, the recovery being more protracted when the lesion occurred before the age of 2. However, this latter relationship is difficult to assess in Basser's (1962) series, because of the low intellectual levels in a majority of the sample. Besides, as in Guttmann's (1942) study, additional information as regards subsequent scholastic achievements unfortunately is not available. Finally, Basser (1962) formulated suggestions as to the pattern of language development in the cerebral hemispheres. We return to this subject when discussing the hypotheses of equipotentiality and progressive lateralization.

That same year, Byers and McLean (1962) reported 12 children who suffered acquired hemiplegia and aphasia of vascular origin. Ten were available at follow-up (which ranged from 3 to 7 years). Their general conclusion that "all 10 children have regained speech spontaneously" (p. 381) fits in well with the common belief that ACA has a good prognosis, but careful examination of the final outcome of these 10 children reveals that only 40% were able to function "back in the community at average level" (p. 382). The other cases displayed "mental irregularities requiring educational concession" (3 cases), "general mental retardation" (2 cases), and an "uncertain status" (1 case).

Riese and Collison's (1964) study provided evidence for a more guarded outcome. They presented observations on six children affected by acquired aphasia. Four of them had a transient language disorder, but two (aged 8 and 9) never fully recovered. Considering the subject of the present chapter, the observation of an instance of sensory aphasia in an 8-year-old right-handed boy is of particular interest. Unfortunately, no description of his neurolinguistic status is provided.

Also that same year, Tomkiewicz (1964) published some theoretical considerations on childhood aphasia. With respect to ACA, he warned against a too optimistic view regarding the recovery of language skills. He put a lot of emphasis on the severe sequelae that could persist in the field of subsequent scholastic achievements, as contrasted to the favorable clinical impression. Consequently, he proposed that it should not be warranted to call the recovery "complete" in those children who afterward fail at school. As to the clinical picture, the author repeated the well-known and widely held notion of nonfluency associated with articulatory disorders and agrammatism, stating that ACA never evolved toward a Wernicke-like picture.

In our opinion, the most frequently quoted study on ACA was conducted by Alajouanine and Lhermitte (1965). They outlined the context of their work by summarizing the current ideas on ACA. In spite of previously reported changes to the description of ACA, in 1965 it was still usual to consider ACA to be a rare and remarkably transitory disorder with very few or no sequelae, characterized by a reduction of verbal expression whatever the locus of the lesion. In order to assess these features, Alajouanine and Lhermitte (1965) studied 32 children (of whom 30 were right-handed) who ranged in age from 6 to 15 years at the onset of the cerebral lesion, which was on the left side in all patients. The etiologies were traumatic, vascular, and tumoral. No precise diagnosis was made in five cases (infectious disease?). With respect to the symptomatology, the authors noted that, in the periacute stage, spontaneous speech was nearly nil in all 32 cases. They stated that this could not be accounted for by the dysarthria, although it frequently occurred (22/32 patients). Vocabulary appeared more or less reduced, and some degree of agrammatism was sometimes displayed. Furthermore the authors observed that:

1. Logorrhea never occurred, even when clinical, surgical, and instrumental data pointed to a temporal or parieto-temporal lesion location.
2. Phonemic or semantic paraphasias were very rare, and occurred only in children over 10 years old.
3. Verbal stereotypies, perseverations, and automatic-voluntary dissociations were absent in all the children.
4. Auditory comprehension difficulties occurred mainly in patients younger than 10 (8/9 children), but rarely in older children (2/23 children); these disorders were marked in 4 out of 32 cases only, and thus the authors considered them to be rare.

Alajouanine and Lhermitte (1965) were also among the first to direct special attention to written language. Writing was severely disordered in 19 out of the 32 children (9/9 in the group younger than 10), and ranged from a total agraphia to a dysorthographia that was dependent on the phonemic disturbances in the verbal output. Reading was affected in 18 out of the 32 children (8/9 in the group younger than 10).

Alajouanine and Lhermitte (1965) also paid attention to the variations of the aphasic disorders according to the age of the patients, thus dividing their sample into two groups. Under the age of 10, the aphasia was characterized by (a) a severe reduction of verbal expression, (b) disorders of articulation and phonetic disintegration, (c) impaired auditory comprehension, (d) severely disturbed writing, and (e) the absence of paraphasias. After 10 years of age, the main features were (a) less frequent disorders of articulation, (b) an increased frequency of paraphasias and some cases of jargon aphasia, (c) disturbed comprehension of written language, and (d) impaired writing. The authors surprisingly did not stop at the finding that in their series, disorders of auditory comprehension were mainly observed in children younger than 10 years of age, despite the fact that instances of jargon aphasia—one would expect auditory comprehension defects to be associated with the latter—were recorded in children above 10 years of age. Alajouanine and Lhermitte (1965) did not try to reconcile the unexpected finding of presence of auditory comprehension disorders in the younger group, then disappearance of such disorders in the older group, with the well-established existence of such comprehension difficulties in adulthood sensory aphasia.

Regarding the recovery, 24 out of the 32 children had regained a normal or nearly normal language at follow-up 1 year or more postonset. None was agrammatic. Age did not appear to affect the speed of recovery. In contrast, the course was unfavorable in 8 children, 6 of whom had large cerebral lesions (3 of these 6 children were less than 10 years old). Alajouanine and Lhermitte (1965) concluded that in 75% of their sample the recovery from ACA was "an indisputable fact and one very particular to children" (p. 660) that could not be explained by the reversibility of the cerebral lesions, as 16 out of the 23 children (1 child died in the course of convalescence) were maintaining severe neurological sequelae. This optimistic conclusion as to the outcome of the language disorder, however, should be tempered by the additional findings that, in spite of the significant remission of the aphasia, "none of the 32 children of this study could follow a normal progress at school" (p. 660). Subjects involving the use of languages appeared to be more difficult than mathematics. The children encountered severe problems in learning lessons, comprehending the general meaning of a course, and applying a logical system to a new problem. In brief, "they were able to regain what had been learned but were unable to acquire new data" (p. 661).

Two years after Alajouanine and Lhermitte's (1965) study, Lenneberg (1967) restated the classical view on ACA that had emerged from clinical experience. He stressed the fact that fluent aphasia and logorrhea were rare "or perhaps altogether absent among pediatric patients" (p. 146). He reviewed 17 cases of ACA published in the literature, and added 8 new cases either examined personally or from available records. Based on this analysis, Lenneberg (1967) claimed that if the aphasia-producing lesion occurred after the onset of language development and was confined to a single hemisphere, language would invariably return if the child was less than 9 years old at the time of lesion occurrence. Lenneberg (1967) concluded that "apparently aphasia runs a different course before the end of the first decade than after it" (p. 146), and stated that aphasia acquired at the time of puberty commonly leaves some traces behind. We return to Lenneberg's (1967) study later when discussing the equipotentiality hypothesis.

In a series of 12 children (9 right- and 3 left-handed), mostly with a traumatic aphasia (9/12), aged 3½ to 13, Collignon, Hécaen, and Angelergues (1968) found a marked initial loss of verbal output in 10 patients, but noted a rapid disappearance of expressive disorders within a month. Logorrhea was not observed in any case. Paraphasias were rare. Dysarthria was mentioned in two children (cases 5 and 10). Auditory comprehension was disturbed in six cases, but completely recovered in five of them. This description closely resembles that of earlier reports (Alajouanine & Lhermitte, 1965; Branco-Lefèvre, 1950; Guttmann, 1942). Collignon et al. (1968) also observed disorders of reading and writing in all their school-aged children. Although reading seemed to recover to a better degree, writing difficulties appeared to be refractory, with their recovery remaining incomplete in seven out of nine cases. Consequently, their study confirmed several features pertaining to the classical view of ACA, but nevertheless casts some doubt on the absence of later sequelae in children who had clinically recovered from their aphasia. An unfavorable outcome seemed to be related to bilateral cerebral lesions.

In a study on acute hemiplegia in infancy and childhood, Aicardi, Amsili, and Chevrie (1969) reported acquired aphasia in 22 out of 122 children. Twenty (91%) had a right- and 2 (9%) a left-sided hemiplegia. The authors suspected that the number of aphasics was lower than the true frequency, because aphasia was possibly overhastily discounted as stupor or unresponsiveness in children who were not thoroughly examined in the acute stage. The language disorder was predominantly expressive in type, but in some children auditory comprehension impairments were also noted. Although the aphasia was usually transitory, persistent difficulties were evident on formal testing in some patients months or years later. These findings are in accordance with other studies from the same period (Alajouanine & Lhermitte, 1965; Collignon et al., 1968; Riese & Collison, 1964) that threw some doubt on the idea of complete recovery from ACA.

One year later, Gloning and Hift (1970) investigated eight preschool children, aged 2½ to 7, who had acquired an aphasia of traumatic (six cases), encephalitic (one case), and epileptic (one case) origin. They did not observe logorrhea. After a period of initial mutism, all patients displayed a nonfluent type of aphasia with reduced verbal output, short sentences, grammatical difficulties, and articulation problems. In some cases, auditory comprehension difficulties were noted. The observations led the authors to the conclusion that a Wernicke-like aphasia with jargon and logorrhea does not occur in childhood. They also assumed that a lack of significant recovery from ACA was related to the presence of severe bilateral cerebral lesions, but did not provide follow-up data.

In a series of 34 children having sustained a severe cerebral trauma, Assal and Campiche (1973) found 18 patients presenting with an acquired language impairment. In the postacute stage, the nonfluent clinical picture was accompanied by dysprosody in all children, and by articulatory difficulties in nine patients. Syntactic difficulties ("troubles de la syntaxe," "phrases agrammaticales") were mentioned in a majority of children. In nine patients, auditory comprehension difficulties were observed. The authors' conclusions were in agreement with the findings of earlier reports in that the clinical picture would be characterized by a "relative monotony" as opposed to the diversified symptomatology of adult aphasia. This general conclusion, however, was tempered somewhat by their observation of a case of lasting alexia with agraphia associated with word-finding difficulties, few phonemic paraphasias, and mild auditory comprehension defects. The occurrence of this peculiar clinical picture, also known as "Wernicke's aphasia type III" in adult studies (Lecours & Lhermitte, 1979), does not fit in with the classical description of ACA, but on the contrary points to a diversity within ACA that has, in our opinion, always been underestimated in previous studies. As a matter of fact, Assal and Campiche (1973) did not dwell on this observation in their general discussion either.

Hécaen (1976) examined 26 cases of cortical lesions in children aged 3½ to 15, and found a disorder of language in 15 out of 17 cases (88%) with left- and 2 out of 6 cases (33%) with right-hemispheric lesion. The sample included instances of traumatic, vascular, tumoral, and infectious etiology. He observed the characteristic features of nonfluency in the majority of cases, including mutism, loss of initiation of speech, the rarity of paraphasias, and the complete absence of logorrhea. Articulatory disorders occurred more frequently than was apparent from the Collignon et al. (1968) study. Auditory comprehension disorders were observed in more than one-third of the cases during the acute period, but they mostly disappeared rapidly and completely. Disturbances in naming and a lexical impoverishment tended to persist at later stages. Reading disorders disappeared quite rapidly in most children, but writing disturbances tended to persist, at times even permanently. The latter observation was in line with Tomkiewicz (1964), Alajouanine and Lhermitte (1965), and Collignon et al. (1968). However, Hécaen (1976) did not provide any information on scholastic status at follow-up. In contrast to Lenneberg's (1967) conclusion that aphasia acquired after 10 years of age unquestionably leaves some traces behind, Hécaen (1976) observed an excellent recovery process in three 14-year-old subjects. In agreement with Collignon et al. (1968) and Gloning and Hift (1970), Hécaen (1976) suggested that the size and the bilaterality of the lesions were one of the most important factors in the recovery process. On the other hand, and as opposed to Assal and Campiche (1973), he did not find any clear relationship between presence and duration of coma, and persistence and severity of linguistic sequelae. Finally, as to the two instances of aphasia associated with right-sided lesions, little can be concluded with respect to the occurrence of this condition in children: The first child was 3½ years of age (handedness can hardly be estimated that early), and the second subject was left-handed.

In regard to the recovery from ACA, Niebergall, Remschmidt, and Lingelbach (1976) were able to distinguish between several types of recovery in a group of six children with traumatic aphasia. The differences resulted from the interpretation of simultaneous measurements of receptive and expressive language modalities. The first group consisted of children whose auditory comprehension and word-finding abilities equally recovered. The language disorder in this group was considered a "mixed motor-sensory aphasia." In the second group, the receptive language component recovered more rapidly than the expressive one; these children had "predominant motor-amnestic aphasia." The third group was composed of children with "clinically predominant sensory aphasia," and was characterized by a better recovery of word-finding abilities as compared to auditory comprehension. The Niebergall et al. (1976) report confirmed the possible occurrence of auditory comprehension disorders in aphasic children and, so to speak, set the tone of ulterior studies that were to shed a new light onto the clinical picture of ACA.

A final study in this part of the historical review comes from Van Dongen and Loonen (1977). They studied the prognosis of ACA in 15 right-handed children, aged 4 to 14. The etiologies were various: nine traumatic, four vascular, one convulsive, and one infectious case. The patients were reexamined up to 3 years postonset. Recovery was observed in 8 children. Seven of them had sustained head trauma. Little recovery was observed in the vascular and convulsive cases. The authors also found a relationship between recovery and type of aphasia. Five out of 6 children with amnestic aphasia showed a greater remission of symptoms, whereas 6 cases with severe comprehension deficits remained aphasic. These findings further confirmed that the prognosis of ACA is not always a good one, and they pointed to both the etiology and the severity of the comprehension disorder as important prognostic indicators. Recovery of language also seemed to be related to the disappearance of electroencephalographic disturbances. With regard to the clinical picture, the description of a 9-year-old boy who displayed the characteristic features of Wernicke's aphasia (fluent speech without articulatory disorder, and with paraphasias) is certainly of interest. This observation clearly does not fit in with the standard doctrine on ACA.

This section has reviewed the ideas on the clinical picture and on the recovery from ACA that were current in the 1960s and 1970s. The prevailing view still corresponded mainly with the standard doctrine. The few anecdotal instances of sensory aphasia in children (Assal & Campiche, 1973; Riese & Collison, 1964; Van Dongen & Loonen, 1977) did not succeed in broadening the traditional notion of nonfluency. However, most authors agreed on the presence of auditory comprehension difficulties in aphasic children, thus disputing Basser's (1962) view that "understanding was intact in spite of complete loss of verbal expression" (p. 435). On the contrary, their findings were in direct line with Pötzl's (1926), Brunner and Stengel's (1932), and Guttmann's (1942) observations of receptive disorders in aphasic children. Moreover, several reports (Aicardi et al., 1969; Alajouanine & Lhermitte, 1965; Collignon et al., 1968; Riese & Collison, 1964; Tomkiewicz, 1964; Van Dongen & Loonen, 1977) contested the claim supported by the earlier literature that recovery of language skills is rapid and complete, and urged others to reconsider some aspects of the traditional description of ACA.

Consequently, in the second half of the 1970s, the formulation of the standard doctrine had slightly been modified. Brown and Hécaen (1976) summarized it in the following way:

1. ACA is characterized by mutism or agrammatism at an early age, and by anomia and nonfluent phonemic paraphasias somewhat later.
2. Articulatory disorders in ACA appear in the context of a nonfluent or borderline fluent state.
3. The picture of fluent phonemic paraphasias in conversation (conduction aphasia) is rarely encountered.
4. Logorrhea and semantic or neologistic jargon do not occur in ACA.
5. Disorders of comprehension are present in about one-third of the patients, but the adult-type correspondence between comprehension loss and logorrheic jargon is not found.
6. Recovery tends to be superior to recovery in adult aphasia.
7. At any early age, there is a relatively even chance that aphasia will occur with injury to either hemisphere.

In the next part of this chapter, we see how this description underwent further changes in the course of the past 21 years.

CURRENT TRENDS IN THE STUDY
OF ACQUIRED CHILDHOOD APHASIA

By presenting the various studies in a chronological way, the first part of this chapter aimed at giving an impression of the birth and growth of the standard doctrine on ACA and of its gradual refinement over the years. This second part concerns recent advances in the study of ACA, and comprises two subsections. The first one addresses the principal aspects of ACA according to subjects: clinical picture, anatomical substrate, etiologies, incidence, recovery, and prognosis. The second subsection introduces the equipotentiality and progressive lateralization hypotheses and briefly discusses the current views on the language organization in children. This section starts in the year Woods and Teuber (1978) published their seminal paper on changing patterns of childhood aphasia, which has led to the development of a new way of thinking about ACA (Paquier & Van Dongen, 1996).

Principal Aspects of Acquired Childhood Aphasia

Clinical Picture. Seven years after the inauguration of a new era in the study of ACA, Swisher (1985) still propagated the classical ideas on the clinical picture of ACA, thus stating that (a) children with an aphasia secondary to a cerebral insult, in most instances a trauma, are initially nonfluent, and then become telegraphic and agrammatic, and (b) fluent aphasias do not appear to occur in children. Yet in their landmark paper Woods and Teuber (1978) had reported an instance of jargon aphasia in a 5-year-old boy. Subsequent studies agreed on the presence of fluent aphasia patterns in children.

Thus, Martins, Ferro, and Castro-Caldas (1981) found 3 cases of fluent aphasia in a follow-up study of 19 children. Van Hout, Evrard, and Lyon (1985) recorded 1 case of Wernicke's aphasia (see also Van Hout & Lyon, 1986) and 1 of transcortical sensory aphasia in a series of 11 children. Other instances of Wernicke's aphasia were observed by Visch-Brink and Van de Sandt-Koenderman (1984) in an 11-year-old girl and by Paquier and Van Dongen (1991) in a 10-year-old anosognosic boy. In a series of 32 children, Basso and Scarpa (1990) found 8 patients who presented with a fluent Wernicke-type aphasia, and 2 who had transcortical sensory aphasia. Cranberg, Filley, Hart, and Alexander (1987) and Van Dongen and Paquier (1991) each documented one case of transcortical sensory aphasia in their respective series of eight and seven children. In a special issue of *Aphasiology* dedicated to ACA (Paquier & Van Dongen, 1993), Ikeda et al. (1993) described an 11-year-old boy showing global aphasia after a left-hemispheric infarct, who demonstrated rapid recovery of speech fluency with poor recovery of language comprehension, thus evolving toward transcortical sensory aphasia.

Klein, Masur, Farber, Shinnar, and Rapin (1992) published the case of a 4½-year-old girl who spoke fluently within 3 weeks of the injury; she was severely anomic and made many semantic paraphasic errors that persisted throughout the 4-year follow-up period. Other instances of acquired anomic aphasia (in children aged 7 and 9, respectively) were provided by Van Hout (1993) in the *Aphasiology* special on ACA. Hynd, Leathem, Semrud-Clikeman, Hern, and Wenner (1995) reported on a case of anomic aphasia in a 10-year-old girl whose spontaneous speech was fluent but empty and circumlocutory. Winter and Prendergast (1995) documented an instance of anomic aphasia caused by simple partial status epilepticus in a 13-year-old boy; the patient spoke fluently in conversation, hiding his word-finding problem by frequently saying "pardon" and by directing the discussion toward rehearsed topics.

Van Dongen, Loonen, and Van Dongen (1985) described three girls aged 9 to 11 years who presented with auditory comprehension difficulties and fluent paraphasic speech associated with acute brain lesions; in all three patients the acute language disorder resembled Wernicke's aphasia, whereas in two children the subsequent evolution progressed toward conduction aphasia. In reporting acquired conduction aphasia in another four children, Van Hout et al. (1985), Martins and Ferro (1987), Tanabe et al. (1989), and Deonna, Davidoff, and Roulet (1993) presented further evidence that the picture of childhood aphasia is heterogeneous. This diversity was further illustrated by Martins and Ferro (1991a), who recorded cases of conduction, anomic, Wernicke's, and transcortical sensory aphasia in their series of 33 children. Skoglund (1979), Makino et al. (1988), and Paquier et al. (1989)

observed children aged 11, 7, and 13 years, respectively, who presented with alexia without agraphia. Finally, Van Dongen, Paquier, Raes, and Creten (1994) succeeded in identifying aphasic children who obviously did not fit the standard doctrine on ACA. By means of an instrumental analysis of phonation times in spontaneous conversational speech, they were able to distinguish children with fluent ACA from children with nonfluent ACA. They suggested that their instrumental method lent further support to the heterogeneity of ACA reported in several clinical descriptions published in the past 19 years.

From these observations, it is clear that the clinical picture of ACA is by no means homogeneous and invariable. As in adults, other aphasic patterns can coexist or appear relatively independently, including impairments of auditory comprehension, naming, reading, and writing. The past decade has consequently underscored the need to reappraise the traditional concept of the clinical features of ACA (Paquier, 1993; Rapin, 1995).

Anatomical Substrate. Before the introduction of modern neuroimaging techniques, data on cerebral lesion localization were derived from clinical, surgical, and laboratory findings. There is adequate reason to believe that these localization methods may sometimes have resulted in a lack of consensus among reports. For instance, Guttmann (1942) had previously suggested that left temporal lesions were associated with more pronounced language disorders than frontal ones. In contrast, Hécaen (1983) concluded that all language modalities were more severely disturbed after anterior than after temporal lesions. The possibility of an undetected bilateral cerebral damage presenting itself clinically as a unilateral disorder, may not have been recognized as such by earlier authors, thus permitting Geschwind (1972) to state several years later: "The curious thing is that even with lesions which in the adult would typically lead to fluent aphasias, the child does not suffer from an obviously fluent aphasia" (p. 265).

The advent of modern brain imaging procedures such as computed tomography (CT) and magnetic resonance imaging (MRI) has permitted investigators to localize structural lesions more precisely, and to establish clinico-anatomical correlations in vivo that appeared to share many similarities with those observed in adults. Thus, when observable, CT anomalies were limited to the left hemisphere in all aphasic children investigated by Loonen and Van Dongen (1990). Children who acquired a nonfluent type of aphasia tend to have suffered the lesion mainly in left pre- or perirolandic areas, either subcortically (Aram, Rose, Rekate, & Whitaker, 1983; Markowitsch, Von Cramon, Hofmann, Sick, & Kinzler, 1990; Martins & Ferro, 1993) or cortico-subcortically (Cranberg et al., 1987; De Bleser, Faiss, & Schwarz, 1995; Martins & Ferro, 1991a, 1993; Pitchford, Funnell, Ellis, Green, & Chapman, 1997). In two children with a nonfluent aphasia associated with a postrolandic lesion, Cranberg et al. (1987) attributed the clinical picture to the anterior extension of the lesion rather than to a specific phenomenon of childhood.

On the other hand, children displaying a fluent type of aphasia seem to have incurred the lesion in posterior brain areas mostly (Paquier & Van Dongen, 1996). Thus, the CT abnormalities in all three patients with fluent aphasia reported by Van Dongen et al. (1985) resided in the posterior part of the left hemisphere encroaching on Wernicke's area. Instances of Wernicke's and of transcortical sensory aphasia were associated with left temporal lesions (Cranberg et al., 1987; Martins & Ferro, 1991a; Paquier & Van Dongen, 1991; Van Dongen & Paquier, 1991; Van Hout & Lyon, 1986; Visch-Brink & Van de Sandt-Koenderman, 1984), whereas conduction aphasia was related to lesions involving the left supramarginal gyrus and arcuate fasciculus (Martins & Ferro, 1987; Tanabe et al., 1989). In the Cranberg et al. (1987) patient with a transcortical sensory aphasia, CT findings of a posterior capsular-putaminal lesion with superior extension were similar to those reported in some adults (Damasio, Damasio, Rizzo, Varney, & Gersh, 1982; Naeser et al., 1982). Paquier et al. (1989) were struck by the similarity between the CT location in their child with alexia without agraphia and the anatomical findings reported in adult cases of subangular alexia (Greenblatt, 1976).

Other modern neuroimaging techniques, such as positron emission tomography (PET) and single photon emission computerized tomography (SPECT), are even more promising in permitting to document cerebral dysfunctions in some pathologies even when CT or MRI fails to demonstrate a corresponding structural abnormality. For instance, Martins, Ferro, and Cantinho (1993) described a 13-year-old right-handed boy who acquired a sensory aphasia following a left subcortical ischemic infarction. A SPECT scan performed during the acute stage disclosed a distant hypoperfusion in the left temporal lobe in addition to the hypoperfusion in the left subcortical region. A repeat SPECT scan, at the time when auditory comprehension had significantly improved, showed a normalization of the left temporal lobe perfusion. The authors concluded that subcortical lesions in ACA may cause distant effects that can explain the "atypical" clinico-radiological correlations.

In contrast to the traditional ideas defending the homogeneity of the nonfluent clinical picture of ACA, irrespective of lesion location (Benson, 1967, 1979; Guttmann, 1942), these studies demonstrate that lesions in different regions of the left hemisphere can be associated with a variety of aphasic syndromes. Generally, the aphasic syndrome resembled that which would be met in adults with similar lesion localizations (Paquier, 1993; Rapin, 1995). These findings relating aphasia to a left-hemisphere lesion, and the occurrence of fluent types of ACA in young children aged 6 or less (Klein et al., 1992; Lees & Neville, 1990; Martins & Ferro, 1991a; Van Hout et al., 1985; Visch-Brink & Van de Sandt-Koenderman, 1984; Woods & Teuber,

1978) support the current view that in right-handed individuals the neuronal substrate for the processing of most aspects of language is present at birth in the left hemisphere (Carter, Hohenegger, & Satz, 1982; Vargha-Khadem, O'Gorman, & Watters, 1985; Woods, 1983).

Etiologies. ACA can be caused by a similar range of central nervous system disorders as adult aphasia. The variety of underlying etiologies primarily includes trauma, vascular lesions, tumors, infections, and convulsive disorders. Although in earlier series (Ford & Schaffer, 1927; Smithies, 1907) aphasia and hemiplegia were frequently associated with infectious diseases, the advent of antibiotics has significantly decreased the incidence of encephalopathies from infections (Woods & Teuber, 1978). In more recent series, the lesions tend to be chiefly of vascular (Aicardi et al., 1969; Byers & McLean, 1962; Fisher & Friedmann, 1959; Isler, 1971) or traumatic origin (Assal & Campiche, 1973; Collignon et al., 1968; Hécaen, 1976; Van Dongen & Loonen, 1977). The incidence of the causes of ACA differs from that of adult aphasia. For instance, cerebrovascular accidents are the most common cause of aphasia in adults, but they rarely occur in children (Giroud et al., 1995; Isler, 1984; Mancini et al., 1997; Nagaraja, Verma, Taly, Veerendra-Kumar, & Jayakumar, 1994; Schoenberg, Mellinger, & Schoenberg, 1978). On the other hand, traumatic head injury is the main cause of ACA but not of adult aphasia (Chadwick, 1985; Ewing-Cobbs, Levin, Eisenberg, & Fletcher, 1987). As etiology and recovery from ACA are interrelated variables (Satz & Bullard-Bates, 1981), this subsection takes into consideration the effect of the former on the latter when addressing the causes of ACA. Other variables influencing the recovery process are considered in a separate subsection.

Aphasic children with traumatic head injury have been reported to improve more than those with other causes (Loonen & Van Dongen, 1990; Martins & Ferro, 1992; Van Dongen & Loonen, 1977; Van Dongen & Visch-Brink, 1988). This might be due to the fact that, because of their more diffuse nature, traumatic brain injuries are less frequently associated with focal damage than are cerebrovascular lesions, and, consequently, they produce less distinct aphasic subtypes (Jordan & Murdoch, 1993; Teasdale, 1995). However, long-term and persistent language deficits such as naming disorders (Hécaen, 1983; Jordan & Murdoch, 1990, 1993; Jordan, Ozanne, & Murdoch, 1988, 1990), impaired syntax production skills (Campbell & Dollaghan, 1990; Chapman et al., 1992), disturbed pragmatic language skills (Dennis & Barnes, 1990; Jordan & Murdoch, 1994), or reading and writing disorders (Chadwick, Rutter, Thompson, & Shaffer, 1981; Ewing-Cobbs, Fletcher, Landry, & Levin, 1985; Hécaen, 1983; Hécaen, Perenin, & Jeannerod, 1984) have been identified in children with head trauma, and may lead to a "subclinical aphasia disorder" (Sarno, Buonaguro, & Levita, 1986) and disruption of academic performance in school-aged children (Cooper & Flowers, 1987; Ewing-Cobbs et al., 1987). The severity of the head injury is likely to determine the degree of residual language impairments (Assal & Campiche, 1973; Ewing-Cobbs et al., 1987; Jordan & Murdoch, 1993).

Lesions that often produce aphasia in adults, such as unilateral cerebrovascular disorders, are less frequent in children. Consequently, relatively few cases of ACA of vascular origin have been described in the literature. However, recent studies have put emphasis on the similitudes with aphasic syndromes of vascular origin in adults (Aram et al., 1983; Cranberg et al., 1987; De Bleser et al., 1995; Lees, 1993; Paquier et al., 1989; Pitchford et al., 1997). Picard, Elghozi, Schouman-Claeys, and Lacert (1989), for instance, reported a case of subcortical aphasia with hemidystonia in a 14-year-old boy, due to a putamino-caudate infarct having occurred at the age of 1 year; the language disorder was similar to that described in adult cases of subcortical aphasia. As to the prognosis for recovery from ACA of vascular origin, the literature contains conflicting data. Martins and Ferro (1991b, 1992, 1993) found that children with stroke exhibited a better recovery than those with trauma or infectious diseases. On the other hand, Loonen and Van Dongen (1990) confirmed Guttmann's (1942) and Van Dongen and Loonen's (1977) observations that children with ACA of vascular origin show a less favorable outcome than children with aphasia of traumatic origin.

Intracerebral tumors can be another cause of ACA (Blauw-Van Mourik, Van Dongen, Loonen, & Paquier, 1989; De Agostini & Kremin, 1986; De Vos, Wyllie, Geckler, Kotagal, & Comair, 1995; Hécaen, 1983; Loonen & Van Dongen, 1990; Martins & Ferro, 1991a). The aphasia generally develops chronically or insidiously, except when it results from an acute bleeding or sudden cystic enlargement (Van Hout, 1990). Usually the evolution of the aphasia parallels the growth of the tumor (De Agostini & Kremin, 1986; Hécaen, 1983), but surgical resection of the neoplasm can provoke a sudden aggravation of the language disorder (Paquier & Van Dongen, 1991). Only a few detailed case reports of ACA with tumoral origin are available in the literature (De Agostini & Kremin, 1986; Martins, Ferro, & Trindade, 1987; Paquier & Van Dongen, 1991). Most often, children with intracerebral tumors have been included in larger series addressing various clinical features of ACA (Hécaen, 1983; Loonen & Van Dongen, 1990).

Infectious diseases of the central nervous system also can produce ACA (Cooper & Flowers, 1987; Martins & Ferro, 1991b; Paquier & Van Dongen, 1991; Van Hout et al., 1985; Van Hout & Lyon, 1986). The frequency of ACA of infectious origin, however, has greatly been reduced since the advent of antibiotics (Woods & Teuber, 1978). Paradoxically, the introduction of antiviral medication reducing the mortality of severe infectious diseases such as herpes simplex encephalitis has permitted aphasic disorders, the existence of which had been denied in the past, to emerge. Indeed, as the herpes virus has a predilection for the temporal lobes, one may diagnose fluent types of aphasia in these children more often nowadays than in earlier days (Van Hout, 1990). For instance, Paquier and Van Dongen (1991) reported a case of Wernicke's aphasia following herpes simplex encephalitis in a 10-year-old anosognosic boy whose CT scan showed a left temporal lesion. The child had severe comprehension disorders, whereas verbal output was characterized by logorrheic neologistic jargon and paragrammatism. As the herpes virus causes devastating necrotic lesions resulting in significant neurologic sequelae in survivors (Kleiman & Carver, 1981; Rantala, Uhari, Uhari, Saukkonen, & Sorri, 1991), the outcome of ACA associated with herpes simplex encephalitis is very poor (Loonen & Van Dongen, 1990; Martins & Ferro, 1992; Paquier & Van Dongen, 1991; Van Hout & Lyon, 1986).

Other epileptic disorders than those seen in the syndrome of acquired aphasia with convulsive disorder (Landau & Kleffner, 1957) can cause expressive or receptive language disturbances depending on the location of the epileptogenic focus, either as ictal or postictal phenomena (Deonna, Chevrie, & Hornung, 1987; Tuchman, 1994; Winter & Prendergast, 1995), and on the type and level of functional organization of the epileptic areas involved (Deonna et al., 1993). The aphasia usually fluctuates along with the electroencephalographic manifestations, and does respond to anticonvulsant medication. For instance, Deonna et al. (1993) described a 7-year-old girl who presented with a brief postictal aphasia of the conduction type, which disappeared once the seizures were brought under control with medication. However, the girl had experienced an isolated, previously unexplained, disorder of written language acquisition that had occurred before the clinically recognized epilepsy and the postictal aphasia. Deonna et al. (1993) emphasized the specific cognitive disorders due to epilepsy in young children, and underlined the vulnerability of recently acquired and incompletely mastered—thus not yet automatized—cognitive skills. They concluded that oral and written language can be differentially involved by cerebral dysfunctions in the young child. When seizures are a consequence of a well-circumscribed cerebral lesion, they can hinder the recovery of the language impairment. As Gaddes (1985) reminded us, focal epilepsies have been shown to be associated with inferior performance on tasks that regularly depend on the normal functioning of the cortical area where the epileptogenic lesion is situated.

Even if this survey of possible causes of ACA is not exhaustive (see Cooper & Flowers, 1987, for cases of ACA associated with anoxic encephalopathy, and Matthes, Walker, Watson, & Bird, 1988, and Kure et al., 1989, for ACA associated with pediatric AIDS), it nevertheless shows that children with a history of acquired aphasia cannot be considered a homogeneous group, as the nature and the outcome of the language impairment apparently vary according to the specific underlying cause (Ozanne & Murdoch, 1990). This finding stands in sharp contrast with the traditional ideas on ACA, and urges us to consider the clinical features of ACA in relation to each etiology separately (Paquier, 1993).

Incidence. Conflicting data on the incidence of ACA are found in the literature. On the one hand, Denckla (1979) stated: "As the sole 'cortical function' consultant in a large neurological institute, between 1969 and 1976 I saw only seven cases of acquired aphasia in children under ten years of age" (p. 537). Marie (1922) had previously questioned whether childhood aphasia even existed. On the other hand, Guttmann (1942) and Hécaen (1976) had remarked that aphasia in childhood is by no means an infrequent disorder.

In order to investigate the incidence of ACA associated with a unilateral hemispheric lesion, Satz and Bullard-Bates (1981) carried out a statistical analysis on data collected in a review of the literature on childhood aphasia. They only took into consideration those studies that met the following criteria: (a) some speech reported before the lesion onset; (b) hand preference reported before lesion onset; (c) patient under the age of 16 at time of lesion; (d) evidence that lesion was unilateral; (e) presence or absence of aphasia had been assessed after the injury. Of 21 studies including 929 cases, only 5 studies comprising 68 cases satisfied these criteria. The results of this survey were also compared to a review of the literature on aphasia in left- and right-handed adults. In conclusion, Satz and Bullard-Bates (1981) stated that:

1. ACA is not rare if the lesion is unilateral and encroaches upon the "speech areas"; however, there is a lower frequency of unilateral vascular disease in children as compared to adults (see Launay et al., 1949).
2. If the left hemisphere has been damaged, the risk of acquired aphasia is approximately the same in right-handed children as it is in right-handed adults.

In another study, Hécaen (1983) found no statistically significant difference between children and adults when comparing the overall frequency of aphasia associated with left-sided hemispheric lesions. Consequently, these studies seriously questioned the presumed differences in the incidence of aphasia between children and adults. Since the early 1980s, ACA has generally been recognized to be not as rare a disorder as previously thought.

Recovery and Prognosis. As exposed in the first part of this chapter, it has long been reported that ACA is transient and has a favorable prognosis. In light of discrepancies between traditional claims and ulterior observations, Satz and Bullard-Bates (1981) critically reviewed the data up to 1978 purporting to show the dramatic recovery from ACA. They concluded that, in general, spontaneous recovery is favorable in a majority of children, although not invariably. Twenty-five to 50% of reviewed cases still presented with aphasia more than 1 year postonset. Moreover, severe cognitive and scholastic sequelae were found even in cases of clinical recovery from aphasia. No relationship appeared to exist between recovery from aphasia and presence or severity of hemiparesis. Finally, Satz and Bullard-Bates (1981) could not unequivocally identify the factors affecting recovery, but suggested that four variables were related to it: etiology, aphasia type, lesion size, and age at lesion onset. However, they warned that they had also found conflicting results for each of these variables regarding their relationship to prognosis.

The preceding subsection dealt with the link between etiology and recovery. Regarding the influence of aphasia type on language recovery, previous studies (Assal & Campiche, 1973; Guttmann, 1942; Van Dongen & Loonen, 1977) had put emphasis on the good prognosis of aphasia without significant auditory comprehension defects, whereas combined motor and sensory aphasia had a more guarded outcome. However, contradictory results emerge from recent reports. In a study on the outcome of ACA 1 year after onset, Loonen and Van Dongen (1990) also investigated the relationship between type of aphasia and recovery from ACA, but were not able to confirm earlier observations. Fluent aphasia was present in four children. Two of them had not recovered at 1 year postonset. Loonen and Van Dongen (1990) remarked that in both cases with favorable outcome, the etiology was traumatic, and that this cause is generally related to a good prognosis. Of 14 children with a nonfluent picture, 9 had not shown a significant improvement of language abilities, thus contradicting previous observations. On the other hand, in a longitudinal study of 32 children younger than 15 years of age with ACA secondary to unilateral focal brain lesions, Martins and Ferro (1992) found the presence of auditory comprehension disorders to be one of the predictors of a poor outcome. They suggested that poor comprehension may prevent the ability to recover to a functional level. However, auditory comprehension defects may be considered an indirect sign of structural or functional damage to Wernicke's area. In their study, damage to Wernicke's area was the single most important factor in predicting an unfavorable prognosis. Therefore, it is not possible to rule out an interaction between the factors of site of lesion and type of aphasia. Moreover, still another variable, the lesion size, may also interact with lesion site and aphasia type, as 80% of the children with damage to Wernicke's area sustained a traumatic or infectious lesion. These are etiologies known to be at risk for bilateral cerebral involvement.

A number of authors had suggested a link between the size or bilaterality of the cerebral lesions and the persistence of aphasic symptoms (Alajouanine & Lhermitte, 1965; Collignon et al., 1968; Gloning & Hift, 1970; Hécaen, 1976). More recent studies (Hécaen, 1983; Van Hout et al., 1985) corroborated these earlier findings, and proposed that bilateral lesions may influence the outcome of ACA in a negative way. Although Loonen and Van Dongen (1990) recently observed a favorable outcome of the aphasia in children with minimal hemispheric damage on CT scan, they could not find a significant relationship between severity of lesion and outcome of the language disorder. For instance, four children with a cerebral tumor initially showed a mild aphasia, whereas the lesions on CT scan were categorized as severe. However, in eight patients whose CT scans showed signs of right hemispheric lesion, a poor outcome was found in all children but one. The authors proposed that not only the bilaterality but also the severity of the lesion could have accounted for the limited recovery, because the severity and the bilaterality of a hemispheric lesion are interrelated. Aram (1991) stated that the role lesion size plays in determining recovery is not clear at present, but that it possibly could interact within the site of the lesion and the age at lesion onset.

The age at lesion onset appears to be the variable to which most attention has been paid in the literature. Lenneberg (1967) stated that the prognosis of ACA is directly related to the age at lesion onset and the language disorders, and that acquired unilateral aphasia-producing lesions incurred before puberty do not leave any permanent residue. However, the evidence from studies on ACA is highly contradictory. In Woods and Teuber's (1978) series, the lesion had occurred before 8 years of age in all aphasic children who showed spontaneous language recovery. In contrast, Woods and Carey's (1979) findings suggested that left-hemisphere lesions having incurred after 1 year of age leave significant residual semantic and syntactic impairment when they had caused initial aphasic disorders. On the other hand, several authors had not been able to identify a single and direct relationship between age at lesion onset and recovery from ACA (Alajouanine & Lhermitte, 1965; Hécaen, 1976). In their study, Loonen and Van Dongen (1990) could not find any difference in recovery of those children aged above or below 11, and consequently, could not confirm the assumption that, the earlier in life a lesion is sustained, the better the outcome. Comparing the performance levels of children and adults with traumatic aphasia, Basso and Scarpa (1990) found that recovery of language disorders in acquired traumatic aphasia was not better in children than in adults. In Martins and Ferro's (1992) analysis, the factor of age at lesion onset did not account for recovery from ACA. The authors suggested that recovery from aphasia depends on the integrity of left posterior language area rather than on a hypothetic age-related plasticity. The fact that a systematic relationship between age at injury and recovery from ACA does not seem to exist appears to be the result of an interaction with other variables such as etiology (Van Hout et al., 1985) or site and size of lesion (Cranberg et al., 1987; Loonen & Van Dongen, 1990). Even in brain-injured groups with carefully controlled subject variables, age does not seem to constitute a significant predictor of language outcome (Aram, 1988).

Although Satz and Bullard-Bates (1981) did not lend a predictive value to the localization of the cerebral lesion, some authors recognized its influence on the recovery process. Alajouanine and Lhermitte (1965) previously stated that language recovery is dependent on the site as well as the extent and reversibility of the cerebral lesions. Unfortunately, they did not provide any specific information as to the lesion location in those eight patients with an unfavorable course of aphasia. More recently, Van Hout et al. (1985) assumed that the site of the lesion may perhaps be more important than the bilaterality of cerebral damage. However, they were unable to specifically assess this factor just because of the presence of bilateral hemispheric involvement in these children in whom left temporal damage had been demonstrated. In contrast, Hécaen (1983) did not discern any apparent relation between the course of recovery and variables such as etiology, age, or lesion localization in a follow-up of 13 cases of ACA for a period ranging from 1½ to 3 months. However, he did not give any detailed information in support of his statements. In a recent study, Martins and Ferro (1992) found that in their series of 32 children with ACA, damage to Wernicke's area was the most significant factor in predicting a poor prognosis. These findings supported previous conclusions (Martins & Ferro, 1991b) suggesting an inverse relation between left temporal lesion extension and recovery in right-handed children. From these conflicting results, any statement relating lesion site to recovery appears tentative at the present time. Fortunately, since the advent of modern neuroradiological techniques, some studies are beginning to address the relationship between intrahemispheric lesion localization and outcome of ACA (Martins & Ferro, 1992).

Finally, some additional variables might also possess a prognostic value. Most clinicians consider the presence of concomitant seizures to have an adverse effect on the outcome of aphasia (Woods, 1985b). This negative effect is most probably related to the spread of abnormal bioelectrical activity that goes far beyond the circumscribed effect of the original lesion. The predictive power of other associated neurological disturbances cannot be established unequivocally. Assal and Campiche (1973) assumed that occurrence and duration of coma were related to outcome of aphasia, but Hécaen (1976) could not discern any clear relationship between these two variables. As to the presence of a hemiplegia, it appeared from several studies (Alajouanine & Lhermitte, 1965; Basser, 1962; Byers & McLean, 1962; Woods & Teuber, 1978) that recovery from ACA is unrelated to the presence or severity of motor sequelae. Finally, diaschisis[9] may account for much of the initial

---

[9]Von Monakow (1914) introduced the concept of diaschisis to explain the generalized but transitory suppression of neural activity that occurs immediately after a sudden insult to the brain. A sudden lesion to the nervous system would disturb regions that are functionally connected to the damage area by inducing deprivation of synaptic activity. After the effect of the "neural shock" has worn off, the unaffected structures regain their function by acquiring innervation from elsewhere (Kertesz, 1984).

regain of functions observed during acute recovery. Riese and Collison (1964) considered transient aphasia to result from diaschisis.

As to the residual linguistic impairments which may persist in the long term, several authors (Cooper & Flowers, 1987; Cranberg et al., 1987; Ewing-Cobbs et al., 1987; Martins & Ferro, 1992) confirmed their impact on subsequent academic achievement (see also Alajouanine & Lhermitte, 1965). Scholastic difficulties as sequelae of ACA seem to be the rule rather than the exception (Van Hout, 1991a), and may affect reading and writing, as well as the acquisition of a second language. In this respect, Watamori, Sasanuma, and Ueda (1990) investigated the nature of residual linguistic impairments when child-onset aphasic subjects reached adulthood. They found that recovery from ACA was not complete, and that syntactic processing difficulties, limitation of lexical-semantic abilities, and alterations in written language processing were present. The case histories of their patients suggested that the effect of residual linguistic impediments was not limited to the area of academic achievement, but had broad generalizing consequences on the subjects' personalities and social development. The Watamori et al. (1990) results also revealed that the strategies for functional compensation that child-onset aphasics used were similar to those seen in recovered adult aphasics. The authors hypothesized that the mechanism of recovery or reorganization of language functions in their patients was not completely different from, but probably analogous to, that of adult aphasics.

In summary, unequivocal data concerning the different factors related to the final outcome of ACA do not seem to be available at present. Different variables have been identified in the past years, but there probably exists an interaction amongst them all. Recovery from ACA is less favorable than witnessed in earlier reports. The age at lesion onset is no longer universally regarded as a positive prognostic factor. Recent reports on ACA have often stressed the presence of persisting linguistic deficits impeding further academic performance of those children who had clinically recovered from aphasia. Tomkiewicz's (1964) warning, more than 30 years ago, becomes all the more actual: It is not possible to speak of complete recovery from aphasia when children keep displaying severe scholastic difficulties relating to orthography and answering questions in classrooms; these lasting impediments show that children who have been aphasic are not capable any more of integrating new data.

The Equipotentiality and Progressive Lateralization Hypotheses

The substratum of the hypotheses of equipotentiality and progressive lateralization is to be traced back to Cotard (1868), Jendrassik and Marie (1885), Steffen (1885), Sachs and Peterson (1890), Freud (1897), Marie (1922), and

Mingazzini (1925) (see the first part of this chapter). The premises are the earlier, apparently contradictory observations that (a) supposing that childhood aphasia exists, it is a rare disorder, and if it does occur, the recovery is rapid and complete; and (b) childhood aphasia is frequently associated with right-hemispheric damage.

These observations gave rise to the viewpoint that in the child, both cerebral hemispheres are capable of developing language: "At birth the two hemispheres are virtually equipotential in regard to the acquisition of language" (Zangwill, 1960, p. 2). Two years later, Basser (1962) examined the effects of unilateral hemispheric lesions and of hemispherectomies both in patients he had come across in clinical practice, and those reported in the literature. He provided new evidence in support of the earlier authors' statements that the right hemisphere can take over language functions after left hemisphere damage and concluded that:

1. "When brain damage was sustained before the acquisition of speech, speech was developed and maintained in the intact hemisphere alone and the right and left hemispheres appeared to be equipotential in this regard irrespective of stock handedness" (p. 448).

2. "The relative frequency of speech disturbance following right hemisphere lesions in right-handed children as compared with adults suggests that often both hemispheres participate in the development of speech before lateralization takes place to the left hemisphere" (p. 450).

The most significant contribution to the study of the ontogenesis of hemispheric dominance for language undoubtedly came from Lenneberg (1967). He derived his evidence from Basser's (1962) study, and from additional cases either reviewed in the literature or examined personally. He interpreted the high incidence of crossed aphasia in children as evidence that initially both hemispheres equally participate in language. From the early clinical observations that recovery from ACA is rapid and complete, he deduced that there must be a critical threshold age below which the right hemisphere is able to take over all language functions from the injured left hemisphere. Lenneberg (1967) formulated his conclusions as follows: "Apparently, there is a period in infancy at which the hemispheres are still equipotential. . . . At the beginning of language development both hemispheres seem to be equally involved; the dominance phenomenon seems to come about through a progressive decrease in involvement of the right hemisphere" (p. 151). Thus, Lenneberg (1967) proposed that during the first 2 years of life, cerebral dominance for language is not well established, and that both hemispheres equally play an active role in language processing. This concept is called the *hypothesis of equipotentiality*. The concept that right-hemisphere involvement in language activity progressively decreases with age, resulting in the establishment of cerebral lateralization of language functions toward the left hemisphere by puberty, is termed the *hypothesis of progressive lateralization.*

Both hypotheses were further advocated in the 1970s. Benson (1972) assumed that rapid recovery of language in ACA was based on shift of language dominance from one hemisphere to the other. He added that, therefore, the prognosis for recovery from ACA was much better than for adults. However, Krashen (1973) reinterpreted Lenneberg's (1967) data and concluded that although the premises of equipotentiality and bilaterality of function remained, the lateralization of language functions toward the left hemisphere was completed by age 5 years.

Some years later, Woods and Teuber (1978) reported on 65 children with unilateral hemispheric brain lesions acquired after onset of language development, somewhere between the ages of 2 and 14 years. Of 34 children with a left-hemisphere lesion, 25 were initially aphasic, whereas only 4 (including 2 left-handers) of 31 right-hemisphere-injured children presented with an initial aphasia. These findings prompted the authors to extensively review the literature on aphasia after childhood lesions. They were the first to remark that in the course of time a dramatic change had occurred in the incidence of crossed aphasia in children. Excluding earlier studies in which reports of diffuse brain involvement due to infectious encephalopathies were frequent, the authors showed that the incidence of crossed aphasia sharply dropped from 33% of the total number of childhood aphasia before 1940, to 5% (after exclusion of known left-handers) in studies undertaken after 1940. Woods and Teuber (1978) attributed the earlier incidence of crossed aphasia in children—which had been used as evidence for early equipotentiality of both hemispheres for language—to undetected bilateral cerebral damage before the introduction of antibiotics and mass immunization programs reducing the common occurrence of neurological complications in diseases such as pneumonia, scarlet fever, measles, pertussis, or diphtheria (Ford & Schaffer, 1927; Smithies, 1907).

In light of Woods and Teuber's (1978) findings that lesion bilaterality could spuriously have inflated the overall incidence of crossed aphasia in early studies, Satz and Bullard-Bates (1981) reviewed the literature on ACA based on reports since 1940 only. Their conclusions were:

1. Regardless of age (at least after infancy), the risk of ACA is substantially greater following left-sided rather than right-sided cerebral lesions.
2. Instances of crossed aphasia do exist, but they are rare after 3 to 5 years of age (or perhaps even earlier) in right-handed children.
3. Crossed aphasia is more commonly observed in left-handed children, regardless of age.

In another study on aphasia and language organization in children, Carter et al. (1982) analyzed the data on ACA in five studies published since 1962 (Basser, 1962; Hécaen, 1977; Isler, 1971; Shillito, 1964; Woods & Teuber, 1978), in order to estimate the (bi)laterality of language representation in children. In light of Krashen's (1973) conclusions, they performed separate analyses for those children aged 5 years or less at the time of lesion onset, and for those aged from 6 to 15 years. The analysis of 107 older children indicated that 97 ± 6% had a left-hemispheric language dominance, whereas only 3 ± 3% were right-hemisphere dominant.[10] The analysis of the 64 younger children was less straightforward, mainly because Basser's (1962) study reported 46% crossed aphasia, whereas the other four studies together found 14% crossed aphasia. Inclusion of Basser's (1962) study resulted in an estimate of 69 ± 20% and 31 ± 36%, respectively, for the proportion of children with left-sided and bilateral language representation. Exclusion of Basser's (1962) study lowered the estimated proportion of language bilaterality to 16 ± 36%, whereas the estimate of left-sided language organization was raised to 84 ± 20%. In spite of these equivocal results, Carter et al. (1982) concluded that their analyses did not support the equipotentiality hypothesis. So, three reasons for this position were put forward:

1. As Woods and Teuber (1978) had already pointed out, Basser's (1962) series may have included some cases with undetected bilateral lesions sustained before antibiotics were in general use.
2. Even the higher estimate of bilateral language representation in children aged 5 years or less (31%) is still inferior to the assumption of universal bilaterality implicit in the equipotentiality hypothesis.
3. They introduced the factor of unrecognized left-handedness among the aphasic children aged 5 years or less.[11] If Basser's (1962) study is excluded, and if a correction for covert left-handedness is introduced, the estimate of the incidence of crossed aphasia in children aged 5 or less drops to 6%.

Hence, Carter et al. (1982) concluded that if Basser's (1962) study is excluded, the ACA data do not support the hypothesis of equipotentiality.

Both the studies of Satz and Bullard-Bates (1981) and of Carter et al. (1982) prompted Hécaen (1983) to reconsider his view regarding the development of language dominance. After having added 30 new cases to his former study (Hécaen, 1976), he concluded that his current series rejected the notion of the equipotentiality of both hemispheres for language during a critical period.

---

[10]Given the authors' assumption that older right-handed children have unilateral language organization.

[11]Some of these younger children may in fact have been undetected left-handers, thus being at higher risk for aphasia associated with right-hemisphere lesions.

In a recent review, Paquier and Van Dongen (1996) emphasized that the presence of persisting language difficulties in right-handed children having acquired an aphasia following an early right-hemispheric lesion (Assal, 1987; Burd, Gascon, Swenson, & Hankey, 1990) is not consistent with the notion of a complete interhemispheric language reorganization toward the left hemisphere, which would be in conformity with Lenneberg's (1967) equipotentiality hypothesis of language development. As a consequence, the rare instances of neurologically and radiologically well-documented cases of acquired crossed aphasia in children followed for a longer period (Assal, 1987; Assal & Deonna, 1977; Burd et al., 1990; Martins et al., 1987; Woods & Teuber, 1978) also support the notion of an early onset of hemispheric dominance for language.

If the hypotheses of equipotentiality and progressive lateralization are no longer tenable, in which way might cerebral language organization in children present itself? The low incidence of crossed aphasia in dextral children makes it likely that in most individuals, the left hemisphere plays the leading role in language from the outset. Moreover, recent studies (Aram, 1988; Aram & Ekelman, 1987; Aram, Ekelman, & Whitaker, 1986; Thal et al., 1991; Vargha-Khadem, O'Gorman, & Watters, 1985; Woods & Carey, 1979) point to the fact that, even in children having sustained a brain injury very early in life, deficits in lexical and syntactic comprehension, syntactic production, and naming and lexical retrieval are all associated with left- but not right-hemisphere lesions. This led Aram (1991) to conclude that "when lesions in children are confined to one hemisphere, just as in adults, aphasia is associated predominantly with left hemisphere involvement" (p. 442).

Observations on the incidence of crossed aphasia in children, and on the presence of persisting linguistic deficits after early left hemisphere damage, are in line with anatomical, behavioral, radiological, and electrophysiological studies (Chi, Dooling, & Gilles, 1977; Davis & Wada, 1977; Duchowny et al., 1996; Foundas, Leonard, Gilmore, Fennell, & Heilman, 1994, 1996; Foundas, Leonard, & Heilman, 1995; Gadian et al., 1996; Hertz-Pannier et al., 1997; Hiscock, 1988; Molfese & Betz, 1988; Nass, Sadler, & Sidtis, 1992; Steinmetz et al., 1990; Steinmetz, Volkmann, Jäncke, & Freund, 1991; Witelson & Pallie, 1973), suggesting that the left hemisphere is predisposed to develop language and that lateralization has already begun at birth.

However, an important remark formulated by Woods (1983) should be mentioned at this point. The potential of the right hemisphere to take over language functions following very early left hemisphere lesions is not being questioned (Vargha-Khadem et al., 1997). What is actually being doubted is the postulate of an initial, simultaneous, and equally active role of the right hemisphere in language activity in normal children. The concept that in dextrals the left hemisphere is dominant for language at birth, and that language representation in the right hemisphere only occurs after the left hemisphere has been lesioned, has been termed the *hypothesis of invariance* (Kinsbourne & Hiscock, 1977).

Finally, one may wonder whether the invariance hypothesis precludes the hypothesis of progressive lateralization. Satz, Strauss, and Whitaker (1990) proposed that progressive lateralization be viewed as a progressive development of language within the left hemisphere, in agreement with Luria (1980), who assumed that functions progressively develop from primary to tertiary cortical areas. Based on studies of myelogenesis, synaptogenesis, and gyral development, Campbell and Whitaker (1986) supported the idea that brain development proceeds from the primary motor and sensory areas (rolandic cortex, calcarine cortex, Heschl's gyrus, planum temporale) outward to the secondary and association areas. Thus Satz et al. (1990) suggested that progressive lateralization is not an inter- but an intrahemispheric process, and stated that "the progressive lateralization hypothesis refers to a dynamic process of increasing cortical specialization of speech and language functions that develops within the left hemisphere in a vertical (subcortical-cortical) and horizontal (anterior-posterior) progression during infancy and childhood" (p. 611). This statement led them to reconsider the invariance hypothesis: "The asymmetry . . . may be invariant but not the type of functional specialization which may change as different structures within the left hemisphere . . . gradually mature and provide the functional . . . substrate for more complex multimodal linguistic functions" (Satz et al., 1990, p. 611). In contrast with the progressive lateralization, the developmental invariance would then be an inter- but not an intrahemispheric concept.

Before concluding this chapter, the question remains, is it justified to relate functional maturation to structural maturation? Satz et al. (1990) presumed that it intuitively seemed reasonable to consider both to be interdependent, but acknowledged that the relationship between them might not always be a straightforward one. One might assume that the level of functional organization is independent of the maturation rate of a given structure when it is already mature at the time of functional development. Woods (1985b), for instance, repeated the viewpoint that the left hemisphere is committed to language much earlier than the right hemisphere is entrusted with its proper functions. One might ask, therefore, whether this is a consequence of the structural organization of the right hemisphere or of its different maturation rate (Reiss, Abrams, Singer, Ross, & Denckla, 1996).

CONCLUSION

From the earliest reports on childhood aphasia to the late 1970s, the study of ACA has mainly concerned itself with highlighting its atypical clinical presentation (Woods, 1985b). Thus, it was claimed that in contradistinction to the heterogeneity of clinical pictures found in adult aphasia, ACA was invariably nonfluent, and occurred frequently in association with right-hemisphere lesions. Furthermore, recovery from ACA was claimed to be rapid and complete. The few scattered counterexamples did not succeed in modifying this standard doctrine. Since the late 1970s, however, this traditional view has been challenged by several reports revealing the presence of neologisms and paraphasias, logorrhea and jargon, impaired repetition abilities, and a host of linguistic deficits in reading and writing. These studies demonstrated that auditory comprehension difficulties can be detected in nearly all aphasic children if appropriate tests are administered.[12] Different varieties of fluent aphasia were thus observed in children (Paquier, 1993). The introduction of new neuroimaging techniques enabled the investigation of relationships between underlying neuropathological processes and clinical manifestations of ACA. Anatomo-clinical correlations were established that appeared to share many similitudes with those found in aphasia syndromes in adults, thus suggesting the presence of an adult-like neural representation of language in childhood. The study of ACA thus moved toward a recognition of the fundamental similitudes between childhood and adulthood aphasia. As Van Hout (1991b) suggested, "the differences between aphasias in children and adults now appear more quantitative than qualitative" (p. 122). One should keep in mind, however, that these similitudes or "quantitative differences" do not fully apply to the etiologies of the aphasia. Traumatic lesions, for instance, are a more frequent cause of ACA than of adulthood aphasia, and the syndrome of acquired aphasia with convulsive disorder (Landau & Kleffner, 1957) typically affects a childhood population only.

The study of ACA has also provided new insights into the cerebral representation of language. Nowadays, it appears that the two cerebral hemispheres are no equal substrate for language representation. Neural plasticity of uncommitted cortical areas rather than hemispheric equipotentiality does facilitate the reorganization of language functions after cerebral damage in childhood (Wetherby, 1985). However, recent reports on ACA have emphasized the either subtle or more evident linguistic deficits persisting in the long term, and have urged tempering of the widely held, optimistic notion of complete recovery. Poor academic performance has been observed in school-aged children even after clinical recovery of language abilities. Such

---

[12]The development of formal and sensitive aphasia test batteries, replacing the less accurate bedside screening methods employed in earlier studies, has made it possible to detect less severe auditory comprehension difficulties (associated with inconspicuous concomitant neurological signs) that might have been missed in the past (Paquier & Van Dongen, 1996). Moreover, because of the preconceived opinion about the clinical features of ACA with which bedside examination was performed in earlier days, an impairment of auditory comprehension may have been missed because it was misinterpreted as acute confusion when neurological deficits were subtle (Van Dongen et al., 1985).

subsequent scholastic difficulties seem to be the rule rather than the exception, and underscore the similarity found between the mechanism of neurologic reorganization in child-onset aphasia and that in adult aphasia. These data also favor the notion of an early onset of hemispheric representation of language functions that is more similar to the adult organization than previously thought.

ACKNOWLEDGMENT

This study was supported by a grant from the Belgian National Fund for Scientific Research (NFWO) awarded to P. F. Paquier.

REFERENCES

Aicardi, J., Amsili, J., & Chevrie, J. J. (1969). Acute hemiplegia in infancy and childhood. *Developmental Medicine and Child Neurology, 11*, 162–173.

Alajouanine, T., & Lhermitte, F. (1965). Acquired aphasia in children. *Brain, 88*, 653–662.

André-Thomas, A. H., Sorrel, E., & Sorrel-Dejerine, Y. (1935). Un cas d'aphasie motrice par traumatisme cranio-cérébral chez l'enfant. *Revue Neurologique, 63*, 893–896.

Aram, D. M. (1988). Language sequelae of unilateral brain lesions in children. In F. Plum (Ed.), *Language, communication, and the brain* (pp. 171–197). New York: Raven Press.

Aram, D. M. (1991). Acquired aphasia in children. In M. T. Sarno (Ed.), *Acquired aphasia* (pp. 425–453). Orlando, FL: Academic Press.

Aram, D. M., & Ekelman, B. L. (1987). Unilateral brain lesions in childhood: Performance on the revised Token Test. *Brain and Language, 32*, 137–158.

Aram, D. M., Ekelman, B. L., & Whitaker, H. A. (1986). Spoken syntax in children with acquired unilateral hemisphere lesions. *Brain and Language, 27*, 75–100.

Aram, D. M., Rose, D. F., Rekate, H. L., & Whitaker, H. A. (1983). Acquired capsular/striatal aphasia in childhood. *Archives of Neurology, 40*, 614–617.

Assal, G. (1987). Aphasie croisée chez un enfant. *Revue Neurologique, 143*, 532–535.

Assal, G., & Campiche, R. (1973). Aphasie et troubles du langage chez l'enfant après contusion cérébrale. *Neuro-Chirurgie, 19*, 399–405.

Assal, G., & Deonna, T. (1977). Aphasie par thrombose de la carotide interne droite, chez un enfant droitier. *Oto-Neuro-Ophtalmologie, 49*, 321–326.

Basser, L. S. (1962). Hemiplegia of early onset and the faculty of speech with special reference to the effects of hemispherectomy. *Brain, 85*, 427–460.

Basso, A., & Scarpa, M. T. (1990). Traumatic aphasia in children and adults: A comparison of clinical features and evolution. *Cortex, 26*, 501–514.

Benson, D. F. (1967). Fluency in aphasia: Correlation with radioactive scan localization. *Cortex, 3*, 373–394.

Benson, D. F. (1972). Language disturbances of childhood. *Clinical Proceedings, Children's Hospital National Medical Center, 28*, 93–100.

Benson, D. F. (1979). *Aphasia, alexia, and agraphia.* New York: Churchill Livingstone.

Bernhardt, M. (1885). Ueber die spastische Cerebralparalyse im Kindesalter (Hemiplegia spastica infantilis), nebst einem Excurse über "Aphasie bei Kindern." *Virchow's Archiv für Pathologische Anatomie und Physiologie und für Klinische Medicin, 102*, 26–80.

Blauw-Van Mourik, M., Van Dongen, H. R., Loonen, M. C. B., & Paquier, P. (1989). Die erworbenen Aphasien bei Kindern: Eine Revision früherer Annahmen. *Aphasie und verwandte Gebiete, 2,* 3–8.

Branco-Lefèvre, A. (1950). Contribuiçao para o estudo da psicopatologia da afasia em crianças. *Arquivos de Neuro-Psiquiatria, 8,* 345–393.

Broca, P. (1861). Remarques sur le siège de la faculté du langage articulé, suivies d'une observation d'aphémie (perte de la parole). *Bulletin de la Société d'Anatomie, 6,* 330–357.

Brown, J. W., & Hécaen, H. (1976). Lateralization and language representation: Observations on aphasia in children, left-handers, and "anomalous" dextrals. *Neurology, 26,* 183–189.

Brunner, H., & Stengel, E. (1932). Zur Lehre von den Aphasien im Kindesalter (Wortstummheit bei linksseitigem otogenem Schläfelappenabscess). *Zentralblatt für die gesamte Neurologie und Psychiatrie, 142,* 430–450.

Burd, L., Gascon, G., Swenson, R., & Hankey, R. (1990). Crossed aphasia in early childhood. *Developmental Medicine and Child Neurology, 32,* 539–546.

Byers, R. K., & McLean, W. T. (1962). Etiology and course of certain hemiplegias with aphasia in childhood. *Pediatrics, 29,* 376–383.

Campbell, S., & Whitaker, H. A. (1986). Cortical maturation and developmental neurolinguistics. In J. E. Obrzut & G. W. Hynd (Eds.), *Child neuropsychology* (pp. 55–72). New York: Academic Press.

Campbell, T. F., & Dollaghan, C. A. (1990). Expressive language recovery in severely brain-injured children and adolescents. *Journal of Speech and Hearing Disorders, 55,* 567–581.

Carter, R. L., Hohenegger, M. K., & Satz, P. (1982). Aphasia and speech organization in children. *Science, 218,* 797–799.

Chadwick, O. (1985). Psychological sequelae of head injury in children. *Developmental Medicine and Child Neurology, 27,* 72–75.

Chadwick, O., Rutter, M., Thompson, J., & Shaffer, D. (1981). Intellectual performance and reading skills after localized head injury in childhood. *Journal of Child Psychology and Psychiatry, 22,* 117–139.

Chapman, S. B., Culhane, K. A., Levin, H. S., Harward, H., Mendelsohn, D., Ewing-Cobb, L., Fletcher, J. M., & Bruce, D. (1992). Narrative discourse after closed head injury in children and adolescents. *Brain and Language, 43,* 42–65.

Chi, J. G., Dooling, E. C., & Gilles, F. H. (1977). Left-right asymmetries of the temporal speech areas of the human fetus. *Archives of Neurology, 34,* 346–348.

Clarus, A. (1874). Ueber Aphasie bei Kindern. *Jahrbuch für Kinderheilkunde, 7,* 369–400.

Collignon, R., Hécaen, H., & Angelergues, R. (1968). A propos de 12 cas d'aphasie acquise de l'enfant. *Acta Neurologica Belgica, 68,* 245–277.

Cooper, J. A., & Flowers, C. R. (1987). Children with a history of acquired aphasia: Residual language and academic impairments. *Journal of Speech and Hearing Disorders, 52,* 251–262.

Cotard, J. (1868). *Etude sur l'atrophie cérébrale.* Thesis, Faculté de Médecine, Paris.

Cranberg, L. D., Filley, C. M., Hart, E. J., & Alexander, M. P. (1987). Acquired aphasia in childhood: Clinical and CT investigations. *Neurology, 37,* 1165–1172.

Creak, E. M. (1950). Discussion on speech defects in children. *Proceedings of the Royal Society of Medicine, 43,* 6–9.

Critchley, M. (1950). Discussion on speech defects in children. *Proceedings of the Royal Society of Medicine, 43,* 4–6.

Damasio, A. R., Damasio, H., Rizzo, M., Varney, N., & Gersh, F. (1982). Aphasia with non-hemorrhagic lesions in the basal ganglia and internal capsule. *Archives of Neurology, 39,* 15–20.

Davis, A., & Wada, J. (1977). Hemispheric asymmetries in human infants: Spectral analysis of flash and click evoked potentials. *Brain and Language, 4,* 23–31.

De Agostini, M., & Kremin, H. (1986). Homogeneity of the syndrome of acquired aphasia in childhood revisited: Case study of a child with transcortical aphasia. *Journal of Neurolinguistics, 2,* 179–187.

De Ajuriaguerra, J. (1958). Troubles du langage chez l'enfant au cours des lésions cérébrales en foyer et des démences. *Journal Français d'Oto-Rhino-Laryngologie, 7*, 225–240.

De Bleser, R., Faiss, J., & Schwarz, M. (1995). Rapid recovery of aphasia and deep dyslexia after cerebrovascular left-hemisphere damage in childhood. *Journal of Neurolinguistics, 9*, 9–22.

de Girardier, J. (1938). Un cas d'aphasie amnésique consécutif à une fracture du crâne chez une enfant de 7 ans. *Bulletin de la Société de Pédiatrie, 36*, 733–736.

de Girardier, J., & Jeannin, J. (1939). Fracture du crâne accompagnée d'aphasie après intervalle libre chez une enfant de 7 ans. *Lyon Chirurgical, 36*, 183–189.

Denckla, M. B. (1979). Childhood learning disabilities. In K. Heilman & E. Valenstein (Eds.), *Clinical neuropsychology* (pp. 535–573). New York: Oxford University Press.

Dennis, M., & Barnes, M. A. (1990). Knowing the meaning, getting the point, bridging the gap, and carrying the message: Aspects of discourse following closed head injury in childhood and adolescence. *Brain and Language, 39*, 428–446.

Deonna, T. (1991). Acquired epileptiform aphasia in children (Landau–Kleffner syndrome). *Journal of Clinical Neurophysiology, 8*, 288–298.

Deonna, T., Chevrie, C., & Hornung, E. (1987). Childhood epileptic speech disorder: Prolonged, isolated deficit of prosodic features. *Developmental Medicine and Child Neurology, 29*, 100–105.

Deonna, T., Davidoff, V., & Roulet, E. (1993). Isolated disturbance of written language acquisition as an initial symptom of epileptic aphasia in a 7-year-old child: A 3-year follow-up study. *Aphasiology, 7*, 441–450.

De Vos, K. J., Wyllie, E., Geckler, C., Kotagal, P., & Comair, Y. (1995). Language dominance in patients with early childhood tumors near left hemisphere language areas. *Neurology, 45*, 349–356.

Duchowny, M., Jayakar, P., Harvey, S., Resnick, T., Alvarez, L., Dean, P., & Levin, B. (1996). Language cortex representation: Effects of developmental versus acquired pathology. *Annals of Neurology, 40*, 31–38.

Ewing-Cobbs, L., Fletcher, J. M., Landry, S. H., & Levin, H. S. (1985). Language disorders after pediatric head injury. In J. K. Darby (Ed.), *Speech and language evaluation in neurology— Childhood disorders* (pp. 97–111). Orlando, FL: Grune & Stratton.

Ewing-Cobbs, L., Levin, H. S., Eisenberg, H. M., & Fletcher, J. M. (1987). Language functions following closed-head injury in children and adolescents. *Journal of Clinical and Experimental Neuropsychology, 9*, 575–592.

Fisher, R. G., & Friedmann, K. R. (1959). Carotid artery thrombosis in persons fifteen years of age or younger. *Journal of the American Medical Association, 170*, 1918–1919.

Ford, F. R., & Schaffer, A. J. (1927). The etiology of infantile acquired hemiplegia. *Archives of Neurology and Psychiatry, 18*, 323–347.

Förster, R. (1880). Mittheilungen über die im neuen Dresdner Kinderhospitale, in den ersten beide Jahren nach seiner Eröffnung, zur Beobachtung gekommenen Lähmungen. *Jahrbuch für Kinderheilkunde, 15*, 261–299.

Foundas, A. L., Leonard, C. M., Gilmore, R. L., Fennell, E. B., & Heilman, K. M. (1994). Planum temporale asymmetry and language dominance. *Neuropsychologia, 32*, 1225–1231.

Foundas, A. L., Leonard, C. M., Gilmore, R. L., Fennell, E. B., & Heilman, K. M. (1996). Pars triangularis asymmetry and language dominance. *Proceedings of the National Academy of Sciences, 93*, 719–722.

Foundas, A. L., Leonard, C. M., & Heilman, K. M. (1995). Morphologic cerebral asymmetries and handedness: The pars triangularis and planum temporale. *Archives of Neurology, 52*, 501–508.

Freud, S. (1897). *Die infantile Cerebrallähmung*. Wien: Alfred Hölder.

Gaddes, W. H. (1985). *Learning disabilities and brain function: A neuropsychological approach*. New York: Springer-Verlag.

Gadian, D. G., Isaacs, E. B., Cross, J. H., Connelly, A., Jackson, G. D., King, M. D., Neville, B. G. R., & Vargha-Khadem, F. (1996). Lateralization of brain function in childhood revealed by magnetic resonance spectroscopy. *Neurology, 46*, 974–977.

Geschwind, N. (1972). Disorders of higher cortical function in children. *Clinical Proceedings, Children's Hospital National Medical Center, 28*, 262–272.

Giroud, M., Lemesle, M., Gouyon, J.-B., Nivelon, J.-L., Milan, C., & Dumas, R. (1995). Cerebrovascular disease in children under 16 years of age in the city of Dijon, France: A study of incidence and clinical features from 1985 to 1993. *Journal of Clinical Epidemiology, 48*, 1343–1348.

Gloning, K., & Hift, E. (1970). Aphasie im Vorschulalter. *Wiener Zeitschrift für Nervenheilkunde, 28*, 20–28.

Gordon, N. (1990). Acquired aphasia in childhood: The Landau–Kleffner syndrome. *Developmental Medicine and Child Neurology, 32*, 270–274.

Greenblatt, S. (1976). Subangular alexia without agraphia or hemianopsia. *Brain and Language, 3*, 229–245.

Grossi, F., & Famiglietti, M. (1934). Un caso di afasia motrice tossica pura in seguito a polmonite. *Pediatria, 42*, 874–878.

Guttmann, E. (1942). Aphasia in children. *Brain, 65*, 205–219.

Hécaen, H. (1976). Acquired aphasia in children and the ontogenesis of hemispheric functional specialization. *Brain and Language, 3*, 114–134.

Hécaen, H. (1977). Language representation and brain development. In S. R. Berenberg (Ed.), *Brain fetal and infant: Current research on normal and abnormal development* (pp. 112–123). The Hague: Martinus Nijhoff Medical Division.

Hécaen, H. (1983). Acquired aphasia in children: Revisited. *Neuropsychologia, 21*, 581–587.

Hécaen, H., & Anglade, L. (1944). Hémiplégie cérébrale infantile et troubles aphasiques. *Bulletin de l'Académie de Médecine, 128*, 259–261.

Hécaen, H., Perenin, M. T., & Jeannerod, M. (1984). The effects of cortical lesions in children: Language and visual functions. In C. R. Almli & S. Finger (Eds.), *Early brain damage: Research orientations and clinical observations* (pp. 277–298). Orlando, FL: Academic Press.

Hertz-Pannier, L., Gaillard, W. D., Mott, S. H., Cuenod, C. A., Bookheimer, S. Y., Weinstein, S., Conry, J., Papero, P. H., Schiff, S. J., Le Bihan, D., & Theodore, W. H. (1997). Noninvasive assessment of language dominance in children and adolescents with functional MRI: A preliminary study. *Neurology, 48*, 1003–1012.

Heuyer, G., Duchene, H., & Roumajon, Y. (1945). A propos d'un cas d'aphasie après hémiplégie congénitale, avec dégénérescence maculaire associée. Considérations sur certains retards de la parole chez l'enfant. *Revue Neurologique, 77*, 31–33.

Heuyer, G., & Lebovici, S. (1947). Hémiplégie droite avec aphasie chez un enfant de 7 ans. *Revue Neurologique, 79*, 40–42.

Heuyer, G., Lebovici, S., Dubois, J. C., & Diatkine, R. (1948). Troubles du langage par hémiplégie droite et aphasie acquise chez une fille de 13 ans. *Archives Françaises de Pédiatrie, 5*, 279–280.

Hiscock, M. (1988). Behavioral asymmetries in normal children. In D. L. Molfese & S. J. Segalowitz (Eds.), *Brain lateralization in children: Developmental implications* (pp. 84–169). New York: Guilford Press.

Hynd, G. W., Leathem, J., Semrud-Clikeman, M., Hern, K. L., & Wenner, M. (1995). Anomic aphasia in childhood. *Journal of Child Neurology, 10*, 289–293.

Ikeda, M., Tanabe, H., Yamada, K., Yoshimine, T., Hayakawa, T., Hashikawa, K., & Nishimura, T. (1993). A case of acquired childhood aphasia with evolution of global aphasia into transcortical sensory aphasia. *Aphasiology, 7*, 497–502.

Isler, W. (1971). *Acute hemiplegias and hemisyndromes in childhood. Clinics in developmental medicine (Nos. 41/42)*. London: William Heinemann Medical Books.

Isler, W. (1984). Stroke in childhood and adolescence. *European Neurology, 23*, 421–424.

Jendrassik, E., & Marie, P. (1885). Contribution à l'étude de l'hémiatrophie cérébrale par sclérose lobaire. *Archives de Physiologie, 1*, 51–105.

Jordan, F. M., & Murdoch, B. E. (1990). Linguistic status following closed head injury in children: A follow-up study. *Brain Injury, 4*, 147–154.

Jordan, F. M., & Murdoch, B. E. (1993). A prospective study of the linguistic skills of children with closed-head injuries. *Aphasiology, 7*, 503–512.

Jordan, F. M., & Murdoch, B. E. (1994). Severe closed-head injury in childhood: Linguistic outcomes into adulthood. *Brain Injury, 8*, 501–508.

Jordan, F. M., Ozanne, A. E., & Murdoch, B. E. (1988). Long-term speech and language disorders subsequent to closed head injury in children. *Brain Injury, 2*, 179–185.

Jordan, F. M., Ozanne, A. E., & Murdoch, B. E. (1990). Performance of closed head-injured children on a naming task. *Brain Injury, 4*, 27–32.

Kertesz, A. (1984). Recovery from aphasia. In F. C. Rose (Ed.), *Progress in aphasiology. Advances in neurology (Vol. 42)* (pp. 23–39). New York: Raven Press.

Kinsbourne, M., & Hiscock, M. (1977). Does cerebral dominance develop? In S. Segalowitz & F. Gruber (Eds.), *Language development and neurological theory* (pp. 171–191). New York: Academic Press.

Kleiman, M. B., & Carver, D. H. (1981). Central nervous system infections. In P. Black (Ed.), *Brain dysfunction in children: Etiology, diagnosis, and management* (pp. 79–107). New York: Raven Press.

Klein, S. K., Masur, D., Farber, K., Shinnar, S., & Rapin, I. (1992). Fluent aphasia in children: Definition and natural history. *Journal of Child Neurology, 7*, 50–59.

Krashen, S. D. (1973). Lateralization, language learning, and the critical period: Some new evidence. *Language Learning, 23*, 63–74.

Kure, K., Park, Y. D., Kim, T. S., Lyman, W. D., Lantos, G., Lee, S., Cho, S., Belman, A. L., Weidenheim, K. M., & Dickson, D. W. (1989). Immunohistochemical localization of an HIV epitope in cerebral aneurysmal arteriopathy in pediatric acquired immunodeficiency syndrome (AIDS). *Pediatric Pathology, 9*, 655–667.

Landau, W. M., Goldstein, R., & Kleffner, F. R. (1960). Congenital aphasia: A clinicopathologic study. *Neurology, 10*, 915–921.

Landau, W. M., & Kleffner, F. R. (1957). Syndrome of acquired aphasia with convulsive disorder in children. *Neurology, 7*, 523–530.

Launay, C., Borel-Maisonny, S., Duchene, H., & Diatkine, R. (1949). *Les troubles du langage chez l'enfant*. Paris: L'Expansion Scientifique Française.

Lecours, A. R., & Lhermitte, F. (1979). Formes cliniques de l'aphasie. In A. R. Lecours & F. Lhermitte (Eds.), *L'aphasie* (pp. 111–151). Paris: Flammarion Médecine-Sciences.

Lees, J. A. (1993). *Children with acquired aphasias*. London: Whurr.

Lees, J. A., & Neville, B. G. (1990). Acquired aphasia in childhood: Case studies of five children. *Aphasiology, 4*, 463–478.

Lenneberg, E. (1967). *Biological foundations of language*. New York: John Wiley.

Loonen, M. C. B., & Van Dongen, H. R. (1990). Acquired childhood aphasia: Outcome one year after onset. *Archives of Neurology, 47*, 1324–1328.

Lovett, R. W. (1888). A clinical consideration of sixty cases of cerebral paralysis in children. *Boston Medical and Surgical Journal, 118*, 641–646.

Ludlow, C. L. (1980). Children's language disorders: Recent research advances. *Annals of Neurology, 7*, 497–507.

Luria, A. R. (1980). *Higher cortical functions in man*. New York: Basic Books.

Makino, A., Soga, T., Obayashi, M., Seo, Y., Ebisutani, D., Horie, S., Ueda, S., & Matsumoto, K. (1988). Cortical blindness caused by acute general cerebral swelling. *Surgical Neurology, 29*, 393–400.

Mancini, J., Girard, N., Chabrol, B., Lamoureux, S., Livet, M. O., Thuret, I., & Pinsard, N. (1997). Ischemic cerebrovascular disease in children: Retrospective study of 35 patients. *Journal of Child Neurology, 12,* 193–199.

Marchman, V. A., Miller, R., & Bates, E. A. (1991). Babble and first words in children with focal brain injury. *Applied Psycholinguistics, 12,* 1–22.

Marie, P. (1922). Existe-t-il dans le cerveau humain des centres innés ou préformés de langage? *La Presse Médicale, 17,* 177–181.

Markowitsch, H. J., Von Cramon, D. Y., Hofmann, E., Sick, C. D., & Kinzler, P. (1990). Verbal memory deterioration after unilateral infarct of the internal capsule in an adolescent. *Cortex, 26,* 597–609.

Martins, I. P., & Ferro, J. M. (1987). Acquired conduction aphasia in a child. *Developmental Medicine and Child Neurology, 29,* 532–536.

Martins, I. P., & Ferro, J. M. (1991a). Type of aphasia and lesion localization. In I. P. Martins, A. Castro-Caldas, H. R. Van Dongen, & A. Van Hout (Eds.), *Acquired aphasia in children: Acquisition and breakdown of language in the developing brain* (pp. 143–159). Dordrecht: Kluwer.

Martins, I. P., & Ferro, J. M. (1991b). Recovery from aphasia and lesion size in the temporal lobe. In I. P. Martins, A. Castro-Caldas, H. R. Van Dongen, & A. Van Hout (Eds.), *Acquired aphasia in children: Acquisition and breakdown of language in the developing brain* (pp. 171–184). Dordrecht: Kluwer.

Martins, I. P., & Ferro, J. M. (1992). Recovery of acquired aphasia in children. *Aphasiology, 6,* 431–438.

Martins, I. P., & Ferro, J. M. (1993). Acquired childhood aphasia: A clinicoradiological study of 11 stroke patients. *Aphasiology, 7,* 489–495.

Martins, I. P., Ferro, J. M., & Cantinho, G. (1993). Acquired childhood aphasia, temporal lobe dysfunction, and comprehension disorder. *Journal of Clinical and Experimental Neuropsychology, 15,* 381.

Martins, I. P., Ferro, J. M., & Castro-Caldas, A. (1981). *Acquired aphasia in children: A longitudinal follow-up study.* Paper presented at the 4th European Conference of the International Neuropsychological Society, Bergen, Norway.

Martins, I. P., Ferro, J. M., & Trindade, A. (1987). Acquired crossed aphasia in a child. *Developmental Medicine and Child Neurology, 29,* 96–100.

Matthes, J., Walker, L. A., Watson, J. G., & Bird, A. G. (1988). AIDS encephalopathy with response to treatment. *Archives of Disease in Childhood, 63,* 545–547.

McNutt, S. J. (1885). Seven cases of infantile spastic hemiplegia. *Archives of Pediatrics, 2,* 20–34.

Miller, H. (1950). Discussion on speech defects in children. *Proceedings of the Royal Society of Medicine, 43,* 1–4.

Mingazzini, G. (1925). Über den heutigen Stand der Aphasielehre. *Klinische Wochenschrift, 4,* 1289–1294.

Minkowski, M. (1930). Gutachten über einen Fall von kindlicher Aphasie nach Trauma. *Nervenarzt, 3,* 411–416.

Molfese, D. L., & Betz, J. C. (1988). Electrophysiological indices of the early development of lateralization for language and cognition, and their implications for predicting later development. In D. L. Molfese & S. J. Segalowitz (Eds.), *Brain lateralization in children: Developmental implications* (pp. 171–190). New York: Guilford Press.

Moschini, S. (1935). Emiplegia destra ed afasia post-scarlattinosa in un bambino di cinque anni. *La Pediatria del Medico Pratico, 10,* 408–420.

Naeser, M. A., Alexander, M. P., Helm-Estabrooks, N., Levin, H. L., Laughlin, S. A., & Geschwind, N. (1982). Aphasia with predominantly subcortical lesion sites: Description of three capsular/putaminal aphasia syndromes. *Archives of Neurology, 39,* 2–14.

Nagaraja, D., Verma, A., Taly, A. B., Veerendra Kumar, M., & Jayakumar, P. N. (1994). Cerebrovascular disease in children. *Acta Neurologica Scandinavica, 90,* 251–255.

Nass, R., Sadler, A. E., & Sidtis, J. J. (1992). Differential effects of congenital versus acquired unilateral brain injury on dichotic listening performance: Evidence for sparing and asymmetric crowding. *Neurology, 42,* 1960–1965.

Niebergall, G., Remschmidt, H., & Lingelbach, B. (1976). Neuropsychologische Untersuchungen zur Rückbildung traumatisch verursachter Aphasien bei Kindern und Jugendlichen. *Zeitschrift für Klinische Psychologie, 5,* 194–209.

Osler, W. (1888). The cerebral palsies of children. *Medical News, 53,* 29–35.

Ozanne, A. E., & Murdoch, B. E. (1990). Acquired childhood aphasia: Neuropathology, linguistic characteristics and prognosis. In B. E. Murdoch (Ed.), *Acquired neurological speech/language disorders in childhood* (pp. 1–65). London: Taylor & Francis.

Palmer, M. F. (1952). Speech therapy in cerebral palsy. *Journal of Pediatrics, 40,* 514–524.

Paquier, P. (1993). *An analysis of the heterogeneity of the clinical pictures of acquired childhood aphasia, with a description of electroencephalographically and neuroradiologically visualized cerebral abnormalities.* Unpublished doctoral thesis, School of Medicine, University of Antwerp (UIA), Belgium.

Paquier, P., Saerens, J., Parizel, P. M., Van Dongen, H. R., De La Porte, C., & De Moor, J. (1989). Acquired reading disorder similar to pure alexia in a child with ruptured arteriovenous malformation. *Aphasiology, 3,* 667–676.

Paquier, P., & Van Dongen, H. R. (1991). Two contrasting cases of fluent aphasia in children. *Aphasiology, 5,* 235–245.

Paquier, P., & Van Dongen, H. R. (1993). Acquired childhood aphasia: A rarity? [Editorial]. *Aphasiology, 7,* 417–419.

Paquier, P., & Van Dongen, H. R. (1996). Review of research on the clinical presentation of acquired childhood aphasia. *Acta Neurologica Scandinavica, 93,* 428–436.

Paquier, P., Van Dongen, H. R., & Loonen, M. C. B. (1992). The Landau–Kleffner syndrome or "acquired aphasia with convulsive disorder": Long-term follow-up of 6 children and a review of the recent literature. *Archives of Neurology, 49,* 354–359.

Picard, A., Elghozi, D., Schouman-Claeys, E., & Lacert, P. (1989). Troubles du langage de type sous-cortical et hémidystonie séquelles d'un infarctus putamino-caudé datant de la première enfance. *Revue Neurologique, 145,* 73–75.

Pitchford, N. J., Funnell, E., Ellis, A. W., Green, S. H., & Chapman, S. (1997). Recovery of spoken language processing in a 6-year-old child following a left hemisphere stroke: A longitudinal study. *Aphasiology, 11,* 83–102.

Pötzl, O. (1926). Über sensorische Aphasie im Kindesalter. *Zeitschrift für Hals- Nasen- und Ohrenheilkunde, 14,* 190–216.

Prandi, G. (1935). Di quattro casi di afasia insorti durante malattie infettive. *Pediatria del Medico Pratico, 10,* 240–245.

Rantala, H., Uhari, M., Uhari, M., Saukkonen, A. L., & Sorri, M. (1991). Outcome after childhood encephalitis. *Developmental Medicine and Child Neurology, 33,* 858–867.

Ranke, H. (1886). Ueber cerebrale Kinderlähmung. *Jahrbuch für Kinderheilkunde, 24,* 78–92.

Rapin, I. (1995). Acquired aphasia in children [Editorial]. *Journal of Child Neurology, 10,* 267–270.

Reiss, A. L., Abrams, M. T., Singer, H. S., Ross, J. L., & Denckla, M. B. (1996). Brain development, gender and IQ in children: A volumetric imaging study. *Brain, 119,* 1763–1774.

Riese, W., & Collison, J. (1964). Aphasia in childhood reconsidered. *Journal of Nervous and Mental Disease, 138,* 293–295.

Roussy, G., & Levy, G. (1933). Un curieux cas d'aphasie par encéphalopathie de l'enfance (Etude comparative de trois observations d'encéphalopathie de l'enfance). *Volume Jubilaire Marinesco,* 579–598.

Sachs, B., & Hausman, L. (1926). *Nervous and mental disorders from birth through adolescence.* New York: Paul B. Hoeber.

Sachs, B., & Peterson, F. (1890). A study of cerebral palsies of early life, based upon an analysis of one hundred and forty cases. *Journal of Nervous and Mental Disease, 17,* 295–332.

Sarno, M. T., Buonaguro, A., & Levita, E. (1986). Characteristics of verbal impairment in closed head injured patients. *Archives of Physical Medicine and Rehabilitation, 67,* 400–405.

Satz, P., & Bullard-Bates, C. (1981). Acquired aphasia in children. In M. T. Sarno (Ed.), *Acquired aphasia* (pp. 399–426). San Diego: Academic Press.

Satz, P., Strauss, E., & Whitaker, H. (1990). The ontogeny of hemispheric specialization: Some old hypotheses revisited. *Brain and Language, 38,* 596–614.

Schoenberg, B. S., Mellinger, J. F., & Schoenberg, D. G. (1978). Cerebrovascular disease in infants and children: A study of incidence, clinical features, and survival. *Neurology, 28,* 763–768.

Seeligmüller, A. (1879). Ueber Lähmungen im Kindesalter. *Jahrbuch für Kinderheilkunde, 13,* 315–376.

Shillito, J. (1964). Carotid arteritis: A cause of hemiplegia in childhood. *Journal of Neurosurgery, 21,* 540–551.

Skoglund, R. R. (1979). Reversible alexia, mitochondrial myopathy, and lactic acidemia. *Neurology, 29,* 717–720.

Smithies, F. (1907). Hemiplegia as a complication in typhoid fever, with report of a case. *Journal of the American Medical Association, 49,* 389–395.

Steffen, A. (1885). Ueber Aphasie. *Jahrbuch für Kinderheilkunde, 23,* 127–143.

Steinmetz, H., Rademacher, J., Jäncke, L., Huang, Y., Thron, A., & Zilles, K. (1990). Total surface of temporoparietal intrasylvian cortex: Diverging left-right asymmetries. *Brain and Language, 39,* 357–372.

Steinmetz, H., Volkmann, J., Jäncke, L., & Freund, H. J. (1991). Anatomical left-right asymmetry of language-related temporal cortex is different in left- and right-handers. *Annals of Neurology, 29,* 315–319.

Stengel, E. (1950). Discussion on speech defects in children. *Proceedings of the Royal Society of Medicine, 43,* 10.

Strümpell, A. (1884). Ueber die acute Encephalitis der Kinder (Poliencephalitis acuta, cerebrale Kinderlähmung). *Jahrbuch für Kinderheilkunde, 22,* 173–178.

Subirana, A. (1960). Visión panorámica de los problemas que comporta la afasia infantil. *Anales de Medicina, 46,* 141–155.

Swisher, L. (1985). Language disorders in children. In J. K. Darby (Ed.), *Speech and language evaluation in neurology—Childhood disorders* (pp. 33–96). Orlando, FL: Grune & Stratton.

Taillens. (1937). L'aphasie chez les enfants. *Schweizerische Medizinische Wochenschrift, 18,* 988–989.

Tanabe, H., Ikeda, M., Murasawa, A., Yamada, K., Yamamoto, H., Nakagawa, Y., Nishimura, T., & Shiraishi, J. (1989). A case of acquired conduction aphasia in a child. *Acta Neurologica Scandinavica, 80,* 314–318.

Taylor, J. (1905). *Paralysis and other diseases of the nervous system in childhood and early life.* London: J. & A. Churchill.

Teasdale, G. M. (1995). Head injury. *Journal of Neurology, Neurosurgery, and Psychiatry, 58,* 526–539.

Thal, D. J., Marchman, V., Stiles, J., Aram, D., Trauner, D., Nass, R., & Bates, E. (1991). Early lexical development in children with focal brain injury. *Brain and Language, 40,* 491–527.

Tomkiewicz, S. (1964). Aphasie chez l'enfant. *Revue de Neuropsychiatrie Infantile, 12,* 109–122.

Tuchman, R. F. (1994). Epilepsy, language, and behavior: Clinical models in childhood. *Journal of Child Neurology, 9,* 95–102.

Van Dongen, H. R., & Loonen, M. C. B. (1977). Factors related to prognosis of acquired aphasia in children. *Cortex, 13,* 131–136.

Van Dongen, H. R., Loonen, M. C. B., & Van Dongen, K. J. (1985). Anatomical basis for acquired fluent aphasia in children. *Annals of Neurology, 17,* 306–309.

Van Dongen, H. R., & Paquier, P. (1991). Fluent aphasia in children. In I. P. Martins, A. Castro-Caldas, H. R. Van Dongen, & A. Van Hout (Eds.), *Acquired aphasia in children:*

Acquisition and breakdown of language in the developing brain (pp. 125–141). Dordrecht: Kluwer.

Van Dongen, H. R., Paquier, P., Raes, J., & Creten, W. L. (1994). An analysis of spontaneous conversational speech fluency in children with acquired aphasia. *Cortex, 30,* 619–633.

Van Dongen, H. R., & Visch-Brink, E. G. (1988). Naming in aphasic children: Analysis of paraphasic errors. *Neuropsychologia, 26,* 629–632.

Van Gelder, D. W., Kennedy, L., & Laguaite, J. (1952). Congenital and infantile aphasia: Review of literature and report of case. *Pediatrics, 9,* 48–54.

Van Hout, A. (1990). *Acquired aphasia in childhood. Its impact on the conception of functional maturation of the brain and its implication for pediatric neuropsychology.* Unpublished doctoral thesis, School of Medicine, Catholic University of Louvain (UCL), Belgium.

Van Hout, A. (1991a). Outcome of acquired aphasia in childhood: Prognosis factors. In I. P. Martins, A. Castro-Caldas, H. R. Van Dongen, & A. Van Hout (Eds.), *Acquired aphasia in children: Acquisition and breakdown of language in the developing brain* (pp. 163–169). Dordrecht: Kluwer.

Van Hout, A. (1991b). Characteristics of language in acquired aphasia in children. In I. P. Martins, A. Castro-Caldas, H. R. Van Dongen, & A. Van Hout (Eds.), *Acquired aphasia in children: Acquisition and breakdown of language in the developing brain* (pp. 117–124). Dordrecht: Kluwer.

Van Hout, A. (1993). Acquired aphasia in childhood and developmental dysphasias: Are the errors similar? Analysis of errors made in confrontation naming tasks. *Aphasiology, 7,* 525–531.

Van Hout, A., Evrard, P., & Lyon, G. (1985). On the positive semiology of acquired aphasia in children. *Developmental Medicine and Child Neurology, 27,* 231–241.

Van Hout, A., & Lyon, G. (1986). Wernicke's aphasia in a 10-year-old boy. *Brain and Language, 29,* 268–285.

Vargha-Khadem, F., Carr, L. J., Isaacs, E., Brett, E., Adams, C., & Mishkin, M. (1997). Onset of speech after left hemispherectomy in a nine-year-old boy. *Brain, 120,* 159–182.

Vargha-Khadem, F., O'Gorman, A. M., & Watters, G. V. (1985). Aphasia and handedness in relation to hemispheric side, age at injury and severity of cerebral lesion during childhood. *Brain, 108,* 677–696.

Vargha-Khadem, F., Watters, G. V., & O'Gorman, A. M. (1985). Development of speech and language following bilateral frontal lesions. *Brain and Language, 25,* 167–183.

Visch-Brink, E. G., & Van de Sandt-Koenderman, W. M. E. (1984). The occurrence of paraphasias in the spontaneous speech of children with an acquired aphasia. *Brain and Language, 23,* 258–271.

Von Monakow, C. (1914). *Die Lokalization im Grosshirn und der Abbau der Funktion durch kortikale Herde.* Wiesbaden: Bergmann.

Wagner, W., & Mayer, K. (1933). Psychologische Untersuchung an der Sprachstörung einer Zwölfjährigen (Psychopathologische Studie zur Frage der Grundfunktionsstörungen). *Monatsschrift für Psychiatrie und Neurologie, 87,* 108–155.

Wallenberg, A. (1886). Ein Beitrag zur Lehre von den cerebralen Kinderlähmungen. *Jahrbuch für Kinderheilkunde, 24,* 384–439.

Watamori, T. S., Sasanuma, S., & Ueda, S. (1990). Recovery and plasticity in child-onset aphasics: Ultimate outcome at adulthood. *Aphasiology, 4,* 9–30.

Wetherby, A. M. (1985). Speech and language disorders in children: An overview. In J. K. Darby (Ed.), *Speech and language evaluation in neurology—Childhood disorders* (pp. 3–32). Orlando, FL: Grune & Stratton.

Winter, E., & Prendergast, M. (1995). Cured of acute lymphoblastic leukaemia but lost for words. *Neuropediatrics, 26,* 267–269.

Witelson, S. F., & Pallie, W. (1973). Left hemisphere specialization for language in the newborn: Neuroanatomical evidence of asymmetry. *Brain, 96,* 641–646.

Woods, B. T. (1983). Is the left hemisphere specialized for language at birth? *Trends in Neurosciences, 6*, 115–117.

Woods, B. T. (1985a). Developmental dysphasia. In J. A. M. Frederiks (Ed.), *Handbook of clinical neurology. Neurobehavioural disorders (Vol. 46)* (pp. 139–145). Amsterdam: Elsevier.

Woods, B. T. (1985b). Acquired aphasia in children. In J. A. M. Frederiks (Ed.), *Handbook of clinical neurology. Neurobehavioural disorders (Vol. 46)* (pp. 147–157). Amsterdam: Elsevier.

Woods, B. T., & Carey, S. (1979). Language deficits after apparent clinical recovery from childhood aphasia. *Annals of Neurology, 6*, 405–409.

Woods, B. T., & Teuber, H. L. (1978). Changing patterns of childhood aphasia. *Annals of Neurology, 3*, 273–280.

Wulff, D. (1890). Cerebrale Kinderlähmung und Geistesschwäche. *Neurologische Zentralblatt, 9*, 343–344.

Zangwill, O. L. (1960). *Cerebral dominance and its relation to psychological function.* Edinburgh: Oliver & Boyd.

CHAPTER FOUR

Aphasia in Tone Languages

Jack Gandour
Purdue University

It was Monrad-Krohn (1947, 1963) who first brought to the attention of aphasiologists the importance of various elements of prosody and their disorders. Such prosodic elements include stress, intonation, rhythm, and tone, as well as different attitudes or emotions. Because the acoustical properties of these prosodic elements overlap to a great extent, we are provided an excellent opportunity for studying the role of the left and right hemispheres in the control of prosodic aspects of language. If physical correlates are of paramount importance in determining hemispheric specialization, then unilateral lesions should result in uniform behavioral deficits regardless of the linguistic status of the prosodic elements. If, on the other hand, linguistic considerations are triggering hemispheric specialization, then we may expect behavioral deficits to vary depending on the specific role of prosodic elements in language. Another possibility is that both hemispheres are engaged in prosody, but attending to different aspects of the speech acoustic signal.

Van Lancker (1980, 1988) proposed a scale of hemispheric specialization associated with different domains (segment, syllable, word, phrase, sentence) of functional pitch contrasts. The scale ranges from *most linguistically structured* pitch contrasts (e.g., Chinese tones, Norwegian word accents) associated with left-hemispheric specialization to *least linguistically structured* pitch contrasts (e.g., emotional tone, personal voice quality) associated with right-hemisphere specialization. That is, hemispheric specialization is determined by the extent to which pitch patterns are linguistic. Another view,

117

espoused by Packard (1986), is that it is not simply the extent to which a prosodic element participates in the linguistic system, but rather the nature of its participation that determines hemispheric lateralization. The issue then becomes what differences in the nature of participation in the linguistic system are correlated with differences in hemispheric specialization. Another view is that different prosodic functions may be generated by the same phonetic mechanism, but that temporal and spectral aspects are hemispherically specialized (Robin, Klouda, & Hug, 1991; Robin, Tranel, & Damasio, 1990; Van Lancker & Sidtis, 1992). The right hemisphere processes F_0 information but not other prosodic features such as timing or intensity. From this perspective, prosody is a multifaceted process that requires integration of multiple cues, some of which appear to be processed in the left hemisphere, others in the right hemisphere. In the same vein, Gandour (1987) proposed that hemispheric lateralization depends on the relationship between the control of F_0 and timing. The size of the temporal domain over which the prosodic pattern extends crucially determines the way the signal is processed in the brain. The right hemisphere is engaged when prosodic functions span larger temporal domains such as clauses or sentences. In this chapter, we evaluate these competing hypotheses in light of evidence from aphasics who are native speakers of tone languages.

In a *tone language*, contrastive variations in pitch at the syllable or word level are used to distinguish the lexical meanings of words. This is what is meant by *lexical tones*. Such languages are to be distinguished from those, such as English, in which pitch variations are usually not contrastive at the syllable or word level. In these *nontone languages*, however, differences in pitch patterns may be used to signal intonation at the phrase and sentence levels. The crucial feature that differentiates between these two types of languages is whether or not pitch variations are contrastive in the lexicon. All languages use pitch variations for intonation, but there are fewer possibilities in tone languages because of the use of pitch variations at the syllable or word level. Although there may be concomitant changes in duration and intensity, as well as phonation, the primary acoustic correlate of tones is generally regarded to be voice fundamental frequency (F_0) states and movements. For the purposes of this review, the important point to remember here is that hypotheses concerning hemispheric specialization for prosody couched in abstract, linguistic terms such as tone and intonation fail to account for the fact that all aspects of prosody beyond the word level are evident in all languages but to varying degrees.

Tone languages are common in the Far East and Southeast Asia. Three of those languages are Mandarin Chinese, Cantonese, and Thai. A brief description of their tonal inventories is in order because the majority of studies to be reviewed in this chapter involve these languages. Mandarin Chinese has four lexical tones: level, rising, falling–rising, falling. Cantonese has six: high level, high rising, high–mid level, low level, low rising, low–mid level. Thai has five: mid, low, falling, high, rising. In Thai, for example, a set of five words can be minimally distinguished by tone: /khaa/, to be stuck; /khàa/, a kind of spice; /khâa/, to kill; /kháa/, to engage in trade; /khǎa/, leg. The tone labels in these languages generally approximate the F_0 patterns associated with citation forms of the lexical tones. In Thai, the mid tone can be described phonetically as mid level with a final drop, the low tone as low falling, the falling tone as high falling, the high tone as high rising, and the rising tone as low rising.

Also reviewed in this chapter are several studies of Norwegian. In this pitch accent language, the tonal oppositions are associated with accented syllables only, and not each syllable as in most tone languages. Every accented syllable carries the F_0 pattern of one of two possible tones. These accents are lexically determined. As in Thai, differences in F_0 patterns are used to distinguish the lexical meaning of a word in Norwegian. For example, word pairs may be minimally distinguished by tone: /[1]vane/, water; /[2]vane/, to water.

It is the presence of lexical tones in tone languages that has led to speculation that the lateralization of language functions in speakers of tone language differs from nontone language speakers (Hu, Qiou, & Zhong, 1990, 1992). It is now felt that a sufficient body of evidence can be assembled from the literature concerning prosody to evaluate whether language representation in the brains of tone language speakers differs substantially from speakers of Indo-European languages. Because the controversy hinges on the role of prosody in a language as opposed to semantic/syntactic properties, studies of agrammatism in tone languages, albeit very interesting in their own right, will not be covered in this review. Moreover, an excellent cross-linguistic comparison of agrammatism is already available in the literature (Menn & Obler, 1990). For readers interested in this topic, agrammatism in tone languages has been addressed in Thai (Gandour, Buckingham, & Dardarananda, 1985) and Mandarin Chinese (Bates, Chen, Tzeng, Li, & Opie, 1991; Chia, Peng, Wang, & Shih, 1986; Chu, Peng, & Yiu, 1986; Packard, 1990; Tzeng, Chen, & Hung, 1991).

According to Fromkin and Rodman (1993), the majority of the world's languages are tone languages. There are more than 1000 tone languages in Africa alone. Many languages of the Far East (Chinese, Taiwanese, Vietnamese, Burmese, Thai) are tone languages, as are many of the Native American languages spoken in both Central and North America. Up to the present, all of the information on aphasia in tone languages comes from aphasics who are native speakers of tone languages spoken in the Far East. Unfortunately, no studies are available on aphasics who are native speakers of tone languages in other parts of the world, especially Africa. Phonologically speaking, African tone languages are typologically different from those in Asia from the standpoint of both tonal inventories and rule systems. Data on tonal breakdown in these languages could potentially shed light on language-universal mechanisms underlying disorders of F_0 and timing. Nevertheless, available information from tone languages of the Far East and nontone languages appears to be sufficient to generate hypotheses that seem likely to apply to African tone languages as well. Earlier reviews that contain relevant information on prosodic disturbances following unilateral lesions, including patients who are speakers of tone languages, had comparatively little data to evaluate from tone languages (Gandour, 1987; Ryalls & Behrens, 1988). In the past decade or so, however, there has been a significant increase in the number of studies focusing on prosodic disturbances in tone languages. In this chapter, we attempt to bring findings from these more recent studies to illuminate issues relating to hemispheric specialization for prosody.

CASE STUDIES

Types of Aphasia

Within the past 15 years, several tests have been developed to assess linguistic abilities in brain-damaged speakers who are speakers of Far Eastern tone languages. Many of these tests have been translations or adaptations of aphasia batteries developed in the West. With the availability of these tests, it is possible to draw better comparisons in patterns of language deficits between tone language speakers and nontone languages. Indeed, the performance of aphasic speakers of tone languages on such tests demonstrates quite convincingly that the classical aphasia patterns of Indo-European language speakers are manifest in tone language speakers as well. To my knowledge, the first such published effort was by Naeser and Chan (1980) who translated the Boston Diagnostic Aphasia Examination (BDAE; Goodglass & Kaplan, 1983). Although they acknowledge "a direct translation was not always possible" (p. 394), it is hard to determine whether their substitutions maintained the organizing principles of the BDAE. Shortly thereafter, the BDAE was adapted into Thai (Gandour, 1982; Gandour, Dardarananda, Buckingham, & Viriyavejakul, 1986). This Thai adaptation was carefully designed to follow the rationale underlying each BDAE subtest. Supplementary language tests (Holasuit Petty & Gandour, 1984a; Holasuit Petty, Gandour, & Jirakupt, 1985) and a handedness questionnaire (Holasuit Petty & Gandour, 1984b) have also been adapted into Thai. The Token Test has been translated into Mandarin Chinese (Chinese) and Cantonese (Naeser & Chan, 1980) and Thai (Akamanon, 1989). More recently, the Western Aphasia Battery (WAB; Kertesz, 1982) has been adapted into Cantonese (Yiu, 1992). This Cantonese aphasia battery is especially significant because the test was standardized on 54 aphasic patients and 24 controls. Gao and Benson (1990) apparently used a modified version of the WAB in classifying their patients. A Thai adaptation of the WAB has also been completed (Dardarananda, Potisuk, Gandour, & Holasuit, in press).

In Mandarin Chinese, the classic aphasia patterns of Indo-European language speakers have been readily demonstrated in case studies of Chinese patients who become aphasic following a stroke. Naeser and Chan (1980) presented the case of a mixed nonfluent aphasic patient using a translation of the BDAE. A computed tomography (CT) scan 17 months after onset of the stroke demonstrated enlargement of the left Sylvian fissure and left lateral ventricle. A small focal lesion was also present higher in the left frontal lobe as well as a larger lesion in the left parietal lobe, including white matter deep to the supramarginal and angular gyri. Her speech output was limited primarily to one-word responses. Speech errors were characterized by incorrect tones, verbal paraphasias, omissions, substitutions, and perseveration. Her production of the four Mandarin Chinese tones, especially Tone 3, the low falling–rising tone, was impaired in word repetition. On one of the repetition tests, she repeated the low falling–rising tone correctly on only 2 out of 15 trials. Errors in tonal production also occurred in her spontaneous speech, elicited speech, object and picture naming, and Chinese character reading. Alajouanine et al. (1973) reported on a right-handed male Chinese Broca's aphasic with a lesion in the left hemisphere. Errors in tonal production occurred in his spontaneous speech. Chang, Peng, and Yü (1986) and Chu et al. (1986) reported on two conduction aphasics who presented with the classic symptoms including verbal self-corrections commonly referred to as *conduites d'approche*. In both cases, a CT scan revealed an infarction over the left parieto-occipital region. Of 81 Chinese patients who became aphasic after a stroke, Gao and Benson (1990) reported that perisylvian aphasia syndromes (Broca's, Wernicke's, conduction) were present in 22%, border-zone aphasia syndromes (transcortical motor, transcortical sensory, mixed transcortical, supplementary motor area) in 24%, global aphasia in 20%, and anomic aphasia in 1%. Subcortical aphasia syndromes (thalamic, basal ganglia) were found in the remaining 33%. The site of brain damage causing the aphasia was determined by CT scan. Almost all right-handed patients with aphasia had lesions located in the left hemisphere. With only a few exceptions, the aphasia syndromes in the Chinese-speaking patients were similar to those reported in the contemporary literature for Indo-European language speakers. Gao and Benson seem to be justified in concluding that "the number of exceptions to anticipated clinical/anatomical correlation was so small that the classic syndrome classification and aphasia syndrome/neuroanatomical locus of lesion correlations can be considered valid for the Mandarin Chinese speakers" (p. 41).

A similar conclusion can be drawn from the language performance of 51 Cantonese-speaking Chinese patients who became aphasic following left hemisphere damage (Yiu, 1992). Using a Cantonese adaptation of the WAB, Yiu reported that perisylvian aphasia syndromes (Broca's, Wernicke's, conduction) were present in 43%, border-zone aphasia syndromes (transcortical motor, transcortical sensory, mixed transcortical, supplementary motor area) in 18%, global aphasia in 10%, and anomic aphasia in 29%. This distribution of aphasia types in Cantonese patients parallels closely those reported in the original WAB studies on English patients (Kertesz, 1979; Kertesz & Poole, 1974).

Detailed case studies have been presented on three right-handed Thai-speaking aphasics using a Thai adaptation of the BDAE plus supplementary language tests. Two involved patients with left hemisphere perisylvian syndromes, one with Broca's aphasia (Gandour, Dardarananda, & Vejjajiva, 1985; Gandour, Holasuit Petty, & Dardarananda, 1989) and another with conduction aphasia (Gandour, Buckingham, Dardarananda, Stawathumrong, & Holasuit Petty, 1982; Gandour, Dardarananda, & Holasuit, 1991). The third was a case of a border-zone aphasia syndrome, transcortical motor aphasia (Gandour, Dardarananda, Vibulsreth, & Buckingham, 1982). In each case, the results of the neurological and language exams characterizing the aphasia syndrome were fully compatible with those associated with the aphasic category in studies of patients of nontone languages.

In sum, these case studies of Mandarin Chinese, Cantonese, and Thai aphasics demonstrate that the clinical/anatomical correlations validated over the past century in nontonal languages are basically the same in tone language speakers who become aphasic following a stroke. There is no evidence from these case studies to suggest that the presence of lexical tones in these languages significantly influenced the anatomical basis of the aphasia syndromes.

Types of Subcortical Aphasia

Subcortical aphasics in earlier studies of nontone languages have been difficult to classify according to traditional aphasia classification systems as their cluster of symptoms is atypical (Alexander & Naeser, 1988; Alexander, Naeser, & Palumbo, 1987; Kennedy & Murdoch, 1989; Robin & Schienberg, 1990). It has been shown that small differences in site of lesion within these structures and tracts may produce dramatic differences in language symptoms (Damasio, Damasio, Rizzo, Varney, & Gersh, 1982). Goodglass (1993) stated that "the production deficits observed in the presence of basal ganglion lesions are probably due to the injury of adjacent white matter, internal capsule and periventricular white matter" (p. 46). Indeed, Robin and Schienberg (1990) concluded that "because many degrees of severity and many different combinations of symptoms can result from lesions of the left basal ganglia, distinct classification of aphasia following basal ganglia strokes is not warranted at this time" (p. 97).

Similar difficulties in classifying subcortical aphasics who are speakers of tone languages have been reported in the literature. In Mandarin Chinese, Gao and Benson (1990) classified 9 cases of thalamic aphasia and 18 of basal ganglia aphasia. Their thalamic aphasics exhibited fluent output with word-finding difficulty, hypophonia, and occasional paraphasia. All cases of thalamic aphasia involved the left thalamus. Most patients in the basal ganglia group were nonfluent with dysarthria. Several, however, had fluent output with word-finding difficulty and hypophonia. Eleven of these patients had hemorrhagic lesions involving the left external capsule, basal ganglia, putamen or deep subcortical region of the parietal lobe, or some combination thereof. Yang, Yang, Pan, Lai, and Yang (1989) evaluated five right-handed patients with subcortical aphasia that involved left hemisphere lesion sites using CT scans and a Mandarin Chinese adaptation of the BDAE. Two of the patients exhibited symptoms that were similar to Broca's aphasia. In both cases, there was involvement of the anterior limb of the internal capsule and of the basal ganglia and an anterior superior extension to the paraventricular white matter in the left hemisphere. One patient exhibited symptoms that were similar to Wernicke's and transcortical sensory aphasia. In this case, there was involvement of the posterior limb of the internal capsule and the thalamus and a posterior extension of the paraventricular white matter. The remaining two patients displayed symptoms of global aphasia. Both had similar infarctions in areas over the left basal ganglia and the left internal capsule and an anterior/posterior extension of the paraventricular white matter.

Two Thai-speaking right-handed patients with subcortical aphasia that involved left-hemisphere lesion sites were evaluated using CT scans and a Thai adaptation of the BDAE and Token Test. One patient exhibited symptoms of mixed nonfluent aphasia (Gandour & Ponglorpisit, 1990). The CT scan revealed involvement of the anterior limb of the internal capsule and the putamen and a superior extension up to the corona radiata. The other patient suffered a hemorrhagic stroke involving the globus pallidus, putamen, and posterior limb of the internal capsule (Gandour & Dechongkit, 1992). Although atypical, the patient's language disorder most closely resembled Wernicke's aphasia.

Although it has been demonstrated that aphasic-like symptoms may be exhibited by tone language speakers who have experienced subcortical lesions, it is difficult to draw any firm conclusions. Robin and Schienberg's (1990) caveat that different combinations of symptoms may result from lesions of the left basal ganglia appears to apply equally as well to native speakers of tone languages. No distinct classification of aphasia following basal ganglion lesions in speakers of tone languages is warranted at this time.

HANDEDNESS

From studies of nontonal languages, it is commonly known that the left hemisphere is dominant for language in almost all right-handed adults as well as in the majority of left-handed adults. Estimates usually state that better than 95% of all right-handed individuals have language function exclusively in the left hemisphere. Estimates for left-hemisphere dominance in left-handers are more variable, ranging from 60% (Goodglass & Quadfasel, 1954) to 87% (Naeser & Borod, 1986). One reason for this variability is that the criteria for classifying people as right-handed, left-handed, or ambidextrous are not standard across studies (Goodglass, 1993).

Clinical surveys of aphasia after stroke in Chinese patients have yielded conflicting findings. Gao and Benson (1990) examined 81 native speakers of Mandarin Chinese who became aphasic following a stroke. The site of brain damage was determined by CT scan; the diagnosis and classification of aphasia were performed using the classical syndromes of aphasia (Benson, 1979). Handedness was determined by asking premorbid hand preference for 10 actions. Those who performed all 10 actions with either the right or the left hand were considered right- or left-handed, respectively. Those who performed all actions but writing with the left hand were also classified as left-handed. Of the 81 patients, 70 were classified as right-handed, 11 as left-handed. Among the 70 right-handed patients with aphasia, 64 had unilateral lesions in the left hemisphere and the other 6 had bilateral lesions. The left hemisphere was considered causative for aphasia in 4 of the bilaterally damaged right-handed patients. Therefore, Gao and Benson (1990) concluded that "in at least 68 right-handed patients (97.1%), the site of brain damage responsible for aphasia was in the left-hemisphere" (p. 41). Only two of the 11 left-handed patients (18%) with aphasia had right-hemisphere lesions.

In their clinical survey of 478 stroke patients who were native speakers of Mandarin Chinese, Hu et al. (1990) reported that the incidence of aphasia was 35% after left-hemisphere damage in right-handed patients. The site of brain damage was determined principally by the presence of hemiplegia; the diagnosis and classification of aphasia included motor, sensory, mixed, and global aphasia. Of 478 patients with hemiplegia, 367 were classified as right-handed, 111 as ambidextrous or left-handed. Handedness was determined by asking premorbid hand preference for 11 actions. Those who performed 9 or more of the actions with either the right or left hand were considered right- or left-handed, respectively. No special consideration was given to writing. Among the 367 right-handed patients, 128 (35%) with right hemiplegia and 57 (16%) with left hemiplegia were diagnosed with aphasia. Hu et al. (1992) reported similar findings for an increased sample of 671 patients with hemiplegia. Among the 509 right-handed patients, 166 (33%) with right hemiplegia and 68 (13%) with left hemiplegia were diagnosed with aphasia.

The incidence of crossed aphasia (i.e., right-handers who suffer aphasia following right cerebral damage) is generally estimated at about 1% from previous reports on nontonal languages (Goodglass, 1993). Gao and Benson's (1990) findings are in agreement with nontonal languages, whereas those of Hu et al. (1990, 1992) are not. April and Tse (1977) and April and Han (1980) reported on two individual cases of crossed aphasia in Chinese speakers. Despite these two independent observations, the authors in a systematic review of patients' hospital charts over a 2–year period found no trend toward increased incidence of crossed aphasia in the Chinese population (April & Han, 1980, p. 346; see Coppens & Hungerford, chapter 7, this volume).

On the basis of the incidence of transient aphasia induced by the Wada test, Hung, Tu, Chen, and Chen (1985) showed that the left hemisphere is dominant for almost all right-handed Chinese patients. Handedness was determined by asking premorbid hand preference for nine actions including special consideration of writing. Those who performed seven or more actions with either the right or the left hand were considered right- or left-handed, respectively. Diagnostic classification of aphasia included nominal, motor, sensory, and mixed. Of 94 right-handed patients, 55 had the injection on the left side, 39 on the right. All but 1 of the 55 patients during the left-sided Wada test exhibited aphasia, whereas only 1 of the 39 patients during the right-sided Wada test did so. Thirty of these patients who underwent the Wada test were found to have surgical lesions in the perisylvian region and subsequently were operated on. The correlation between the Wada test and surgical confirmation was perfect. An operation performed on the dominant side determined by the Wada test always resulted in "transient postoperative aphasia or aggravation of aphasia" (p. 157), but an operation performed on the nondominant side determined by the Wada test never resulted in subsequent aphasia. Their findings are congruent with those reported earlier for speakers of nontonal languages (Milner, Branch, & Rasmussen, 1964).

Contrary to Hu et al. (1990, 1992), who speculated that the Chinese are either right dominant or bilaterally dominant for language, the evidence from the other clinical/anatomical correlation studies just reviewed suggests overwhelmingly that the organization of language in the brain of tone language speakers is comparable to that of nontone language speakers. It is clearly premature for Hu et al. to claim that Wernicke's area does not exist in the left brain of Chinese speakers or that the neural pathways of language in Chinese speakers are different from those who are speakers of a phonetic language (Hu et al., 1990, pp. 353–354). First, all spoken languages are based on sound, including Chinese. Hu et al. (1992) falsely assumed that Chinese people speak "a nonphoneticizing or ideographic language" (p. 766). They argued that the writing system of Chinese, which, they correctly pointed out, is not sound-based, is the principal determinant of brain lateralization for language function. Yet nearly half of their own patients were illiterate! Second, their linguistic naiveté is further evident when they asserted that comprehending a sentence in Chinese requires the recognition of word meanings, "but identifying the tone . . . is not as important" (p. 766). Why should tone be any less important than consonants or vowels when, in each case, word meanings can be minimally distinguished by substituting one linguistic element for another? And it already has been demonstrated that left-brain damage in right-handed Chinese patients has an adverse effect on tonal recognition and production (Naeser & Chan, 1980; Packard, 1986). Third, their view that their patients "represent the *pure* [emphasis mine] native population of China" (p. 767) is linguistically unsound as well as irrelevant. They contended that neither the patients in Taiwan nor the Chinese immigrants in America speak their "pure mother language" (p. 767). The issue is not whether the patient is a speaker of a particular dialect of Chinese, but rather whether the patient is a speaker of Chinese as an exemplar of a tone language. If, as they contend, the writing system determines language laterality, then one would predict homogeneity in performance anyway regardless of geographic origin.

Rather than viewing Hu et al. (1990) as a "major contribution to the broader question of the possible influences of nonbiological factors on cerebral language organization" (Gitterman & Sies, 1992, p. 163), it can be argued that methodological problems and naive linguistic assumptions make it difficult to draw any firm conclusions from their study. They classified patients by ethnic group, and their aphasia tests were minimal. Finally, it is not clear how they inquired about hand preference for writing. Because their findings are at odds with all earlier relevant studies on Chinese, and inconsistent with what has already been established in the contemporary aphasia literature, we conclude that the cerebral dominance for language functions in Chinese speakers is the same as that for speakers of Indo-European languages.

AFFECTIVE PROSODY

A number of experimental studies have suggested that the right hemisphere is generally dominant for emotional processing (Ross, 1981; Ross & Mesulam, 1979; for reviews, see Bryden & Ley, 1983; Silberman & Weingartner, 1986), and therefore for *affective prosody*, the use of speech in emotional contexts. Other research has implicated right-hemisphere involvement for *linguistic prosody*, the use of speech in propositional or nonemotional contexts as well (Behrens, 1989; Shapiro & Danly, 1985; Weintraub, Mesulam, & Kramer, 1981; for review, see Ryalls & Behrens, 1988). The question then arises of whether the dysprosodic speech of right-hemisphere-damaged patients results from an emotional deficit or, alternatively, from a phonetic deficit in the control of prosody in both propositional and emotional contexts.

Another view on lateralization of prosody is that linguistic and affective prosody may be generated by the same phonetic mechanism, but that temporal and spectral aspects are hemispherically specialized. The right hemisphere processes F_0 information but not other prosodic features such as timing or intensity (Robin et al., 1990, 1991). Left-hemispheric contributions to prosody may be related to the processing of timing information. Van Lancker and Sidtis (1992), indeed, claimed that models attributing linguistic prosody to the left hemisphere and affective prosody to the right hemisphere (Ross, 1981) or models attributing all prosodic processing to the right hemisphere (Blumstein & Cooper, 1974; Shipley-Brown, Dingwall, Berlin, Yeni-Komshian, & Gordon-Salant, 1988) are no longer tenable. Prosody is a multifaceted process that requires integration of multiple cues, some of which appear to be processed in the left hemisphere, others in the right hemisphere.

The results of studies examining the production of linguistic or affective prosody in right-hemisphere-damaged patients of nontonal languages are mixed and sometimes contradictory (for review, see Ryalls & Behrens, 1988). Shapiro and Danly (1985) reported abnormal intonation patterns in both emotional and nonemotional contexts. Their findings, however, are not without controversy (Ryalls, 1986; Colsher, Cooper, & Graff-Radford, 1987). In nonemotional contexts, phonemic and contrastive stress patterns appear to be relatively intact (Behrens, 1988), but certain aspects of intonational contours are abnormal (Behrens, 1989). On the other hand, some acoustic investigations of linguistic prosody in right-hemisphere-damaged patients have reported no or only small differences in intonational contours between right-hemisphere-damaged patients and normal controls (Cooper, Soares, Nicols, Michelow, & Goloskie, 1984; Ryalls, Joanette, & Feldman, 1987).

Up to the present, only a few studies on affective prosody have been completed on tone languages. Hughes, Chan, and Ming (1983) found that 11 of 12 Mandarin Chinese-speaking patients with right-hemisphere damage exhibited a deficit in the production and comprehension of prosody in affective contexts. Conversely, none of these patients were impaired in the production of Mandarin Chinese tones, and only 5 of the 12 were mildly impaired in the comprehension of tones. Taiwanese right-hemisphere-damaged patients were also found to be impaired in their production of affective prosody (Edmondson, Chan, Seibert, & Ross, 1987; Ross, Edmondson, Seibert, & Chan, 1992). They were especially unable to vary the global range of F_0 throughout the utterance as appropriate for different types of emotion. In a companion study, Ross, Edmondson, Seibert, and Homan (1988) reported that English-speaking patients who underwent the Wada test experienced a deficit in signaling affective prosody in both local as well as global measures of F_0 when injected in the right hemisphere. Taken together, the findings of Ross and colleagues suggest that, although affective prosody itself is lateralized to the right hemisphere, the phonetic manifestation of affective prosody may differ depending on whether the language is tonal or not.

The production of affective prosody has also been examined in 12 Thai patients with unilateral right-hemisphere damage (Gandour, Larsen, Dechongkit,

Ponglorpisit, & Khunadorn, 1995). In agreement with the studies on Mandarin Chinese and Taiwanese, a severe deficit in affective prosody was found in Thai right-hemisphere-damaged patients. They especially had difficulty in utilizing global measures of F_0, intensity, and timing to signal differences in affect type. Despite their loss of affective prosody, the same right-hemisphere-damaged speakers of Thai are able to control F_0 (Gandour, Holasuit Petty, & Dardarananda, 1988; Gandour, Ponglorpisit, & Dardarananda, 1992; Gandour, Ponglorpisit, Khunadorn, Dechongkit, Boongird, Boonklam, & Potisuk, 1992; Gandour, Ponglorpisit, Dechongkit, Khunadorn, Boongird, & Potisuk, 1993a) and timing (Gandour, Ponglorpisit, Khunadorn, Dechongkit, Boongird, & Boonklam, 1992a, 1992b; Gandour, Dechongkit, Ponglorpisit, Khunadorn, & Boongird, 1993; Gandour, Dechongkit, Ponglorpisit, & Khunadorn, 1994) successfully in nonemotional contexts. Similarly, right-hemisphere-damaged Mandarin Chinese-speaking patients are able to produce lexical tones successfully in a nonemotional context (Hughes et al., 1983).

As mentioned earlier, the findings from nontone languages are less conclusive about the question of whether prosodic disturbances found in right-hemisphere-damaged patients are confined to emotional utterances. Interestingly, right-hemisphere-damaged speakers of English appear to be able to produce phonemic and contrastive stress patterns successfully (Behrens, 1988), but exhibit disturbances in modulating some aspects of F_0 contours at the sentence level (Behrens, 1989). These combined findings led Behrens to hypothesize that the integrity of prosodic abilities in right-hemisphere-damaged patients may be a function of the size of the linguistic domain. They are able to produce prosodic patterns that are manifested locally at the word level, but display a deficit in prosodic patterns that are manifested globally at the sentence level. No empirical data are yet available on F_0 contours at the sentence level in nonemotional contexts in right-hemisphere-damaged patients of tone languages. If lateralization depends on the affective–linguistic dichotomy, it is predicted that prosodic disturbances would occur only in emotional contexts regardless of the size of the linguistic unit. If, instead, lateralization depends on the local–global dichotomy, it is predicted that smaller sized linguistic units would be preserved in both emotional and nonemotional contexts, but that larger sized linguistic units would be disrupted in those same contexts.

In sum, the prosodic deficit observed in right-hemisphere-damaged speakers of tone languages (Mandarin Chinese, Taiwanese, Thai) is restricted to the emotional content of sentences only. The right hemisphere appears to assume a dominant role in modulating the affective components of language only. Some caution, however, is to be exercised in drawing firm conclusions about the lateralization of affective prosody across languages. The three aforementioned studies on affective prosody in tone languages are the only ones published to date. Moreover, the findings on hemispheric specialization for linguistic and affective prosody in nontone languages are much less clearcut.

TONAL BREAKDOWN AFTER
UNILATERAL BRAIN DAMAGE

Perception

The few reports on tone perception in brain-damaged speakers that are available in the contemporary literature consistently point to the left hemisphere as being dominant for the perception of lexical tones. In Mandarin Chinese, Naeser and Chan (1980) found that perception of Mandarin Chinese tones was impaired for their Mandarin Chinese–Cantonese bilingual mixed nonfluent aphasic. Her score of 55% on a listening identification test of the four Mandarin Chinese tones was abnormal in comparison to a score of 100% obtained by a normal control. Her performance was poor across all four tones. A CT scan revealed that she had suffered an intracerebral bleed resulting in extensive cortical and subcortical damage to the left hemisphere. There was no involvement of the right hemisphere. In their study of a Cantonese–English bilingual with crossed nonfluent aphasia, April and Han (1980) reported scores of 70% and 80%, respectively, on Cantonese tonal discrimination and identification tests. No scores were given for a normal control subject. A CT scan indicated hemorrhagic infarction in the right frontotemporal region. The left hemisphere was normal. The patient's relatively high scores may reflect the intactness of the left hemisphere. In the case of bilinguals, however, it is difficult to determine unequivocally whether their tonal deficits stem from language interference or language pathology.

Group studies of tone perception in brain-damaged monolingual speakers have been carried out in Mandarin Chinese, Cantonese, and Thai. In their study of 12 Mandarin Chinese patients with right-hemisphere lesions, Hughes et al. (1983) found no significant difference between the performance of the right-hemisphere group and normal controls on a Mandarin Chinese tonal identification test. Most of the patients achieved a perfect or near-perfect score. Yiu and Fok (1995) reported on identification of Cantonese tones by 21 aphasic subjects (11 anomic, 2 conduction, 2 Wernicke's, 2 Broca's, 4 transcortical motor), 3 dysarthric patients, and 8 normal controls. All subjects were right-handed. Left-hemisphere damage was verified by CT scan for all but four of the aphasic subjects. Results indicated that the aphasics (50%) performed significantly worse than either the normals (93%) or dysarthrics (91%). The normal performance of the dysarthrics suggests that the tone perception deficit can be attributed directly to hemisperic lesions causing aphasia. No differences in performance were found between nonfluent (Broca's, transcortical motor) and fluent (anomic, conduction, Wernicke's) aphasics. Neither aphasia severity nor auditory comprehension ability correlated with the tone perception scores. Gandour and Dardarananda (1983) examined identification of Thai tones by 4 aphasic patients (2 Broca's, 1 transcortical motor, 1 conduction), 1 right-hemisphere-damaged patient, and 1 normal control. Results of the perception tests on both natural speech and synthetic speech stimuli indicated that all 4 aphasic patients performed significantly worse than either the right-hemisphere-damaged patient or the normal control. The near perfect scores achieved by the right-hemisphere-damaged patient suggest that the tone perception deficit exhibited by left-hemisphere-damaged aphasics is not due to a general brain damage effect. Taken together, these findings clearly point to a tone perception deficit secondary to aphasia in left-hemisphere-damaged patients who are speakers of a tone language.

These findings are largely confirmed with dichotic listening studies of the perception of tones by normal speakers. Van Lancker and Fromkin (1973) found that normal Thai speakers show a right-ear advantage, which indicates left-hemisphere specialization, when the pitch configurations of the Thai tones are presented in a linguistic context (real words), but that they demonstrate no ear preference when the same pitch configurations are presented in a nonlinguistic context (hums). English speakers, on the other hand, do not show an ear advantage in either context. Van Lancker and Fromkin (1978) further found that neither musically trained nor musically untrained English speakers show a right-ear advantage for the tone words. Thus, the function of the stimuli rather than its physical composition determines whether it is lateralized to the left hemisphere or not. The perception of pitch contrasts is lateralized to the left hemisphere when these pitch variations serve to minimally distinguish words for native speakers of a tone language. Similarly, a right-ear advantage has been reported in a dichotic listening study of the perception of pitch accent contrasts by Norwegian listeners (Moen, 1993). Woerner (1992), however, reported a right-ear advantage for Thai listeners ($n = 45$) for both linguistic and nonlinguistic stimuli. A left-ear advantage was found for German listeners ($n = 44$) irrespective of stimulus type. In dichotic listening tests of Mandarin Chinese, the failure to find a right-ear advantage for tones is most likely due to methodologically induced artifacts of experimental design (Baudoin-Chial, 1986).

The evidence for a selective deficit in the perception of particular kinds of lexical tones is inconclusive at present. Naeser and Chan (1980) reported no evidence of selective impairment in their Mandarin-speaking patient. Her performance was poor across all four Mandarin tones. Gandour and Dardarananda (1983) found that although two (mid, low) of the five Thai tones accounted for a large proportion of tonal misidentifications, no rank order of difficulty could be established for the group of aphasic patients. Their deficit appeared to be general across all five tones instead of specific to individual tones. Yiu and Fok (1995), on the other hand, found that the high falling and low falling tones were somewhat easier to identify than the other Cantonese tones. In all studies, it appears that tonal confusions for aphasics are qualitatively similar to those for normal subjects. Their deficit is primarily quantitative in nature, meaning that aphasic patients are simply making more of the same kinds of perceptual errors made by normals. Those tones most susceptible to perceptual confusion are precisely those that are phonetically similar in height and shape to others in the tone space.

Production

Although findings across studies in tone production are not as uniform as in tone perception, the weight of the evidence shows that tones, like consonants and vowels, may be disrupted subsequent to left-hemisphere damage. T'sou (1978) reported on a Cantonese–English bilingual conduction aphasic with a lesion in the left temporoparietal region. His patient had difficulty in producing only one of the six Cantonese tones, the low falling tone. Naeser and Chan (1980), in their study of a Mandarin Chinese–Cantonese bilingual mixed nonfluent aphasic, reported that her production of Mandarin Chinese tones, especially Tone 3, the low falling–rising tone, was impaired in word repetition. Errors in tonal production also occurred in her spontaneous speech, elicited speech, object and picture naming, and Chinese character reading. In case studies of Thai conduction and transcortical motor aphasics, tonal paraphasias were observed on both speaking and writing tasks (Gandour, Buckingham, Dardarananda, Stawathumrong, & Holasuit Petty, 1982; Gandour, Dardarananda, Vibulsreth, & Buckingham, 1982; Gandour et al., 1991). In a case study of sequences of phonemic approximations produced by another Thai conduction aphasic, Gandour, Akamanon, Dechongkit, Khunadorn, and Boonklam (1994) found that tones, although frequently in error, were corrected earlier during the course of such sequences than consonants or vowels. However, in a study of a Thai-speaking Broca's aphasic (Gandour, Dardarananda, & Vejjajiva, 1985; Gandour et al., 1989), tones were relatively well preserved both in isolated words and in connected speech. Despite the fact that sentence timing and intensity patterns were abnormal in her connected speech, she was still able to produce F_0 patterns of the five Thai tones. In subcortical aphasia, tonal production was disrupted in a Thai patient with aphasia secondary to a left-hemisphere subcortical lesion (Gandour & Ponglorpisit, 1990). Collectively, it seems clear from these case studies that tone production may be impaired subsequent to left-hemisphere lesions.

Group studies of tone production in brain-damaged monolingual speakers have been carried out in Mandarin Chinese, Cantonese, and Thai. Although tonal breakdown has been observed to occur across tone languages, variability in the magnitude of the deficit appears to be related primarily to aphasia severity and time since onset of the stroke. Packard (1986) investigated the production of Mandarin Chinese consonants and tones in eight left-hemisphere-damaged patients with mild to moderate nonfluent aphasia. As measured by average error rate, their production deficit for tones (22%) was not significantly different from that for consonants (27%), indicating that tones are just as vulnerable to disruption following aphasia as are segmental phonemes. These error rates were significantly higher than those for normals. More than half of the aphasics' errors involved production of Tone 3. Gandour et al. (1988, pp. 230–231) pointed out that 75% of the tone production errors were made by severely aphasic patients within 2 months postonset. Yiu and Fok (1995) reported on production of Cantonese tones by 21 aphasic subjects (11 anomic, 2 conduction, 2 Wernicke's, 2 Broca's, 4 transcortical motor). Eight of the 21 aphasics were tested at 2 months or less postonset. The aphasics (64%) performed significantly worse than either the normals (98%) or dysarthrics (90%). Nonfluent aphasics (34%; Broca's, transcortical motor) had more difficulty in producing the six Cantonese tones than fluent aphasics (75%; anomic, conduction, Wernicke's). The aphasics experienced difficulty in producing all six Cantonese tones. Tone production scores correlated significantly with aphasia severity. The more severe the aphasic impairment, the more difficulty the patient had in tonal production. Gandour et al. (1988) investigated the production of Thai tones by 6 aphasic subjects (2 Broca's, 1 transcortical motor, 1 global, 1 conduction, 1 Wernicke's), 1 cerebellar dysarthric, and 1 right-hemisphere-damaged patient. With the exception of the global aphasic (63%) and one of the Broca's aphasics (78%), tonal production was relatively spared in aphasic patients (90% or higher) as compared to normals (95–100%). Interestingly, the aphasia severity ratings were lower for those 2 patients whose performance was worse than the others. The global aphasic was also tested at 2 months postonset, whereas the other aphasics ranged from 5 months to 9 years postonset. The dysarthric (96%) and right-hemisphere-damaged (92%) patients produced the Thai tones at a performance level comparable to that of normals. In agreement with Hughes et al. (1983), tonal production in Thai appears not to be impaired following unilateral lesions to the right hemisphere.

In a follow-up study that contained a much larger subject sample, Gandour, Ponglorpisit, Khunadorn, Dechongkit, Boongird, Boonklam, and Potisuk (1992) examined 48 subjects including 10 young normals, 10 old normals, 11 right-hemisphere-damaged patients, 9 left-hemisphere fluent aphasics (3 conduction, 4 Wernicke's, 2 anomic), and 8 left-hemisphere nonfluent aphasics (6 Broca's, 1 mixed nonfluent, 1 global). Only 2 of the aphasic patients were tested at less than 2 months postonset. Despite a relatively high level of proficiency, the nonfluent aphasics (85%) performed significantly worse than the young normals (97%), old normals (96%), right-hemisphere-damaged patients (93%), or fluent aphasics (96%). Although the extent of disruption varied widely among left nonfluent aphasics depending on severity level, none of the right-hemisphere-damaged patients encountered much difficulty in the production of the five Thai tones. At least for lexical tones produced in isolated words, these findings on Thai patients coupled together with Chinese patients demonstrate unequivocally that lesions to the right hemisphere are not likely to result in difficulties of tone production. Ryalls and Reinvang (1986) similarly reported that pitch accent contrasts in Norwegian were more perturbed in left-hemisphere-damaged patients than in right-hemisphere-damaged patients.

The evidence for a selective deficit in the production of particular kinds of tones (e.g., level vs. contour) is inconclusive at present. The data from Mandarin Chinese suggest perhaps that Tone 3 is especially vulnerable to disruption (Naeser & Chan, 1980; Packard, 1986). It accounts for over half of tonal confusions in response to tones produced by aphasic speakers. Its complex rising F_0 contour may contribute to its difficulty in production for aphasic patients. Falling tones are considered to be easier to produce than rising tones (Ohala, 1978; Sundberg, 1979). Tone 3's close phonological relationship to Tone 2 may also be a contributing factor. In Cantonese, production errors appear to be more or less evenly distributed across the six lexical tones (Yiu & Fok, 1995). Contrary to the notion that level tones are more resistant to disruption than contour tones, their data would indicate otherwise. Indeed, three out of seven of the tonal error patterns for nonfluent aphasics involved a change of a level tone to a contour tone. In Thai, however, the fact that almost all tonal substitutions resulted in a mid, low, or falling tone is compatible with the notion that tones exhibiting a falling F_0 contour are somehow articulatorily less complex than others (Ohala, 1978; Sundberg, 1979). Of the five Thai tones, the mid, low, and falling tones are characterized primarily by a falling F_0 trajectory throughout their duration, whereas the high and rising tones are not.

Among aphasic patients in tone languages, no one has yet to report that their performance on tone perception was superior to that on tone production (Gandour et al., 1988; Packard, 1986; Yiu & Fok, 1995). Similarly, Naeser and Chan's (1980) mixed nonfluent Mandarin Chinese–Cantonese bilingual had more difficulty with tone perception than production. Left-hemisphere-damaged patients are likely to suffer from a deficit in tone perception regardless of aphasic syndrome, whereas nonfluent aphasics are more impaired than fluent in tone production. These findings suggest that their difficulties in tone perception and production do not stem from a central disorder in language processing.

In studies of intonation in nontone languages, Ryalls (1982) and Cooper et al. (1984) showed that French- and English-speaking aphasics exhibit a narrowing of the F_0 range, especially in longer sentences. The inability of aphasic patients to maintain a sufficiently wide F_0 range is believed to be responsible for their dysprosody. Similarly, Danly and Shapiro (1982) found that F_0 declination for English-speaking Broca's aphasics was intact in short sentences only. The Gandour et al. (1988) and Gandour, Ponglorpisit, Khunadorn, Dechongkit, Boongird, Boonklam, and Potisuk (1992) findings in Thai aphasics, however, showed the opposite effect. Not only is there no compression of the F_0 range in Thai-speaking aphasics, but the tone space in these brain-damaged patients actually has a wider than normal range. Thus, the extent to which left-hemisphere nonfluent aphasics have difficulty in producing tonal contrasts, at least for tones in isolated words, cannot be attributed to a narrowing of the F_0 range.

There is an intimate relationship between the control of timing and F_0. Danly and Shapiro (1982) and Danly, Cooper, and Shapiro (1983) demonstrated that preservation of F_0 patterns in aphasic patients depends on sentence length, and that F_0 patterns may be less disrupted than timing. In a linguistic analysis of Monrad-Krohn's (1947) famous patient with deviant prosody, Moen (1991) argued that the patient's apparently deviant sentence intonation could be secondary to an underlying timing disorder. In a case study of a Thai-speaking Broca's aphasic, Gandour et al. (1989) showed that timing and amplitude were aberrant at the sentence level, whereas F_0 contours of the five tones were relatively preserved. These findings, coupled with the relative sparing of tone production in isolated words in Thai aphasics, led Gandour et al. (1988) and Gandour, Ponglorpisit, Khunadorn, Dechongkit, Boongird, Boonklam, and Potisuk (1992) to hypothesize that disruption of F_0 contours is due primarily to malfunctions in timing mechanisms that span larger linguistic units. That is, tonal patterns may be less disrupted than intonational patterns because of the smaller temporal domain over which they extend. Even though tonal contrasts may be preserved, phonetic deterioration may occur due to the absence of sentence-level effects on the shape of F_0 contours that are present in normal speech. With this different conceptualization of dysprosody in aphasia, the critical variable is the size of the domain over which prosodic patterns extend. Deviant timing at the sentence level necessarily disrupts F_0 contours associated with intonation but not tone.

To test this hypothesis, it is necessary to examine the production of tones in larger contexts. As a measure of tonal production beyond the word level, a series of studies were carried out on tonal coarticulation in Thai aphasic patients (Gandour, Ponglorpisit, Dechongkit, Khunadorn, Boongird, & Potisuk, 1993a, 1993b; Gandour, Potisuk, Ponglorpisit, Dechongkit, Khunadorn, & Boongird, 1994). *Coarticulation* refers to the phenomenon whereby a given speech sound is altered in its phonetic manifestation depending on influences from adjacent sounds. In tones, coarticulatory effects occur in much the same way as in consonants and vowels. Of particular interest is anticipatory coarticulation, which involves one speech sound being influenced by subsequent sounds, and perseverative coarticulation, which involves one speech sound being influenced by preceding sounds. Gandour, Ponglorpisit, Dechongkit, Khunadorn, Boongird, and Potisuk (1993a, 1993b) found tonal coarticulation to be relatively intact in bisyallabic words and phrases. This, however, was not the case when tonal coarticulation occurs in larger sentence contexts. Gandour, Potisuk, Ponglorpisit, Dechongkit, Khunadorn, and Boongird (1994c) investigated all 25 possible sequences of two tones from the five Thai tones embedded in a carrier sentence. Anticipatory and perseverative tonal coarticulation were markedly reduced in left fluent aphasics ($n = 9$), totally absent in left nonfluent aphasics ($n = 5$), but reasonably well preserved in right-hemisphere-damaged patients ($n = 13$). The disparity in performance between the left- and right-hemisphere-damaged patients supports the notion that tonal coarticulation is primarily a function of the left hemisphere.

In sum, tonal production is disrupted following unilateral lesions to the left hemisphere in patients who are native speakers of a tone language. None of the studies to date have found tonal production to be disturbed in right-hemisphere-damaged patients. The magnitude of the deficit appears to vary somewhat depending primarily on aphasia severity. A production deficit is clearly more evident in nonfluent aphasics as compared to fluent aphasics. The relative sparing of tones in isolated words produced by Thai-speaking aphasics, combined with intonational deficits observed in longer sentences in nontone language aphasics, suggests that aberrant F_0 contours may not reflect reduced control of tones per se, but instead may be a secondary effect resulting from lack of timing control. Studies on tonal coarticulation produced by Thai-speaking aphasics in sentence contexts appear to support this hypothesis.

CONCLUSIONS

From this survey of contemporary aphasia literature, we are led to conclude that language representation in the brains of tone language speakers is essentially the same as that in nontone language speakers. We are not claiming that there will be no surface differences in language behavior, but rather that the underlying brain mechanisms are language universal. For example, dysprosody in a Cantonese Broca's aphasic may look somewhat different from that of a nontone language Broca's, not because different brain mechanisms are implicated but instead because their effects on the surface phonetic output vary as a function of the prosodic categories that are present in the language. In this way, we can begin to search for language-universal mechanisms whose differential effects on prosodic output can be predicted from language structure. There is some evidence that differences in behavioral manifestations of prosodic disturbances in aphasic patients between these two language types may likely be attributed to the size of the temporal domain over which the prosodic unit extends. By focusing our attention on both timing and F_0 simultaneously, and perhaps intensity as well, we can obtain a much clearer picture of abstract linguistic elements in relation to their acoustic/phonetic and neurological correlates. A number of case studies as well as handedness–aphasia correlations, anatomical–clinical syndrome correlations, and Wada test studies generally indicate that the presence of tone in a language does not influence lateralization of language function. That is, the left hemisphere is dominant for language function in tone language speakers just as in speakers of Indo-European languages.

In contrast to nontone languages in which findings are mixed or even contradictory, affective prosody appears to be lateralized to the right hemisphere and linguistic prosody to the left hemisphere in speakers of tone language. None of the studies reviewed suggests that the right hemisphere of tone language speakers is engaged in linguistic prosody. It should be pointed out, however, that most studies that investigated this question in right-hemisphere-damaged patients of tone languages employed sentence-length stimuli in emotional contexts without comparable sentence-length stimuli in nonemotional or propositional contexts. Thus, the possibity remains that linguistic prosody may also be disturbed in right-hemisphere-damaged patients of tone languages when sentence-length stimuli are taken into account.

And finally, although the precise mechanisms underlying impairment of both tone perception and production remain elusive at present, the data clearly suggest that tonal processing is impaired following unilateral lesions to the left hemisphere in tone language speakers. The only caveat is that all studies on tone perception have examined tones in citation forms. With the exception of a few studies on Thai, the same is true for studies that have investigated tone production. We can look forward to future studies of aphasic patients who are native speakers of tone languages that focus on sentence-length stimuli.

ACKNOWLEDGMENT

This material is based on work supported in part by the National Institute on Deafness and other Communication Disorders under grant DC00515-07.

REFERENCES

Akamanon, C. (1989). The assessment of auditory comprehension ability with a Thai adaptation of the Token Test. *Ramathibodi Medical Journal (Thailand)*, *12*, 104–108.

Alajouanine, R., Cathala, H. P., Metellus, J., Siksou, M., Alleton, V., Cheng, F., DeTurckheim, C., & Chang, M. C. (1973). La problématique de l'aphasie dans les langues à écriture non-alphabetique. A propos d'un cas chez un Chinois. *Revue Neurologique*, *128*, 229–243.

Alexander, M., & Naeser, M. (1988). Cortical-subcortical differences in aphasia. In F. Plum (Ed.), *Language, communication, and the brain* (pp. 215–228). New York: Raven Press.

Alexander, M., Naeser, M., & Palumbo, C. (1987). Correlations of subcortical CT lesion sites and aphasia profiles. *Brain, 110,* 961–991.

April, R. S., & Han, M. (1980). Crossed aphasia in a right-handed bilingual Chinese man, a second case. *Archives of Neurology, 37,* 342–346.

April, R. S., & Tse, P.-C. (1977). Crossed aphasia in a Chinese bilingual dextral. *Archives of Neurology, 34,* 766–770.

Bates, E., Chen, S., Tzeng, O., Li, P., & Opie, M. (1991). The noun-verb problem in Chinese aphasia. *Brain and Language, 41,* 203–223.

Baudoin-Chial, S. (1986). Hemispheric lateralization of Modern Standard Chinese tone processing. *Journal of Neurolinguistics, 2,* 189–199.

Behrens, S. J. (1988). The role of the right hemisphere in the production of linguistic stress. *Brain and Language, 33,* 104–127.

Behrens, S. J. (1989). Characterizing sentence intonation in a right hemisphere-damaged population. *Brain and Language, 37,* 181–200.

Benson, D. F. (1979). *Aphasia, alexia, and agraphia.* New York: Churchill Livingstone.

Blumstein, S., & Cooper, W. (1974). Hemispheric processing of intonational contours. *Cortex, 10,* 146–158.

Bryden, M. P., & Ley, R. G. (1983). Right-hemispheric involvement in the perception and expression of emotion in normal humans. In K. Heilman & P. Satz (Eds.), *Neuropsychology of human emotion* (pp. 6–44). New York: Guilford Press.

Chang, C. G.-S., Peng, F., & Yü, J.-Y. (1986). Patterns of information retrieval from LTM in the process of verbalization by a fluent (conduction) aphasic: A Chinese case. *Journal of Neurolinguistics, 2,* 277–296.

Chia, Y.-W., Peng, F., Wang, Y.-C., & Shih, C.-J. (1986). Agrammatism of Chinese transcortical aphasics. *Journal of Neurolinguistics, 2,* 233–259.

Chu, Y.-T., Peng, F., & Yiu, H.-K. (1986). Agrammatism and conduction aphasia: A Chinese case. *Journal of Neurolinguistics, 2,* 209–232.

Colsher, P., Cooper, W., & Graff-Radford, N. (1987). Intonational variability in the speech of right-hemisphere damaged patients. *Brain and Language, 32,* 379–383.

Cooper, W., Soares, C., Nicol, J., Michelow, D., & Goloskie, S. (1984). Clausal intonation after unilateral brain damage. *Language and Speech, 27,* 17–24.

Damasio, A., Damasio, H., Rizzo, M., Varney, N., & Gersh, F. (1982). Aphasia with nonhemorrhagic lesions in the basal ganglia and internal capsule. *Archives of Neurology, 39,* 15–20.

Danly, M., & Shapiro, B. (1982). Speech prosody in Broca's aphasia. *Brain and Language, 16,* 171–190.

Danly, M., Cooper, W., & Shapiro, B. (1983). Fundamental frequency, language processing, and linguistic structure in Wernicke's aphasia. *Brain and Language, 19,* 1–24.

Dardarananda, R., Potisuk, S., Gandour, J., & Holasuit, S. (in press). Thai adaptation of the Western Aphasia Battery (WAB). *Chiangmai Medical Bulletin (Thailand).*

Edmondson, J., Chan, J.-L., Seibert, G. B., & Ross, E. D. (1987). The effect of right-brain damage on acoustical measures of affective prosody in Taiwanese patients. *Journal of Phonetics, 15,* 219–233.

Fromkin, V., & Rodman, R. (1993). *An introduction to language* (5th ed.). New York: Harcourt Brace Jovanovich.

Gandour, J. (1982). A diagnostic aphasia examination for Thai. *Linguistics of the Tibeto-Burman Area, 6*(2), 65–76.

Gandour, J. (1987). Tone production in aphasia. In J. Ryalls (Ed.), *Phonetic approaches to speech production in aphasia and related disorders* (pp. 45–57). Boston: College Hill Press.

Gandour, J., Akamanon, C., Dechongkit, S., Khunadorn, F., & Boonklam, R. (1994). Sequences of phonemic approximations in a Thai conduction aphasic. *Brain and Language, 46,* 69–95.

Gandour, J., Buckingham, H., Jr., & Dardarananda, R. (1985). The dissolution of numeral classifiers in Thai. *Linguistics, 23,* 547–566.

Gandour, J., Buckingham, H., Jr., Dardarananda, R., Stawathumrong, P., & Holasuit Petty, S. (1982). Case study of a Thai conduction aphasic. *Brain and Language, 17,* 327–358.

Gandour, J., & Dardarananda, R. (1983). Identification of tonal contrasts in Thai aphasic patients. *Brain and Language, 18,* 98–114.

Gandour, J., Dardarananda, R., Buckingham, H., Jr., & Viriyavejakul, A. (1986). A Thai adaptation of the Boston Diagnostic Aphasia Examination. *Crossroads: An Interdisciplinary Journal of Southeast Asian Studies, 2*(3), 1–39.

Gandour, J., Dardarananda, R., & Holasuit, S. (1991). Nature of spelling errors in a Thai conduction aphasic. *Brain and Language, 41,* 96–119.

Gandour, J., Dardarananda, R., & Vejjajiva, A. (1985). Case study of a Thai Broca aphasic with an adaptation of the Boston Diagnostic Aphasia Examination. *Journal of the Medical Association of Thailand, 68,* 552–563.

Gandour, J., Dardarananda, R., Vibulsreth, S., & Buckingham, H., Jr. (1982). Case study of a Thai transcortical motor aphasic. *Language and Speech, 25,* 127–150.

Gandour, J., & Dechongkit, S. (1992). Aphasia in a Thai speaking patient with a hemorrhagic lesion in the left basal ganglia. *Ramathibodi Medical Journal (Thailand), 15,* 111–116.

Gandour, J., Dechongkit, S., Ponglorpisit, S., Khunadorn, F., & Boongird, P. (1993). Intraword timing relations in Thai after unilateral brain damage. *Brain and Language, 45,* 160–179.

Gandour, J., Dechongkit, S., Ponglorpisit, S., & Khunadorn, F. (1994). Speech timing at the sentence level in Thai after unilateral brain damage. *Brain and Language, 46,* 419–438.

Gandour, J., Holasuit Petty, S., & Dardarananda, R. (1988). Perception and production of tone in aphasia. *Brain and Language, 35,* 201–240.

Gandour, J., Holasuit Petty, S., & Dardarananda, R. (1989). Dysprosody in Broca's aphasia: A case study. *Brain and Language, 37,* 232–257.

Gandour, J., Larsen, J., Dechongkit, S., Ponglorpisit, S., & Khunadorn, F. (1995). Speech prosody in affective contexts in Thai patients with right hemisphere lesions. *Brain and Language, 51,* 422–443.

Gandour, J., & Ponglorpisit, S. (1990). Disruption of tone space in a Thai-speaking patient with subcortical aphasia. *Journal of Neurolinguistics, 5,* 333–351.

Gandour, J., Ponglorpisit, S., & Dardarananda, R. (1992). Tonal disturbances in Thai after brain damage. *Journal of Neurolinguistics, 7,* 133–145.

Gandour, J., Ponglorpisit, S., Dechongkit, S., Khunadorn, F., Boongird, P., & Potisuk, S. (1993a). Anticipatory tonal coarticulation in Thai noun compounds after unilateral brain damage. *Brain and Language, 45,* 1–20.

Gandour, J., Ponglorpisit, S., Dechongkit, S., Khunadorn, F., Boongird, P., & Potisuk, S. (1993b). Tonal coarticulation in Thai disyllabic utterances after unilateral brain damage: A preliminary study. *Nopparat Rajathanee General Hospital Medical Journal (Thailand), 4,* 24–47.

Gandour, J., Ponglorpisit, S., Khunadorn, F., Dechongkit, S., Boongird, P., & Boonklam, R. (1992a). Timing characteristics of speech after brain damage: Vowel length in Thai. *Brain and Language, 42,* 337–345.

Gandour, J., Ponglorpisit, S., Khunadorn, F., Dechongkit, S., Boongird, P., & Boonklam, R. (1992b). Stop voicing in Thai after unilateral brain damage. *Aphasiology, 6,* 535–547.

Gandour, J., Ponglorpisit, S., Khunadorn, F., Dechongkit, S., Boongird, P., Boonklam, R., & Potisuk, S. (1992). Lexical tones in Thai after unilateral brain damage. *Brain and Language, 43,* 275–307.

Gandour, J., Potisuk, S., Ponglorpisit, S., Dechongkit, S., Khunadorn, F., & Boongird, P. (1994). Tonal coarticulation in Thai after unilateral brain damage. *Brain and Language, 46,* 419–438.

Gao, S., & Benson, D. F. (1990). Aphasia after stroke in native Chinese speakers. *Aphasiology, 4,* 31–43.

Gitterman, M., & Sies, L. (1992). Nonbiological determinants of the organization of language in the brain: A comment on Hu, Qiou, and Zhong. *Brain and Language, 43,* 162–165.

Goodglass, H. (1993). *Understanding aphasia.* San Diego: Academic Press.

Goodglass, H., & Kaplan, E. (1983). *The assessment of aphasia and related disorders* (2nd ed.). Philadelphia: Lea & Febiger.

Goodglass, H., & Quadfasel, F. (1954). Language laterality in left-handed aphasics. *Brain, 77,* 523–548.

Holasuit Petty, S., & Gandour, J. (1984a). Some auditory language comprehension tests for Thai aphasic patients. *Nursing Newsletter (Thailand), 11*(1), 25–29.

Holasuit Petty, S., & Gandour, J. (1984b). A handedness questionnaire for Thai aphasic patients. *Nursing Newsletter (Thailand), 11*(1), 20–24.

Holasuit Petty, S., Gandour, J., & Jirakupt, S. (1985). A picture arrangement test for eliciting connected discourse from Thai aphasic patients. *Nursing Newsletter (Thailand), 12*(4), 42–48

Hu, Y.-H., Qiu, Y.-G., & Zhong, G.-Q. (1990). Crossed aphasia in Chinese: A clinical survey. *Brain and Language, 39,* 347–356.

Hu, Y.-H., Qiou, Y.-G., & Zhong, G.-Q. (1992). A reply to Gitterman and Sier "Nonbiological determinants of the organization of language in the brain: A comment on Hu, Qiu, and Zhong." *Brain and Language, 43,* 764–767.

Hughes, C. P., Chan, J.-L., & Ming, S.-S. (1983). Aprosodia in Chinese patients with right cerebral hemisphere lesion. *Archives of Neurology, 40,* 732–736.

Hung, C.-C., Tu, Y.-K., Chen, S.-H., & Chen, R.-C. (1985). A study on handedness and cerebral speech dominance in right-handed Chinese. *Journal of Neurolinguistics, 1,* 143–163.

Kennedy, M., & Murdoch, B. (1989). Speech and language disorders subsequent to subcortical vascular lesions. *Aphasiology, 3,* 221–247.

Kertesz, A. (1979). *Aphasia and associated disorders: Taxonomy, localization, and recovery.* New York: Grune & Stratton.

Kertesz, A. (1982). *Western aphasia battery.* New York: Grune and Stratton.

Kertesz, A., & Poole, E. (1974). The aphasia quotient: The taxonomic approach to measurement of aphasic disability. *Canadian Journal of Neurological Sciences, 1,* 7–16.

Menn, L., & Obler, L. (Eds.). (1990). *Agrammatic aphasia: Cross-language narrative sourcebook.* Amsterdam: John Benjamins.

Milner, B., Branch, C., & Rasmussen, T. (1964). Observations on cerebral dominance. In A. V. S. de Reuck & M. O'Connor (Eds.), *Ciba Foundation symposium on disorders of language* (pp. 200–214). London: J. & A. Churchill.

Moen, I. (1991). Functional lateralisation of pitch accents and intonation in Norwegian: Monrad-Krohn's study of an aphasic patient with altered "melody of speech." *Brain and Language, 41,* 538–554.

Moen, I. (1993). Functional lateralization of the perception of Norwegian word tones—Evidence from a dichotic listening experiment. *Brain and Language, 44,* 400–413.

Monrad-Krohn, G. H. (1947). Dysprosody or altered melody of language. *Brain, 70,* 405–423.

Monrad-Krohn, G. H. (1963). The third element of speech: Prosody and its disorders. In L. Halpern (Ed.), *Problems of dynamic neurology* (pp. 101–118). Jerusalem: Hebrew University Press.

Naeser, M., & Borod, J. C. (1986). Aphasia in left-handers. *Neurology, 36,* 471–488.

Naeser, M. A., & Chan, S. W.-C. (1980). Case study of a Chinese aphasic with the Boston Diagnostic Aphasia Exam. *Neuropsychologia, 18,* 389–410.

Ohala, J. (1978). The production of tone. In V. Fromkin (Ed.), *Tone: A linguistic survey* (pp. 5–39). New York: Academic Press.

Packard, J. L. (1986). Tone production deficits in non-fluent aphasic Chinese speech. *Brain and Language, 29,* 212–223.

Packard, J. L. (1990). Agrammatism in Chinese: A case study. In L. Menn & L. Obler (Eds.), *Agrammatic aphasia: Cross-language narrative sourcebook* (Vol. 2, pp. 1191–1223). Amsterdam: John Benjamins.

Robin, D., Klouda, G., & Hug, L. (1991). Neurogenic disorders of prosody. In M. Cannito & D. Vogel (Eds.), *Treating disordered speech motor control: For clinicians by clinicians* (pp. 241–271). Austin, TX: Pro-Ed.

Robin, D., & Schienberg, S. (1990). Subcortical lesions and aphasia. *Journal of Speech and Hearing Disorders, 55,* 90–100.

Robin, D., Tranel, D., & Damasio, H. (1990). Auditory perception of temporal and spectral events in patients with focal left and right cerebral lesions. *Brain and Language, 39,* 539–555.

Ross, E. D. (1981). The aprosodias: Functional-anatomic organization of the affective components of language in the right hemisphere. *Archives of Neurology, 38,* 561–569.

Ross, E. D., Edmondson, J., Seibert, G. B., & Chan, J.-L. (1992). Affective exploitation of tone in Taiwanese: An acoustical study of "tone latitude." *Journal of Phonetics, 20,* 441–456.

Ross, E. D., Edmondson, J., Seibert, G. B., & Homan, R. (1988). Acoustic analysis of affective prosody during right-sided Wada test: A within-subjects verification of the right hemisphere's role in language. *Brain and Language, 33,* 128–145.

Ross, E. D., & Mesulam, M. (1979). Dominant language functions of the right hemisphere? Prosody and emotional gesturing. *Archives of Neurology, 36,* 144–148.

Ryalls, J. (1982). Intonation in Broca's aphasia. *Neuropsychologia, 20,* 355–360.

Ryalls, J. (1986). What constitutes a primary disturbance of speech prosody?: A reply to Shapiro and Danly. *Brain and Language, 29,* 183–187.

Ryalls, J., & Behrens, S. (1988). An overview of changes in fundamental frequency associated with cortical insult. *Aphasiology, 2,* 107–115.

Ryalls, J., Joanette, Y., & Feldman, L. (1987). An acoustic comparison of normal and right-brain-damaged speech prosody. *Cortex, 23,* 685–694.

Ryalls, J., & Reinvang, I. (1986). Laterality of linguistic tones: Acoustic evidence from Norwegian. *Language and Speech, 29,* 389–398.

Shapiro, B., & Danly, M. (1985). The role of the right hemisphere in the control of speech prosody in propositional and affective contexts. *Brain and Language, 25,* 19–36.

Shipley-Brown, F., Dingwall, W., Berlin, C., Yeni-Komshian, G., & Gordon-Salant, S. (1988). Hemispheric processing of affective and linguistic intonation contours in normal subjects. *Brain and Language, 33,* 16–26.

Silberman, E., & Weingartner, H. (1986). Hemispheric lateralization of functions related to emotion. *Brain and Cognition, 5,* 322–353.

Sundberg, J. (1979). Maximum speed of pitch changes in singers and untrained subjects. *Journal of Phonetics, 7,* 71–79.

T'sou, B. K. (1978). Some preliminary observations on aphasia in a Chinese bilingual. *Acta Psychologica Taiwanica, 20,* 57–64.

Tzeng, O., Chen, S., & Hung, D. (1991). The classifier problem in aphasia. *Brain and Language, 41,* 184–202.

Van Lancker, D. (1980). Cerebral lateralization of pitch cues in the linguistic signal. *Papers in Linguistics, 13*(2), 201–277.

Van Lancker, D. (1988). Nonpropositional speech: Neurolinguistic studies. In A. Ellis (Ed.), *Progress in the psychology of language* (Vol. 3, pp. 49–118). Hillsdale, NJ: Lawrence Erlbaum Associates.

Van Lancker, D., & Fromkin, V. A. (1973). Hemispheric specialization for pitch and tone: Evidence from Thai. *Journal of Phonetics, 1,* 101–109.

Van Lancker, D., & Fromkin, V. A, (1978). Cerebral dominance for pitch contrasts in tone language speakers and in musically untrained and trained English speakers. *Journal of Phonetics, 6,* 19–23.

Van Lancker, D., & Sidtis, J. (1992). The identification of affective-prosodic stimuli by left- and right-hemisphere-damaged subjects: All errors are not created equal. *Journal of Speech and Hearing Research, 35,* 963–970.

Weintraub, S., Mesulam, M., & Kramer, L. (1981). Disturbances in prosody: A right hemisphere contribution to language. *Archives of Neurology, 38,* 742–744.

Woerner, W. (1992). Tone processing and the brain. In *Proceedings of the Third International Symposium on Language and Linguistics: Pan-Asiatic linguistics* (Vol. 1, pp. 588–603). Bangkok: Chulalongkorn University Press.

Yang, B.-J., Yang, T.-C., Pan, H.-C., Lai, S.-J., & Yang, F. (1989). Three variant forms of subcortical aphasia in Chinese stroke patients. *Brain and Language, 37,* 145–162.

Yiu, E. (1992). Linguistic assessment of Chinese speaking aphasics: Development of a Cantonese aphasia battery. *Journal of Neurolinguistics, 7,* 1–46.

Yiu, E., & Fok, A. (1995). Lexical tone disruption in Cantonese aphasic speakers. *Clinical Linguistics and Phonetics, 9,* 79–92.

CHAPTER FIVE

Aphasia in Ideograph Readers: The Case of Japanese

Atsushi Yamadori
Tohoku University, Sendai, Japan

A BRIEF REVIEW OF APHASIA STUDIES IN JAPAN

Aphasia studies in Japan can be traced back to 1893, when Onishi (1893) published the first known treatise on aphasia (Hamanaka, 1994). The interesting fact that Kanji (logograph) and Kana (syllabograph) processing ability can sometimes be dissociable in aphasia was first reported by Miura in 1901 (Hamanaka, 1994).

In this section I briefly review several substantial facts about aphasia in Japan, and then in subsequent sections introduce in some detail its symptom characteristics, which might be of some interest to non-Japanese aphasiologists. Generally speaking, it has been repeatedly confirmed that there is no difference in the aphasic symptomatology between the aphasia in Euro-American languages and that in Japan (Hamanaka, 1994; Ohashi, 1965; Sasanuma, 1986). In other words, all the essential features found in Euro-American aphasia were also found in Japanese aphasia (Yamadori, 1985).

A lesion situated anterior to the central sulcus of the left cerebral hemisphere in the majority of right-handers would produce a nonfluent aphasia. For instance, lesions of 49 Broca's aphasics studied by computed tomography (CT) scans were found to be concentrated in the left posterior inferior frontal gyrus, left precentral gyrus, and the adjacent deep white matter including the striatum (Watanabe et al., 1986), implicating a rather large lesion as a prerequisite for a typical Broca's aphasia. The interesting thesis that a typical and persistent Broca's aphasia does not occur in a circumscribed lesion limited to Broca's area (Zangwill, 1975) was also found to be true in Japanese

143

cases, as the studies by Tanabe et al. (1982) and Ohashi and Hamanaka (1985) clearly suggested. A partial lesion of Broca's area, a lesion anterior and superior to Broca's area, a lesion in the left superior frontal gyrus, a diffuse left frontal lesion, and a deep white matter lesion affecting the antero-lateral portion of the anterior horn of the left lateral ventricle all would produce a transcortical motor aphasia (Enokido, 1988).

On the other hand, a lesion situated posterior to the left central sulcus would produce a fluent type of aphasia. All the CT scan-confirmed lesions of 13 cases of typical Wernicke's aphasia were shown to conform to the posterior third of the left superior temporal lobe, that is, Wernicke's area (Fujii & Kurachi, 1988). A CT scan analysis of 32 cases of Wernicke's aphasia by Watanabe et al. (1986) also reached the same conclusion. Not unlike the cases of Broca's area aphasia, a circumscribed small lesion confined in Wernicke's area would produce a Wernicke's aphasia, but might ameliorate rapidly leaving no residual symptoms (Yamadori, 1984). An extensive autopsy study (Enokido, 1988) listed a lesion involving the left superior temporal gyrus, a lesion involving the left middle and inferior temporal gyri, a left basal temporal lesion, and a left deep parietal lobe lesion as a cause of a transcortical sensory aphasia.

Conduction aphasia, in which a repetition difficulty stands out of proportion to other linguistic difficulties, has been found to be related with a lesion in the cortico-subcortical region of the left posterior superior temporal gyri including Wernicke's area and cortico-subcortical areas of the left supramarginal gyrus partially extending to the angular gyrus (Watanabe et al., 1986). All of the seven cases of conduction aphasia analyzed by Koyama (1988) also had a common cortico-subcortical lesion in the left supramaginal gyrus.

The localizing value of anomic aphasia is said to be poor, because a lesion producing this type of aphasia can be found in various regions of the left hemisphere (Benson, 1979). Japanese studies are also consistent with this view. CT scan-confirmed lesions of 24 anomics (Totsuka, Funai, Fujibayashi, Fukusako, & Sasanuma, 1979) and of 20 anomics (Watanabe et al., 1986) tended to be small and were found almost everywhere in the left hemisphere.

Aphasia following a left thalamic lesion has also been frequently reported in Japan. Common symptoms included difficulty in confrontation naming, word-finding difficulty in running speech, verbal paraphasias, perseveration, mild comprehension difficulty, and mild agraphia. A mild degree of anterograde amnesia for verbal material is associated without exception. Lesions attributable to these symptoms included ventroanterior (VA), ventrolateral (VL), medial (M), laminar, and centromedian (CM) nuclei of the left thalamus (Mori, Yamadori, & Mitani, 1986; Yamadori, 1987).

Symptom clusters caused by damage in the left supplementary motor area have been confirmed to be identical with those described in the Euro-

American literature (Rubens, 1975). It is characterized by early mutism, low voice volume, difficulty in initiating speech, transient aphasia, preserved repetition, preserved comprehension, preserved confrontation naming, and absence of paraphasias and agrammatism (Motomura, 1994; Motomura & Nagae, 1985).

A subcortical lesion including parts of the basal ganglia is a frequent cause of aphasia (Naeser et al., 1982). Whether it is due to nuclear or to surrounding white matter lesions is still an unsolved question. Although the latter mechanism is much more likely (Alexander, Naeser, & Palumbo, 1987), definite conclusions are yet to be reached. Although many studies appeared on subcortical aphasia in Japan, they also failed to reach a common conclusion concerning the role of the basal ganglia.

Crossed aphasia, that is, aphasia caused by a right-hemisphere lesion in right-handers, is also seen in Japanese patients. The clinicopathological characteristics of this atypical syndrome are essentially the same between Japanese and Euro-American populations (Kishida, 1991; Coppens & Hungerford, chapter 7, this volume). Some would show a complete mirror pattern of a typical aphasic syndrome observed in a left hemispheric lesion, but others would show rather atypical symptoms like a prominent agrammatism. Kishida found 4 cases of crossed aphasia out of 454 aphasic cases (Kishida, Tsuruoka, Otsuka, Tsukuda, & Uemura, 1976). This incidence of 0.9% is slightly higher than the number reported by Hécaen, Mazars, Ramier, Goldblum, and Merienne (1971), who found only 1 case (0.38%) out of 239 cases.

The incidence of aphasia in non-right-handed subjects, as well as its symptomatology, is also not particularly different from the Euro-American one (Basso & Rusconi, chapter 1, this volume). Thus, Kawachi and Takeuchi (1987) found 37 cases of non-right-handed aphasia that had a unilateral cerebral lesion during a 7-year period at a large rehabilitation hospital. Twenty-one cases (15 males and 6 females) had a lesion in the left hemisphere (61.8%), and 13 cases (10 males and 3 females) had a lesion in the right hemisphere (38.2%). This incidence is approximately comparable with the one reported by Gloning (1977). Further, severe aphasia was less frequently encountered in these non-right-handed aphasics than in right-handed ones (Kawachi et al., 1987).

All these facts firmly establish an important principle that a common biological organization of the brain underlies linguistic activity across speakers of different languages. However, this principle should not lead to the conclusion that linguistic difference does not matter at all in studying brain organization of language. Emergence of different languages might not have been possible if the brain had a rigid organization. Different languages employ different psychological units of speech sounds (syllables) to create a unit of meaning (morpheme), and different rules to combine these morphemes into a meaningful whole (word and sentence). Words also represent different concepts in different linguistic cultures. This apparent arbitrariness of linguistic units and rules among the human races demonstrates a plastic nature of the brain in incorporating linguistic activities. In other words, this must be a reflection of the fact that a small difference in strategies does not affect a grand function of the brain to communicate between the peoples.

This being said, Japanese neuropsychologists including the present author have been fascinated by a dissociation in performance between Kanji and Kana scripts seen in some cases of Japanese aphasics and in some visual hemifield reading experiments in normal subjects. For instance, in some of the tachistoscopic left visual field exposure experiments, Kanji symbols were said to be processed more accurately than Kana symbols (Hatta, 1977; Sasanuma, Itoh, Mori, & Kobayashi, 1977; for more detail, see a compilation of the related literature by Kess & Miyamoto, 1994). Inspired by these reports, there appeared quite a few arguments that because Kanji reading requires a more "holistic" processing than Kana processing, the involvement of the right hemisphere in reading might be larger in Japanese speakers than in users of the alphabetic code. Thus, a linguistic difference like the written code may be employed as an effective cue to a deeper understanding of brain organization (Nagae, 1992), because the difference might work as a kind of magnifier in detecting a subtle functional difference between different parts of the brain, like between the left and right cerebral hemisphere.

The use of the different linguistic codes among the different linguistic cultures does not necessarily mean that it reflects a difference of the essential function of the brain, but it probably means that the strategies employed to realize the common linguistic function may be different. Studying the difference in symptomatology among aphasics of the different languages may help elucidate these strategic differences, and would contribute in obtaining a clearer understanding of the neurological organization of the brain participating in the universal linguistic activity.

In the following sections, the author attempts to pinpoint some of the unique features of the Japanese language and their impact on aphasic symptomatology.

SOME CHARACTERISTICS
OF THE JAPANESE LANGUAGE

Spoken Language

Japanese is composed of only 108 syllabic sounds (Amanuma, Otsubo, & Mizutani, 1978). The number of syllabic sounds varies by region but it is always less than 120 sounds. Each syllable in principle has the same duration, and is pronounced with the same interval. In practice, these sounds may be pronounced at different speeds and durations, but psychologically this feature is clear to all native Japanese speakers. For instance a word NIHON (Japan) is pronounced as NI-HO-N, all three syllables being pronounced with the same speed divided by the same interval. Japan may sometimes be called NIPPON, which is pronounced as NI-P-PO-N, with a rhythm of four beats. In this case, a pause is placed between NI and PO. Mentally this pause has the same duration than the other three syllables. This equitemporal nature of the Japanese pronunciation has long been recognized by some linguists as one of the important features of the Japanese language and is called haku (beat). Haku has been approximated to the concept of mora, which is defined as the length of a short syllable. Tokieda (1941) stated that haku is a form of language and a syllable is the content of haku. By this, he probably meant that language has two aspects, that is, information to be conveyed and a vehicle on which the information is carried.

Theoretically speaking, syllables can be dissected into vowel and consonants. However, because the Japanese language has no alphabetical writing system, a mental unit of the Japanese language seems to be always a syllable or haku. An average Japanese speaker is not accustomed to separate a syllable into vowels and consonants. Japanese is produced and received as a sequence of syllabic sounds.

Written Language

Kana. As is well known, the Japanese writing system is characterized by the hybrid use of Kana and Kanji characters. Kana is a syllabic system and a character represents a syllable. The contemporary writing system employs 46 essential Kana characters (see Fig. 5.1). By adding signs that represent a prolongation or a pause after a certain syllable for the length of a haku, and signs representing lip sounds, all 108 syllabic sounds in standard Japanese can be transcribed into Kana code.

All pronounceable Japanese sounds can be transcribed into Kana characters. Because the correspondence between a Kana character and a syllable is very regular with only a few exceptions, writing in Kana script would pose no difficulty to average Japanese speakers once they memorize all the Kana characters and a few rules of transcription. Above all, some individual variations in transcription are tolerated as far as it can be read as acceptable Japanese.

Kana has two types of characters, namely, Hiragana and Katakana. Hiragana is used in transcribing all the grammatical words and many of the substantive words. Katakana is mainly used to transcribe imported foreign words or if a writer wants to emphasize a particular word. The ability to write both types of Kana characters is mastered by the end of the first year of primary school. Because the syllable constitutes the smallest unit of writing

	a	あ	i	い	u	う	e	え	o	お
k	ka	か	ki	き	ku	く	ke	け	ko	こ
s	sa	さ	shi	し	su	す	se	せ	so	そ
t	ta	た	chi	ち	tsu	つ	te	て	to	と
n	na	な	ni	に	nu	ぬ	ne	ね	no	の
h	ha	は	hi	ひ	fu	ふ	he	へ	ho	ほ
m	ma	ま	mi	み	mu	む	me	め	mo	も
y	ya	や	(i)	(い)	yu	ゆ	(e)	(え)	yo	よ
r	ra	ら	ri	り	ru	る	re	れ	ro	ろ
w	wa	わ	(i)	(い)	(u)	(う)	(e)	(え)	o	を
	n	ん								

FIG. 5.1. Essential Hiragana characters. Characters in parentheses indicate the
repetition of the same characters.

in transcribing the Japanese sounds, a problem of "spelling" in which alphabetical letters have to be sequenced in a specific order to represent a
particular syllabic sound in a particular word does not occur.

   Kanji. Kanji has a longer history than Kana. Japanese had known no
written symbols until Kanji was imported from China at the time of the Han
Dynasty, hence Han (= Kan) character (= Ji). Over the course of their natu-
ralization, Japanese names were associated to an original Kanji character or
a combination of characters that had a similar meaning. As a result, most
of the Kanji characters have come to have more than two sound labels. The
original sound of a Kanji is called On (= sound) reading or Chinese reading,
and the associated Japanese name Kun (= national) reading, or Japanese
reading. Thus, an extremely complicated way of handling Kanji characters

has developed. A Kanji symbol may have more than two pronunciations. In other words, heterography (same letter with many sounds) is the norm rather than the exception (see Fig. 5.2).

For instance, the Kanji I-SHI shown in Fig. 5.2 has three On readings, namely, SE-KI, KO-KU, and SYA-KU, and one Kun reading, namely, I-SHI. Which pronunciation should be selected is strictly determined by both meaning and context (see Fig. 5.3). Thus, three two-character Kanji words containing the character I-SHI shown in Fig. 5.3 are pronounced differently. An old word meaning the amount of the rice produced in a certain province should be read as KO-KU-DA-KA, whereas another one meaning magnet should be read as JI-SYA-KU. Yet another two-character word, meaning a falling stone, should be read as RA-KU-SE-KI. Finally, if it appears in a sentence as a single character, it is read as I-SHI and means stone. No other reading is permitted. These specific combinations of Kanji characters make a single word. If another reading was applied like *RA-KU-I-SHI for RA-KU-SE-KI, it would become a meaningless sound sequence. Thus, Japanese speakers not only have to memorize each Kanji character but also learn its pronunciation in specific sequences. It is highly irregular.

The number of Kanji characters in current use is huge. A small and average dictionary contains more than 5,000 Kanji characters at least. In order to lessen the burden of Kanji learning, the Japanese government tried to limit the number of Kanji characters. As of 1988, 1,005 essential Kanji characters should be learned by the end of the 6-year primary school education. Average adult readers have to process at least 1,945 Kanji characters at their command to read newspapers and magazines. The former group of Kanji characters are called Educational Kanji and the latter is called Everyday Kanji by the Ministry of Education, Culture, and Science.

An example of a Kanji

On-reading: se-ki; ko-ku; sya-ku

Kun-reading: i-shi

FIG. 5.2. Example of a Kanji character: stone.

Examples of two-Kanji words

石高   **KO-KU-DA-KA**

磁石   **JI-SYA-KU**

落石   **RA-KU-SE-KI**

FIG. 5.3. Examples of two-character Kanji words. Note the same characters are pronounced differently.

Kanji has sometimes been cited as a typical example of ideograms. Although a Kanji character does represent meaning most of the time, it does not necessarily mean you can have a meaning at a glance. Sometimes it represents more than one meaning, and the various meanings can be very different. For instance, the Kanji I-SHI means stone most of the time. But sometimes it has quite a different meaning, like a unit of rice. Thus, when the Kanji character I-SHI is combined with the Kanji character TA-KA meaning amount, it means the amount of rice produced in a particular province and should be read as KO-KU-DA-KA (see Fig. 5.3). So the Japanese Kanji is not an ideograph in the strictest sense of the meaning; it should be regarded as a type of logogram, which is defined as a grapheme representing a word or a morpheme, rather than a concrete meaning (Sampson, 1985).

Because Japanese is composed of such a small number of sounds as mentioned earlier, it is no wonder that there exist many homophones. If you want to type the Kanji stone with a Japanese word processor, first you have to type I-SHI in Kana. You may wonder why in Kana? Why can't you type I-SHI just in Kanji? The reason: The number of keys on a keyboard is limited. Even for Kana you have to have at least 45 keys. If you want to accommodate a keyboard with all the keys for the Kanji characters you must have more than 2,000 keys at the least! So, you type I and SHI in Kana. The word processor then searches all the possible words it has in memory for I-SHI. My present word processor, for example, displayed a list of Kanji words, which included physician, intention, one's dying wishes, and stone, all in different Kanji script (see Fig. 5.4). Finally you choose from this list the correct target for the Kanji "stone" for your text. This type of wild array of homophonic heterographs has

Examples of homophones "I-SHI"

医師   physician

意志   intention

遺志   wish of a deceased

石   stone

FIG. 5.4. Examples of Japanese two-syllable words: I-SHI in Kanji script.

no equivalent in the alphabetical script system. You may think this happens in English. For instance, the word "act" could mean an action, a part of a play, or a legal deed. Its meaning, however, is related and comes from a common origin. On the other hand, I-SHI with the meaning of physician and I-SHI with the meaning of intention have nothing in common in their meanings, and are expressed in completely different Kanji symbols. The use of the Kanji code is the only way to avoid confusion.

SYMPTOMATIC PECULIARITIES OF JAPANESE APHASICS

Severe Broca's Aphasia and Preservation of Haku Rhythm

When you speak, you produce not only a sequence of syllables but also a specific prosody that is a vehicle for sounds. As mentioned at the beginning of this chapter, the Japanese language has a specific rhythm characterized by an equitemporal beat, namely, haku. This rhythmic characteristic of Japanese has long been recognized by the Japanese themselves and is symbolically crystallized in many poetic forms or in theatrical conversations in dramas. For instance, Haiku, a type of poem known worldwide for its shortness, has a strict rhythmic form made up with 5-7-5 beats. Every expression should be molded into this short and rigid form. The TA-N-KA, meaning short poem, which has a longer history than Haiku, is believed to have originated in the 7th century and is still popular; the form is made up with 5-7-5-7-7 haku.

We encountered two patients with severe aphasia who showed preserved rhythm of haku (Sugiura, Yoneda, Yoshida, & Yamadori, 1992). Case K.I. was a 71-year-old right-handed male, a university graduate. He was found unconscious in his room on 31 May 1989. On admission to an emergency hospital a left putaminal hemorrhage was found and the hematoma was surgically removed on day 3 postonset.

On tranfer to our Neurology Service of Hyogo Brain and Heart Center 2 months later, he was alert but severely aphasic. His spontaneous speech was extremely limited. Several distorted syllables were produced with effort. These syllables were produced one by one in an explosive way, or they were produced with two rather long beats followed by a shorter beat. When this 2-1 beat pattern was produced, the amount of sounds increased. Repetition was impossible. However, haku number was correctly repeated up to 12 beats. Thus a sentence was repeated with a 2-1 rhythm using neologistic jargon. Naming was also impaired. For each stimulus a neologism was produced. In these neologisms, a haku rhythm of 3 to 6 beats was clearly discernible. Comprehension was limited to a few commands involving whole-body movement. Writing and reading were also severely impaired.

A sample of his spontaneous speech recorded on a sound spectrogram is shown in Fig. 5.5. The sound was produced as an answer to a question asking the name of his resident town. It was jargon but syllables were produced with an approximately same interval, suggesting the preservation of haku rhythm.

This case demonstrated that haku production ability can be preserved even when the sounds become unintelligible. There seems to be a stage in which the native rhythm of language is independently produced. This vehicle of rhythmic pattern, so to speak, is used for carrying linguistic contents. Thus, an appropriately placed lesion in the brain may produce a dissociation of form, that is, haku rhythm in this particular instance, and content, that is, a sequence of meaningful syllables.

In my experience, in contrast to this type of neologisms, which preserves a distinctly clear haku rhythm, the neologisms often observed in subcortical aphasia, characterized by a combination of dysarthria and jargon-like output (mumbling, according to some authors), often lose their intrinsic rhythm. Thus, the syllables produced are not separated by equitemporal intervals but are condensed into a continuous production of sounds.

Broca's Aphasia and Kanji Writing

In Broca's aphasia, one sometimes encounters a patient who has extreme difficulty in producing Kana characters, yet can produce Kanji characters easily. This surprising characteristic in Japanese Broca's aphasia was first

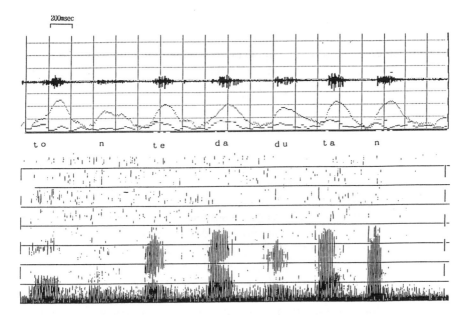

200msec

t o   n   t e   d a   d u   t a   n

FIG. 5.5. Sound spectrographic recording of a sample of a patient's verbal output. These sounds were produced in response to the question: "In what city do you live?" Note the regularity of the duration of syllables and the interval in-between syllables. From Sugiura et al. (1992). Reprinted with permission.

reported by Yamamoto in 1911 and to the medical world outside Japan by Asayama in 1914. The following is a summary from the original Japanese paper published 2 years before the 1914 paper (Asayama, 1912).

In March 1911, a 33-year-old merchant developed a disturbance of consciousness and right hemiplegia. He was mute but could express his basic physiological needs by gesture. By the end of May, he became quite alert but still lacked spontaneous speech. In October, he was examined by Dr. Asayama.

Neurologically, there was a mild right hemiparesis sparing the face. There was also a mild hemisensory deficit on the right side of the body. No Babinski signs were present.

Spontaneous speech was severely impaired. He could only state his name and produce some fragmented words. Repetition was severely impaired. Oral comprehension was fair for simple commands but difficult for complex ones. Naming of objects was severely impaired, but he could identify the objects by nonverbal means.

In oral reading, he could read more than half of the Kana characters slowly but could not read Kanji characters. In writing, he had a clear difficulty in the Kana code. When he was asked to write the I-RO-HA song, which is a song composed of 46 essential Kana characters for primary school students to facilitate their learning of Kana, he produced only a few characters of the first portion. No other Kana characters were produced. In striking contrast, he could produce many Kanji characters. He could write the date correctly in Kanji. He could correctly write the name of his doctor and the commercial school where he graduated from. He also could write a receipt form quite well.

In written comprehension, a dissociation between Kanji and Kana was again observed. For instance, he could not understand the sentence "What is your age?" when all the words were written in Kana characters, but could immediately respond with a correct answer of "33 years" in Kanji when the question was presented in a Kanji–Kana sentence. Even when he could read a Kana sentence one word at a time correctly, he never grasped the meaning. But when presented with a Kanji–Kana sentence, even though he could not read Kanji characters aloud, he grasped the meaning easily. Copying of characters was normal both for Kanji and Kana characters.

In order to read and write phonological characters, Asayama argued, a close coordination between the sensory language center (Wernicke area) and motor language center is required. According to Wernicke, this coordination forms an inseparable functional unit, that is, the word concept or Wortbegriff. Kana requires a syllable–grapheme association process, so words written in Kana code may be explained with this concept. Kanji, however, is qualitatively different from Kana. According to Asayama, Kanji depends more on the function of the visual center and could be spared in case of damage to Broca's area or Wernicke's area.

Kanji preservation in some cases of Broca's aphasia has since been established as a very important feature of Japanese aphasics (Imura, Nogami, & Asakawa, 1971; Sasanuma, 1975; Sasanuma & Fujimura, 1971, 1972). In my personal file, I have a couple of cases with this pattern of writing impairment (Yamadori, 1980).

A 57-year-old right-handed housewife developed severe Broca's aphasia with a right hemiplegia following an ischemic stroke of the left middle cerebral artery in 1978. In spontaneous speech she only produced a stereotypic word "HI-DE-KO" (a name) and sound of "yeah." Her comprehension was also disturbed. Pointing to objects was inconsistent. However, with a pencil in the left hand, she responded to a question about the date of the onset of her disease correctly in Kanji. When asked about her family she wrote a Kanji character CHI-CHI (father), then wrote his age. In Japan, it is a custom to call a husband "father" and a wife "mother" as a child would do. Next, she wrote her own name, then wrote a two-Kanji-character word meaning "myself" (JI-BU-N), and her age, which were all correct. However, she could not produce any Kana characters even with repeated instructions.

This phenomenon would often be seen in severe cases of Broca-type aphasia, but the distinction might blur as the patient's writing ability recovers.

It is by no means a constant feature of Broca's aphasia, but when encountered it would amaze an examiner. Imagine a patient who during a bedside observation not only seemed to be mute but also not to comprehend precisely what was said, and seemed to have regressed into communicative isolation, and who would start responding correctly in Kanji code when provided with a pencil! Without the Kanji code the patient may be categorized as globally aphasic or even severely demented.

It is absurd to postulate a linguistic code system that is totally independent of phonological influence, but it has to be emphasized that, at least in part, the Kanji code can operate without an exact phonological support. Because Kanji is a code in which a single character represents a morpheme, a strategy to evoke this grapheme may be quite different from the one to evoke a Kana grapheme, which has a regular association with the phonological system. This phenomenon is remotely similar to phonological agraphia (Shallice, 1981).

Apraxia of Speech (Pure Anarthria)

In 1934, Kiyoshi Kimura, a neuropsychiatrist, reported an interesting phenomenon, the parallel improvement of articulatory and Kana writing capacity (K. Kimura, 1934). A 35-year-old female suddenly became aphasic and unable to communicate. There was no weakness. She could walk. For several days she remained unable to formulate any meaningful syllables and tried many gestures to communicate, but to no avail. She happened to try to communicate by writing, and found she could still write Kanji well but could not write Kana anymore. A family member reported she wrote words like grandmother, telegram, Tokyo, husband, child, and so on in Kanji in normal calligraphy, but could not write them in Kana. When some Kana characters were produced, most of them were so distorted that they could not be identified. Even when correct characters were produced, they became a jargon. Over the next week, her articulatory ability recovered. Recovery of Kana writing was observed at the same time.

When Dr. K. Kimura saw the patient at 3 months postonset, her spontaneous speech still showed hesitation, dysprosody, and occasional syllabic paraphasias. Word finding was impaired with circumlocutions. Comprehension of spoken language was good. Oral reading was slow but normal. Writing on dictation as well as copying of characters was normal. Head's aphasia battery was performed and was normal. The results showed that she was normal both in symbolic formulation and expression of language. Thus, at this time, it seems that she showed a syndrome of pure anarthria (Lecours & Lhermitte, 1976; or in another terminology, apraxia of speech) and mild anomia.

In this case, articulatory difficulty and Kana agraphia showed a nonparallel amelioration. I have been using this feature as a diagnostic key to clinically differentiate mild Broca's aphasia from pure anarthria. When a patient presents with a rather typical symptom cluster consistent with pure anarthria, the co-occurrence of Kana agraphia would indicate that the disturbance extends beyond the domain of articulatory encoding (Mori, Yamadori, & Furumoto, 1989).

Conduction Aphasia

In 1975, Yamadori and Ikumura reported a case of conduction aphasia. The case was a 66-year-old right-handed widow who had suffered from a ruptured aneurysm at the bifurcation of the left middle cerebral artery. She presented with a relatively pure syndrome of conduction aphasia. She spoke fluently and comprehension was fair. But her spontaneous speech, naming, and repetition were filled with syllabic paraphasias.

When she was asked to repeat, her difficulty increased as the number of syllables in the task increased. In naming objects, the same difficulty with increasing syllabic length was observed. We wondered whether the same phenomenon might be seen in oral reading of Kanji characters, because Kanji includes multiple syllables. Therefore, we prepared 5 sets of 10 Kanji characters. The first 10 Kanji group had one syllable. The second had two, the third three, and the fourth four syllables, respectively. It was difficult to collect Kanji characters with five syllables in a character. All the Kanji words were comprehended well, just like materials in naming and repetition. As shown in Fig. 5.6, her performance of oral reading deteriorated as the number of syllables in a character increased. In contrast to this difficulty, she clearly showed better performance of oral reading if the same name used in single Kanji reading was presented in Kana script as is also shown in Fig. 5.6.

In reading multisyllabic Kanji characters, the patient has to produce a correct syllabic sequence mentally before it is actually articulated, just like in a naming or a repetition task. This process of mental representation of auditory word image seems to have been impaired in this patient. In Kana, what the patient had to do was to read the series of Kana characters one by one, making the task much easier.

The reverse of the performance pattern was observed in the same patient in writing. When she was asked to write a certain word in Kanji, her performance was fairly good up to the level of three-syllable words. However, when she was asked to write the same name in Kana script, her performance was much worse. For instance, when she was asked to write WA-TA-SHI (me) in Kanji, she wrote down a correct Kanji character, but when she had to write it down in Kana, she only wrote WA-SHI. In the former task the three-syllable word is represented in a single Kanji character, whereas in the latter task three Kana characters are required. When she was asked to write KU-RU-MA (car), she wrote it correctly in Kanji, which requires a single character, but failed in Kana, which requires three characters. She wrote

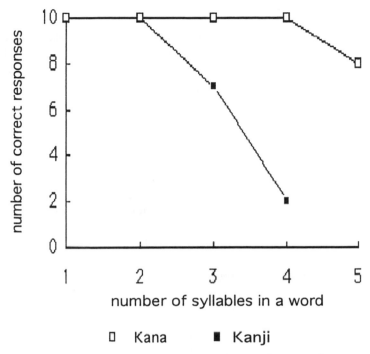

FIG. 5.6. Dissociation pattern of oral reading of Kanji and Kana words in terms of syllabic numbers involved. From Yamadori et al. (1975). Reprinted with permission.

KU-MA-I for KU-RU-MA. Thus, it was clear that when given a noun for dictation, she not only grasped the sound correctly but also grasped the meaning correctly. She could write the name in Kanji because it required no exact sound sequencing, but she failed in transcribing it into Kana because it required an exact sequencing of the syllables involved.

This is another example where a different culture with a different writing system can contribute to elucidate the pathophysiological mechanism of an aphasic syndrome. By utilizing a unique characteristic of the Japanese written system we could confirm that there exists a subtype of conduction aphasia characterized by a clear difficulty in sequencing the group of syllabic sound images into a correct word. This sequencing difficulty is manifested as a dissociation between oral reading of Kanji and Kana words and between Kana and Kanji word writing.

The existence of this specific type of reading and writing dissociation in conduction aphasia has since been confirmed (Sasanuma, 1986; Yamadori, 1979; Yamadori, Yoshida, & Sugiura, 1992). The lesion converges to the supramarginal gyral area of the dominant hemisphere, confirming European studies (Damasio & Damasio, 1983).

Word Meaning Aphasia or Go-gi Aphasia

In 1943, Imura reported a type of transcortical sensory aphasia characterized by a set of dissociations in Kanji and Kana processing (Imura, 1943; Imura, Nogami, & Asakawa, 1971; Sasanuma & Monoi, 1975). A typical patient is able to repeat an auditorily presented word quite normally but cannot comprehend its meaning or match the orally presented word with the corresponding object. This loss of word meaning constitutes the core symptom (Ito et al., 1990; Matsubara, 1987; Tanabe et al., 1992). When such a patient is asked to read a two-character Kanji word, he or she would read it incorrectly. Most importantly, reading of each Kanji character may be correct but in a word it is not. This means that the patient recognizes each Kanji characters and knows their pronunciation but cannot recognize a combination of Kanji characters as a meaningful word. On the other hand, oral reading of words written in Kana script is correct. Comprehension of the word, however, is not possible. Writing to dictation in Kana is usually better than Kanji. In Kanji dictation, each character produced may be phonetically correct, but the final combination of characters does not form the correct target word.

The syndrome was named Go-gi (word-meaning) aphasia by Imura. The lesion was not clearly identified but was thought to involve the posterior part of the middle and inferior temporal lobe of the dominant left hemisphere. In Japan, this symptom complex has been recognized as a pathognomonic feature of Pick's disease of the temporal lobe type at its early stage (Kurachi & Matsubara, 1991; Matsubara, 1987; Matsubara, Enokido, Torii, Hiraguchi, & Ainoda, 1984; Tanabe et al., 1992). In these degenerative cases, the lesion responsible for the loss of word meaning as an atrophy of the left temporal lobe from its anterior to middle portion. This type of Go-gi aphasia, which would be typically seen in the course of the temporal type of Pick's disease, has to be distinguished from so-called "slowly progressive aphasia" (Mesulam, 1982), in which it has been argued that aphasia stands out as the only cognitive disorder for a long time and whose pathological characteristic is said not to conform with Pick's or Alzheimer's disease. Following is an illustrative case.

The patient was a 54-year-old right-handed housewife. For the previous 5 years, her family noted a progressive difficulty in recalling words. On one occasion a family member cautioned her that a pot had been boiling over. She responded to the warning: "What do you mean by pot?"

On admission, no physical neurological signs were observed. Her spontaneous speech was effortless and fluent, but was contaminated with verbal paraphasias and often incomprehensible. Oral comprehension was severely disturbed. Her comprehension difficulty was marked by frequent questions about the word the examiner had used. Thus she responded to the author's question: "Do you have a difficulty with words?" by the question: "What are words?" To a command to write down her name, she said "What is name?

How do you write name?" As is clear from these examples her repetition capacity of verbal materials was quite good. Naming was severely disturbed on confrontation naming as well as on category naming.

Detailed examination of her written language showed a complex dissociation between Kana and Kanji tasks. She was good at oral reading (90% correct) and pointing (80% correct) to single Kana characters. Her Kana word reading was fair (60% correct). But she was unable to read aloud any of the single Kanji characters presented. Comprehension was null both for the Kana words and the Kanji words tested. On dictation, she was able to write single Kana characters (80% correct) and Kana words (80% correct). However, she was unable to write any Kanji characters or Kanji words on dictation. This dissociation of Kanji and Kana reading ability was so remarkable that we designed a specific test to further elucidate her basic difficulties.

Oral reading of single characters was tested for 10 Kanji, 10 Hiragana, and 10 Katakana characters. Oral reading and comprehension of meaningful words were tested for 20 Kanji, 20 Hiragana, and 20 Katakana words. Of these 20 words for each type of script, 10 were selected from a low-frequency word list and the other 10 from a high-frequency word list. Further, each 10-word set was designed to contain five sets of 2 words from five categories: kitchen utensils, stationery, animals, vegetables, and plants. Comprehension of the words was tested by having the patient select the appropriate target from six drawings belonging to the same category. Oral reading ability of nonwords was also tested for 10 Kanji, 10 Hiragana, and 10 Katakana nonwords.

The results of the tests are displayed in Fig. 5.7. Oral reading of single characters was good for Katakana (9/10), followed by Hiragana (6/10). No

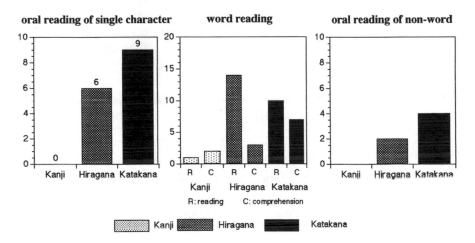

FIG. 5.7. Reading test results from a patient with Go-gi aphasia. Note the extreme difficulty in Kanji reading and the superior performance of oral reading over comprehension.

Kanji character was read correctly (0/10). Oral reading of words was fair for Hiragana (14/20), poor for Katakana (10/20), and worst in Kanji (1/20). Comprehension of words was slightly preserved for Katakana (7/20), but severely impaired for Hiragana (3/20) and Kanji (1/20). Oral reading of nonwords was worse than word reading, that is, Katakana (4/10), Hiragana (2/10), and Kanji (0/10).

An analysis of errors showed no difference between low- and high-frequency words and among the five categories. As for errors in reading Kanji, almost all responses were of the no-response type and no paralexic response was noted. Of 18 incorrect responses out of the 40 stimuli in Hiragana, no verbal paraphasias were found. All the errors were literal paraphasias. There were 102 characters in these 18 stimulus words. Only 17 characters were read incorrectly. Of the 17 errors, 12 were classified as visual errors and the remaining 5 as phonetic. Of 17 incorrect responses out of 40 stimulus words in Katakana, there was no no-response type error. There were 110 characters in these 17 words. Eighteen of these characters were read incorrectly. Eleven of the 18 characters were mistaken for visually similar ones. The remaining 7 errors were judged to be phonetic. Through the whole test, no semantic paraphasic errors were noted. An example of reading error of a Kanji word is shown in Fig. 5.8 and of a Kana word in Fig. 5.9.

The essential feature of word-meaning aphasia is the loss of the meanings of words. This loss of word meaning was typically reflected in severe impairment of Kanji processing. Kanji reading was totally lost, because this code cannot be processed without support from the word-meaning system. Kana word comprehension was also severely impaired. However, oral reading of Kana words was fairly well preserved because its processing does not require support from meaning in the initial stage. Thus, this can be called a Japanese version of surface dyslexia (Sasanuma, 1985). Kana, a

target word: 大豆 (soybean)

reading of each Kanji: 大 da-i or o-o (big)
　　　　　　　　　　　　豆 zu or ma-me (bean)

correct reading: da-i-zu (soybean)

patient's reading: o-o-ma-me (jargon)
　　　　　　　　　　　大 o-o; 豆 ma-me

FIG. 5.8. Example of a Kanji word reading error: soybean.

target word: えんぴつ (pencil)

reading of each Kana: え e; ん n; ぴ pi; つ tsu

correct reading: e-n-pi-tsu (pencil)

patient's reading: へhe-ん n-び bi-つ tsu (jargon)

nature of error: visual   び bi for ぴ pi
　　　　　　　　phonetic   へ he for え e

FIG. 5.9. Example of a Hiragana word reading error: pencil.

written code that has a very regular grapheme–syllable conversion rule, can be read aloud without comprehension, whereas Kanji, which is completely irregular in its grapheme–morpheme conversion rule, cannot be read without support from meaning.

A difficult problem remains. There was a complicated difference between Hiragana and Katakana reading in this case. The patient was better at oral reading of single characters and nonwords in Katakana, whereas she read words better in Hiragana. On the other hand, her comprehension of words was better in Katakana than Hiragana. The data are too small to comment on this matter.

A magnetic resonance imaging (MRI) study of the brain showed bilateral temporal lobe atrophy that was more prominent on the left (see Fig. 5.10). Based on the pattern of atrophy and the clinical course of the disease, Pick's disease is the most likely etiology. Clinically, it is identical with the semantic dementia beautifully summarized by recent English studies (Snowden, Goulding, & Neary, 1989; Hodges, Patterson, Oxbury, & Funnel, 1992).

Alexia With Agraphia

Alexia With Agraphia and the Left Angular Gyrus. Alexia with agraphia as an independent symptom complex has been known since the days of Dejerine (1891). The lesion usually involves the left angular gyrus. Here again, the Kanji–Kana impairment presents a very interesting pattern.

In a typical case, the reading difficulty is more severely impaired in Kana than in Kanji, as first observed by Kotani (1935). Patients would have difficulties reading even a single Kana character. Many "literal" paralexias would

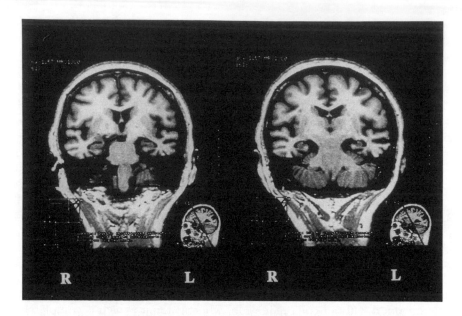

FIG. 5.10.   MRI study of the brain of a patient with Go-gi aphasia. Two oblique coronal sections of T1-weighted images showed bilateral temporal-lobe atrophy that was more prominent on the left. The images are consistent with Pick's disease.

be observed. Kana word reading would also be severely impaired. No word-level comprehension in Kana is possible, whereas in Kanji the reading performance would be much better. A two- or three-character Kanji word might be read correctly or replaced by a semantically related paraphasia, betraying that the meaning represented by the word was processed up to a certain degree (Yamadori, 1975, 1982). One of my patients, for instance, was able to understand the meaning of a three-character Kanji word NI-HO-N-SYU (Japanese sake) at a glance, but could not read or comprehend the Kana word NI-HO-N-SYU at all.

It has been proposed that the emergence of the angular gyrus area is a basis for the emergence of language in the human being, because association among different sensory modalities became possible in this "association area of association areas" (Geschwind, 1965). If the hypothesis is valid, damage to this area would pose a great difficulty in auditory–visual association. Grapheme–syllable conversion, that is, Kana reading, must be one of the typical visual–auditory association activities. In reading Kanji, this area may not be essential, because the activity involves more than simple visual–auditory association. The pattern of dissociation is the opposite of the word-meaning aphasia, and could be compared to the deep dyslexia reported in the European literature.

Alexia With Agraphia and the Left Inferior Posterior Temporal Gyrus. The most interesting and intriguing problem for Japanese aphasiology has surfaced through the analysis of the alexia with agraphia syndrome. Iwata reported in 1984 a case of alexia with agraphia with an unusual Kanji–Kana dissociation. Unlike the well-accepted cases, his patient showed a difficulty in reading Kanji whereas Kana was read perfectly well. In writing also the patient showed difficulty in Kanji but his Kana writing ability was spared. Semantic comprehension was said to be disturbed. According to Iwata, the lesion was situated in the left inferior posterior temporal region (Iwata, 1984, 1985).

The present author encountered the same type of patient around the same period. In 1984, I read a paper in a symposium in Hong Kong reporting two cases who showed a selective reading and writing difficulty in Kanji (Yamadori, Motomura, Endo, & Mitani, 1985; Yamadori, 1986). Both patients had a lesion in the posterior portion of the left middle and inferior temporal gyri. Reports of similar cases followed (see review of the literature in Soma, Sugishita, Kitamura, Maruyama, & Imanaga, 1989). It now seems to be firmly established that a lesion in the posterior portion of the left middle and inferior temporal gyri plays an important role in Kanji processing.

For example, a 64-year-old right-handed housewife suffered from an embolic infarction of the inferior branch of the right middle cerebral artery. Neurologically she was normal, including the visual fields. No apraxia or visual agnosia was noted. Her spontaneous speech was fluent with a few paraphasias. Repetition was normal. Comprehension was good at the conversational level. The Token Test was 75% correct. Copying of characters was normal. Naming was poor (0/25), but pointing ability was better preserved (13/25). The most interesting finding in this patient was in reading tasks. Oral reading of single Kanji characters was tested for the 221 characters used at the first and second grade of primary school. Oral reading of single Kana characters was tested for 45 Hiragana characters. Also, word reading was tested for four categories, that is, 30 concrete nouns, 30 abstract nouns, 20 verbs, and 20 adjectives, which were tested both in Kanji and Kana. Comprehension was tested by having the patient select an appropriate picture from four pictures to a written stimulus word. Fifty words were used for Kanji and Kana, respectively.

In Kana character reading, 39 characters out of 45 were read correctly (87%), whereas in Kanji character reading, only 27 characters out of 221 were read correctly (12%). In the Kana task, four of the six errors belonged to the visual type. In the Kanji task, 87% of the errors belonged to the no-response type. The patient responded for a presented Kanji character by saying either that she didn't know or that she had no idea. Paralexic errors constituted only 5% of all the errors. The other errors included partial reading of a stimulus Kanji character. In Kana word reading, she read 89% of the

100 stimuli correctly. In Kanji word reading, on the other hand, she succeeded in only 15 words, which all belonged to the category of adjectives (15%). Not a single word in the other three categories was read correctly. In the comprehension task she was 62% correct for Kanji words and 90% correct for Kana words. When these 50 words were presented auditorily she comprehended the meaning 98% correctly.

In writing, single Kana characters were 78% correct whereas Kanji characters were 40% correct. With words, Kana words were 80% correct, whereas no two-character Kanji words were correctly written.

An MRI study of the brain revealed a rather large lesion in the posterior portion of the left middle and inferior temporal gyri (see Fig. 5.11).

The syndrome is consistent with other reported cases affecting this part of the brain. The patient had rather good comprehension for words written in Kana and almost perfect comprehension for the auditorily presented words, but the same words could not be processed if they were expressed in Kanji code. Writing showed the same pattern.

Iwata proposed that the processing of Kanji involves a different neural pathway than Kana processing. According to this hypothesis, the angular gyrus is important for syllable–grapheme conversion but is not indispensable for ideographic character processing. The latter processing is realized through the left inferior posterior temporal structure.

It has been well established that in the primate brain the inferior temporal cortex is critical in shape identification (Kandel, 1991; Miyashita, 1993). This had not been clear in humans, however. Recently, Howard et al. (1992) demonstrated an increase in blood flow in the posterior part of the left middle temporal gyrus when subjects were reading a stimulus word containing a nonexistent letter. Howard et al. argued that a lexicon for written

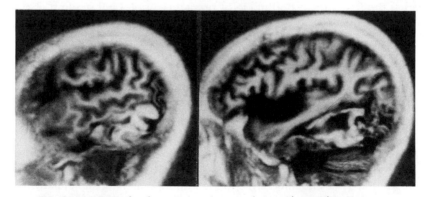

FIG. 5.11. MRI study of a patient with Kanji alexia with agraphia. Two consecutive sagittal views of the left hemisphere are shown in T1-weighted images. Hemorrhagic high signal area is seen in the posterior portion of the left middle and inferior temporal gyri.

word recognition should be localized in this region. On the other hand, a positron emission tomography (PET) study of Kanji reading confirmed an increase of blood flow in the left posterior inferior temporal area (Sakurai et al., 1992). These basic data are consistent with the Japanese clinical cases of the Kanji-type alexia with agraphia.

Callosal Disconnection Agraphia

When the corpus callosum is lesioned, the left hand may become agraphic. It had been assumed that this agraphia was a partial symptom of the left-sided ideomotor apraxia, which was caused by a disconnection of the dominant left hemispheric sensorimotor engram from the right hemisphere (Liepmann & Maas, 1907). Geschwind and Kaplan (1962), however, through a shrewd analysis of one patient, demonstrated that left-sided agraphia was a manifestation of a disconnection of the left-hemisphere language zone from the right hemisphere. Their argument was based on the fact that the left hand of their patient was not only unable to write but also unable to arrange anagrams into meaningful words.

We presented further evidence that the left agraphia is not necessarily caused by an apractic mechanism (Yamadori, Osumi, Ikeda, & Kanazawa, 1980). This patient, whose corpus callosum was damaged by occlusion of the left anterior cerebral artery, presented a left agraphia and a left tactile anomia without any apractic signs. The agraphia was characterized by the production of many illegible characters and some graphically correct characters on dictation. Graphically correct characters contained perseverations, missequencing of characters, and paragraphic errors. Copying of characters and words was not disturbed. The most interesting feature was that the left hand was definitely better in producing Kanji characters than Kana characters. This was amazing because Kanji is more complicated in its shape than Kana, and is less automatized in its motor output. As described in an earlier section, this type of dissociation has been known as one of the characteristic features of some types of Broca's aphasia (Imura et al., 1971; Paradis, Hagiwara, & Hildebrandt, 1985; Yamamoto, 1911). Thus, we concluded that at least in some cases the left-sided agraphia could be independent from apraxia and be a result of a disconnection of the right hemisphere from the left language hemisphere.

Similar case reports of this Kanji–Kana dissociation in left-sided callosal agraphia started to appear around the same time (Sugishita, Toyokura, Yoshioka, & Yamada, 1980; Yamadori, Nagashima, & Tamaki, 1983).

A reverse pattern of Kanji–Kana dissociation was also reported in left callosal agraphia without accompanying apraxia. Thus, Kawamura's case showed writing difficulties with Kanji characters but not with Kana characters (Kawamura, Hirayama, & Yamamoto, 1989). This patient could copy the

Kanji characters that he could not write accurately on dictation. These dou-
ble-dissociation cases strongly support the argument that left agraphia is
caused by a linguistic dysfunction and not by a praxic disorder.

Pure Agraphia of Kana Words

This type of disturbance is rare but does occur (Abe, Yokoyama, Yorifuji,
& Yanagihara, 1993; Fukui, Kuzuhara, Toyokura, & Sugishita, 1986; B.
Kimura, Matsuda, Kuroiwa, & Tohgi, 1986; Kojima, Uno, & Kato, 1991; Sato
et al., 1983; Tanaka, Yamadori, & Murata, 1987; Tsuduki & Indo, 1986). In
all reports where the Kanji–Kana dissociation was clear, the capacity to
produce the graphemes themselves was retained in either code. Patients
were able to copy characters as well. No dissociation of writing ability with
the hand used was observed.

As an illustration, Tanaka et al. (1987) described a 52-year-old right-
handed businessman who suddenly developed dysarthria, drooling from the
right corner of the mouth, and weakness of the right side of the body.

A neuropsychological profile, performed after the patient's condition had
stabilized, showed a slight recent memory deficit, a slight comprehension
deficit (78% on the Token Test), and mild anomia. Spontaneous speech was
fluent without paraphasias, and repetition was normal. Reading comprehension was impaired for complex sentences. Oral reading was 90% correct.
No difference between Kanji and Kana was observed. On the contrary, his
writing was disproportionally impaired for Kanji and Kana.

The analysis of the error pattern of writing showed two interesting facts
(Fig. 5.12): (1) the error was more prominent with Kana words than Kanji
words, and (2) the difficulty in Kana word writing increased with the increase
of the number of Kana characters necessary for a word. The results suggested
that the deficit was most likely at the locus where an acoustic image of a
word is transformed into a Kana grapheme sequence. The difference between Kana and Kanji performance might be due to the difference in the
number of graphemes involved. As a rule, the number of graphemes necessary for a word is less in Kanji than in Kana. For instance the word *mother*
is written in two Kanji characters, that is, HA-HA (mother) and O-YA (parent),
but requires four Kana characters, that is, HA-HA-O-YA. He could write
HA-HA and O-YA in Kanji correctly but wrote HA-HA-GO-YA in Kana,
which is a neologism (Fig. 5.13).

Also, writing a Kanji word requires less support from the acoustic system
than writing Kana. In Kanji writing, HA-HA-O-YA is expressed as a combination of two morphemes, that is, *mother* and *parent*. The two graphemes
could be recalled if the meaning of *mother* was clear to the patient. In Kana,
all four graphemes corresponding to each syllable Ha, Ha, O, Ya, should
be recalled and be put into a correct sequence. If the total capacity of this

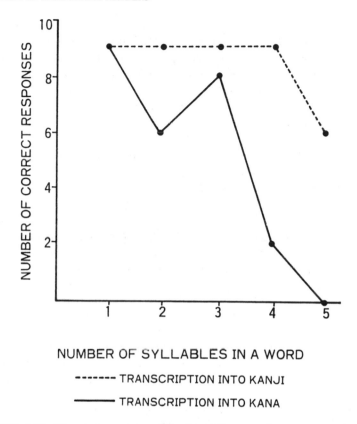

NUMBER OF SYLLABLES IN A WORD

------- TRANSCRIPTION INTO KANJI

———— TRANSCRIPTION INTO KANA

FIG. 5.12. Dissociation pattern of Kanji and Kana word writing. Note the deterioration of Kana writing as the number of necessary Kana characters increased. From Tanaka et al. (1987). Reprinted with permission.

acoustico-graphemic interface was decreased to a point where processing of no more than two or three graphemes at a time was possible, the patient's error pattern could be explained.

Another possibility is that Kanji and Kana writing systems employ closely related but different anatomical systems. In the face of a double dissociation between Kanji and Kana writing reported in the callosal left agraphia, this possibility cannot be ruled out.

This type of agraphia resembles phonological agraphia reported in the European literature (Shallice, 1981). In this type of agraphia, the ability to write words is said to be preserved but the ability to write nonsense syllables or nonsense words is severely disturbed. Kanji words may be approximated with alphabetic words and Kana words with alphabetic nonsense words. But in phonological agraphia, the letters used in writing words and nonsense words are the same, whereas in the Japanese writing system, Kanji and Kana belong to different classes of graphemes. Also, there exists no "spelling"

Example of Kana writing error for mother: HA-HA-O-YA

Kanji target: 母親 (HA-HA-O-YA)
response: 母親

Hiragana target:ははおや(HA-HA-O-YA)
response: はは ご や(HA-HA-*GO*-YA)

FIG. 5.13. Example of writing of a patient with pure Kana agraphia. Kanji was correctly written. Kana became jargon.

operation in Japanese writing because a Kana character represents a syllabic unit, as described previously. Thus, facile comparison should be avoided.

COMMENT

Language is organized in the brain and utilizes the extremely complex neural networks to realize its purpose, that is, communication between people. The way this function of communication is realized in the brain must be the same across people speaking different languages. However, the subtle but distinctive difference of the linguistic units and rules among different languages must make it unavoidable to employ different strategies in mobilizing neural modules to realize this common purpose of linguistic activity. I believe that these strategic differences exist at all linguistic levels, that is, phonetics, phonology, lexicon, syntax, pragmatics, and paralinguistic aspects like prosody, however subtle they may be.

In the phonological system, for instance, the number of speech sounds and the nature of sounds detectable to a hearer-speaker are clearly different between the linguistic cultures. For instance, many linguists are familiar with the fact that Japanese speakers are unable to differentiate between the /r/ sound and the /l/ sound. The Japanese language has a single sound that is neither /r/ nor /l/, but somewhere in between. These cultural differences can already be detected by the sixth month after birth (Kuhl, Williams, Lacerda, Stevens, & Lindblom, 1992).

Prosody is another variable that differs between languages. English is said to be a stress language and has a unique stress pattern. Japanese is monotonous and has no such stress pattern, but does have a unique rhythmic structure, which is haku. Chinese has a four-tone system for each syllabic sound, which is so complicated for foreigners to master. These differences may require a different mode of operation for utilizing the anatomical structures engaging in the prosodic realization in general (see chapter 4, Aphasia in Tone Language, this volume). The case that showed preservation of haku rhythm in spite of the severe breakdown of the speech output can be quoted as evidence that the implementation of the haku rule may be realized through a closely related yet separate neural substrate of the articulation of syllables.

Syntax, which I skipped in the text, is another domain in need of cross-cultural aphasic studies. Although concrete data are still to come, it is the general impression of Japanese aphasiologists that agrammatism in most of the Japanese Broca's aphasias is very difficult to confirm. In other words, it is difficult to determine whether a particular sentence is agrammatic or not (Yamadori, 1985). At least, it may be said that agrammatism is not a typical characteristic of the speech of Japanese Broca's aphasia (Sasanuma, 1986). My personal unconfirmed explanation for this fact is that the syntactic rules governing the Japanese are probably much less strict than for most of the European languages.

Writing also differs between the linguistic cultures. The dissociated impairment of the Kanji–Kana codes gives us a clue for understanding the level of processing that is impaired in a given patient. When Kanji is more impaired than Kana, it may help us to speculate that the dysfunction involves the lexical–semantic system. This semantic disturbance may be diffuse or confined. If the semantic system for words is impaired, Kanji processing is disturbed along with the lexical system in general, as is the case in Go-gi aphasia. The impairment can also be limited to the Kanji processing system, as is the case in Kanji alexia with agraphia. When Kana is more impaired than Kanji, it points to the possibility that a system related to phonological processing is affected, as in the case of Kana alexia with agraphia or Broca's aphasia.

Another important implication is that written language systems can be organized into different neurological networks according to the kind of symbols employed. The double dissociation observed in Kanji–Kana impairment in cases of alexia with agraphia and left unilateral agraphia strongly suggests that the strategy employed to process these two codes may be different. This leads to the further implication that strategies employed in Kana and the alphabetical codes may also be different, because the unit of representation of speech sound is different between the two. In this regard, an easy comparison between alphabetical code impairment and Kanji–Kana impairment should be avoided. The paradigm of surface-deep processing may be valid for the alphabetical systems, but may not apply to the Kana-Kanji system.

The interesting implication is that the reading strategy may not be the same even among people who use the same code. In Japanese, the difference between lexical (or morphemic) code and phonological code is overemphasized because the code itself is different. But even in alphabetic systems there are strictly regular words that can be processed automatically at phonological level and quite a few irregular words that require general or ideographic processing. The tendency to use the latter strategy even for regular words may increase in educated people and in highly literate individuals. This then may lead to a different operational utilization of the brain, a hypothesis that was first mentioned by Wernicke in the dawning days of aphasiology and that remains unverified (Wernicke, 1874/1966–1968).

The last but not the least relevant comment I want to make is that these differences I enumerated are a by-product of the linguistic uniqueness, that is, a product of a particular culture, and the essential biological organization of the brain is unequivocally universal, as my short review of aphasia research in Japan at the beginning of the chapter clearly demonstrated.

ACKNOWLEDGMENTS

I thank my colleagues for their collaboration in completing this manuscript. Among others, Drs. Kazuko Sugiura, Etsuro Mori, Goro Ikumura, Misato Fujimori, Michimasa Ohi, and Yasufumi Tanaka contributed in collecting the data and caring for the patients quoted in the study. I particularly thank the editors of this volume for their indefatigable corrections and suggestions in brushing up the chapter.

REFERENCES

Abe, K., Yokoyama, R., Yorifuji, S., & Yanagihara, T. (1993). A jargon agraphia and selective agraphia of Kana resulting from an infarct in the left middle frontal gyrus. *Japanese Journal of Neuropsychology, 9,* 196–201. (in Japanese)

Alexander, M. P., Naeser, M. A., & Palumbo, C. L. (1987). Correlations of subcortical CT lesion sites and aphasia profiles. *Brain, 110,* 961–991.

Amanuma, Y., Otsubo, K., & Mizutani, O. (1978). *Japanese phonology.* Tokyo: Kuroshio Syuppann. (in Japanese)

Asayama, T. (1912). Aphasia in Japanese. *Psychiatria et Neurologia Japonica, 11,* 473–480. (in Japanese)

Asayama, T. (1914). Uber die Aphasie bei Japanern. *Deutsche Archive für Klinische Medizin, 113*, 523–529.

Benson, D. F. (1979). *Aphasia, alexia and agraphia.* New York: Churchill Livingstone.

Damasio, H., & Damasio, A. R. (1983). Localization of lesions in conduction aphasia. In A. Kertesz (Ed.), *Localization in neuropsychology* (pp. 231–243). New York: Academic Press.

Dejerine, J. (1891). Sur un cas de cécité verbale avec agraphie, suivi d'autopsie. *Compte rendus de Séance Société Biologie, 3*, 197–201.

Enokido, H. (1988). Transcortical aphasia. In E. Kishimoto, T. Miyamori, & A. Yamadori (Eds.), *Neuropsychology and neuroimaging* (pp. 69–78). Tokyo: Asakura Shoten. (in Japanese)

Fujii, T., & Kurachi, M. (1988). Wernicke's aphasia. In E. Kishimoto, T. Miyamori, & A. Yamadori (Eds.), *Neuropsychology and neuroimaging* (pp. 49–58). Tokyo: Asakura Shoten. (in Japanese)

Fukui, T., Kuzuhara, S., Toyokura, Y., & Sugishita, M. (1986). Writing disturbance similar to "pure" agraphia caused by left frontal infarction. *Neurological Medicine, 25*, 545–550. (in Japanese)

Geschwind, N. (1965). Disconnexion syndromes in animals and man. *Brain, 88*, 237–294, 585–644.

Geschwind, N., & Kaplan, E. (1962). A human cerebral deconnection syndrome. *Neurology, 12*, 675–685.

Gloning, K. (1977). Handedness and aphasia. *Neuropsychologia, 15*, 355–358.

Hamanaka, T. (1994). One hundred years of neuropsychology in Japan: Retrospect and prospect. *Neuropsychology Review, 4*, 289–298.

Hatta, T. (1977). Recognition of Japanese Kanji in the left and right visual fields. *Neuropsychologia, 15*, 685–688.

Hécaen, H., Mazars, G., Ramier, A. M., Goldblum, M. C., & Mérienne, L. (1971). Aphasie croisée chez un sujet droitier bilingue. *Revue Neurologique, 124*, 319–323.

Hodges, J. R., Patterson, K., Oxbury, S., & Funnel, E. (1992). Semantic dementia. Progressive fluent aphasia with temporal lobe atrophy. *Brain, 115*, 1783–1806.

Howard, D., Patterson, K., Wise, R., Brown, W. D., Eriston, K., Weiller, C., & Frackowiak, R. (1992). The cortical localization of the lexicons. *Brain, 115*, 1769–1782.

Imura, T. (1943). Aphasia: Characteristic symptoms in Japanese. *Folia Psychiatrica Neurologica Japonica, 47*, 196–218. (in Japanese)

Imura, T., Nogami, Y., & Asakawa, K. (1971). Aphasia in Japanese language. *Nihon University Journal of Medicine, 13*, 69–90.

Ito, K., Tanabe, H., Hariguchi, Y., Nishimura, K., Egawa, I., & Shiraishi, J. (1990). Gogi aphasia and Pick's disease. *Clinical Records of Osaka Kaisei Hospital, 150*, 77–84. (in Japanese)

Iwata, M. (1984). Kanji versus Kana. Neuropsychological correlates of the Japanese writing system. *Trends in NeuroSciences, 7*, 290–293.

Iwata, M. (1985). Neural mechanisms of reading and writing. In Y. Tsukada (Ed.), *Perspectives of neuroscience* (pp. 297–298). Tokyo: University of Tokyo Press.

Kandel, E. R. (1991). Perception of motion, depth, and form. In E. R. Kandel, J. H. Schwartz, & T. M. Kandel (Eds.), *Principles of neural science* (3rd ed., pp. 440–466). London: Prentice-Hall International Inc.

Kawachi, J., & Takeuchi, A. (1987). Course and prognosis of non-right-hander's aphasia. In I. Sobue, K. Fukui, & A. Yamadori (Eds.), *Course and prognosis of aphasia* (pp. 149–167). Tokyo: Igaku Kyoiku Syuppansya. (in Japanese)

Kawamura, M., Hirayama, K., & Yamamoto, H. (1989). Different interhemispheric transfer of Kanji and Kana writing evidenced by a case with left unilateral agraphia without apraxia. *Brain, 112*, 1011–1018.

Kess, J. F., & Miyamoto, T. (1994). *Japanese psycholinguistics: A classified and annotated research bibliography* (pp. 167–177). Philadelphia: John Benjamins.

Kimura, B., Matsuda, K., Kuroiwa, Y., & Tohgi, H. (1986). Pure agraphia in left parietal subcortical infarction. *Neurological Medicine, 24,* 484–488. (in Japanese)

Kimura, K. (1934). Zu erklärung des der japanischen Schrift eigentümlichen agraphischen Symptombildes. *Folia Psychiatria et Neurologica Japonica, 37,* 437–459. (in Japanese)

Kishida, K. (1991). Aphasia with right hemisphere lesion. In M. Sugishita (Ed.), *Neuropsychology of the right hemisphere* (pp. 147–185). Tokyo: Asakura Shoten. (in Japanese)

Kishida, K., Tsuruoka, H., Otsuka, A., Tsukuda, I., & Uemura, G. (1976). Aphasia and localization of brain lesions. *Clinical Neurology, 16,* 677–686. (in Japanese)

Kojima, T., Uno, A., & Kato, M. (1991). Training in Kana writing in a case of pure agraphia. *Higher Brain Function Research, 7,* 172–179. (in Japanese)

Kotani, S. (1935). A case of alexia with agraphia. *Japanese Journal of Experimental Psychology, 2,* 333–348. (in Japanese)

Koyama, Y. (1988). Conduction aphasia. In E. Kishimoto, T. Miyamori, & A. Yamadori (Eds.), *Neuropsychology and neuroimaging* (pp. 59–67). Tokyo: Asakura Shoten. (in Japanese)

Kuhl, P. K, Williams, K. A., Lacerda, F., Stevens, K. N., & Lindblom, B. (1992). Linguistic experience alters phonetic perception in infants by 6 months of age. *Science, 255,* 606–608.

Kurachi, M., & Matsubara, S. (1991). Clinicopathology and brain imaging of Pick's disease. *Japanese Journal of Neuropsychology, 7,* 10–18. (in Japanese)

Lecours, A. R., & Lhermitte, F. (1976). The "pure form" of the phonetic disintegration syndrome (pure anarthria): Anatomo-clinical report of a historical case. *Brain and Language, 3,* 88–113.

Liepmann, H., & Maas, O. (1907). Fall von linksseitiger Agraphie und Apraxie bei rechtseitiger Lähmung. *Journal of Psychology and Neurology, 10,* 214–227.

Matsubara, S. (1987). Clinical course of Gogi aphasia seen in a case of presenile dementia. In I. Sobue, K. Fukui, & A. Yamadori (Eds.), *Course and prognosis of aphasia* (pp. 211–226). Tokyo: Igaku Kyoiku Syuppan. (in Japanese)

Matsubara, S., Enokido, H., Torii, H., Hiraguchi, M., & Ainoda, N. (1984). A case of presenile dementia with Gogi aphasia. *Higher Brain Function Research, 4,* 586–596.

Mesulam, M.-M. (1982). Slowly progressive aphasia without generalized dementia. *Annals of Neurology, 11,* 592–598.

Miyashita, Y. (1993). Inferior temporal cortex: Where visual perception meets memory. *Annual Review of Neuroscience, 16,* 245–263.

Mori, E., Yamadori, A., & Furumoto, M. (1989). Precentral gyrus and Broca's aphasia. *Neurology, 39,* 51–54.

Mori, E., Yamadori, A., & Mitani, Y. (1986). Left thalamic infarction and disturbance of verbal memory: A clinicoanatomical study with a new method of computed tomographic stereotaxic lesion localization. *Annals of Neurology, 20,* 671–676.

Motomura, S. (1994). *Handbook of clinical aphasiology* (pp. 60–62). Tokyo: Igakushoin. (in Japanese)

Motomura, S., & Nagae, K. (1985). Medial frontal lobe and language. *Clinical Pychiatry, 27,* 665–670. (in Japanese)

Naeser, M. A., Alexander, M. P., Helm-Estabrooks, N., Levine, H. L., Laughlin, S. A., & Geschwind, N. (1982). Aphasia with predominantly subcortical lesion sites. *Archives of Neurology, 39,* 1–14.

Nagae, S. (1992). Kanji information processing as manifested in studies of divided visual field. *Psychology Review, 35,* 269–292. (in Japanese)

Ohashi, H. (1965). *Clinical neuropsychology.* Tokyo: Igaku Shoin Medical Publishers. (in Japanese)

Ohashi, H., & Hamanaka, T. (1985). *The enigma of Broca's center.* Tokyo: Kongo Shuppan. (in Japanese)

Onishi, K. (1893). *On aphasia.* Ijikaiho (Medical Society Proceedings) No 50, 10–13. (in Japanese)

Paradis, M., Hagiwara, H., & Hildebrandt, N. (1985). *Neurolinguistic aspects of the Japanese writing system.* New York: Academic Press.

Rubens, A. (1975). Aphasia with infarction in the territory of the anterior cerebral artery. *Cortex,* *11,* 239–250.

Sakurai, Y., Momose, T., Iwata, M., Watanabe, T., Ishikawa, T., Takeda, K., & Kanazawa, I. (1992). Kanji word reading process analyzed by positron emission tomography. *NeuroReport,* *3,* 445–448.

Sampson, G. (1985). *Writing systems.* Stanford, CA: Stanford University Press.

Sasanuma, S. (1975). Kana and Kanji processing in Japanese aphasics. *Brain and Language,* *2,* 369–383.

Sasanuma, S. (1985). Surface dyslexia and dysgraphia: How are they manifested in Japanese? In K. M. Patterson, J. C. Marshall, & M. Coltheart (Eds.), *Surface dyslexia: Neuropsychological and cognitive studies of phonological reading* (pp. 225–249). Hillsdale, NJ: Lawrence Erlbaum Associates.

Sasanuma, S. (1986). Universal and language-specific symptomatology and treament of aphasia. *Folia Phoniatrica,* *38,* 121–175.

Sasanuma, S., & Fujimura, O. (1971). Selective impairment of phonetic and non-phonetic transcription of words in Japanese aphasic patients: Kana vs. Kanji in visual recognition and writing. *Cortex,* *7,* 1–18.

Sasanuma, S., & Fujimura, O. (1972). An analysis of writing errors in Japanese aphasic patients: Kanji vs. Kana words. *Cortex,* *8,* 265–282.

Sasanuma, S., Itoh, M., Mori, K., & Kobayashi, Y. (1977). Tachistoscopic recognition of Kana and Kanji words. *Neuropsychologia,* *15,* 547–553.

Sasanuma, S., & Monoi, H. (1975). The syndrome of Gogi (word-meaning) aphasia. *Neurology,* *25,* 627–632.

Sato, M., Yasui, N., Suzuki, A., Kawamura, S., Sayama, I., & Kobayashi, T. (1983). Agraphia from frontal lesion: A case of Moyamoya disease. *Brain and Nerve,* *35,* 1145–1151. (in Japanese)

Shallice, T. (1981). Phonological agraphia and the lexical route in writing. *Brain,* *104,* 413–429.

Snowden, J. S., Goulding, P. J., & Neary, D. (1989). Semantic dementia: A form of circumscribed cerebral atrophy. *Behavioural Neurology,* *2,* 167–182.

Soma, Y., Sugishita, M., Kitamura, K., Maruyama, S., & Imanaga, H. (1989). Lexical agraphia in the Japanese language. *Brain,* *112,* 1549–1561.

Sugishita, M., Toyokura, Y., Yoshioka, M., & Yamada, R. (1980). Unilateral agraphia after section of the posterior half of the trunkus of the corpus callosum. *Brain and Language,* *9,* 215–225.

Sugiura, K., Yoneda, Y., Yoshida, T., & Yamadori, A. (1992). Preservation of intrinsic rhythm ability (Haku) in severe aphasia. *Higher Brain Function Research,* *12,* 313–322. (in Japanese)

Tanabe, H., Ikeda, M., Nakagawa, Y., Yamamoto, H., Ikejiri, Y., Kazui, H., Hashikawa, K., & Harada, K. (1992). Gogi (word meaning) aphasia and semantic memory for words. *Higher Brain Function Research,* *12,* 153–167. (in Japanese)

Tanaka, Y., Yamadori, A., & Murata, S. (1987). Selective Kana agraphia: A case report. *Cortex,* *23,* 679–684.

Tokieda, M. (1941). *A principle of Japanese.* Tokyo: Iwanami Publishers.

Totsuka, M., Funai, H., Fujibayashi, M., Fukusako, Y., & Sasanuma, S. (1979). Differential diagnosis of aphasia and lesions in the brain. *Japanese Journal of Logopedics and Phoniatrics,* *20,* 197–205.

Tsuduki, S., & Indo, T. (1986). "Pure" agraphia following left frontotemporal lobe infarction. *Neurological Medicine,* *25,* 160–165. (in Japanese)

Watanabe, S., Hojo, T., Tasaki, H., Kazono, T., Sato, T., Medoki, H., & Tozuka, M. (1986). CT analysis of aphasic lesions. *Higher Function Studies,* *6,* 972–980. (in Japanese)

Wernicke, C. (1966–1968). The symptom complex of aphasia. In R. S. Cohen & M. W. Wartofsky (Eds.), *Boston studies in the philosophy of science* (Vol. 4, pp. 34–97). (Original work published in 1874 as *Der Aphasische Symptomencomplex.* Breslau: Max Cohn & Weigert)

Yamadori, A. (1975). Ideogram reading in alexia. *Brain,* *98,* 231–238.

Yamadori, A. (1979). On conduction aphasia. *Brain and Nerve, 31,* 891–897. (in Japanese)

Yamadori, A. (1980). Cerebral laterality and Kanji–Kana processing. *Progress in Neurological Sciences, 24,* 556–564. (in Japanese)

Yamadori, A. (1982). Alexia with agraphia and angular gyrus. *Higher Brain Function Research, 2,* 236–242. (in Japanese)

Yamadori, A. (1984). Wernicke's aphasia. Its symptoms and lesion. *Clinical Psychiatry, 26,* 693–699. (in Japanese)

Yamadori, A. (1985). *Introduction to neuropsychology.* Tokyo: Igakushoin Medical Publishers. (in Japanese)

Yamadori, A. (1986). Category specific alexia and a neuropsychological model of alexia. In H. S. R. Kao & R. Hoosain (Eds.), *Linguistics, psychology and the Chinese language* (pp. 255–264). Hong Kong: University of Hong Kong.

Yamadori, A. (1987). Dysphasia caused by the left thalamic infarction. *Japanese Journal of Stroke, 9,* 554–558. (in Japanese)

Yamadori, A., & Ikumura, G. (1975). Central (or conduction) aphasia in a Japanese patient. *Cortex, 11,* 73–82.

Yamadori, A., Motomura, N., Endo, M., & Mitani, Y. (1985). Category specific alexia and a neuropsychological model of reading. *Higher Brain Function Research, 5,* 817–821. (in Japanese)

Yamadori, A., Nagashima, T., & Tamaki, N. (1983). Ideogram writing in a disconnection syndrome. *Brain and Language, 19,* 346–356.

Yamadori, A., Osumi, Y., Ikeda, H., & Kanazawa, Y. (1980). Left unilateral agraphia and tactile anomia. *Archives of Neurology, 37,* 88–91.

Yamadori, A., Yoshida, T., & Sugiura, K. (1992). A case of crossed conduction aphasia. *Journal of Neurolinguistics, 7,* 187–196.

Yamamoto, S. (1911). Motor aphasia: A case report. *Report of the Third Conference of the Medical Society of Japan,* 1233–1234. (in Japanese)

Zangwill, O. L. (1975). Excision of Broca's area without persistent aphasia. In J. Zülch, O. L. Creutzfeldt, & G. L. Galbraith (Eds.), *Cerebral localization* (pp. 258–263). Berlin: Springer-Verlag.

C H A P T E R   S I X

Aphasia in Illiterate Individuals

Patrick Coppens
Moorhead State University, Moorhead, Minnesota

Maria Alice de Mattos Pimenta Parente
Universidade de São Paulo, São Paulo, Brazil

André Roch Lecours
Centre Hospitalier Côte des Neiges, Montreal, Quebec, Canada

A clinician assessing an aphasic patient without knowing that the patient is illiterate may erroneously diagnose alexia and agraphia. Although this example is overly simplistic, can we be sure that all the measured impairments are attributable to the aphasia or could they be due in part, either directly or indirectly, to a premorbid lack of literacy training? The clinician is unable to answer this question because there are no norms for illiterate patients in the aphasia or neuropsychological batteries. Clearly, we first need to understand how the development of literacy impacts on cognitive processing as a whole before focusing on the aphasia population. Then we will be able to focus on the intriguing interaction between language lateralization and localization and learning a writing system. This is one instance of the potential influence of a social factor on biological characteristics.

Unlike spoken language, literacy neither represents an inherent necessity to the evolution of the human species, nor, *a fortiori*, an essential attribute of the human brain. The development of writing is a phylogenetically recent phenomenon, and, as an agent of social and individual change, is perceived as the frontier between prehistory and history, between "primitive" and "civilized," between traditional and modern cultures. Furthermore, whereas individuals who cannot express themselves using oral language are generally considered physically abnormal, entire cultures are able to function effectively without written language. In fact, Ardila, Rosselli, and Rosas (1989) reported that a full one-third of the world population is illiterate.

Studies on the influence of literacy skills on cognition typically compared task performance in literate and illiterate population samples. The definition

175

of *illiteracy*, however, can vary with the cultural and social strata between countries or even within a country. In developed countries, illiteracy rates primarily include school dropouts who have little or no reading or writing skills. In such cases, it is possible that cognitive or genetic factors have impeded the acquisition of these skills. This is not the case in poor countries, where significant subgroups of the general population have normal cognitive potential but no access to schooling. This chapter concentrates on the latter group of illiterate subjects.

First, we define literacy and attempt to isolate its effects from confounding variables by reviewing the studies that have analyzed the influence of literacy skills on cognitive processing. Second, we review the available literature on the question of cerebral dominance and aphasia among illiterate individuals.

DEFINITION OF LITERACY

Literacy is defined as the acquisition of a written code. This particular learning process usually takes place in a structured schooling environment. However, in addition to literacy skills, many other abilities are directly or indirectly developed or taught in schools. Therefore, the potential influence of literacy on cognitive processes is confounded by schooling (e.g., Laboratory of Comparative Human Cognition, 1983). Thus when comparing literate and illiterate populations, authors have for all intents and purposes compared schooled and unschooled subjects. Moreover, the illiterate subjects are usually recruited from rural areas, where illiteracy is more frequent, or from Third World countries with higher illiteracy rates. These comparisons are confounding the effects of literacy with cultural or socioeconomic status (SES) factors (e.g., Reis & Castro-Caldas, 1997). Ideally, in order to analyze the effects of literacy per se, the influence of culture, SES, and schooling should be removed. Indeed there is some indication in the literature that all these variables affect performance on a variety of neuropsychological tasks.

VARIABLES INFLUENCING COGNITIVE PROCESSES

Cultural Effects

From a theoretical and phylogenetic perspective, Goody (1977) focused on the impact of written language development on a given culture, more specifically how the representation of the world was modified as a consequence of the development of a written system. Goody viewed written language as "semipermanent" and "timeless." Therefore people became able to analyze and criticize the written production much more effectively than they were the evanescent spoken words. He listed an impressive series of features that may have developed thanks to the advent of a written code: a more critical and more logical thinking, more skepticism or rationality, a decontextualization of language, the development of syllogisms and algebra, a linear time measurement instead of a cyclical one, and so on. In addition, because one of the most important purposes for early written language was lists, Goody (1977) claimed that this new way of organizing words triggered the development of categories and hierarchies. Moreover, Goody maintained that those changes in cognitive processes would also take place in illiterate members who share that culture, by merely being exposed to the new way of thinking. This point has often been overlooked in subsequent discussions of Goody's contribution, but is of paramount importance because it implies a difference of cognitive processing between literate and illiterate cultures, but not necessarily between literate and illiterate members of a same culture.

Luria (1976) examined five groups of subjects: three illiterate groups and two barely literate groups. His goal was to describe the possible changes in cognitive processing brought about by the fight against illiteracy and the birth of the collectivist system of the New Economic Policy in the USSR in the 1920s. To find the differences, Luria compared farmers (untouched by the changes) and villagers (affected by the new policy) from different regions of the country. The test battery included tasks of perception, word association, conceptual thinking, and classification. The illiterate subjects undertook the tasks in a very concrete way, attaching more importance to the context, whereas the villagers relied more on the perceptual and functional characteristics of the items presented. For example, the illiterate subjects would interpret syllogisms based on personal experience rather than on logical associations. Although the illiterate individuals could not solve the "odd word out" task (out of four words), they seemed to possess the superordinate needed but did not grant that analysis precedence upon the concrete approach. For example, a subject acknowledged that three items were tools, but could not dismiss the fourth item "wood" because without the latter, the first three would be "useless." Luria (1976) concluded that the social and cultural changes did indeed cause cognitive changes, mostly expressed as a more abstract way of thinking. The most important variable appeared to be the level of literacy, which he implicitly equated with schooling.

Laurendeau-Bendavid (1977) attempted to distinguish between the effects of culture by comparing children of various grades from Canada and Rwanda on several measures of cognitive development (e.g., the concept of "life," conservation of surface, probability reasoning). She noted that the Rwandese children reached her criterion of success significantly later than Canadian children. Furth (1981, in Ostrosky-Solis et al., 1985) also showed that children from rural areas needed 3 years more than urban children to understand the liquid conservation paradigm.

Orsini, Schiappa, and Grossi (1981) focused on environmental and cultural differences by comparing verbal and nonverbal memory in children from rural and urban areas. All children were attending school or kindergarten. The results showed that the urban children performed significantly better in both measures for all age groups. This study confirms that environmental/cultural variables influence cognitive measures. Orsini et al. (1986, 1987) replicated these findings in children and adults, but they included schooling as a variable. Level of schooling was a significant variable, but the study did not separate the schooling effect from the cultural variable. Indeed, it is likely that most of the illiterate or semiliterate subjects came from rural areas. The authors themselves considered education one aspect of cultural differences (Orsini et al., 1986).

In conclusion, cultural/environmental factors have been shown to produce differences in cognitive measures, such as memory. The most obvious strategy difference between the groups is that rural subjects performed at a more concrete level whereas urban subjects were able to reach a higher level of abstraction. Nevertheless, the authors noted that the influence of education/schooling seemed to be the most powerful variable between the groups. However, Scribner and Cole (1981) stated that reading habits and a greater exposure to graphic stimuli in urban areas influence cognitive processing characteristics.

Socioeconomic Effects

Greenfield (1972) and Greenfield and Bruner (1966) observed that the communication style of Senegalese children was context dependent rather than abstract. They hypothesized that in oral societies the children learn exclusively by watching and imitating adults. Similarly, they contended that lower SES mothers in developed countries tend to teach their children more by pointing and showing, whereas higher SES mothers tend to explain verbally the task at hand, thereby making the communicative exchange more abstract. Although the differences are expressed in terms of SES, they noticed that the schooling variable was the most important in explaining the shift from concrete to abstract thinking. Ostrosky-Solis et al. (1985) used an adaptation of Luria's battery to assess the influence of SES on neuropsychological and linguistic measures. All measures were significantly different, with the high SES group scoring higher than the low SES subjects. The most striking differences included the more complex aspects of language, such as passive structure, antonyms, and reading low-frequency words. The authors interpreted their results as a consequence of SES and schooling group differences (the two groups had very different levels of education), with schooling being implicitly considered as an integral part of SES. The authors further interpreted the differences in cognitive processing in terms of abstractness of thought.

Amante, VanHouten, Grieve, Bader, and Margules (1977) specifically focused on the influence of SES on neuropsychology measures. Schooling was assumed to be equivalent among the subject groups because the children were from the same nine schools in the same town. For the general intelligence measure, the subjects were divided into two groups: manual and nonmanual workers. Results showed significantly higher scores for the nonmanual SES level. For the visuoperceptual subtest, the subjects were divided into three groups: nonmanual, working class, and lower class. Again, results showed a significant difference between all groups: the higher the SES, the better the performance. The authors interpreted their findings as partly genetic and partly environmental in nature, because the lower the SES level, the higher the probability of malnutrition, undernutrition, or intrauterine pathology. Finally, Bertolucci, Brucki, Campacci, and Juliano (1994) observed differences between their three SES groups on a mental status questionnaire. The groups were of comparable education level.

In sum, SES levels seem to influence cognitive strategies to some extent. Again, the differences were interpreted as a consequence of schooling differences (Greenfield & Bruner, 1966; Ostrosky-Solis et al., 1985). However, the group differences seem to be present even when schooling level is controlled (Amante et al., 1977; Bertolucci et al., 1994).

Schooling Effects

After reviewing the literature on the influence of culture on cognitive processing, Greenfield and Bruner (1966) noted that "it is always the schooling variable that makes qualitative differences" (p. 104). They added that "the huge impact of school" (p. 104) has been clearly demonstrated.

Laurendeau-Bendavid (1977) analyzed the effects of schooling by comparing schooled and unschooled Rwandese children on several measures of cognitive development (e.g., the concept of "life," conservation of surface, probability reasoning). Although not all variables were significant, Laurendeau-Bendavid concluded that "school experience is thus not a necessary condition for the appearance of concrete operational thinking, but certainly is a facilitating one" (p. 156). This implies that some cognitive skills may be acquired in some cases by concrete experience outside a school environment. Similarly, Dauster (1975) found that on Piagetian tests of formal and concrete operation stages, illiterate adults were limited to a strategy "better conditioned to the concrete, to the perceptual, to live experience and the contingent" (p. 76). Tfouni (1983) noted that illiterate adults tended to interpret syllogisms on the basis of personal experience. Garcia and Guerreiro (1983) compared the results of illiterate, semiliterate (i.e., less than 4 years of schooling), and literate subjects on a mental status questionnaire. They found significant differences in performance between the literate subjects and the other two groups, but not between the illiterate and semiliterate subjects. This result confirms that the influence of schooling on cognition requires a significant schooling period to become measurable.

Lecours et al. (1987) used an aphasia screening test with literate and illiterate (i.e., schooled and unschooled) individuals. Using subtests of the Portuguese adaptation of the Examen Linguistique de l'Aphasie, Version Alpha (Lecours et al., 1986), they tested 100 normal adults without history of neurological problems. All were Portuguese-speaking right-handed monolinguals. Fifty-seven were totally unschooled and illiterate, whereas the remaining 43 had from 4 to 15 years of schooling (mean: 8.2 years). The subtests selected were a directed interview, auditory comprehension, repetition, and picture naming. In the spontaneous speech condition, no statistical differences were present between the two groups, although occasional phonemic and verbal "deviations" were detected in the spontaneous speech of a few subjects. However, the illiterate subjects made significantly more errors than the literate subjects on each of the remaining subtests. The results of the auditory comprehension subtest showed that significantly more illiterate than literate subjects produced at least one inadequate response on each of the three types of stimuli (words, simple sentences, and complex sentences). The most frequent errors in the illiterate subject group involved the visually similar foils, such as *rake* for *comb*, or *the girl runs* for *the girl walks*. In both tasks of the repetition subtest (words and sentences), significantly more illiterate than literate subjects produced at least one inadequate response. Also, the illiterate subjects made significantly more phonemic errors. Mostly, the illiterate subjects made frequent repetition errors on grammatical morphemes in single words (*pratos* repeated as *prato*, and *cruzeiros* as *cruzeiro*), and tended to delete adjectives or free morphemes in the sentence repetition task. In the naming subtest, once again, significantly more illiterate than literate subjects produced at least one inadequate response. The errors of the illiterate subjects were mostly of the anomic type (i.e., no response), and their paraphasias seemed to be related to a difficulty in visually decoding the iconographic nature of some items (e.g., *duck head* for *pipe*; *horse* for *ear*). In addition, they seemed to have particular difficulty recognizing a part of a whole presented in isolation (e.g., the picture of a human ear), whereas when the part of a whole was not presented in isolation, they tended to answer correctly (e.g., whiskers on a cat). The authors concluded that most of the errors in naming and comprehension were due to the illiterate subjects' unfamiliarity with two-dimensional representations. Interestingly, significant differences in naming have been described between a low schooling (<9 years) and a high schooling group (>9 years) as well (Dordain, Nespoulous, Bourdeau, & Lecours, 1983). The errors in repetition are probably due to phonological processing difficulties (rather than morphemic), and either a particular difficulty with functors or a limited short-term memory span. Because functors may have a less concrete semantic representation, this observation could be linked with the difficulties illiterate subjects experienced with abstract thinking in previous studies. Similarly, some semantic misinterpretations could also be associated with the concreteness of previous experiences. Some illiterate subjects interpreted the sentence *the boy pulls the horse* by inverting subject and object. The authors argued that the inverted sentence *the horse pulls the boy* is more logical at a concrete level, hence the error.

Kolinsky, Morais, Content, and Cary (1987) submitted their subjects to a visual postperception task. Visual postperception is a secondary analysis, albeit simple, of an incoming visual stimulus. The subjects are asked whether a specific shape is a part or not of a larger figure. Memory is not involved; both shapes remained in front of the subjects. Their subject groups included schooled illiterate children of 4 and 5 years old (kindergartners), schooled literate children of 6 and 7 years old (first and second graders), unschooled illiterate adults, and ex-illiterate adults who had been taught to read and write later in life. There were significant differences between the second graders and all the other groups and between the first graders and the unschooled illiterate adults. The authors concluded that this particular skill does not develop with cognitive maturation or as a consequence of literacy, but that the critical variable was schooling, since the ex-illiterate adult group did not perform significantly better than the illiterate children.

Ardila et al. (1989) compared illiterate subjects (of illiterate parents) with professional subjects (of professional parents) on measures of memory and visuospatial skills. The authors reported a significant difference between the two groups for all the measures tested. To be sure, some of their tasks dealt with very specific skills clearly taught in school, such as labeling maps of the country, or recalling historical facts. In addition, the illiterate subjects showed a particular difficulty with two-dimensional representations. The authors noted the similarities of these productions with children's drawings. They also were unable to represent a cube in three dimensions, a result replicating previous conclusions (Parente, 1984). The results of the visuospatial tasks showed that they could not separate embedded line drawings, adequately copy the Rey–Osterrieth figure, or make a map of the room in which they were. The memory score differences were attributed to the fact that literate subjects used organizational strategies to help recall. The authors concluded that the cognitive abilities needed to perform these tasks adequately are the result of school training. Therefore, they argued that normative neuropsychological tests are biased against illiterate individuals.

Using the same groups of subjects, Rosselli, Ardila, and Rosas (1990) extended the previous study to include language variables. Again, all measurements showed a significant difference in performance between the groups, in favor of the literate subjects. Several of these results warrant a closer examination. In naming real objects, the discrepancy between the two groups was present but interpreted as marginal. However, in picture naming the group difference dramatically increased, thereby indicating that illiterate subjects had particular difficulties in naming two-dimensional representations. The verbal paraphasias observed during this subtest confirmed this hypothesis. In the verbal fluency task, the illiterate subjects showed difficulty with letter fluency as compared to fluency in animal naming. Indeed, the authors reported that these subjects showed difficulties simply understanding this task. Moreover, the illiterate subjects made phonological errors when repeating complex words. From these observations, Rosselli et al. (1990) concluded that these subjects were unable to master the notion of phoneme. In addition, the illiterate subjects demonstrated a significantly lower performance understanding verbal commands, particularly longer, more syntactically complex sentences, an observation confirming the results of Ostrosky-Solis et al. (1985) and Lecours et al. (1987). Rosselli et al. (1990) presented two hypotheses to explain these results. First, either these patients were unfamiliar with complex syntax or their overall use of verbal strategies was lower. Second, illiterate subjects have difficulty with spatial relationships expressed verbally, because they made a significant number of errors on relational words such as *above, into,* or *under.* Again, the authors' main conclusion was that the effects of schooling (and not literacy only) are also measurable in language tasks, and that the norms of formal neuropsychological tests cannot be applied to the illiterate population.

One problem in the previous two studies is that the potential influence of SES differences confounds the schooling effect. Grossi et al. (1993) compared 189 literate and illiterate elderly subjects with comparable SES using a custom-made neuropsychological battery, including mental status, verbal and nonverbal memory, constructional apraxia, and Raven's progressive matrices. They found that the literate group performed significantly better than the illiterate group on all measures. However, when illiterate subjects were compared to a group of semiliterate subjects (3 years of education), only the differences found in constructional apraxia and the progressive matrices subtests reached significance. The authors concluded that schooling improves cognitive functioning. We may also add that some cognitive changes seem to take place before others during the development of literacy, and hence that literacy and semiliteracy are recognizably different stages.

Taken together, the results of these studies leave little doubt that schooling influences cognitive processing. By teaching the skills that a society values, the educational system unifies cognitive processing to a certain extent (Castro-Caldas, 1993). The main group differences identified include more abstract thinking (removed from personal concrete experience), difficulties with phoneme manipulation and two-dimensional representations, visual postperception, and poor organizational strategies to enhance recall. These changes appear to take place progressively because they are much less obvious between illiterate and semiliterate subjects. On the other hand, evidence of more abstract thinking does appear in a subset of the illiterate population, an indication that it is possible for some of these skills to develop from experience outside a formal schooling environment.

Literacy Effects

The influence of writing on cognition was already of concern to the Greek philosophers. Socrates believed that acquiring the skills to read and write diminished one's memory capacity, in that the information is readily available instead of being held in memory (Scribner & Cole, 1981).

Many authors have equated literacy and schooling (education), but the two experiences are clearly different. Literacy is the acquisition of a linguistic code in a written modality, whereas schooling involves exposure to numerous new experiences. For example, Greenfield and Bruner (1966) contended that school not only taught to read and write, but also to use oral language in a more abstract way; also, Ardila et al. (1989) noted that literacy was more than learning to read and write, but actually a small part of the skills taught in school. They defined schooling as an entirely new culture in which new cognitive strategies are acquired. Consequently, we need to be able to distinguish between the effects of literacy and those of schooling.

Only one study has attempted to distinguish between the schooling and the literacy variables. Scribner and Cole (1981) investigated the Vai culture of Liberia where the elders traditionally teach literacy skills to the children. The authors tested categorization, abstraction, memory, logical reasoning, and metalinguistic skills in three groups of adults: illiterate, elder-taught literate, and school-taught literate. The Vai script is taught during one-on-one social interactions between younger and older members of the culture. Interestingly, this literacy training begins rather late, usually during adolescence (late teens, early twenties) and is completed in a matter of a few months. The Vai script is used mostly for social purposes (letter writing) and record keeping. In schools, literacy includes Arabic (exclusively for religious purposes) and English. In this case, the children start the learning process earlier, usually under age 10. The results showed that a schooling effect was consistently present. The authors attributed this effect mainly to the fact that the school-taught subjects were typically able to justify their answers verbally. They also noted that the effect was small probably because the school-taught subjects only had 2 or 3 years of education. Those who had just left school or who were still involved in school activities at the time of testing performed distinctly better. Again, this observation confirms the hypothesis that the cognitive changes need a significant amount of time to take place. Few differences emerged between the illiterate and the elder-taught groups. However, in the metalinguistic tasks, all the literate subjects, including the non-schooled elder-taught subjects, performed significantly better than the illiterate subjects. This observation suggests that the development of metalinguistic skills does depend on literacy training specifically. Also, among the illiterate subjects, urbanization proved to be a significant factor: Villagers tended to perform better than country-dwelling subjects. The fact that cultural/environmental factors (i.e., richness of experience) play a part in cognitive development has already been established. The authors concluded that literacy per se probably did not influence cognitive functions, but only developed metalinguistic skills. However, they offered the caveat that Vai literacy is more specific, not as broadly used as written language in Western societies. We would also argue, in the same vein, that Vai schooling probably does not offer the same variety of topics and experiences as education in developed countries.

Discussion

Taken together, these studies clearly show that external/environmental variables influence cognitive processing. Knowingly or unknowingly, many authors have combined several of these variables in their studies. Therefore, it seems extremely tentative to associate a given variable with specific group differences in cognitive processing. However, there is no doubt that literacy and schooling are different experiences and that their respective influence on cognitive processing is also different (Scribner & Cole, 1981). It appears that all but one study (Scribner & Cole, 1981) analyzed the influence of schooling rather than that of literacy. To express the results in terms of literacy per se is therefore misleading. Because literacy is virtually impossible to separate from schooling, it would be more accurate to refer to *unschooled, semischooled,* and *schooled* (or *uneducated, semieducated,* and *educated*) individuals rather than to express the group differences in terms of literacy levels.

The most frequently reported differences between the schooled and unschooled populations fall into three main categories: concrete versus abstract thinking, phonemic difficulties, and difficulties with two-dimensional representations. Many authors have commented on the fact that uneducated individuals seem to be unable to think at a more abstract level. In other words, schooling aids in the development of abstract thinking by decontextualizing the referents. Vygotsky (1978) maintained that illiterate individuals, like children, have a "natural memory" that operates at a more concrete level, without symbolization. However, children and illiterate individuals do possess symbolic processes, because oral language makes use of symbols, but only the written modality "*forces* remoteness of reference on the language user" (Greenfield & Bruner, 1966, p. 104, emphasis added). Moreover, writing is more abstract than speech, because speech symbolizes situations and writing symbolizes speech. Writing is then a second-generation symbolic activity (Vygotsky, 1978).

The second major difference identified between schooled and unschooled subjects concerns phonological issues. Phonemic difficulties were observed in repetition (Lecours et al., 1987; Reis & Castro-Caldas, 1997; Rosselli et al., 1990) and letter fluency (Reis & Castro-Caldas, 1997; Rosselli et al., 1990). The fact that uneducated subjects were hardly able to understand the task of finding words beginning with a specific sound indicates that phonological parsing (a metaphonological skill) may be at the core of the problem (see also Morais, 1994). Moreover, Scribner and Cole (1981) noted that metalinguistic skill development was specifically associated with literacy rather than schooling. Morais, Cary, Alegria, and Bertelson (1979) investigated metaphonological skills in illiterate adults and ex-illiterate adults who had learned to read and write after 15 years of age. Both groups originated from the same rural area, so that literacy was purportedly the only variable differentiating the groups. The task involved adding or removing the first phoneme of words and nonwords. The illiterate group performed significantly worse than the ex-illiterate group, particularly for nonwords. The authors concluded that the awareness of the phonemic makeup of a word and the ability to manipulate these basic elements do not develop spontaneously but are linked with learning a written language. This development can occur at any age, because their subjects were adults. However, we know that preliterate children (and hence illiterate subjects) are able to process the difference between minimal pairs. This apparent contradiction disappears if one considers that phonological decoding is a perceptual process whereas metalinguistic skills are a postperceptual skill (Kolinsky et al., 1987). Read and Ruyter (1985) compared the metaphonological skills of adults and children matched for reading level. They found that the adults performed very poorly in reading nonwords (i.e., grapheme–phoneme transformation) and in manipulating phonemic units (e.g., adding an initial consonant). They performed better with rhymes. The authors concluded that the interruption of literacy skills also interrupts the development of metaphonological skills. These adults remained poor readers. This conclusion confirms the results of Morais et al. (1979), who also observed that metalinguistic skills do not develop without exposure to a written language. Interestingly, Read and Ruyter (1985) further reported that verbal memory correlated significantly with the subjects' poorest metaphonological measures. According to the authors, the subjects were unable to maintain a phonological representation in memory. Other authors have indeed reported a lower performance on verbal memory measures with unschooled individuals (Ardila et al., 1989; Grossi et al., 1993; Orsini et al., 1981, 1986, 1987). If phonological encoding is poor, one could also argue that the phonological route for lexical access is insufficiently developed. This mechanism explains the observed lower performance in letter naming, and may be involved in possible confrontation naming difficulties in some cases. The repetition difficulties of unschooled subjects also could be ascribed to phonological difficulties, particularly for nonwords or digit span. Reis, Guerreiro, and Castro-Caldas (1996) showed that there was a difference in repetition skills between schooled and unschooled transcortical aphasia subjects because the latter did not have access to a phonological input buffer.

Further analysis of metaphonological development was carried out by Bertelson and de Gelder (1989). They noted that illiterate subjects, like preliterate children, were able to manipulate rhymes but not phonemes. They concluded from their review of the literature that metalinguistic knowledge of rhymes (i.e., at the syllable level) can develop in illiterate subjects, but not metaphonological skills. This observation was further investigated by Bertelson, de Gelder, Tfouni, and Morais (1989). They compared the performance of literate and semiliterate (at most second grade level) adult subjects on three tasks: rhyme judgment, initial vowel deletion, and initial consonant deletion. There were no group differences in the first two tasks, but a highly significant difference in favor of the semiliterate subjects on the first consonant deletion task. These results suggest that some parsing skills at the syllable level can be acquired by illiterate subjects, but that phonemic manipulation requires literacy training, albeit a minimal exposure to a written code. Implicitly, the vowel deletion task was interpreted as a syllable rather than a phoneme manipulation. Bowey and Francis (1991) also investigated this issue. They gave syllable and phonemic manipulation tasks to preschoolers, first graders, and second graders. The schooled subjects outscored the preschoolers on all measures; however, the extremely poor results of the preschoolers on phonemic manipulation tasks prompted the authors to conclude that "alphabetically illiterate children do not develop sensitivity to the phonemic structure of language in the absence of special environmental support" (p. 116). In addition, the performance on these tests seemed to improve gradually with literacy instruction and/or "general linguistic maturity" (Bowey & Francis, 1991, p. 117). Contrary to Morais et al. (1979), these latter two studies did not specifically link metaphonological skills with literacy training. In de Gelder, Vroomen, and Bertelson (1993), however, the methods allowed for the distinction between schooling and literacy. The subjects were all Chinese speakers who had emigrated to the Netherlands. Although they all could speak some Dutch, some were exposed to alphabetic literacy (in Dutch) and others were not. The tasks included rhymes and phonemic manipulation. There were no differences on the rhyme task, but the alphabetically trained subjects were significantly better at phonological manipulation, which brought the authors to the conclusion that "sensitivity to rhyme, unlike sensitivity to segments, develops to some extent spontaneously, and independently of school experience, but can still be promoted by instruction" (p. 320). From this literature review, there seems to be little doubt that unschooled subjects will show particular difficulties with phonemic manipulation, and that this distinction has been specifically linked with literacy training.

The third major difference observed between schooled and unschooled individuals concerns the perception/interpretation of two-dimensional representations. Two-dimensional representations do not occur in all cultures. Several cultures were described in which the members were unable to infer a three-dimensional representation from a drawing (Greenfield & Bruner, 1966). Also, well-known optic illusions that are considered normal phenomena in Western cultures were shown not to be universal (Greenfield & Bruner, 1966; Luria, 1976). Greenfield and Bruner (1966) concluded that "members of different cultures differ in the inferences they draw from perceptual cues" (p. 91). Differences in visuospatial test results were identified based on SES level (Amante et al., 1977) and educational level (Ardila et al., 1989); also, difficulties with two-dimensional representations displayed by uneducated subjects were observed in naming (Dordain et al., 1983; Lecours et al., 1987; Reis, Guerreiro, & Castro-Caldas, 1994; Rosselli et al., 1990), constructional praxis (Ardila et al., 1989; Grossi et al., 1993; Parente, 1984), and oral comprehension (Lecours et al., 1987). Reis et al. (1994) specifically investigated picture and object naming according to level of schooling. The authors compared unschooled, semischooled (<4 years), and schooled (>4 years) subjects from the same community on naming real objects, photographs, and line drawings. The objects were the same in each condition. The results showed no difference between the groups on real object naming. In naming photographs and line drawings, there was a significant difference between unschooled and schooled subjects and between unschooled and semischooled subjects. These results confirmed previous studies, but also indicated that the semischooled individuals performed better than the unschooled subjects. The authors interpreted the results in terms of level of abstraction (which implies that this characteristic is but an expression of the previous variable: concrete vs. abstract); that is, the unschooled individuals have difficulty as a group in recognizing two-dimensional representations of objects because of the higher level of abstractness. Indeed, more visuoperceptual errors (e.g., *thermometer* for *cigarette*) were reported for pictures than drawings. Interestingly, there was a significant difference between the semischooled and the schooled subjects in naming drawings but not photographs. It seems that semischooled individuals reached an intermediate level of abstractness.

The observed differences in cognitive processing between the groups triggered by environmental factors do not take place overnight. Laurendeau-Bendavid (1977) reported a relationship between level of schooling and the development of Piagetian stages, such as formal and concrete operations. The uneducated and the highly educated children performed at the two extremes, and the children who left school after 3 and 6 years fell in between, thereby showing a progressive development according to level of schooling. This development was interrupted when schooling was discontinued. Luria (1976) observed changes in classification skills and syllogism interpretation between totally uneducated subjects and subjects with 2 years of schooling. The change was not categorical, because "barely literate" subjects scored in between the other two groups. When comparing unschooled with schooled adults, the differences in performance are often highly significant (e.g., Ardila et al., 1989; Rosselli et al., 1990). However, when comparing unschooled with semischooled subjects, the differences are more limited. Luria (1976) showed that a more abstract cognitive processing already appeared with very little schooling. Similarly, Garcia and Guerreiro (1983) found significant differences between unschooled and semischooled subjects (<4 years of education) on all nine cognitive variables investigated, whereas the difference was present only in six variables between semischooled and schooled subjects (>4 years of education). Moreover, all the measures used by Grossi et al. (1993) could significantly differentiate schooled and unschooled subjects, but only constructional apraxia and Raven's progressive matrices performances showed significant differences between unschooled and semischooled (<3 years) subjects. These results indicate that the appearance of abstract thinking and the familiarity with two-dimensional representations may be the first skills to appear with even limited schooling.

Other less well studied areas have highlighted differences between schooled and unschooled individuals. The studies of Reis, Guerreiro, Garcia, and Castro-Caldas (1995) and of Carraher, Carraher, and Schliemann (1982) showed that the abilities involved in mathematical operations and reasoning may develop from daily life situations, and not necessarily from a formal education or as a result of the use of numbers. Such a dissociation shows that schooling may facilitate the development of a variety of arithmetic operations, whereas, for unschooled individuals, the lexical component of numbers may have more to do with the concept of quantity. This difference can again be interpreted as a more concrete level of mathematical processing.

The variability of the results on most of the tasks investigated has been underscored by several authors. Read and Ruyter (1985), for example, linked this individual variability with the progressive development of the skills. They stated that "awareness of phonological structure as it relates to reading and spelling is not all-or-none but exists at varying levels" (p. 49). The group differences between schooled and unschooled subjects reported in these studies make us overlook that the samples (and hence probably the populations) do overlap. Unschooled subjects, as a group, tend to score lower on various measures compared to schooled subjects. The unschooled subjects also typically show a wide individual variability. Indeed, a proportion of unschooled individuals achieves results that are comparable to those of schooled subjects (e.g., de Gelder et al., 1993). It is possible that schooling homogenizes cognitive processing in a culture, and thus, individuals with no formal education may or may not develop such skills through living experiences or internal motivation. How these individuals developed these skills without schooling remains unexplained. As mentioned earlier, Goody (1977) predicted that illiterate members of a culture would show the same global cognitive changes as the literate individuals by exposure to the new way of thinking. The results suggest that it is a possible but not a necessarily spontaneous change.

All these studies provide ground for skepticism regarding the value of formally testing those who have not been to school. Gregory (1984) summarized in two points what he believed to be a paradoxical notion of intelligence in psychometric examinations: (a) Presumably, intelligence does not increase with education, and (b) presumably, education improves various skills, which are those measured in IQ testing. To illustrate this paradox, Oliveira (1983) tested adults from a São Paulo shanty town to obtain descriptive information on reasoning and problem-solving processes in everyday life situations and to compare these processes to IQ test performance. The test scores clearly placed the subjects in the extremely low intelligence range and yet the author noted that these individuals were quite capable of dealing with the demands of their environment, thereby suggesting that IQ measurements may not be ecologically valid for the illiterate population. This logic can be generalized to any other type of standardized tests including language or visuospatial measures for which skill differences have been identified between schooled and unschooled subjects.

The analysis of the literature on normal illiterate subjects clearly shows that there are cognitive processing differences between this population and schooled subjects. Unschooled individuals show a more concrete level of cognitive processing that seems pervasive enough to have consequences in visuospatial skills (two-dimensional representation), language (e.g., naming, metaphonology), memory, and potentially several other abilities (e.g., computation of quantities). These results should alert clinicians to the validity issues associated with the use of formal tests standardized on a schooled population for an unschooled individual.

These differences also raise the important question of the organization of these skills in the brain. Do the differences in performance between schooled and unschooled individuals represent an underlying functional or an organizational difference? In other words, are these skills organized similarly in the brain but used with different strategies, or organized altogether differently? Researchers have investigated language lateralization and localization in unschooled subjects. Indeed, by analogy with children, it has been hypothesized that the acquisition of literacy skills was the factor responsible for the typical cortical language representation. From an empirical research standpoint, two different research avenues have been explored: The first approach compared the performance of schooled and unschooled normal subjects on dichotic listening tasks, which are supposed to reflect cerebral lateralization, and the second approach focused on aphasia symptoms or aphasia recovery rates between schooled and unschooled patients following left-hemisphere lesions. The second part of this chapter presents these studies.

LANGUAGE LATERALIZATION AND LOCALIZATION IN UNSCHOOLED INDIVIDUALS

Dichotic Listening Research

Damasio, Damasio, Castro-Caldas, and Hamsher (1979) submitted 16 un-schooled, 10 semischooled (4 years of education), and 21 schooled (>12 years of education) normal right-handed adults to three dichotic tasks: digit pairs, word pairs, and minimal word pairs. Because no difference appeared between the unschooled and semischooled subjects, they were combined into a new "dysliterate" group. For each condition, the schooled subjects outperformed the dysliterate group in accuracy (number of correct answers). The authors interpreted this result as a sign of the schooled subjects' higher linguistic training. Moreover, Damasio et al. (1979) found a significant difference between the dysliterate and the schooled subject group in the minimal word pair condition. The right-ear advantage remained in the schooled group, but they found a left-ear advantage in the dysliterate group. For the other two tasks, involving digits and dissimilar words, both groups showed a right-ear advantage. The authors concluded that language lateralization was the same for both groups, but that the linguistic decoding difficulty level of minimal pairs presented dichotically was beyond the capabilities of dysliterate subjects. Damasio et al. (1979) hypothesized that the dysliterate subjects treated the minimal difference as sound differences rather than phonemic differences. In that sense, these results would stem from the same underlying difficulty already discussed, namely, that the unschooled individuals cannot handle phonemic manipulation (in this case, simultaneous discrimination) at the postperceptual level. Furthermore, although they denied a difference in language lateralization between schooled and unschooled subjects, the authors acknowledged that "poor linguistic training and poor linguistic use contributed to a less capable language processor, e.g., a less mature dominance, calling for particular perceptual strategies in specific circumstances" (p. 337).

Tzavaras, Kaprinis, and Gatzoyas (1981) compared schooled (>12 years of education) and unschooled subjects on a digit pair paradigm with and without directed attention. Although this paradigm had not revealed group differences in the Damasio et al. (1979) study, Tzavaras et al. (1981) did find a significantly stronger right-ear advantage for unschooled subjects. The authors hypothesized that literacy develops spatial abilities, thereby increasing the role of the right hemisphere in linguistic processing. In unschooled individuals, however, the more strongly linguistic left hemisphere inhibits the right-hemisphere participation in language processing. These results were recently replicated by Tzavaras, Phocas, Kaprinis, and Karavatos (1993) with semischooled (<6 years of education) versus schooled (>12 years of education) subjects. In this study, the significantly stronger right-ear advantage of semischooled subjects also applied to word pairs. Unfortunately, the authors did not compute a separate comparison for the minimal pair stimuli. Castro and Morais (1987) dismissed the results of Damasio et al. (1979) and Tzavaras et al. (1981), in the former case because of lack of control over free orientation and attention, and in the latter because of an age discrepancy between the groups. In this carefully controlled experiment, Castro and Morais (1987) submitted unschooled, semischooled (>4 years of education), and schooled (<12 years of education) subjects to dissimilar word pairs and minimal word pairs (the phonemic difference being limited to voicing, place of articulation, or both). All groups showed a similar right-ear advantage for all the dichotic conditions.

In summary, these results are difficult to reconcile with each other. For example, Damasio et al. (1979) showed a stronger right-ear advantage for schooled subjects on the dissimilar word pair task, Tzavaras et al. (1981, 1993) a stronger right-ear advantage for unschooled subjects on the same task, and Castro and Morais (1987) no difference at all. It should also be noted that dichotic testing procedures have recently come under fire for reasons of validity (Efron, 1990). This caveat notwithstanding, it appears that dichotic studies of schooled and unschooled normal subjects have not established any group differences in language lateralization. At best, only a subtle difference in processing specific phonological contrasts was noted by Damasio et al. (1979), a difference that disappeared in a better controlled study (Castro & Morais, 1987).

Aphasia Studies

In 1904, 40 years after the publication of Paul Broca's famous paper (1865) in which he claimed a left cerebral dominance for language, Ernest Weber (1904) suggested—without actually challenging Broca's claim—that actualization of the left-hemisphere language dominance might depend on the acquisition of reading and writing skills. This hypothesis thus implied that to achieve a "normal" complete functional organization of cerebral language dominance an interaction between the environment (i.e., learning to read) and the human genetic program must take place. Weber's hypothesis was based on his observations of a few left-brain-damaged subjects who were either literate[1] or semiliterate. His hypothesis predicted that, compared to literate individuals, right-handed illiterate patients would show (a) a lower incidence of aphasia, (b) a greater incidence of crossed aphasia, and (c) a better recuperation of language skills.

In his dissertation, Moutier (1908) stated that the illiterate may not present with aphasia after left cerebral lesions. About 50 years later, Critchley (1956) hypothesized that language lateralization in illiterate individuals is probably comparable to that in children. Although he recognized that "clinical experience does not support the belief that aphasia is rare in illiterate persons" (Critchley, 1956, p. 335), the author posited that in aphasic patients with a premorbid superior mastery of language, the symptoms would be more severe and longer lasting. The following year, Gorlitzer von Mundy (1957), a German neurologist who had worked in India, described a case of a right-handed butler who presented with a severe right hemiplegia but no linguistic problems after a left anterior sylvian lesion. Von Mundy was also surprised at the low incidence of aphasia among right-handed illiterate adults with right hemiplegia. He further noted that in cases where aphasia did occur, the symptoms were only mild or transitory. More recently, based on single case reports, Wechsler (1976) and Métellus, Cathala, Aubry-Issartier, and Bodak (1981) argued that the cerebral representation of language might be somewhat different in the illiterate, as opposed to the school-educated. In 1964, Eisenson also put forth this view in a debate with Roman Jakobson. He based his opinion on a subjectively observed lower frequency of aphasia among low-ranking American soldiers.

In addition to the case reports and other incidental unsupported observations, several authors have investigated this issue by comparing subject samples. Smith (1971) compared two groups of chronic aphasic patients: 21 subjects with less than a high school degree (mean: 9.4 years of education), and 57 subjects with more than a high school degree (mean: 14.3 years of education). The results showed that there were no qualitative symptomatology differences between the groups. However, the less educated group displayed more severe sequelae at this chronic stage. The author concluded that the difference was not in symptom severity between the groups, but simply reflected the premorbid discrepancy in language competence. Although these results are not pertinent to complete illiteracy issues, they show that level of education does not seem to influence language lateralization or rate of recovery.

---

[1]Although the effects of literacy versus those of schooling are not distinguishable in the studies reviewed in this section, most authors have linked language lateralization with the acquisition of a written code.

Cameron, Currier, and Haerer (1971) reviewed the hospital records of 65 adults with left-hemisphere strokes. Unfortunately, their definition of aphasia was heavily biased. To be labeled aphasic a patient must have had a right-sided weakness and have "completely or nearly completely lost his ability to speak" (Cameron et al., 1971, p. 161). Their groups included schooled (mean: 10.5 years of education), semischooled (mean: 5.6 years of education), and illiterate (but somewhat schooled with a mean of 2.5 years of education). The authors did not specify how illiteracy was determined. They observed that aphasia (as defined) occurred in 78% of the schooled subjects, 64% of the semischooled, and 36% of the subjects considered illiterate. A chi-square analysis only revealed a significant difference between the literate and the illiterate subject groups. The authors stated that "language is not as well 'planted' in the dominant hemisphere in illiterates as it is in literate persons," and that "language patterns are more bilaterally represented" (1971, p. 163). Although this study has many obvious flaws, such as the definitions of aphasia and illiteracy, and the lack of control for lesion site and size, the biggest challenge to their conclusions comes from their own figures. Indeed, within their illiterate group, the subjects who were aphasic had actually less schooling than the nonaphasic illiterate subjects (a mean of 1.8 years of education for the aphasic subjects versus a mean of 2.9 years for the nonaphasic individuals).

The conclusions of Damasio, Castro-Caldas, Grosso, and Ferro (1976), however, do not support the Cameron et al. conclusions. Damasio et al. (1976) used a Portuguese adaptation of the Boston Diagnostic Aphasia Examination to test a random series of 247 subjects with focal lesions. The procedure led to a diagnosis of aphasia in 114 out of 209 schooled subjects (54.5%) and in 21 out of 38 unschooled subjects (55.2%). These percentages are remarkably similar. The authors further reported that the aphasia type and severity between the two groups were comparable. They matched 20 unschooled aphasic subjects with 20 schooled subjects for age, gender, lesion site, and aphasia type, and compared the performance of the subjects on the Token Test. No significant differences were found. Although the average education level of the schooled group was not stated, Damasio et al. (1976) still were able to conclude that "brain specialization for language does not depend on literacy" (p. 300). Ferro, Santos, Castro-Caldas, and Mariano (1980) looked for differences in the distribution of aphasia types according to four education levels (uneducated, less than 4, 5 to 10, and more than 10 years of education). Their results showed that the frequency distributions for the aphasic syndromes did not differ between the various literacy level groups. Further, Miceli et al. (1981) compared educational level (low, <5 years; mid, 5 to 8 years; and high, >8 years) with presence, severity, and type of aphasia in 390 right-handed left-hemisphere-lesioned subjects. The results showed that educational level did not correlate with either of these three variables, thereby confirming the observations of Damasio et al.

(1976) and contradicting the results of Cameron et al. (1971) and Smith (1971).

More recently, Parreira et al. (1995) compared the Western Aphasia Battery performances of 5 schooled and 12 unschooled patients with Wernicke's aphasia. A computerized tomography (CT) scan comparison study between the groups showed that the lesion sites were similar between the groups, thereby suggesting that the location of the language areas is typical. The authors further observed that the illiterate subjects scored lower on the comprehension and repetition subtests. Although no details about the type of errors are presented, the authors concluded that these variations are the result of different strategies used by unschooled individuals. Furthermore, they posited that these differences reflected the premorbid cognitive processing strategies characteristics already observed between schooled and unschooled normal subjects.

Lecours et al. (1988) divided a sample of 296 right-handed monolingual adult Portuguese speakers into six different groups: three unschooled groups (62 normal controls, 48 left-hemisphere stroke patients, 47 right-hemisphere stroke patients) and three schooled groups (46 normal controls, 61 left-hemisphere stroke patients, 32 right-hemisphere stroke patients). All six groups were statistically homogeneous for age, and the three' groups of literate subjects were homogeneous for level of education (means: 8.3, 8.6, and 8.3 years of education, respectively). The testing protocol included a spontaneous speech sample, and auditory comprehension, picture naming, and repetition tasks. Consistent with previous studies, the unschooled normal controls made significantly more errors across the board than the schooled normal controls.

In the spontaneous speech sample, more phonemic deviations were reported in unschooled versus schooled right-hemisphere stroke subjects. The naming subtest, however, revealed significant group differences. Using a chi-square paradigm (proportion of the sample reaching a set criterion), there were significant differences between the normal controls and both left-hemisphere stroke patient groups, between the illiterate right-hemisphere stroke group and the illiterate control group, but not between the literate control group and the right-hemisphere stroke literate patients. This observation prompted the authors to conclude that a naming difficulty appears in unschooled individuals after right-hemisphere involvement, but not in schooled subjects. Unfortunately, the raw data presented (Table 6.1) represent error rates and thus are not directly illustrative of the statistical analysis performed. The data in Table 6.1 show that both right-hemisphere stroke groups performed worse than their respective controls in frequency of naming errors. It would be interesting to run comparisons of means based on these data to confirm the result obtained with the chi-square analysis.

The repetition subtest showed the expected pattern of results (Table 6.1). The two left-hemisphere experimental groups differed from normal controls

TABLE 6.1
Results of the Naming, Repetition, and Auditory Comprehension Subtests in Three Groups of
Subjects in Percentages of Errors

	Controls		Left Stroke		Right Stroke	
	Illiterate	Literate	Illiterate	Literate	Illiterate	Literate
Naming	14.1	4.7	32.2	27.7	20.6	10.7
Repetition	25.5	6.9	44.0	27.7	24.1	13.4
Auditory comprehension	24.0	7.1	43.0	24.5	36.4	21.9

but not the two right-hemisphere experimental groups. As expected, only the unschooled left-hemisphere stroke group made a significant number of phonemic paraphasias.

The auditory comprehension subtest did not reveal overall significant differences between the control groups and any of the experimental groups (Table 6.1). However, after controlling for unilateral neglect in the sentence-picture matching tasks, significant differences appeared for both left-hemisphere stroke groups, as compared with their appropriate control group, but not for the right-hemisphere stroke groups.

The authors reported that the expected differences between schooled and unschooled populations were present in their results. They further noted that their results supported the principles of classical aphasiology except for the unexpected naming difficulties exhibited by the unschooled right-hemisphere stroke patients. Lecours et al. (1988) claimed that the recognized difficulty of unschooled subjects with two-dimensional representation could not have been responsible for the discrepancy because both unschooled groups (controls and right-hemisphere stroke) were faced with the same task. However, these two groups were very different in their gender makeup (unschooled controls, 22 males, 40 females; unschooled right-hemisphere stroke, 31 males, 16 females), and the potential confounding influence of the gender variable was not controlled.

Lecours et al. (1988) concluded that the lateralization of language skills in unschooled individuals is the same as for schooled subjects, and hence that learning a written language does not influence the predetermined pattern of language lateralization. However, they posited that unschooled individuals may use different strategies when performing specific language tasks (i.e., lexical access) that tend to recruit their right hemisphere to a greater extent than schooled individuals. They further acknowledged that the cause of this strategy difference could be attributed either to literacy or to schooling, because both variables have been shown to influence certain aspects of

cognitive and language processing. Lecours (1989) reiterated these conclusions and added that there does not seem to be any difference in the presence
of aphasia between schooled and unschooled subjects.

Castro-Caldas (1993) and Castro-Caldas, Ferro, Guerreiro, Mariano, and
Farrajota (1995) concluded from their review of the literature that there are
no differences in language lateralization between schooled and unschooled
individuals. The authors also acknowledged that there are differences in
strategies between the two populations. These conclusions seem to be in
agreement with those of Lecours (1989) and Lecours et al. (1988), but they
proposed different underlying causative factors. Where Lecours (1989) posited a more important right-hemisphere language involvement in lexical
access, Castro-Caldas (1993) and Castro-Caldas et al. (1995) concluded that
unschooled individuals require a greater visuospatial involvement because
of their unfamiliarity with the task. These authors reinterpreted the results
of Lecours et al. (1988) by stating that "naming of iconographic materials
by illiterates requires a greater effort and there is probably a larger weight
of non-verbal processing of the stimuli, which depends on right-hemisphere
mechanisms" (Castro-Caldas, 1993, p. 207). In other words, these individuals
need a more active participation of right-hemisphere "mechanisms not exactly related to linguistic processing" (Castro-Caldas et al., 1995, p. 88).
Castro-Caldas et al. (1995) also rejected one of the implications of a more
bilaterally distributed language representation, namely, the increase in the
incidence of crossed aphasia in the unschooled population. They viewed
crossed aphasia as a biological aberration of language lateralization, completely independent of external influences such as schooling or literacy.
They reported that they could not find an increased frequency of crossed
aphasia in their unschooled population (Castro-Caldas, 1991; see Coppens
& Hungerford, chapter 7, this volume).

In conclusion, although some early incidental reports have suggested that
language is not as strongly lateralized in unschooled as compared to schooled
individuals, more recent investigations have consistently concluded that language lateralization is similar in both populations. The implications of a
lateralization difference, such as a lower incidence of aphasia, or a greater
incidence of crossed aphasia in unschooled subjects, have also been rejected
by most authors. Nevertheless, researchers do agree that there is a difference
in language processing between the two populations. It reflects the premorbid processing differences, which are usually expressed as differences in
processing "strategies." Specifically, naming tasks may recruit more involvement from the right hemisphere. Although the results leading to this hypothesis (Lecours et al., 1988) are in need of replication, the two current
views attribute the observed processing strategy difference either to linguistic
(Lecours, 1989; Lecours et al., 1988) or to visuospatial causes (Castro-Caldas,
1993; Castro-Caldas et al., 1995).

Aphasia Recovery

Métellus et al. (1981) reported a case of Wernicke's aphasia in an unschooled patient. They noted a significant improvement of the patient's oral language after 1 year postonset. However, they also described a severe aphasic symptomatology at 2 months postonset. Such an observation hardly qualifies as an unschooled rapid rate of aphasia recovery. In contradistinction to that incidental case study, Smith (1971) reported that in his sample of subjects, education level influenced symptom severity in chronic aphasia patients. Unexpectedly, Smith noticed that aphasic patients with less schooling displayed a more severe aphasic symptomatology than patients with a higher level of education, an observation that clearly contradicts the hypothesis of more bilateral language strategies in the former population. Smith (1971) attributed this difference in severity of symptoms to the premorbid group discrepancy in language abilities, rather than to a difference in recovery rates. To be sure, this study did not look at totally unschooled aphasic patients.

Castro-Caldas et al. (1995) followed schooled and unschooled right-handed global aphasia patients longitudinally. The subjects in the two groups were matched for type of aphasia, severity of aphasia at onset, age, and gender. There was no difference in the aphasia quotient between the samples at 6 months postonset. Unfortunately, individual symptoms were not compared.

Parente and Lecours (in press) retested 59 stroke patients after 6 months, using the same elementary bedside aphasia screening test used initially. All subjects had remained stroke-free, surgery-free, and did not receive speech/language services during the interval. Of the 59 subjects, 31 unschooled (18 left-hemisphere and 13 right-hemisphere strokes), and 28 schooled (21 left-hemisphere and 7 right-hemisphere strokes) subjects were tested. These four groups were statistically identical in terms of gender, and the two literate subgroups in terms of education level. Yet these four subgroups were not homogeneous in age, as the schooled left-hemisphere stroke group was significantly younger than the other three.

More aphasic subjects improved in the unschooled left-hemisphere stroke group than in any other group in motor and sensory measures and in naming abilities. The superior improvement in naming skills in the unschooled left-hemisphere stroke group was still present after controlling for the sensory and motor variables. However, no difference was observed in auditory comprehension or repetition. The authors concluded that the right hemisphere of unschooled individuals may be able to assume some linguistic function (i.e., naming) more easily than in schooled individuals in case of damage to the language-dominant left hemisphere. However, this hypothesis cannot account for the fact that no significant improvement in naming was observed in right-hemisphere lesioned unschooled subjects.

To sum up, it does not appear that unschooled aphasia patients improve significantly better overall than their schooled counterparts. One study has even reported more severe sequelae for chronic aphasic subjects with less schooling. Focusing on individual symptoms, Parente and Lecours (in press) reported that naming abilities seemed to show a more favorable outcome following a left-hemisphere lesion in unschooled versus schooled aphasic patients. However, the expected corollary that unschooled subjects with right-hemisphere lesion should also improve better than their schooled counterparts was not observed. Taken together, these results are still too scarce and conflicting to allow major conclusions to be drawn. However, there is no overwhelming indication to date suggesting that unschooled aphasic subjects recover better than schooled aphasic individuals.

CONCLUSIONS

Literacy is a fairly easy construct to define; however, the effects of literacy on cognitive processing are very difficult to isolate from other confounding variables such as culture, SES, or schooling. There is a convincing body of literature showing that all of these variables influence the development or even the nature of cognition to some extent. However, most authors indicated that the schooling variable was the most influential even when comparing cultures or SES levels. The observed differences in cognitive processing included a more abstract thinking (including two-dimensional representations), better proficiency at more complex linguistic tasks, higher IQ measurements, and better results in naming, repetition, and verbal and nonverbal memory tasks. The only difference in performance associated with the literacy variable was metaphonological manipulation. More specifically, the results of these studies suggest that syllable-level metaphonological skills can develop in preliterate or illiterate individuals, but that phoneme-level manipulation skills need literacy training to further develop. Interestingly, most of the group differences in cognitive development seemed to require a few years of schooling to be clearly established, whereas metaphonological manipulation skills associated with literacy seem to appear fairly quickly. These results clearly show that unschooled individuals perform less well than schooled subjects when faced with a variety of cognitive and language tasks, which invalidates using the norms of most formal measurements used clinically in psychology and speech-language pathology. Moreover, the greater individual variability noted in the unschooled population is linked to idiosyncratic learning environments, whereas a formal educational system is believed to homogenize cognitive processing within the schooled population.

What do these differences mean in terms of language lateralization and localization? Does schooling affect the representation of language or only the strategies for language use? The results of the few studies involving dichotic tasks are contradictory and hence no strong conclusions can be drawn. Interestingly, the most carefully designed experiment (Castro &

Morais, 1987) among those reviewed did not show any influence of schooling on language lateralization.

The older reports of aphasia in illiterate individuals are incidental observations without supporting evidence or case studies without generalizable value. A review of more recent investigations suggests that the frequency and type of aphasia following left-hemisphere focal lesions do not differ between schooled and unschooled subjects. Similarly, there is no indication that the frequency of crossed aphasia is higher in unschooled aphasic individuals, and no report presents convincing data pointing to a more rapid overall recovery rate in unschooled aphasic patients. Still, specific differences in language processing performance between schooled and unschooled aphasic subjects have been reported. These differences can be interpreted as a reflection of the already noted premorbid discrepancies. In other words, clinicians can expect unschooled aphasic patients to perform worse than schooled aphasic patients on tasks involving an increased potential reliance on phonemic analysis (e.g., repetition of nonwords, verbal memory tasks), and two-dimensional representations (e.g., oral/picture matching, picture naming, or visuospatial tasks). Moreover, the purported absence of a phonological lexical access route in unschooled aphasic patients, because of their unfamiliarity with the phonological system, may further hamper lexical retrieval, and hence verbal memory performance.

These observations suggest that the language and cognitive processing differences between schooled and unschooled populations can be reduced to a limited but influential set of basic processing principles, the effects of which percolate to affect a variety of tasks usually involved in neuropsychological or linguistic testing. In some instances, the underlying cause of the observed task performance discrepancy is not yet identified. For example, Lecours et al. (1988) concluded that picture naming seems to recruit more right-hemisphere strategies in unschooled individuals, but it is not yet clear whether visuospatial or language systems are activated. Nevertheless, researchers do agree that language lateralization and localization are identical in schooled and unschooled populations, but that there are differences in language processing strategies. The causes of these differences lie in several variables such as SES, cultural background, schooling, and literacy training. It appears that schooling is the most influential of these variables, but also that metaphonological manipulation is the only skill exclusively linked with exposure to a written code.

REFERENCES

Amante, D., VanHouten, V. W., Grieve, J. H., Bader, C. A., & Margules, P. H. (1977). Neuropsychological deficit, ethnicity, and socioeconomic status. *Journal of Consulting and Clinical Psychology, 45,* 524–535.

Ardila, A., Rosselli, M., & Rosas, P. (1989). Neuropsychological assessment in illiterates: Visuospatial and memory abilities. *Brain and Cognition, 11,* 147–166.

Bertelson, P., & de Gelder, B. (1989). Learning about reading from illiterates. In A. M. Galaburda (Ed.), *From reading to neurons* (pp. 1–23). Cambridge, MA: MIT Press.

Bertelson, P., de Gelder, B., Tfouni, L. V., & Morais, J. (1989). Metaphonological abilities of adult illiterates: New evidence of heterogeneity. *European Journal of Cognitive Psychology, 1*(3), 239–250.

Bertolucci, P., Brucki, S. M. D., Campacci, S. R., & Juliano, Y. (1994). O mini-exame do estado mental em uma população geral: Impacto da escolaridade. *Arquivos de Neuropsiquiatria, 52*(1), 1–7.

Bowey, J. A., & Francis, J. (1991). Phonological analysis as a function of age and exposure to reading instruction. *Applied Psycholinguistics, 12,* 91–121.

Broca, P. (1865). Sur le siège du language articulé. *Bulletin de la Société d'anthropologie, 6,* 337–393.

Cameron, R. F., Currier, R. D., & Haerer, A. F. (1971). Aphasia and literacy. *British Journal of Disorders of Communication, 6,* 161–163.

Carraher, T. N., Carraher, D. W., & Schliemann, A. D. (1982). Na vida dez; Na escola zero: Os contextos culturais da aprendizagem da matemática. *Cadernos de Pesquisa, 42,* 79–86.

Castro, S. L., & Morais, J. (1987). Ear differences in illiterates. *Neuropsychologia, 25,* 409–417.

Castro-Caldas, A. (1991). Crossed aphasia as a model of atypical specialization. In I. P. Martins, A. Castro-Caldas, H. R. van Dongen, & A. van Hout (Eds.), *Acquired aphasia in children: Acquisition and breakdown of language in the developing brain* (pp. 83–93). Dordrecht, The Netherlands: Kluwer.

Castro-Caldas, A. (1993). Problems of testing aphasia in illiterate subjects. In F. J. Stachowiak (Ed.), *Developments in the assessment and rehabilitation of brain-damaged patients* (pp. 205–210). Tübingen: Gunter Narr Verlag.

Castro-Caldas, A., Ferro, J. M., Guerreiro, M., Mariano, G., & Farrajota, L. (1995). Influence of literacy (vs illiteracy) on the characteristics of acquired aphasia in adults. In C. K. Leong & R. M. Joshi (Eds.), *Developmental and acquired dyslexia* (pp. 79–81). Dordrecht, The Netherlands: Kluwer.

Critchley, M. (1956). Premorbid literacy, and the pattern of subsequent aphasia. *Proceedings of the Royal Society of Medicine, 49,* 335–336.

Damasio, A. R., Castro-Caldas, A., Grosso, J. T., & Ferro, J. M. (1976). Brain specialization for language does not depend on literacy. *Archives of Neurology, 33,* 300–301.

Damasio, H., Damasio, A. R., Castro-Caldas, A., & Hamsher, K. (1979). Reversal of ear advantage for phonetically similar words in illiterates. *Journal of Clinical Neuropsychology, 1,* 331–338.

Dauster, T. (1975). *Análise do nível operatório do adulto analfabeto.* Unpublished doctoral dissertation, Mobral, Rio de Janeiro.

de Gelder, B., Vroomen, J., & Bertelson, P. (1993). The effects of alphabetic-reading competence on language representation in bilingual Chinese subjects. *Psychological Research, 55,* 315–321.

Dordain, J. L., Nespoulos, M., Bourdeau, M., & Lecours, A. R. (1983). Capacités verbales d'adultes normaux soumis a un protocole linguistique de l'aphasie. *Acta Neurologica Belgica, 83,* 5–16.

Efron, R. (1990). *The decline and fall of hemispheric specialization.* Hillsdale, NJ: Lawrence Erlbaum Associates.

Eisenson, J. (1964). Discussion. In A. V. S. de Reuck & M. O'Connor (Eds.), *Disorders of language* (p. 259). London: Churchill.

Ferro, J. M., Santos, M. E., Castro-Caldas, A., & Mariano, M. G. (1980). Gesture recognition in aphasia. *Journal of Clinical Neuropsychology, 2,* 277–292.

Garcia, C., & Guerreiro, M. (1983, June). *Pseudo-dementia from illiteracy.* Poster session presented at the sixth European meeting of the International Neuropsychological Society, Lisbon, Portugal.

Goody, J. (1977). *The domestication of the savage mind.* Cambridge: Cambridge University Press.

Gorlitzer von Mundy, V. (1957). Zur Frage der paarig veranlagten Schachzentren. *Der Nervenartz, 28,* 212–216.

Greenfield, P. M. (1972). Oral or written language: The consequences for cognitive development in Africa, the United States and England. *Language and Speech, 15,* 169–178.

Greenfield, P. M., & Bruner, J. S. (1966). Culture and cognitive growth. *International Journal of Psychology, 1*(2), 89–107.

Gregory, R. L. (1984). *Mind in science.* London: Penguin.

Grossi, D., Correra, G., Calise, C., Ruscitto, M. A., Vecchione, V., Vigliardi, M. V., & Nolfe, G. (1993). Evaluation of the influence of illiteracy on neuropsychological performances by elderly persons. *Perceptual and Motor Skills, 77,* 859–866.

Kolinsky, R., Morais, J., Content, A., & Cary, L. (1987). Finding parts within figures: A developmental study. *Perception, 16,* 399–407.

Laboratory of Comparative Human Cognition. (1983). Culture and cognitive development. In P. H. Mussen (Series Ed.) & W. Kessen (Vol. Ed.), *Handbook of child psychology: Vol. 1. History, theory, and methods* (4th ed., pp. 295–356). New York: John Wiley & Sons.

Laurendeau-Bendavid, M. (1977). Culture, schooling, and cognitive development: A comparative study of children in French Canada and Rwanda. In P. R. Dasan (Ed.), *Piagetian psychology: Cross cultural contributions* (pp. 123–168). New York: Gardner Press.

Lecours, A. R. (1989). Literacy and acquired aphasia. In A. M. Galaburda (Ed.), *From reading to neurons* (pp. 27–39). Cambridge, MA: MIT Press.

Lecours, A. R., Mehler, J., Parente, M. A., Beltrami, M. C., de Tolipan, L. C., Cary, L., Castro, M. J., Carrono, V., Chagastelles, L., Dehaut, F., Delgado, R., Evangelista, A., Fajgenbaum, S., Fontoura, C., Karmann, D. F., Gurd, J., Torne, C. H., Jakubovicz, R., Kac, R., Lefevre, B., Lima, C., Maciel, J., Mansur, L., Martinez, R., Nobrega, M. C., Osorio, Z., Paciornik, J., Papaterra, F.,Penedo, M. A. J., Saboya, B., Scheuer, C., da Silva, A. B., Spinardi, M., & Teixeira, M. (1988). Illiteracy and brain damage: 3. A contribution to the study of speech and language disorders in illiterates with unilateral brain damage (initial testing). *Neuropsychologia, 26,* 575–589.

Lecours, A. R., Mehler J., Parente, M. A., Caldeira, A., Cary, L., Castro, M. J., Dehaut, F., Delgado, R., Gurd, J., Karmann, D. F., Jakubovitz, R., Osorio, Z., Cabral, L. S., & Junqueira, A. M. S. (1987). Illiteracy and brain damage: 1. Aphasia testing in culturally contrasted populations (control subjects). *Neuropsychologia, 25,* 231–245.

Lecours, A. R., Nespoulous, J.-L., Joanette, Y., Lemay, A., Lafond, D., Cot, F., & Rascol, A. (1986). *Protocole MT-86 d'examen linguistique de l'aphasie.* Montreal: Les Editions de la Côte-des-Neiges.

Luria, A. R. (1976). *Cognitive development. Its cultural and social foundations.* Cambridge, MA: Harvard University Press.

Métellus, J., Cathala, H. P., Aubry-Issartier, & Bodak, A. (1981). Une observation d'aphasie chez une illettrée (analphabète): Reflexions critiques sur les fonctions cérébrales concourant au langage. *Annales de Médecine et Psychologie, 139,* 992–1001.

Miceli, G., Caltagirone, C., Gainotti, G., Masullo, C., Silveri, M. C., & Villa, G. (1981). Influence of age, sex, literacy and pathologic lesion on incidence, severity and type of aphasia. *Acta Neurologica Scandinavica, 64,* 370–382.

Morais, J. (1994). *L'art de lire.* Paris: Editions Odile Jacob.

Morais, J., Cary, L., Alegria, J., & Bertelson, P. (1979). Does awareness of speech as a sequence of phones arise spontaneously? *Cognition, 7,* 323–331.

Moutier, F. (1908). *L'aphasie de Broca.* Paris: Steinheil.

Oliveira, M. K. (1983). Inteligência e vida cotidiana: Competências cognitivas de adultos de baixa renda. *Cadernos de Pesquisa, 4,* 45–54.

Orsini, A., Chiacchio, L., Cinque, M., Cocchiaro, C., Schiappa, O., & Grossi, D. (1986). Effects of age, education and sex on two tests of immediate memory: A study of normal subjects from 20 to 99 years of age. *Perceptual and Motor Skills, 63*, 727–732.

Orsini, A., Grossi, D., Capitani, E., Laiacona, M., Papagno, C., & Vallar, G. (1987). Verbal and spatial immediate memory span: Normative data from 1355 adults and 1112 children. *Italian Journal of Neurological Sciences, 8*, 539–548.

Orsini, A., Schiappa, O., & Grossi, D. (1981). Sex and cultural differences in children's spatial and verbal memory span. *Perceptual and Motor Skills, 53*, 39–42.

Ostrosky-Solis, F., Canseco E., Quintanar, L., Navarro, E., Meneses, S., & Ardila, A. (1985). Sociocultural effects in neuropsychological assessment. *International Journal of Neuroscience, 27*, 53–66.

Parente, M. A. (1984). *Habilidades Construtivas em analfabetos: Um estudo através de desenho e construção do cubo.* Unpublished dissertation, Pontifícia Universidade Católica de São Paulo, Brasil.

Parente, M. A. P., & Lecours, A. R. (in press). Participação do hemisfério direito na recuperação lingüística de analfabetos. *Neuropsychologia Latina.*

Parreira, E., Alburquerque, L., Guerreiro, M., Leal, M. G., Farrajota, L., Fonseca, J., & Castro-Caldas, A. (1995). Wernicke's aphasia in illiterate subjects: CT scan and clinical correlations [abstract]. *Journal of the International Neuropsychological Society, 1*, 206.

Read, C., & Ruyter, L. (1985). Reading and spelling skills in adults of low literacy. *Remedial and Special Education, 6*(6), 43–52.

Reis, A. I., & Castro-Caldas, A. (1995). Illiteracy: A cause for biased cognitive development. *Journal of the International Neuropsychological Society.*

Reis, A., Guerreiro, M., & Castro-Caldas, A. (1994). Influence of educational level of non brain-damaged subjects on visual naming capacities. *Journal of Clinical and Experimental Neuropsychology, 16*(6), 939–942.

Reis, A., Guerreiro, M., & Castro-Caldas, A. (1996, February). *The illiterate brain: The influence of an untrained phonological input buffer in oral repetition and digit span of transcortical aphasics.* Poster session presented at the Nineteeth Annual International Neuropsychological Society Mid-Year Conference, Veldhoven, The Netherlands.

Reis, A. I., Guerreiro, M., Garcia, C., & Castro-Caldas, A. (1995). How does an illiterate subject process the lexical component of arithmetics? [abstract]. *Journal of the International Neuropsychological Society, 1*, 206.

Rosselli, M., Ardila, A., & Rosas, P. (1990). Neuropsychological assessment in illiterates: Language and praxic abilities. *Brain and Cognition, 12*, 281–296.

Scribner, S., & Cole, M. (1981). *The psychology of literacy.* Cambridge, MA: Harvard University Press.

Smith, A. (1971). Objective indices of severity of chronic aphasia in stroke patients. *Journal of Speech and Hearing Disorders, 36*, 167–207.

Tfouni, L. V. (1983). *O resgate da identidade. Investigação sobre o uso da modalidade por adultos não-alfabetizados.* Campinas: IEL-UNICAMP.

Tzavaras, A., Kaprinis, G., & Gatzoyas, A. (1981). Literacy and hemispheric specialization for language: Digit dichotic listening in illiterates. *Neuropsychologia, 19*, 565–570.

Tzavaras, A., Phocas, C., Kaprinis, G., & Karavatos, A. (1993). Literacy and hemispheric specialization for language: Dichotic listening in young functionally illiterate men. *Perceptual and Motor Skills, 77*, 195–199.

Vygotsky, L. S. (1978). *Mind in society. The development of higher psychological processes.* Cambridge, MA: Harvard University Press.

Weber, E. (1904). Das Schreiben als Ursache der einseitigen Lage des Sprachzentrums. *Zentralblatt für Physiologie, 18*, 341–347.

Wechsler, A. F. (1976). Crossed aphasia in an illiterate dextral. *Brain and Language, 3*, 164–172.

CHAPTER SEVEN

Crossed Aphasia

Patrick Coppens
Suzanne Hungerford
Moorhead State University, Moorhead, Minnesota

Crossed aphasia (CA) is defined as an acquired language impairment following a right-hemisphere lesion in a right-handed patient. The definition, the inclusion/exclusion criteria, and what was once considered "typical" symptomatology have undergone changes over time. However, the rarity of the phenomenon has been underscored by many authors. In the present chapter, CA refers to persistent language impairments caused by a single neurological event localized in the right hemisphere of right-handed individuals. This definition is purposely inclusive rather than exclusive.

One aim of this chapter is to review the literature on CA. The review of the literature yielded 136 cases of CA that are presented in a table format in the appendices. The 114 CA cases with vascular etiology appear in Appendix A, the 20 cases of CA with tumor are in Appendix B, and finally, 2 cases of CA in children are in Appendix C. Both the language and nonverbal characteristics are noted. In most cases, the investigators' diagnoses are reported. In other cases, we have attempted to label the symptomatologies using the classical aphasia categories. On occasion, judgments needed to be made from the descriptions provided in the case reports concerning the presence or the absence of specific signs, such as apraxias, or discrepancy between written and oral language.

Another purpose of this chapter is to attempt to determine in what measure CA can be compared to aphasia following left-hemisphere lesions, or uncrossed aphasia (UCA), in right-handed individuals. Is CA clearly distinguishable from UCA? Or, conversely, are CA and UCA similar because both are acquired language impairments following a lesion in the language-dominant hemisphere?

Finally, we also address the possibility of subgroups in CA, based on the presence or absence of typical right-hemisphere symptoms such as neglect, and prosodic disturbances. Similarly, the involvement or sparing of typical left-hemisphere skills in CA, such as praxis or writing, may also provide a basis for the identification of subgroups.

HISTORICAL BACKGROUND

Paul Broca declared in 1865 that speech was represented in the left hemisphere of the brain, more specifically in the foot of the third frontal convolution. However, at the same time, he readily acknowledged the existence of a small number of cases in which the right hemisphere was dominant for speech (Broca, 1865). In 1899, Byrom Bramwell coined the term *crossed aphasia* to indicate a language dysfunction following a cerebral lesion ipsilateral to the dominant hand. In other words, CA also referred to left-handers with a lesion in the left hemisphere. Bramwell proceeded to specify that CA is very rare (also in left-handers), that it usually causes transient deficits, and that he was not aware of any cases involving right-handed patients. The hypothesis of the purported rarity of CA in left-handers resisted analysis for many years (Anastasopoulos & Kokkini, 1962). In 1921, Claude and Schaeffer believed that CA in left-handed individuals was even more unusual than CA in right-handers. Although some authors noticed that aphasia following left-hemisphere damage in left-handers was more frequent than expected (Conrad, 1949, cited in Subirana, 1952), it was only in 1960 that Zangwill recognized the "possibility that even in those who are fully left-handed the dominant hemisphere may be the left" (p. 5). Consequently, the term CA progressively came to refer only to right-handed aphasic individuals with a lesion in the right hemisphere. Still, some authors prefer the older definition of CA (Nagaraja et al., 1989).

Search for a Cause

Although Broca recognized the possible dissociation of handedness and hemispheric dominance for language, he believed it to be pathological in nature, and thus necessarily the result of a lesion or dysfunction in the early stages of brain development (Broca, 1865). Mendel (1912, 1914) considered three potential explanations for CA: the absence of pyramidal decussation, a concomitant left-hemisphere lesion, or a language-dominant right hemisphere. The first two hypotheses needed to be considered because of the unavailability of imagery at the time to unequivocally locate the lesion. Still, Mendel rejected them for the latter.

Early authors interpreted the right-handedness of CA patients as acquired instead of developmental. Because it was still believed that left-handed individuals were right-hemisphere-dominant for language, it logically followed that in these patients, handedness changed whereas right-hemisphere language dominance persisted. Jackson (1880) reported on a left-handed patient who became aphasic following a right-hemisphere lesion. During childhood, this patient was forced to use his right hand for several activities including writing. Bramwell (1899) also reported the case of a CA patient whose left hand was tied to his chair when he was learning to write. Forced switching of handedness as the underlying cause of CA became a prominent explanation of left hemiplegia with aphasia in right-handers, and was even evoked in cases where there was no history of forced handedness switch (Ettlinger, Jackson, & Zangwill, 1955; Joffroy, 1903; Marinesco, Grigoresco, & Axente, 1938). Thus, very early, authors were aware of this phenomenon, and only patients with "natural" right-handedness were considered as acceptable candidates for the diagnosis of CA.

Bramwell (1899) believed that three factors were responsible for directing language abilities to a specific hemisphere, namely, heredity, handedness, and hand preference for writing. Heredity refers to the handedness of parents and ancestors, handedness refers to an individual's natural hand preference, and hand preference for writing refers to "learning to write and the act of writing with the right hand" (p. 1478). According to Bramwell, each of these variables tends to lateralize language in the contralateral hemisphere. For example, left-handedness would cause language to lateralize to the right hemisphere, but the presence of right-handed family members and learning to write with the right hand would "drive" language dominance to the left hemisphere. In this fashion, Bramwell explained the supposedly rare cases of CA in left-handers, that is, language impairment following left-hemisphere lesions in left-handers. In right-handers, however, the presence of left-handed family members is the only one of the three hypotheses that could transfer the "leading speech centers" (p. 1477) to the right hemisphere, and therefore could account for CA in right-handers. Bramwell acknowledged having no possible explanation for CA in right-handers without familial sinistrality. This concept of familial sinistrality was later coined *stock-brainedness* by Kennedy (1916).

Since then, many authors have embraced stock-brainedness as the most probable cause of CA. For example, Anastasopoulos and Kokkini (1962) stated that "a relationship between handedness and brainedness for speech exists always, even if such a relationship is not found in the individual but is revealed through family investigation only" (p. 9). However, in certain cases of CA, no familial sinistrality could be identified. In order to explain them, the stock-brainedness hypothesis was carried to the extreme by suggesting that stock-brainedness could bypass several generations and suddenly reappear (Cosman, 1923), an explanation clearly rejected by Pillon, Desi, and Lhermitte (1979) who only took one generation into consideration for familial sinistrality decisions. One of their patients had one grandfather and one granddaughter left-handed; the other had a left-handed granddaughter as well but no information was available for the grandparents. Although not explicitly stated, this selection criterion implied that familial sinistrality two generations removed is not powerful enough to explain CA.

Brown and colleagues (Brown, 1976; Brown & Hécaen, 1976) revived a hypothesis proposed in 1962 by Anastasopoulos and Kokkini that compared CA with acquired aphasia in children and left-handers. They maintained that CA was the result of an interruption of the normal progression of the lateralization pattern from bilateral language representation to a strong left-hemisphere localization. According to this view, CA is characterized either by bilateral language representation or diffuse intrahemispheric language representation. Brown and Hécaen (1976) stated that the common ground between acquired childhood aphasia, aphasia in left-handers, and CA is the "bilateral language representation, rather than a strict or truly anomalous language lateralization to the right hemisphere" (p. 188). This hypothesis is contradicted by the cases of CA in which the symptoms mirror those in UCA, the cases in which a strong right-hemisphere lateralization is indubitable (e.g., Delreux, de Partz, Kevers, & Callewaert, 1989), and by the CA cases associated with jargonagraphia (Assal, 1982; Assal, Perentes, & Deruaz, 1981; Basso, Capitani, Laiacona, & Zanobio, 1985; Fournet et al., 1987; Habib, Joanette, Ali-Cherif, & Poncet, 1983; Ihori, Kashiwagi, Kashiwagi, & Tanabe, 1994; Pillon et al., 1979; Puel et al., 1982), which Brown and Hécaen (1976) themselves described as the consequence of strongly lateralized language abilities. As a consequence, many authors have argued against Brown's theory (e.g., Basso, Capitani, Laiacona, & Zanobio, 1985; Henderson, 1983; Joanette, Puel, Nespoulous, Rascol, & Lecours, 1982).

Further, Holmes and Sadoff (1966) proposed that CA is essentially caused by subcortical lesions. They attempted to explain CA in the light of Pierre Marie's theory of the cortico-subcortical quadrilateral. According to Marie, a subcortical right-hemisphere lesion could cause language disturbances. This hypothesis implies that there is no such thing as CA, that the cortex of the right hemisphere does not process language in CA, and that patients with CA are "normal patients with unusual lesions" (p. 395), namely, subcortical lesions. This hypothesis is of course contradicted by numerous case studies of CA (e.g., Hécaen, Mazars, Ramier, Goldblum, & Mérienne, 1971). Interestingly, Raggi (1915, cited in Deleni, 1917), instead of explaining CA with Marie's theory, proposed that Marie developed his theory by observing CA cases.

Habib et al. (1983) presented a CA case with right basal ganglia infarction. The patient showed crossed fluent aphasia and jargonagraphia but little oral comprehension difficulties. The authors concluded that subcortical aphasia can be crossed as well, and postulated that left and right subcortical language structures are possibly less lateralized in function than cortical areas. Although additional reports of subcortical CA have been published (Alexander & Annett, 1996, case 6; Perani, Papagno, Cappa, Gerundini, & Fazio, 1988; Sapir, Kokmen, & Rogers, 1986), many subsequent authors have rejected this hypothesis because their CA patients' lesions did not encroach on subcortical structures (e.g., Basso, Capitani, Laiacona, & Zanobio, 1985). Although there is little validity in explaining CA exclusively in terms of subcortical lesions, there is an argument to be made for the significance of subcortical extension of lesions. The same argument is valid for UCA as well.

The same idiosyncratic approach was followed by Puel et al. (1982) in an attempt to explain the presence of CA in their patient. They suggested that their patient's early right-ear deafness may have caused a primacy of the right hemisphere for receiving auditory signals, thereby creating an advantage for language decoding. To their credit, they also noted that CA is still rare even compared with the frequency of right-ear deafness.

Pillon et al. (1979) and Habib et al. (1983) reiterated a hypothesis first proposed by Levy and Nagylaki (1972, cited in Habib et al., 1983), in that hand dominance and language laterality are represented in two neighboring genes or alleles. Their proximity would account for the typical picture of left-hemisphere language dominance in right-handed individuals, but they could nevertheless be dissociated in some cases, such as in CA. It is well known that there is a genetic component in handedness, although it is but a part of the explanation. However, a reliable genetic pattern for language laterality has not yet been established, particularly a theory that could apply to left-handed individuals, in whom there would be more exceptions than cases following the rule.

It has been shown that the hypometabolic region after a cerebrovascular accident is much more extensive than the lesion visualized by CT scanning (Metter et al., 1981, cited in Schweiger, Wechsler, & Mazziotta, 1987). Consequently, Schweiger et al. (1987) hypothesized that CA might result from a massive cross-callosal inhibition of the left-hemisphere language areas by the right-hemisphere lesion. Their patient did not show a decreased left-hemisphere metabolism, although the hypometabolic area in the right hemisphere was larger than the lesion on the CT scan. However, on a repetition task, the left hemisphere did not show an increased metabolism, thereby suggesting a right-hemisphere processing for this particular skill. More recently, functional imaging studies (Bakar, Kirschner, & Wertz, 1996; Gomez-Tortosa, Martin, Sychra, & Dujovny, 1994) clearly showed a right-hemisphere language dominance for CA patients. On the other hand, Cappa et al. (1993) did demonstrate a hypometabolism in the left hemisphere in two CA patients. It is not known whether this "transcallosal diaschisis" phenomenon (Dobkin et al., 1989) contributes to the symptoms of CA. If confirmed, this hypothesis could extend the distance effect variable to all CA cases. However, there is no reason to believe that this distant hypometabolic effect is present in CA alone, and not in UCA.

Castro-Caldas, Confraria, and Poppe (1987) discussed the hypothesis that CA can be caused by an early silent brain lesion, the so-called "pathological" CA (Castro-Caldas, 1991). The authors rejected that hypothesis because such a language reorganization should give rise to a higher incidence of history of learning disabilities, including dyslexia, in CA patients, which does not seem to be the case.

In addition, several hypotheses for the genesis of CA were based on what Demeurisse, Hublet, Coekaerts, Derouck, and Capon (1986) called *cultural factors*. These hypotheses share the premise that the right hemisphere of individuals who are illiterate, use an ideographic or a tone language, or are bilingual or multilingual could somehow be involved in language processing. However, none of these approaches can provide a general explanation for CA, and there is no reliable evidence indicating that CA is more frequent in those populations (see other chapters, this volume).

Inclusion/Exclusion Criteria

Inclusion/exclusion criteria have been proposed in an attempt to define "true" CA (Table 7.1). In the 1970s, the typical criteria were delineated by Brown and Hécaen (1976), and included no familial sinistrality, a clear right-hemisphere lesion, and strong right-handedness. The only criterion dealing with the patient's own experience was childhood brain injury, which could conceivably alter early language lateralization. In the 1980s, investigators included more cultural factors, which were thought to also possibly affect language lateralization (Basso, Capitani, Laiacona, & Zanobio, 1985; Habib et al., 1983; Henderson, 1983; Joanette et al., 1982). Joanette et al. (1982), for example, added the absence of illiteracy, bilingualism, tone language use, and ideographic language use as inclusion criteria. Implied in such a rationale is that CA does not exist in regions of the world, such as Vietnam and China, where tone or ideographic languages are used. More recently, however, the tendency has been for authors to reduce the list of exclusion criteria (Castro-Caldas et al., 1987; Coppens & Robey, 1992; Faglia, Rottoli, & Vignolo, 1990). The criteria are discussed individually, and a decision about their value is taken and applied to this review of the cases from the literature.

Right-Handedness. Although right-handedness is usually associated with hand dominance for writing, even early investigators have recognized that other types of everyday activities needed to be included in the assessment, such as fencing and playing billiards, or using a hammer, a needle, and utensils (Jackson, 1880; Joffroy, 1903; Lewandowsky, 1911; Souques, 1910). There is no a priori reason then to doubt the accuracy of handedness assessments even in very early reports of CA, even if the precision of a formal test protocol is lacking.

TABLE 7.1
Suggested Inclusion Criteria for CA

Brown & Wilson (1993)
    Thorough language testing
    Right-hemisphere lesion only
    Absence of childhood brain injury
    No familial sinistrality

Brown & Hécaen (1976)
    Thorough language testing
    Right-hemisphere lesion only
    Absence of childhood brain damage
    Strong right-handedness
    No familial sinistrality

Urbain et al. (1978)
    Thorough description of the aphasia
    Unilateral right-hemisphere lesion
    Right-handed individual
    No childhood brain lesions
    No familial sinistrality

Goldstein et al. (1979)
    Right-handedness
    No familial sinistrality
    No previous brain damage
    Right-hemisphere lesion only

Pillon et al. (1979)
    Right-hemisphere lesion only
    No childhood brain damage
    No familial sinistrality (one generation)

Joanette et al. (1982)
    No familial sinistrality or ambidexterity
    No previous brain damage
    Absence of environmental factors susceptible to affect language lateralization
        Illiterate
        Bi- or multilingualism
        Tone language
        Ideographic language
    Good description of the aphasia
    Right-hemisphere lesion only

Habib et al. (1983)
    Exclusively right-handed subject
    No history of sinistrality in siblings or parents
    Right-handed lesion only
    Good description of the aphasia
    Absence of environmental factors susceptible to affect language lateralization
        Illiterate
        Bi- or multilingualism
        Tone language

Henderson (1983)
    Strongly right-handed
    Adult
    Unilingual

(continued)

TABLE 7.1
(Continued)

Absence of childhood brain damage
Adequate language testing
Right-hemisphere lesion only
Ischemic etiology only

Basso, Capitani, Laiacona, & Zanobio (1985)
    Right-handed patient (minimum 10/12 on the Edinburgh)
    No familial sinistrality
    At least 3 years of schooling
    Unilingual
    Absence of previous brain damage
    Right lesion only
    Patient clearly aphasic

Castro-Caldas et al. (1987)
    Unequivocal diagnosis of aphasia
    Explicitly reported as right-handers
    Only one documented lesion in the right hemisphere

Faglia, Rottoli, & Vignolo (1990)
    Right-handedness (on standardized tests)
    Absence of left-handers in the family
    Integrity of left hemisphere

Coppens & Robey (1992)
    Right-handedness
    Clear unilateral right-hemisphere lesion
    Absence of previous brain damage

Familial Sinistrality.   As shown in Table 7.1, a majority of authors have excluded cases of CA on the basis of familial sinistrality. Denes and Caviezel (1981) even used familial sinistrality to question CA as a syndrome. In other words, because a CA patient had a left-handed family member, the diagnosis of CA was believed to be erroneous. However, Pillon et al. (1979) suggested that left-handedness in grandparents or grandchildren was probably not powerful enough to trigger a transfer of language dominance to the right hemisphere in a right-handed patient. Also, many CA cases in the literature do not have any information about grandparents and grandchildren.

This theory of "stock-brainedness" (Kennedy, 1916) was put forth when it was believed that the right hemisphere was dominant for language in left-handed individuals. The fact that it is now known that this is the exception rather than the rule considerably weakens this theory. For example, Holmes and Sadoff (1966) stated that "in more than half of left-handed patients with aphasia the causal lesion will be in the left hemisphere. We believe, therefore, that the finding of left-handed relatives does not explain the aphasia of the right-handed, right hemisphere dominant patient" (p. 395). Other authors have also recognized that the presence of left-handed family members is quite a weak causative factor for a shift in language laterality (Castro-Caldas & Confraria, 1984; Clarke & Zangwill, 1965; Henderson, 1983; Holmes & Sadoff, 1966; Sweet, Panis, & Levine, 1984; Zangwill, 1979). Already in 1965, Clarke and Zangwill noted that "the incidence of left-handedness in the pedigree of dextrals with 'crossed aphasia' may well have been exaggerated and may turn out to have less significance than has been traditionally supposed" (p. 85). Later, Zangwill (1979) confirmed that: "familial left-handedness is evidently neither a necessary nor a sufficient condition for the incidence of aphasia from a right hemisphere lesion in right-handed individuals" (p. 170). In two papers, Bishop (1980, 1990) compellingly argued that the probability of having a left-handed relative is biased by the number of relatives that the individual actually has. Moreover, Bishop (1990) stated that the "usual rationale given for subdividing handedness groups according to familial sinistrality is logically indefensible" (p. 155).

In a rare direct comparison between CA and UCA populations, Donoso, Vergara, and Santander (1980) did not find any significant differences based on the presence of familial sinistrality. Also, the influence of familial sinistrality implies that CA must be similar to aphasia in left-handed individuals, a hypothesis far from established (Joanette et al., 1982). Table 7.2 shows the results of our review of 114 CA cases with vascular etiologies.

Although there are some discrepancies between the columns in Table 7.2, they do not necessarily represent significant differences. The number of CA cases with a positive history of familial sinistrality is too small to allow for reliable statistical analyses. At this point, familial sinistrality does not appear to be a satisfactory explanation for CA. However, one needs to underscore the importance of recording familial sinistrality, so that the impact it might have on the symptomatology can be analyzed in the future. Also, investigators should report CA cases even in the presence of familial sinistrality.

Aphasia Diagnosis. There is little argument about the necessity to clearly diagnose aphasia in a CA patient. The case of Brust, Plank, Burke, Guobadia, and Healton (1982), for example, leaves some doubts as to the nature of their patient's difficulties. The authors recognized that their patient's symptomatology could be due to severe akinesia. Similarly, the patient described by Guard, Fournet, Sautreaux, and Dumas (1983) shows confusion, thought disorder, incoherence, bombastic style in expressive language, but no comprehension impairment—certainly not a typical aphasia. On the other hand, it is reasonable to include patients who show a specific symptomatology such as pure agraphia, or alexia–agraphia (e.g., Basso, Capitani, Laiacona, & Zanobio, 1985, case 5), although these patients are not aphasic *stricto sensu.*

Transient Symptomatology. Some authors concluded that transient CA symptoms cannot be considered, as they may be due to the influence of diaschisis on the left hemisphere, rather than the right. The notion of transient symptoms is not universally defined, however. For example, Gloning, Gloning, Haub, and Quatember (1969) considered transient aphasia an

TABLE 7.2
Breakdown of Characteristics Based on Familial Sinistrality in 84 CA Patients (Out of 114) With
Reported Presence or Absence of Familial Sinistrality (Unknown in 30 Cases)

	Positive History of Familial Sinistrality (n = 14)	Negative History of Familial Sinistrality (n =70)
Mirror-image[a]	Unknown (n = 4) Yes (n = 5), 50% No (n = 5), 50%	Unknown (n = 22) Yes (n = 29), 60.4% No (n = 19), 39.6%
Apraxia	Unknown (n = 2) Present (n = 8), 66.7% Absent (n = 4), 33.3%	Unknown (n = 10) Present (n = 35), 58.3% Absent (n = 25), 41.7%
Neglect	Unknown (n = 5) Present (n = 8), 88.9% Absent (n = 1), 11.1%	Unknown (n = 28) Present (n = 26), 61.9% Absent (n = 16), 38.1%
Discrepancy between oral and written language	Unknown (n = 2) Present (n = 6), 50% ⠀⠀Written worse (n = 3), 50% ⠀⠀Oral worse (n = 3), 50% Absent (n = 6), 50%	Unknown (n = 11) Present (n = 23), 39% ⠀⠀Written worse (n = 15), 65.2% ⠀⠀Oral worse (n = 8), 34.8% Absent (n = 36), 61%%

[a]Mirror-image refers to CA cases in which the aphasic symptomology is identical to that expected from a similar lesion site in the left hemisphere.

aphasia of less than one day in duration, whereas Alexander, Fischette, and Fischer (1989) considered that true CA patients must still display obvious aphasic disturbances in the subacute stage, that is, 3 weeks to 2 months. The latter approach seems more reasonable than the former. Therefore, case 1 in Carr, Jacobson, and Boller (1981), case 1 in Perani et al. (1988), and case 3 in Bakar et al. (1996) were not included in the present review. These patients' aphasic symptomatology resolved in a matter of days. On the other hand, the patient presented by Denes and Caviezel (1981) is included in our review. This patient, despite a rapid recovery, still showed anomia in conversational speech at 6 months postonset.

Previous History of Brain Damage. Some researchers did not consider subjects with histories of previous brain dysfunction, such as stroke, head injury, or epilepsy. Excluding these patients, a priori, implies that CA should not be defined as the consequence of a reorganization of skills, including language, following an acquired lesion, but rather as the consequence of a "natural" process of still unknown etiology. For example, the case of Rapcsak, Gonzalez Rothi, and Heilman (1987) was excluded from this review because the patient suffered a head trauma in 1951 that caused a chronic seizure disorder (the same patient was discussed in Ochipa & Gonzalez Rothi, 1989). The patient described by Sollberg (1963) was excluded for the same reason. The patient of Alexander et al. (1989) was not included in our review on the grounds that she had a large left-hemisphere lesion in addition to the right-hemisphere lesion. The same holds for the case described by Kitayama, Yamazaki, Shibahara, and Nomura (1990). The exclusion of these cases from the present study does not diminish their importance in elucidating the brain's ability to reorganize language after trauma.

On the other hand, the CA patient described by Trojanowski, Green, and Levine (1980) was included although the autopsy showed a small lesion in the left hemisphere. The lesion was older, had been asymptomatic, and was probably much too small to trigger a major reorganization of language. The same rationale can be applied for the case of Sweet et al. (1984). They reported a large lesion in the right hemisphere, and two minuscule lesions in the left hemisphere, probably much too small to be symptomatic, let alone cause the extensive language symptomatology displayed by the patient. Moreover, both lesions were outside the traditional language areas. The CA case presented by Kapur and Dunkley (1984) was also included is this review. Their CA patient showed some structures in the right hemisphere that were abnormally small (e.g., thalamus, hippocampus, mammillary body). Additionally, this patient had congenitally small and narrow or malformed cerebral arteries in the right hemisphere only. Notwithstanding this congenital inequality, the right hemisphere was still evidently responsible for language processing.

Sass, Novelly, Spencer, and Spencer (1990) reported on language lateralization measured by the Wada technique in epileptics. Three patients out of their sample of 32 were right-handed and had language lateralized to the right hemisphere. This frequency of 9.4% is significantly higher than the frequency of CA usually accepted (Fernández-Martín, Martínez-Lage, Madoz, & Maraví, 1968). Similar results were reported by Kurthen et al. (1994). This suggests that, indeed, the presence of epilepsy can affect language lateralization. Therefore, cases reported by, for example, Botez and Wertheim (1959), Hadar, Ticehurst, and Wade (1991), Ettlinger et al. (1955), and Loring et al. (1990) were excluded from our analysis because the patients had histories of seizure disorder. These may be considered cases of "pathological" CA rather than "natural" CA (Castro-Caldas, 1991).

Etiology. Traumatic brain injury undoubtedly causes widespread damage to the brain. The focal lesions are visible on CT scan, but diffuse axonal injury is not. Also, it is well recognized that a traumatic etiology will give rise to both verbal and nonverbal difficulties as well as other types of cognitive deficits (memory, attention), thereby confirming the generalized impact of this type of etiology. Boller (1973) noted that the most frequent etiology of CA was trauma. The poor localizing value of traumatic brain injury, therefore, must disqualify this etiology as a meaningful source of information regarding CA. More recent authors have excluded trauma as a possible etiology for CA (see Table 7.1).

Tumors have also often been rejected as etiology for the study of CA. The rationale, of course, is that tumors may have distant effects and that the symptoms are of little localizable value. Also, Boller (1973) reported an increased incidence of tumors in the CA population, an observation that is consistent with the idea that right-hemisphere tumors may, in fact, be impacting on left-hemisphere function. However, in the cases in which tumor resection leads to nontransient language symptoms, the aphasia can hardly be explained by distant effects. On the other hand, Martins, Ferro, and Trindale (1987) reported the case of a CA patient who displayed a fluent aphasia with a posterior right-hemisphere tumor. Surgery was not performed, but as the tumor progressed to more anterior brain areas, the patient progressively became nonfluent. It could be convincingly argued that the symptoms were a direct consequence of the tumor itself in such a case. It seems reasonable, then, not to reject the tumor cases out of hand, but to interpret them cautiously. Were there differences in symptomatology between CA cases caused by tumor as compared to those caused by cerebrovascular accidents, these could only be brought to light by a comparison of the various etiologies. Therefore, the cases of CA due to tumors are reviewed separately and compared to the cases of CA of vascular origin.

Age.   CA may not be more frequent in children than in adults (Carter et al., 1982, cited in Nass & Myerson, 1985; Martins et al., 1987; Woods & Teuber, 1978). There are only two cases of nontraumatic CA in children reported in the literature, a 5-year-old (Assal & Deonna, 1977), and a 4-year-old child (Burd, Gascon, Swenson, & Hankey, 1990). Again, it is only by studying CA in children that we will be able to determine whether the features are similar to or different from those in adult CA patients.

Cultural Factors.   Illiteracy, bilingualism, and ideographic or tone language use were used as exclusion criteria for CA (see Table 7.1). Demeurisse et al. (1986) collectively referred to these variables as *cultural factors.* One case of CA in an illiterate patient has been described (Wechsler, 1976). Wechsler (1976) suggested that learning to read and write contributes to the establishment of left-hemisphere language dominance, and conversely, that the absence of learning to read and write at a critical age causes a failure to strongly lateralize language to the left hemisphere. However, Wechsler also stated that his patient's language was strongly lateralized to the right hemisphere. If the language lateralization process is interrupted, one would expect a bilateral distribution of language, or at least a weak or partial lateralization. Also, Castro-Caldas (1991) reported a comparable rate of occurrence of CA in illiterate and literate patients (see Coppens, Parente, & Lecours, chapter 6, this volume).

Zangwill (1979) described a bilingual CA patient who seemed to display the same expressive difficulties in French as in English. Some authors would exclude such a case because the patient was bilingual. The underlying assumption is that the right hemisphere can take over some aspects of language in bilinguals or multilinguals because the left hemisphere is somehow overloaded. This hypothesis implies that originally these patients have a typical left-hemisphere dominance. This view cannot be easily reconciled with a long-lasting aphasia following a right-hemisphere lesion, particularly in those instances where all languages are equally affected in all modalities. A more reasonable explanation would be that such cases represent CA in patients who happened to be bilingual and that it is not different in nature from other cases of CA. Wechsler (1976), April and Han (1980), and Hécaen et al. (1971) reported similar cases. These patients showed a persistent CA, equally severe in both languages. The trilingual CA patient reported by Holmes and Sadoff (1966) was probably aphasic in all three of his mastered languages. Although the authors did not explicitly state that fact, a significantly better preserved language would have been easily noticed and reported. Barroche, Presles, Ramel, Weber, and Arnould (1979) reported a similar case of a CA bilingual patient. The only exception is the patient presented by Paradis and Goldblum (1989). This patient became aphasic only in one of his three languages following the removal of a cyst in the right prerolandic area (see Paradis, chapter 2, this volume).

Karanth and Rangamani (1988) reported a population study of the frequency of CA in bi- and multilinguals. In their sample of 94 unilateral stroke patients from India, 25% of the bi- or multilinguals had CA versus 0% of unilinguals. In a sample of 48 aphasic patients, they reported a frequency of 12.5% of CA in unilinguals and 6.25% of CA in bi- and multilinguals. They acknowledged that if mastering more than one language caused CA, their figures should have been higher, and the latter discrepancy should have been inverted. In addition, there are other peculiarities in their results. For example, they reported finding an abnormally low proportion of left-handed individuals in their sample (1.1%), and none of these subjects had language represented in the right hemisphere. However, the authors mentioned that left-handed individuals are still stigmatized in Indian society and are usually forced to switch handedness when writing. Consequently, the authors conceded that "the high incidence of crossed aphasia could well be due to the factor of an increased incidence of forced or apparent right-handedness" (p. 177).

April and Tse (1977) reported a bilingual CA patient in whom Chinese was more affected than English, although Chinese was his native and most used language. Although the patient was clearly aphasic in both languages, he tended to use English spontaneously even if addressed in Chinese. This observation could be interpreted in the following fashion: Chinese is lateralized to the right hemisphere because of the intrinsic visuospatial qualities and

English is mostly processed in the left hemisphere as shown by the better preservation of the latter language. Interestingly, however, the only comparable case the authors cite from the literature, that is, a Chinese-English bilingual patient with English better preserved than Chinese, became aphasic following left-hemisphere damage. This patient shows that the former hypothesis is unlikely (see Yamadori, chapter 5, this volume). This fact illustrates the point that few if any characteristics of CA cannot also be described in UCA.

April (1979) and April and Tse (1977) specifically discussed the possibility that early learning of an ideographic language, that is, with more emphasis on visuospatial perception, such as Chinese, could promote language lateralization to the right hemisphere. This hypothesis implies that CA must be more frequent in Chinese aphasic patients; however, the authors still recognized that "the paucity of *crossed* aphasic patients of any language origin suggests that other factors must play equally important roles" (p. 770). Hamasaki, Suzuki, Hirakawa, Imahori, and Nakajima (1987) also rejected that hypothesis for the same reason. After surveying New York's hospitals for aphasia in Chinese patients, April (1979) and April and Han (1980) acknowledged that they were unable to demonstrate a higher incidence of CA in nonalphabetical language users. April and Han (1980) stated that the incidence of CA in a Taiwanese hospital was no more than what has traditionally been cited in the European literature. Winterling (1978) also argued against this idea, stating that spoken Chinese is no more visuospatial in nature than any other spoken language, so the learning of spoken Chinese should, logically, have no influence on the lateralization of language to the right. He also added that all written languages, to some extent, have a visuospatial component. Further, he cited research showing no difference in handedness distribution between the Chinese and other populations.

Hamasaki et al. (1987) described a crossed Broca's aphasia patient for whom the Kana writing system was more impaired than Kanji. Because this is usually the rule in UCA Japanese patients, and because of the absence of traditional right-hemisphere symptoms, the authors postulated a reversal of dominance. Conversely, Yamada, Nakamura, and Kobayashi (1977) reported a crossed Broca's aphasia patient in whom Kana was better preserved than Kanji. They stated that this discrepancy is unusual. Although it is beyond the scope of this chapter to review the lateralization pattern of the two Japanese writing systems, it appears that the lateralization of the Japanese written language can be dissociated from that of oral language, as is the case in alphabetical languages (see Yamadori, chapter 5, this volume).

The use of a tone language has been considered an exclusion criterion because prosody of language is a right-hemisphere characteristic. Consequently, the mastery of tones could theoretically involve the right hemisphere to a larger degree than in nontone languages, even if such a hypothesis is not widely accepted. Two CA patients were tested for the linguistic tones, one in Vietnamese (Hécaen et al., 1971) and one in Cantonese Chinese

(April & Han, 1980). The former patient could produce and understand the tonal nuances, but the latter patient was moderately impaired on a tonal same/different paradigm (7/10) and on a receptive task (12/15). Here again, the data do not provide a sound rationale for the automatic exclusion of these patients from the CA population (see Gandour, chapter 4, this volume).

To conclude, these "cultural factors" (Demeurisse et al., 1986) have been invoked as causative factors for CA. Data on the prevalence of CA, for example, in these populations are conflicting. There are reports of increased frequency of CA, for example, in illiterates (Cameron, Currier, & Haerer, 1971) and in speakers of Chinese (Hu, Qiou, & Zhong, 1990). However, other studies dispute these findings (April, 1979; April & Han, 1980; Castro-Caldas, 1991; Hyodo, Maki, Nakagawa, Enomoto, & Akimoto, 1979; Kishida, 1976, cited in Sakurai et al., 1992; see Coppens, Parente, & Lecours, chapter 6, and Yamadori, chapter 5, this volume). These cultural factors, however, considered together or separately, cannot explain the majority of CA cases. Moreover, their influence on language lateralization is far from established. Consequently, there is no compelling reason to use these variables as exclusion criteria for CA.

Conclusions. Some authors have attempted to homogenize the CA population by introducing extremely strict inclusion criteria (Joanette et al., 1982). Essentially, whenever the CA could be "explained" by a criterion, the case was rejected. For example, CA patients who were bilingual, illiterate, or had one ambidextrous or left-handed family member were believed to be at an increased probability of having language abilities lateralized to the right hemisphere, even if that hypothetical risk is not necessarily supported by data. The consequence was that CA was viewed as a homogeneous group of patients in whom the cause of the CA was supposedly unknown, and the most common characteristics of these patients' symptomatology were then considered the "real" CA. The rationale was to try to decide whether CA is comparable to aphasia in left-handers (Brown's theory) or truly a separate type of aphasia once the confounding variables are removed. Joanette et al. (1982), after analyzing the 10 cases they retained as the only valid CA patients, had to conclude that no one hypothesis could explain the origin of the particular language dominance. Similarly, Sweet et al. (1984) noted the "inadequacy of the current theories" (p. 479), such as latent ambidexterity, illiteracy, familial sinistrality, or anatomical differences between hemispheres, to account for CA.

It is true that no single hypothesis can explain all the cases of CA, and indeed there may not be one single causal factor. It is becoming obvious that there may be several different explanations for right-hemisphere language dominance in right-handed individuals. This is the reason why it is of paramount importance to collect as many cases as possible without stringent exclusion criteria. The patterns will appear from the comparison of possible subgroups of patients with CA. In each syndrome, there is an unavoidable amount of individual variation. Striving to completely suppress it can only lead to an unworkable multitude of small, well-defined syndromes, or to the majority of patients being ignored because they do not fit the definition.

The analysis of the CA population would benefit from a simple distinction between natural (functional) and pathological (organic) CA. The former includes the cases reviewed here, and the latter the cases that have a recognizable organic explanation such as childhood brain damage, or an etiology of tumor. Also, within the population of functional CA, the symptoms may vary based on characteristics such as the presence of familial sinistrality, or bilingualism, for example. These characteristics should be recorded, and when a sufficient number of cases are compiled, the possible differences between the groups, if any, will then come to light. Accordingly, the present review has compiled a total of 136 CA cases from the literature. Among these, 114 are adults (over 15 years of age) with vascular etiology, 20 are adults with tumor etiology, and 2 are children (Appendixes A, B, and C).

POPULATION CHARACTERISTICS

Various incidence measures of CA have been reported, ranging from very low frequency, for example, 0.0 (none out of 105 right-handed aphasics, Zangwill, 1960), or 0.38 (Hécaen et al., 1971), or "less than one percent" (Castro-Caldas, 1991) up to 18% (Mohr et al., 1980). Intermediate values include 1% (Borod, Carper, Naeser, & Goodglass, 1985; Gloning et al., 1969), 1.8% (Zangwill, 1979), 2.6% (Roberts, 1969), and 3% (Carr et al., 1981). The higher frequency of CA has been found in traumatic brain injury populations. For example, Mohr et al. (1980), who reported a CA frequency of 18%, studied patients with penetrating head injuries. This observation underscores the importance of controlling for etiology when studying CA.

It is interesting to note that the percentages reported by the various authors are not necessarily comparable. Usually, the incidence of aphasia is used, that is, the proportion of aphasic patients among a sample of right-handed patients with right-hemisphere lesions. However, Gloning et al. (1969) used the incidence of right-hemisphere damage, that is, the proportion of right-hemisphere lesions among a sample of right-handed aphasic patients. Although the results of this method do not dispute the rarity of CA, the latter approach is probably an overestimation of the frequency of CA. For example, from the figures reported by Weisenburg and McBride (1964) CA represented 1.11% of a sample of right-handed patients with brain lesions, but 1.85% of a sample of right-handed aphasic patients.

CA patients have been reported to be younger than UCA patients (Brown & Hécaen, 1976; Donoso et al., 1980; Goldstein, Vaillant, Laplanche, & Pépin, 1979; Urbain et al., 1978). Brown and Hécaen (1976) reported a mean age of

41 years in their selected sample of 8 CA patients, and in an unselected sample of 29 CA patients from the literature, a mean age of 44.7 years. Donoso et al. (1980) reviewed a sample of 24 CA cases from the literature and reported a mean age for CA of 47.9 years versus a mean age for UCA of 52.9 years. In their selective sample of only 10 subjects, Joanette et al. (1982) reported the mean age of CA patients as 56.6 years. Finally, Castro-Caldas and Confraria (1984) compared 39 CA subjects with 390 UCA patients. They found no age differences between the two groups, in fact, the means were identical (CA = 57.4 years; UCA = 57.4 years). The authors suggested that the age difference reported in previous articles was due to the inclusion of other etiologies, such as head trauma. The present sample includes a total of 136 CA patients, 114 with a vascular etiology, 20 with tumor, and 2 children. The average age of our sample of CA adults (over 15 years of age) with a vascular etiology is 57.3 years (Appendix A), a figure comparable to that of Castro-Caldas and Confraria (1984). Overall, these results seem to contradict the hypothesis that CA patients tend to be younger than UCA patients. However, our compilation of CA cases with tumors shows that these patients are somewhat younger (Appendix B), with an average of 47.4 years.

The CA population has been said to include more female than male patients (Urbain et al., 1978). Donoso et al. (1980) agreed that because females are believed to have less lateralized language abilities, there should be more female than male CA patients. However, their sample of 24 CA cases included more males than females. Also, Joanette et al. (1982) described their sample as containing 7 men and 3 women. Similarly, Castro-Caldas and Confraria (1984) reported 32 males and 7 females among CA cases from the literature. The present sample of adult CA with vascular etiology includes 76 males (67.3%) and 37 females (32.7%) (Appendix A). These results contradict the view that there are more female than male CA patients. Moreover, in the group of CA patients with tumor (Appendix B), the male to female ratio is similar: 14 males (73.7%) and 5 females (26.3%).

CA SYMPTOMATOLOGY

Rigid inclusion criteria may have led to a homogenization of reported CA cases and their symptomatology. It has been stated that "typical" CA is nonfluent with agrammatism regardless of lesion site, and involves initial mutism. Naming was reported to be good, whereas repetition and comprehension varied. Jargon was believed to be always absent (Barraquer-Bordas, 1965; Barroche et al., 1979; Barroche, Marchal, Ascaillas, Rivail, & Lepoire, 1981; Brown, 1976; Brown & Hécaen, 1976; Brown & Wilson, 1973; Donoso et al., 1980; Goldstein et al., 1979; Hécaen et al., 1971; Pillon et al., 1979; Taylor & Solomon, 1979; Urbain et al., 1978). However, it has now been shown that many cases of CA do not fit this pattern (Appendix A). Joanette et al. (1982) analyzed 10 CA cases from the literature and concluded that Broca's aphasia with agrammatism was the most frequent symptomatology, but that other types of clinical pictures were encountered as well.

One explanation for this underrepresentation of fluent aphasias is related to imaging techniques. Indeed, before the widespread use of scanners, lesion location was usually deduced from motor impairments. The frequent absence of associated motor signs in fluent aphasias and the lack of brain imaging techniques may have obscured the right-hemisphere lesion location. This underrepresentation may also simply be due to a greater number of anterior lesions in CA (Yarnell, 1981), which is also the case in UCA. After the advent of CT scanning, fluent types of CA became more frequently reported in the literature (Castro-Caldas, 1991; Yarnell, 1981), although "typical" CA cases were still being described. For example, Delreux et al. (1989) report a case of crossed Broca's aphasia with a posterior lesion site and initial mutism.

Castro-Caldas and Confraria (1984) compared the aphasia types of 39 CA patients from the literature with 390 UCA patients. They found that the two populations were strictly comparable in terms of type of aphasia distribution, with Broca's aphasia being the most frequent, followed by global, Wernicke's, transcortical, and finally conduction aphasia. Similarly, Carr et al. (1981) reported that every major aphasic syndrome has been described as a consequence of CA. Moreover, the authors noted that the distribution of fluent and nonfluent aphasias was similar between CA and UCA, with about 72% nonfluent CAs (Broca's and globals) and 27% fluent CAs. Thus, nonfluent aphasias are represented more often than fluent aphasias in CA, but nonfluent aphasias are also more frequent in UCA. These results contradicted Mendez and Benson's hypothesis (1985) that conduction aphasia is more likely to occur than Wernicke's aphasia in CA following a posterior lesion. Interestingly, Castro-Caldas and Confraria (1984) reported that the typical age difference between the various aphasia types was observed in CA as well. Crossed Broca's aphasia patients were found to be younger, crossed Wernicke's aphasia patients were older, and crossed global aphasia patients fell in between.

Although many authors have recently found many similarities between CA and UCA (Alexander et al., 1989; Carr et al., 1981; Henderson, 1983; Schacter, 1977; Sweet et al., 1984), some authors have noted differences. According to Schacter (1977), CA is essentially indistinguishable from UCA, except possibly for its transient character and a possible discrepancy between written and oral language abilities. Joanette et al. (1982) noted the frequent presence of CA symptom complexes that do not correspond to what can be observed following a left-hemisphere lesion in right-handed patients, thereby rejecting the idea of CA being merely UCA in the opposite hemisphere. Also, Puel et al. (1982) described a CA patient whose expressive language seemed to evolve from agrammatic and nonfluent to fluent and dyssyntactic. The authors noted that such a change is unusual for both CA and UCA. Basso, Capitani, Laiacona, and Zanobio (1985) considered CA patients, in general, "slightly different from prototypical left-hemisphere-brain-damaged patients with aphasia" (p. 40). They based their conclusion on better overall auditory comprehension scores in CA and oral versus written language performance discrepancies.

There are indeed CA cases in which some features are unusual, such as Broca's aphasia with preserved reading, Wernicke's aphasia with only mild comprehension difficulties (Basso, Capitani, Laiacona, & Zanobio, 1985; Demeurisse et al., 1986; Gonzalo Barrio, Pareja Grande, Romero López, & Pérez García, 1986; Lanoë et al., 1992) or mixed transcortical aphasia with preserved naming (Fujii, Yamadori, Fukatsu, Ogawa, & Suzuki, 1997). It must be underscored that most unusual or unexpected features in CA have also been described in UCA (e.g., Fujii et al., 1997). Still, any specific CA case is usually compared to an "average" or a "typical" UCA symptomatology, making many CA cases appear "anomalous." Because some CAs appear to mirror UCAs, but others do not, it seems reasonable to postulate the existence of two subgroups of CA, a logical step taken by Alexander et al. (1989). These authors divided CA into *mirror-image* and *anomalous* CA. A mirror-image CA has a symptomatology comparable to that following an analogous lesion in the left hemisphere, whereas an anomalous CA displays unexpected symptoms given the lesion site. The next step, then, is to compare the two CA subgroups to highlight the possible symptomatology and possible causal differences. Another challenge for future research is to determine whether the frequency of these "anomalous" cases is higher than that reported in UCA (Basso, Lecours, Moraschini, & Vanier, 1985).

Anatomical asymmetries are another way some authors have tried to distinguish CA from UCA. In UCA, it has been reported that the width and length of the right frontal lobe and left occipital lobe are greater in right-handed individuals with an assumed left-hemisphere language lateralization, the so-called petalias (LeMay & Kido, 1978, cited in Haaland & Miranda, 1982). Assal (1982) reported the right occipital pole to be longer in one of his CA patient, and atypical right frontal lobe asymmetries in another (Assal, 1987), both half typical and half atypical measurements. Haaland and Miranda (1982) reported three out of the four petalia measurements in their CA patient to be atypical for right-handed individuals and to be closer to what may be observed in left-handers. However, Sweet et al. (1984) reported that their CA patient's petalias are comparable to those in right-handed subjects with left-hemisphere dominance for language. In one case (Junqué, Litvan, & Vendrell, 1986), a complete functional reversal (language in the right hemisphere, visuospatial skills in the left) was nevertheless still associated with the typical asymmetries encountered in right-handed individuals with left-hemisphere language dominance. Overall, frontal and occipital asymmetries were shown to be poorly correlated with CA (Henderson, Naeser, & Chui, 1983).

Berthier and Starkstein (1994) reported that their patient and several other CA patients with catastrophic reactions displayed reversed frontal and occipital anatomical asymmetries. The authors suggested that reversed anatomical asymmetries could be a sign associated with reversed affect lateralization rather than reversed language lateralization (i.e., CA). Moreover, Castro-Caldas et al. (1987) found a correlation between brain asymmetries and neglect in CA. When neglect was absent, the asymmetries were reversed. Taken together, these results indicate that the anatomical asymmetries could be better indicators of atypical lateralization of nonverbal skills rather than of linguistic abilities. More studies are needed to confirm that hypothesis.

Some attention has also been given to the speed and extent of recovery in CA. Some authors have stated that CA has a faster recovery and a better prognosis than UCA (Barraquer-Bordas, 1965; Brown, 1976; Brown & Hécaen, 1976; Brown & Wilson, 1973; Donoso et al., 1980; Foroglou, Assal, & Zander, 1975; Goldstein et al., 1979; Joanette et al., 1982; Urbain et al., 1978), or even that CA was essentially transient in nature (Holmes & Sadoff, 1966). There are indeed CA cases associated with rapid recovery (Basso, Capitani, Laiacona, & Zanobio, 1985, cases 2 & 6; Cappa et al., 1993, case 2; Claude & Schaeffer, 1921; Denes & Caviezel, 1981; Davous & Boller, 1994; Sapir et al., 1986; Sartori, Bruno, Serena, & Bardin, 1984; Urbain et al., 1978). However, these 10 cases represent only slightly less than 9% of the present sample of 114 CA patients with a vascular etiology (Appendix A). Moreover, these patients do not appear to have any common characteristic, other than their rapid recovery. One patient showed a positive history of familial sinistrality, eight do not, and it is unknown in the last case. The lesion sites vary and the aphasia diagnosis varies: three were Broca's, two Wernicke's, one conduction, one mixed transcortical, one "motor," one "fluent," and one unknown aphasia type. Three are mirror-image type CA, three are anomalous, and the type is uncertain for four cases.

Sartori et al. (1984) presented a CA patient with Broca's aphasia who showed significant recovery, and at 2 months postonset, only mild articulatory difficulties were observed. In the acute stage, the patient underwent a tachistoscopic examination that revealed a left-hemisphere superiority for language. The authors concluded that the left hemisphere played a part in the patient's language recovery. Basso, Capitani, Laiacona, and Zanobio (1985) noted that some of their patients showed a rapid recovery but chose not to draw any conclusions from that observation because no data were available to compare speed of recovery with a sample of matched controls. Similarly, Sapir et al. (1986) noted the rapid recovery of their CA patient, but went on to state that they could not tell whether the recovery was different from UCA. Donoso (1984) remarked that the rate of recovery varies in CA, thereby making it difficult to create a generalized recovery rate for CA as a syndrome. It appears that CA does not have a good recovery as an intrinsic characteristic, and the rate of recovery is as variable as it is in UCA. Moreover, the judgments of rate of recovery for both CA and UCA in the literature are highly subjective. More objective measures of recovery should be devised before a meaningful comparison can take place between recovery rates of CA and UCA.

Conversely, many authors underscored the persistent character of their patients' CA (e.g., Barroche et al., 1979; Hamasaki et al., 1987; Nagaraja et al., 1989; Sweet et al., 1984). For Carr et al. (1981), the recovery pattern of CA is comparable to that of UCA. Wertz (1982) focused on rehabilitation issues in a case of CA. He concluded that the rate and extent of improvement paralleled those in UCA. Moreover, he also concluded that his CA patient responded to therapy in a similar fashion as UCA patients.

Furthermore, cases of rapid amelioration of symptoms following left-hemisphere lesions in right-handed individuals without familial sinistrality have also been described (Denes & Caviezel, 1981; Mohr, 1973). It is reasonable to postulate that in some aphasic patients, nondamaged brain regions can reorganize language more easily than in other patients. For example, Kinsbourne and Durham (1971) described two UCA patients whose aphasia remained unchanged after left-hemisphere sodium amytal injections, but who lost their remaining language following right-hemisphere injection. Without Wada testing, it is impossible to ascertain whether these regions of reorganized language are ipsilateral or contralateral to the original insult.

The notion that CA has a better prognosis than UCA led to the hypothesis that the language skills of CA patients are more bilaterally distributed; that is, the left hemisphere is able to compensate for the right-hemisphere aphasia (e.g., Brown & Hécaen, 1976). However, Denes and Caviezel (1981) described a patient with what they believe to be a "very good recovery" from CA. Still they interpreted the dichotic listening tasks as indicating a strong right-hemisphere language lateralization. Similarly, Carr et al. (1981, case 1) described a CA patient whose aphasia was transient and who did not display any signs of aphasia following a subsequent left-hemisphere CVA. The authors concluded that this patient did not have a bilateral language representation, notwithstanding the transient symptoms of the initial CVA in the right hemisphere. This leaves open the possibility that language in these patients was diffusely organized in the right hemisphere, and noninjured right brain areas aided the recovery.

In conclusion, it does not appear that CA has an overall more rapid or favorable recovery compared to UCA, or that rapid recovery is linked either to the mirror-image or to the anomalous type of CA. Also, what is considered a rapid recovery is largely subjective for both CA and UCA.

LANGUAGE LATERALIZATION

The debate about language lateralization in CA has focused on two opposite viewpoints. On the one hand, CA essentially represents a strong right-hemisphere language lateralization; on the other, CA indicates a bilateral language

representation. A bilateral language representation implies that some dissociation of skills is taking place. Using bilateral Wada experiments, Kurthen
et al. (1994) postulated three distinct patterns of language distribution: positive, negative, and general bilaterality. Positive bilaterality refers to a double
representation of some language abilities; that is, these language skills are
preserved regardless of the side of the sodium amytal injection. Negative
bilaterality refers to a required collaboration between the two hemispheres
for the efficient processing of specific language abilities; that is, these abilities
are impaired regardless of the side of the sodium amytal injection. Finally,
general bilaterality refers to the bilateral distribution of language skills; that
is, certain skills are affected by the left sodium amytal injection, and others
with the contralateral injection. It is usually assumed either that language
lateralization in CA is completely lateralized to the right hemisphere or that
there is a dissociation of skills (general bilaterality). Little attention has been
given to positive or negative bilaterality in CA. Although Kurthen et al. (1994)
were analyzing a population of epileptic patients, and generalizing to other
populations is unwise, it could nevertheless theoretically be possible to
encounter positive or negative bilaterality in CA, or even in UCA. Nass and
Myerson (1985) argued that even when bilateral and symmetric representation of language skills has been assessed by Wada testing, both hemispheres may be necessary to process language (negative bilaterality). Their
left-handed 13-year-old patient showed persistent language impairment following surgery for a vascular malformation in the left hemisphere, although
Wada testing clearly showed bilateral language representation.

Mendel (1912, 1914) was the first author to explicitly articulate the hypothesis of a interhemispheric dissociation of skills. His patient presented with
Broca's aphasia without comprehension difficulties or writing impairment.
Mendel concluded that this particular patient was right-hemisphere dominant
for oral expressive language and left-hemisphere dominant for all comprehension abilities and writing. Mendel used the term *dissociated aphasia* to refer
to his patient. This hypothesis of bilateral language representation was later
championed by Jason Brown (Brown, 1976; Brown & Chobor, 1987; Brown
& Hécaen, 1976; Brown & Wilson, 1973). This theory posits that CA is similar
to aphasia in left-handers and children, and represents a stage of incomplete
lateralization. These statements imply that CA is incompatible with a strong
right-hemisphere language lateralization and that CA must be different from
UCA as a symptom complex. That hypothesis was heralded by Anastasopoulos
and Kokkini (1962), who stated that when "handedness and brainedness for
speech do not coincide, a part at least of the language functions are [*sic*]
represented on the hemisphere opposite to the preferred hand" (p. 7). For
example, Demeurisse, Coekaerts, and Hublet (1984) reported a CA patient
with a frontal lesion including Broca's area presenting with apraxia of speech
but hardly any aphasic symptoms. In this patient, cerebral blood flow studies
showed that language was bilaterally distributed.

Although there are CA patients whose language abilities seem to be bilaterally distributed, Brown's theory of an interruption in the normal progression from bilateral to unilateral language representation is contradicted by CA cases in which a strong right-hemisphere language lateralization is highly probable (e.g., Assal, 1987; Delreux et al., 1989; Demeurisse et al., 1986; Larrabee, Kane, & Rodgers, 1982; Zangwill, 1979) or in cases of jargon in the symptomatology (e.g., Assal, 1982; Pillon et al., 1979, cases 1 & 2; Sweet et al., 1984; Yarnell, 1981, case 3). Indeed, jargon was viewed by Brown as incompatible with an incomplete language lateralization pattern. An opposite point of view was presented by Barraquer-Bordas, Mendilaharsu, Peres-Serra, Acevedo de Mendilaharsu, and Grau-Veciana (1963). Their CA patient displayed a persistent aphasia essentially comparable to a UCA. The authors concluded that right-handed individuals tended to be strongly lateralized regardless of the hemisphere, a conclusion also reached by Fernández-Martín et al. (1968). This suggests that mirror-image CA must be the rule. The interesting case presented by Assal and Deonna (1977) also argues against Brown's theory. Their patient was a 5-year-old child with persistent CA with severe comprehension disorders. The patient was reexamined 12 years postonset (Assal, 1987) and still showed impaired language abilities and poor verbal memory skills. The severity and the persistent character of the symptoms suggest a strong right-hemisphere language lateralization in that right-handed child. This case argues against the incomplete lateralization hypothesis in both acquired aphasia in children (see Paquier & van Dongen, chapter 3, this volume) and in CA. Interestingly, the fact that this patient's brother was ambidextrous did not prevent a strong right-hemisphere language lateralization.

Bilateral language has been described in UCA as well. Cambier, Masson, Guillot, and Robine (1985) described a UCA right-handed patient with severe ideomotor apraxia, visuospatial difficulties (including hemiasomatognosia), agraphia, but without aphasia and with only mild oral apraxia. The lesion involved the entire left hemisphere except the territory of the posterior cerebral artery. The authors concluded that this is a case of reversed laterality, except for writing and praxis, skills that were affected by the lesion. However, this case also shows that bilateral language representation is sometimes present in UCA as well.

Although Wada tests are crude examinations compared to the complex character of language processing, they can provide information about the lateralization of broad systems. Language lateralization in CA has been established by the Wada technique in only five cases (Angelergues, Hécaen, Djindjian, & Jarrié-Hazan, 1962; Delreux et al., 1989; Lanoë et al., 1992; Larrabee et al., 1982; Zangwill, 1979). In three cases, it was clearly established that language abilities were strongly lateralized to the right hemisphere (Delreux et al., 1989; Larrabee et al., 1982; Zangwill, 1979). The fourth patient

(Angelergues et al., 1962) displayed a transcortical motor aphasia with intact written and oral comprehension. Oral language was agrammatic with apraxia of speech, but repetition, reading, and comprehension were preserved. Writing skills were severely impaired, more so than oral language. Left injection of sodium amytal was associated with severe comprehension difficulties and a jargonaphasia. It appears then that expressive and receptive language were clearly dissociated in this particular patient and lateralized in opposite hemispheres. This pattern suggests that the patient had expressive language lateralized in the right hemisphere and her receptive language in the left. In other words, it seems that Broca's area was located in the right hemisphere and Wernicke's area in the left. The integrity of oral reading, however, cannot be interpreted. The last patient (Lanoë et al., 1992) suffered from an atypical form of Wernicke's aphasia. This patient's receptive language was superior to what can be expected with Wernicke's aphasia and his expressive language showed elements of conduction aphasia, such as *conduites d'approche*. A left-hemisphere Wada procedure caused apraxia of speech and a significant worsening of oral comprehension abilities. This observation may be the only recognized example of negative bilaterality described so far in the CA literature.

Demeurisse et al. (1986) used "atraumatic methods" to establish the language dominance of their CA patient. Both dichotic listening tasks and regional cerebral blood flow testing indicated a strong right-hemisphere dominance for language in their patient. Recently, Kurthen et al. (1994) reported language lateralization data for 173 epileptic patients who underwent bilateral Wada techniques. The authors found that incomplete right-hemisphere language lateralization did not occur at all. It seems that language tends to lateralize strongly rather than partly, even in the right hemisphere. Taken together, these results suggest that strong right-hemisphere language lateralization is frequent but does not necessarily imply a mirror image in terms of intrahemispheric organization. Bilateral language representation is also possible. It is interesting to note that among these cases only one CA patient with a demonstrated bilateral language representation (Angelergues et al., 1962) showed a discrepancy between written and oral language performance, with written language more severely affected than oral language skills. Incidentally, this case also demonstrated that bilateral language representation does not necessarily entail a rapid and complete recovery.

More recently, the discussion about lateralization of abilities included more specific language subsystems. For example, Basso, Capitani, Laiacona, and Zanobio (1985) compared six CA patients to matched UCA controls in terms of Token Test scores. Every CA patient showed a higher score on the test, including the crossed Wernicke's aphasic patients. The authors concluded that the greater amount of residual receptive language in CA is "possibly due to a greater participation of the non-specialized hemisphere" (p. 40). Similarly,

Trojano, Balbi, and Russo (1994) raised the possibility that their patient's good improvement in phonological skills may signal a left-hemisphere transfer of competence. Although Trojano et al. noted that an intrahemispheric reorganization was also a viable hypothesis, it seems that the clear-cut picture of lateralization of skills or abilities needs to be replaced by a more "dynamic" view (Barroche et al., 1981). This view implies that certain subsystems could be lateralized independently of broader systems. The latter point implies in turn that our examination of patients needs to be more detailed and focus on more specific aspects of language.

As a general rule, one should be careful in drawing conclusions based on the absence of symptoms. That is, the intact or residual skills should not necessarily be attributed to the hemisphere opposite the lesion. The remaining language abilities could reside in the undamaged areas of the right hemisphere (Taylor & Solomon, 1979). In a CA patient, when a symptom is not present, there is a tendency to conclude that that particular skill is subserved by the opposite hemisphere, a conclusion researchers would not automatically draw in a left-hemisphere-lesioned aphasic patient. For example, Giovagnoli (1993) presented a CA patient with a lesion in the right parietal lobe without any apraxic symptoms. The author concluded that "the absence of oral and limb apraxia suggested a dissociation of motor planning and language, with shift of motor dominance to the left hemisphere" (p. 331). The same claim would probably not have been made in the case of a left-hemisphere-lesioned aphasic patient. As an exception, Boller (1973) presented a UCA patient with destruction of Wernicke's area without any reported signs of aphasia, and concluded that the patient's language was lateralized to the right hemisphere. Still, the hypothesis that this patient had a different interhemispheric lateralization pattern instead of a different intrahemispheric language organization cannot be confirmed.

However, in the case of a massive right-hemisphere lesion it is more difficult to reject the possibility of bilateral language representation. Several CA cases have been described with extensive lesions that should have caused global aphasia but were less severe (Assal et al., 1981; Puel et al., 1982). Assal et al. (1981) presented a CA patient who became globally aphasic following a large right-hemisphere perisylvian lesion. The patient improved dramatically within about 5 weeks, much more rapidly than expected, according to the authors. The lesion was so extensive that it is difficult to attribute recovery to an intrahemispheric language reorganization. Assal et al. (1981) concluded that this patient had an increased ability for the left hemisphere to process language. Similarly, Selnes, Rubens, Risse, and Levy (1982) described a right-handed UCA patient with an extensive left-hemisphere lesion. The patient showed only a moderate aphasia with ideomotor apraxia, verbal fluency difficulties, and agraphia in the acute stage. Expressive speech showed no evidence of agrammatism or paraphasic errors. Only some mild anomic difficulties were observed. Comprehension was more involved. After 34 months, only spelling mistakes were evidenced. The authors noted that such a massive perisylvian lesion should have caused a severe and persistent aphasia. They concluded that their patient had a pre-morbid bilateral language representation.

In conclusion, there is no doubt that some unusual characteristics have been observed in CA. It is also possible that some of these features may be observed more often than others, such as disproportionately good naming or compre-hension (Basso, Capitani, Laiacona, & Zanobio, 1985; Kapur & Dunkley, 1984). However, these observations have to be systematically compared with UCA. A difference such as the one reported by Basso, Capitani, Laiacona, and Zanobio (1985) would suggest that CA can be differentiated from UCA as a group. Another interpretation, however, is that there is a subgroup of CA that is not similar to UCA, and a subgroup of CA that is comparable to UCA.

LANGUAGE ORGANIZATION

Alexander et al. (1989) reviewed the literature and identified two subtypes of CA: mirror-image and anomalous. Their categories refer exclusively to the aphasic symptomatology. A CA case is mirror-image if a symmetrical lesion in the left hemisphere is believed to produce the same set of language disturbances. Conversely, the anomalous type of CA displays an aphasic symptomatology that would not be expected following a similarly located lesion in the left hemisphere. The authors referred to both the intrahemi-spheric organization and the discrepancy between oral and written language. It should be obvious that this basic distinction is based not only on possible intrahemispheric differences, but also interhemispheric variability, or even both. As an example, Delreux et al. (1989) reported a case of crossed Broca's aphasia in which the initial mutism and comprehension difficulties resolved within 48 hr. The strong right-hemisphere language representation was un-doubtedly established by the Wada technique; however, the intrahemi-spheric language organization was different. The patient had a posterior lesion with a Broca's aphasia. This case exemplifies the possibility of an exclusively intrahemispheric disorganization of the classic language areas. Conversely, Martins et al. (1987) reported the case of a CA patient who displayed a fluent aphasia with a posterior right-hemisphere tumor. As the tumor progressed to more anterior brain areas, the patient progressively became nonfluent. This case is a good example of mirror-image CA.

Barroche et al. (1979) and Urbain et al. (1978) suggested that CA differs from UCA in that there are more right-hemisphere posterior lesions. In ad-dition, these authors also agreed with the "typical" CA symptomatology (i.e., nonfluent, agrammatic, good comprehension, good repetition), and under-scored the tendency of a more rapid recovery in CA compared to UCA. The combination of posterior lesions with nonfluent aphasia types implies that there must be many more anomalous type than mirror-image type CA. The authors indeed postulated that the language areas of the right hemisphere in CA patients are organized more diffusely. Conversely, Castro-Caldas (1991) conducted a blind study of lesion size, location on the antero-posterior axis, and subcortical involvement between CA patients and left-hemisphere aphasia patients matched for aphasia type, age, gender, and education level. He found that there was no difference between the groups on any of the three variables. This indicates that the mirror-image type of CA may be the rule rather than the exception.

Alexander et al. (1989) reported that a majority of the cases they reviewed matched their mirror-image category. They listed 22 mirror-image CA cases (64.7%) and 12 anomalous CA cases (35.3%). In this review of 114 CA patients with vascular etiologies, 48 cases (64.9%) were considered mirror-image and 26 (35.1%) anomalous. Another 40 could not be classified with a reasonable degree of certainty. For the 20 cases with tumor etiology, 10 could not be classified, 8 (80%) were considered mirror-image CA, and 2 (20%) were anomalous. The results of these two reviews seem to indicate that mirror-image CA is twice as frequent as anomalous CA.

Intuitively, anomalous cases reflect an abnormal language distribution linked to the CA. Basso, Capitani, Laiacona, and Zanobio (1985) described seven CA cases. Their case 2 presented with an anterior lesion and a fluent type aphasia. Although the authors recognized the unusual character of the anatomopathological correlation, they stressed that such cases have been described in UCA as well (Basso, Lecours, Maraschini, & Vanier, 1985; Lhermitte & Derouesné, 1974). Similarly, Davous and Boller (1994) described a patient with a diagnosed mixed transcortical aphasia associated with a right temporoparietal lesion. Although such a lesion site is unusual for this aphasia type and we classified it as a anomalous type of CA (Appendix A), the authors nevertheless reported that such an anatomopathological correlation was indeed described following a left-hemisphere lesion (Davous & Boller, 1994).

Basso, Lecours, Maraschini, and Vanier (1985) identified 267 right-handed patients with a left-hemisphere lesion. The authors excluded patients without aphasia, with normal computerized tomography (CT) scans, and patients with subcortical lesions. Among the remaining 207 patients, 36 showed an abnormal anatomopathological correlation. In other words, 17.4% of the sample showed unexpected symptomatology based on lesion location, a decidedly high number. Among the unusual cases, seven patients showed a fluent aphasia with anterior lesions (3.4%) and six displayed a nonfluent aphasia with a posterior lesion (2.9%). The authors concluded that "even for a highly localized function such as language anatomopathological correlations are less absolute than current tenets would have them and that 'exceptions' are to be expected" (pp. 226–227). That conclusion should apply to CA as well.

Classifying the CA cases into mirror-image and anomalous hinges on several prerequisites (Alexander et al., 1989). First, the time postonset has to be taken into consideration. For example, a massive perisylvian lesion encompassing all language areas with a symptomatology of Broca's aphasia could be anomalous in the acute stage, but mirror-image in the chronic stage. Walker-Batson, Wendt, Devous, Barton, and Bonte (1988) studied a CA patient 10 years postonset. Although there may not be any doubt that we are dealing with a CA patient, we cannot comment on inter- or intra-hemispheric language representation issues after such a long post-facto delay. Sakurai et al. (1992) presented a case of CA following an extensive perisylvian lesion. They contended that their case could not be a mirror-image CA because the lesion should have caused a global aphasia instead of the Wernicke's aphasia displayed by their patient. However, they assessed their patient 3 months postonset, and the case history does not refute the possibility of an acute global aphasia. They stated that "it was not clearly reported whether his speech was fluent" (p. 144) and that "3 weeks after admission he could make himself understood in one way or another" (p. 144). The evolution from a global aphasia to a Wernicke's aphasia is not frequent, but possible. This uncertainty is represented by a question mark for the mirror-image category for this patient in Appendix A. Alexander et al. (1989) recommended the postacute period (3 weeks to 2 months postonset) as the most reliable for the description of the symptoms.

Second, the subcortical extension of the lesion has to be reported. A lesion with an anterior subcortical white matter extension will cause nonfluent types of symptoms even if the cortex of Broca's area is intact. These remarks are valid for UCA as well.

In conclusion, CA seems to include patients with a strong right-hemisphere language lateralization as well as patients with a bilateral language representation. The former group argues against Brown's theory of an interruption in the progressive lateralization of language. In addition, a strong right-hemisphere language lateralization does not preclude an unusual language organization within the right hemisphere. This group of patients will also be labeled anomalous. It is not clear, however, that this type of anomalous language representation occurs more often in CA as compared to UCA.

ORAL VERSUS WRITTEN LANGUAGE DISCREPANCY

Although some authors have reported that, in general, oral and written language skills are affected to the same extent in CA (Donoso, 1984; Urbain et al., 1978), others have underscored a frequent discrepancy between written and oral language in CA (Assal, 1982; Basso, Capitani, Laiacona, & Zanobio, 1985; Joanette et al., 1982; Puel et al., 1982). Authors usually referred to a discrepancy either between written and auditory comprehension and/or written and oral expression. For example, Zangwill (1979) reported a CA patient in whom written language was better preserved than oral language. The patient was able to write and read aloud, but his written comprehension was comparable to his oral comprehension.

In most cases where such a discrepancy is present, written language is more affected than oral language (Aboo-Baker & Labauge, 1987; Angelergues et al., 1962; April & Tsc, 1977; Assal et al., 1981; Basso, Capitani, Laiacona, & Zanobio, 1985, cases 1, 5, & 6; Carr et al., 1981, case 3; Claude & Schaeffer, 1921; Coppens & Robey, 1992, case 1; Davous & Boller, 1994; Demeurisse et al., 1986; Donoso et al., 1980; Habib et al., 1983; Hamasaki et al., 1987; Ihori et al., 1994; Ogden, 1984; Puel et al., 1982; Rétif, Lebrun, Leleux, Coppens, & Dachy, 1987, case 1; Roeltgen & Heilman, 1983; Sapir et al., 1986; Trojano et al., 1994). This type of discrepancy can also include jargonagraphia (Assal, 1982; Fournet et al., 1987; Pillon et al., 1979, cases 1 & 2). Conversely, in some cases, oral language is more affected than written language (Alexander & Annett, 1996, case 7; Barroche et al., 1979; Berndt, Mitchum, & Price, 1991; Brown & Wilson, 1973; Cappa et al., 1993, case 2; Carr et al., 1981, cases 2 & 4; Gomez-Tortosa et al., 1994; Hamasaki et al., 1987; Mendel, 1912, 1914; Rétif et al., 1987, case 2; Zangwill, 1979, case 1). Nagaraja et al. (1989) proposed that there are two groups of CA patients: a group with bilateral language representation with usually mild or transient aphasia and a discrepancy between written and oral language, and a group with strong right-hemisphere language lateralization, with severe and persistent aphasic symptoms and with writing as affected as oral language.

The discrepancy between the two modalities appeared in 90% of the 10 CA patients reviewed by Joanette et al. (1982). In the present sample of 114 CA patients with vascular etiology (Appendix A), 2 patients were illiterate, and 19 cases were lacking information allowing for a reasonably valid decision. Among the 93 cases remaining, 60 (64.5%) showed a written language symptomatology similar to the oral language symptoms, and 33 (35.5%) displayed a discrepancy between written and oral language performance. Among the latter group, 21 (63.6%) displayed a more severe disturbance in writing, and 12 (36.4%) showed more severe impairments in oral language. These results do not support the observation of Joanette et al. (1982).

Diagnosing a discrepancy between oral and written language is not without difficulties. Some cases of discrepancy between the two modalities could be misinterpreted. For example, Hamasaki et al. (1987) reported the case of a Japanese patient who performed much better in the written modality. He remained essentially mute for the 2 months the authors followed the patient. The patient had severe crossed Broca's aphasia with oral apraxia and normal comprehension. One could hypothesize that the persistent mutism was due to severe apraxia rather than to an underlying language impairment. In this case, a true discrepancy in written and oral language may not have existed.

The degree of the discrepancy between written and oral language can also vary, as the different modalities recover at different rates (Berndt et al., 1991). Puel et al. (1982) described a CA patient in whom a qualitative change occurred over time. In the more acute stage, oral language was characterized by nonfluent agrammatism and written production was fluent and dyssyntactic. In the chronic stage, oral language was much superior to written production which remained severely dyssyntactic. The authors concluded that oral and written language modalities are independent in CA. Similarly, Trojano et al. (1994) noted that "the dissociation between oral and written output was present at some stages but had disappeared by the last examinations" (p. 654). The same observation was made by Brown and Wilson (1973) and Coppens and Robey (1992). Also, Assal et al. (1981) observed that their CA patient's writing skills were worse than his oral language abilities. However, the discrepancy appeared around 5 weeks postonset, after oral language had significantly improved. To remedy this problem, the time postonset period should always be reported. Additionally, the discrepancy between the two modalities could be defined by a specific postonset testing time, for instance, the postacute period (Alexander et al., 1989). Furthermore, written and oral language skills have been shown to improve differently not only in CA, but in UCA as well.

Finally, diagnosing a discrepancy is largely subjective. Carr et al. (1981) reported a discrepancy between written and oral language in every one of their four CA patients. Either their sample of CA patients was very unusual or the authors were recognizing more subtle discrepancies than previous researchers. Unfortunately, the authors did not describe the differences quantitatively. Moreover, even objective measures can be inadequate in defining a potential discrepancy. Kapur and Dunkley (1984) used a blind study to evaluate oral versus written language skills in one CA patient. The examiners rated the patient's "oral output as more accurately reflecting the content of the pictures, whereas his written output was found to be more grammatically correct. Neither written nor oral expression, however, was rated as being consistently better than the other on both measures" (pp. 138–139). Here is a case in which both modalities were judged to be equal overall, but one had better content and the other better form. Comparing CA to UCA on the basis of such a discrepancy will require a more objective approach and a better understanding of the frequency of such a discrepancy in UCA. A molecular analysis of the two modalities will undoubtedly yield a higher frequency of discrepancies in CA. However, the same standards for identifying discrepancies between oral and written language should also be applied to UCA. Presently, little is known about similar potential discrepancies in UCA.

Basso, Taborelli, and Vignolo (1978) specifically addressed the issue of the discrepancy between written and oral language in UCA. They found such a discrepancy in 2.8% of their sample (14 subjects out of 500). Seven subjects presented with a selective impairment of writing and 7 with selective oral language difficulties. The CA literature includes only one patient with pure alexia (Ogden, 1984), one with pure agraphia (Basso, Capitani, Laiacona, & Zanobio, 1985, case 5), and one with alexia with agraphia (Aboo-Baker & Labauge, 1987). Only 7 patients in the Basso et al. (1978) study (3 with more severe written impairment and 4 with more severe oral impairment) showed written language difficulties associated with aphasia and a clear discrepancy between the two modalities (1.4%). That frequency is believed to be much higher in CA. However, Basso et al. (1978) included patients with a wide variety of time postonset periods, and we already have established that the discrepancy between written and oral language can appear or disappear with the evolution of the aphasic symptomatology. Moreover, the authors' criterion to identify a difference as a discrepancy between the two modalities is quite large. We also already underscored the fact that the authors working with CA patients are more willing to call a smaller difference a discrepancy. This observation again highlights the importance of developing a more objective tool to measure the difference between written and oral abilities, and also to follow the possible change over time. In conclusion, the data currently available do not allow a valid comparison between CA and UCA in terms of the discrepancies between written and oral language. Interestingly, Basso et al. (1978) and Hier and Mohr (1977) explained the discrepancy in UCA exclusively in localizationist terms within the left hemisphere. Similarly, Lhermitte and Derouesné (1974) and Bub and Kertesz (1982) interpreted the modality difference in terms of language processing entirely within the left hemisphere. However, the dominant tendency with CA is to hypothesize an interhemispheric representation.

Pillon et al. (1979) maintained that a discrepancy between oral and written language involving either jargonagraphia or jargonaphasia in CA is entirely comparable to what can be observed in UCA. Indeed, some similar cases have been described in UCA as well. Lhermitte and Derouesné (1974, case 1) reported a UCA patient with jargonaphasia following a posterior left-hemisphere lesion in whom written language was essentially normal. Hier and Mohr (1977) and Bub and Kertesz (1982) reported uncrossed Wernicke's aphasia patients whose written naming skills were superior to their oral naming abilities. However, Lhermitte and Derouesné (1974) described the symptomatology at 2 weeks postonset, Bub and Kertesz (1982) reported the discrepancy between modalities at 3 months postonset, and Hier and Mohr (1977) analyzed the discrepancy more than 1 year postonset. Hier and Mohr (1977) also referred to Mohr et al. (1973) where the authors "reported several patients recovering from total aphasia whose written naming *improved more rapidly* [italics added] than did their oral naming" (Hier & Mohr, 1977, p. 123). Similarly, Bub and Kertesz (1982) noted that "semantic access of spoken and written words, though affected during acute stages, *rapidly improved* [italics added] until a near normal level was attained three months postonset" (p. 702). Clearly, discrepancies between oral and written language can be found in UCA also, and identifying these discrepancies is as problematic as it is for CA because of inherent difficulties in defining differences across modalities, the subjective nature of the endeavor, and the varying rates of recovery between the different modalities.

Furthermore, a syndrome of Wernicke's aphasia with jargonagraphia has been recognized as a separate entity by Lecours and Lhermitte (1979) as Wernicke type III. The characteristics of the syndrome include normal fluency, prosody, and articulation, with word-finding difficulties and severe alexia and agraphia, including disproportionate impairment of reading comprehension compared to the fair to good oral comprehension. Consequently, the discrepancy between oral and written modalities is the cardinal symptom of this syndrome. Moreover, Lecours and Lhermitte (1979) also mentioned the possibility of anosognosia for the written but not the oral production. Such a case was described by Fournet et al. (1987) and diagnosed as such, but similar cases can be found in the CA literature. For example, Habib et al. (1983) presented a comparable case that was retrospectively diagnosed as conduction aphasia by Alexander et al. (1989), but that parallels closely the Wernicke type III syndrome of Lecours and Lhermitte (1979). This observation suggests that the discrepancy between oral and written language has been recognized as a type of syndrome following left-hemisphere damage in right-handed patients. We must caution against overstating that discrepancy as a landmark of CA.

PRAXIS

In their review of 66 CA cases from the literature, Castro-Caldas et al. (1987) found that limb apraxia was present in 17% of the cases, and oral apraxia in 52%. In a sample of 34 CA cases, Alexander et al. (1989) reported that 11% of CA patients had limb apraxia and 46% had oral apraxia. In the present sample of 114 CA patients with a vascular etiology, 25 cases did not include information on apraxia. Among the 89 cases remaining, oral apraxia was diagnosed in 30 patients (33.7%) and ideomotor apraxia was present in 15 patients (16.9%). Taken together, these results suggest that oral apraxia is more common in CA than ideomotor apraxia. In addition, Castro-Caldas et al. (1987) maintained that the incidence of oral apraxia in CA is comparable to that in UCA, whereas the frequency of ideomotor apraxia is lower in CA than in UCA. This observation indicates that oral apraxia tends to lateralize with language, whereas limb praxis seems to lateralize with handedness. Several cases of reversed laterality have confirmed this latter observation (Alexander & Annett, 1996, case 2; Cambier et al., 1985; Judd, 1989; Junqué et al., 1986; Selnes, Pestronk, Hart, & Gordon, 1991). Following massive lesions in the left hemisphere, these patients presented with typical right-hemisphere signs (e.g., visuospatial impairments, neglect) and limb apraxia, but no aphasia. Again, these cases point to the tendency of limb praxis to lateralize with handedness, even when language abilities are represented in the right hemisphere.

Kapur and Dunkley (1984) postulated that praxic skills may be independent of both verbal and nonverbal abilities. Rey, Levin, Rodas, Bowen, and Nedd (1994) described a patient with crossed Broca's aphasia without apraxia. They concluded that praxis and linguistic skills are dissociable, in that they can lateralize independently. Alexander and Annett (1996, case 9) and Marchetti and Della Sala (1997) reported patients with crossed oral and limb apraxia but no CA. Similarly, Kramer, Delis, and Nakada (1985) and Mani and Levine (1988) described patients with crossed oral apraxia only. These latter cases show that not only can praxic abilities lateralize contralaterally to the dominant hand, but also that a specific type of apraxia can be dissociated and lateralize independently. Moreover, Heilman, Gonyea, and Geschwind (1974), Fischer, Alexander, Gabriel, Gould, and Milione (1991), and Alexander and Annett (1996, case 2) presented four right-handed patients with severe oral and limb apraxia, but no oral language impairment, following left-hemisphere lesions. In addition, Alexander and Annett (1996, case 1) described a patient in whom a left-hemisphere lesion entailed a severe visuospatial impairment, but without aphasia, oral apraxia, or limb apraxia. Puel et al. (1982) reported a CA patient with an extensive perisylvian lesion and noted the preserved quality of speech, good mechanics of writing, and intact ideomotor praxis, despite a severe aphasia. They concluded that their patient's left hemisphere was still responsible for ideomotor, speech, and writing praxis. On the other hand, Demeurisse et al. (1984) reported a CA patient with a frontal lesion encompassing Broca's area who presented with apraxia of speech, mild oral apraxia, poor mechanics of writing (apraxic agraphia), but no ideomotor apraxia and minimal aphasic signs. These examples show that praxic skills can be dissociated from both handedness and language. Taken together, these cases strongly suggest the dissociability of praxis and language abilities.

In many CA cases, the absence of impairment in a specific skill prompts investigators to assume a contralateral representation of that skill. For example, Assal (1982) proposed that the absence of ideomotor apraxia and the usual preservation of mechanics of writing in CA indicated a left-hemisphere dominance for those skills. Haaland and Miranda (1982) also concluded that the absence of ideomotor apraxia in their CA patient with a lesion in the depth of the supramarginal gyrus suggested a left-hemisphere dominance for praxis. However, the CA patient described by Delreux et al. (1989) was tested with the Wada technique. He was able to perform ideomotor praxis tasks flawlessly when the left hemisphere was inactivated. This case exemplifies the danger in automatically assuming contralateral representation of intact skills.

A type of praxis that has received relatively little attention is writing praxis. Some CA patients who are agraphic also appear to have preserved mechanics for writing; that is, the ability to produce well-formed letters is preserved. Although intact mechanics of writing can be observed with posterior lesions in fluent UCA, it is very unusual in nonfluent UCA. In CA cases, crossed Broca's aphasia can be associated with the typical effortful and limited written production (Trojanowski et al., 1980), but, on the other hand, nonfluent types of CA patients can be agraphic with preserved mechanics of writing (Barroche et al., 1979; Brown & Wilson, 1973; Coppens & Robey, 1992, case 2; Kapur & Dunkley, 1984). It is possible that, in some CA cases, writing praxis lateralizes with handedness rather than language. A significant number of reversed laterality cases (right-hemisphere lesions without aphasia) showed the presence of apraxic agraphia (Alexander & Annett, 1996, case 1; Cambier et al., 1985; Junqué et al., 1986). Interestingly, the patient described by Alexander and Annett (1996, case 1) displayed apraxic agraphia in the absence of oral or limb apraxia. Again, in these cases, writing praxis lateralized with handedness and not with language. However, Roeltgen and Heilman (1983) described a fluent CA patient who had apraxic agraphia. The patient was able to spell aloud but not write the words. In their patient, writing praxis had lateralized with language skills in the right hemisphere, rather than with handedness or ideomotor praxis. In conclusion, it appears that writing praxis is dissociable from ideomotor praxis, handedness, and language. Writing praxis seems to lateralize more frequently with handedness and/or ideomotor praxis than with language skills.

Castro-Caldas et al. (1987) noted that among the CA patients who displayed limb apraxia, one-third had a history of familial sinistrality. In the present review of 114 CA cases (Appendix A), 15 patients reportedly displayed limb apraxia. In 2 cases, familial sinistrality was unknown or not reported, and only 3 patients with limb apraxia had a history of familial sinistrality, whereas in 10 patients that characteristic was absent. In other words, this survey found a ratio of 1:5 rather than the 1:3 ratio observed by Castro-Caldas et al. (1987).

TYPICAL RIGHT-HEMISPHERE SYMPTOMS

Although Donoso et al. (1980) concluded from their sample of 24 CA cases that typical right-hemisphere symptoms, such as neglect and constructional apraxia, were infrequent and mild when present, many authors reported the high frequency of typical right-hemisphere symptomatology, such as visual neglect and visuospatial difficulties in CA patients (Alexander et al., 1989; Castro-Caldas et al., 1987; Hécaen et al., 1971; Joanette et al., 1982). For example, Sweet et al. (1984) described a CA patient with a right temporo-parietal lesion with Wernicke's aphasia and clearly impaired visuospatial skills. The patient would become lost in familiar environments, and his attempts to copy Rey's complex figure resulted in haphazard production of isolated fragments.

Other very specific right-hemisphere symptoms have been reported in CA patients. Pillon et al. (1979) described a case of hemiasomatognosia. That is, following a right parietal infarction and the onset of aphasia, their patient stated that, although he was aware of his difficulties, his left arm did not appear to belong to him. Also, some CA patients have reportedly presented with prosopagnosia (Aboo-Baker & Labauge, 1987; Stone, 1934).

Some CA patients, however, did not appear to display any signs of "typical" right-hemisphere symptomatology (Brown & Wilson, 1973). In the cases where visuospatial difficulties are not present, the term *reversed laterality* was coined (Larrabee et al., 1982). In these cases, the left hemisphere purportedly houses the skills usually subserved by the right hemisphere. Because there are CA cases with typical right-hemisphere symptoms, and cases with apparent reversed laterality, it appears that visuospatial skills can either remain in the right hemisphere, or be lateralized to the left hemisphere. Therefore, the lateralization process of verbal and that of nonverbal skills seem to be independent. However, it needs to be emphasized again that the absence of typical right-hemisphere signs in a case of CA does not necessarily confirm a contralateral representation. Furthermore, Alexander et al. (1989) reported that associated typical right-hemisphere signs occur in both the mirror-image and the anomalous type of CA. This observation is consistent with the fact that language and visuospatial skills lateralize independently.

A number of cases have been described with extensive lesions of the left hemisphere associated with typical and persistent right-hemisphere symptomatology and without aphasia (Alexander & Annett, 1996, cases 1 & 2; Cambier et al., 1985; Cohen, Rémy, Leroy, Gény, & Degos, 1991; Han & Foo, 1983; Heilman et al., 1974; Judd, 1989; Junqué et al., 1986; Kellar & Levick, 1985; Sclnes et al., 1991; Taylor & Solomon, 1979), a condition labeled "crossed right-hemisphere syndrome" by Judd (1989) and "crossed nonaphasia" by Alexander and Annett (1996). For example, the patient described by Taylor and Solomon (1979) presented with a large left-hemisphere lesion entailing massive and persistent visuospatial impairments but no aphasia. Wada testing revealed strong right-hemisphere language lateralization. These cases, which could be viewed as "potential CAs," show that a complete reversal of laterality (functional situs inversus) is possible (Kellar & Levick, 1985). From their review of the CA literature, Castro-Caldas et al. (1987) hypothesized the presence of "clusters of functions" that tend to lateralize as a unit by genetic predetermination. A particular lateralization of a cluster does not impact on the lateralization of another. This could explain the frequency of typical right-hemisphere signs in CA. The visuospatial "clusters" are not affected by the right-hemisphere lateralization of language. The corollary is that a functional situs inversus is an example of a more disturbed, more abnormal lateralization pattern than the co-occurrence of visuospatial symptoms in CA, because more clusters are lateralized aberrantly.

Kreindler, Fradis, and Sevastopol (1966) postulated the possibility of a double dissociation between linguistic and visuospatial skills. They hypothesized four types of hemispheric ability distribution: the typical lateralization, the inverse, both types of skills in the right hemisphere, or both in the left. They claimed that all four of these lateralization patterns have been observed in clinical practice and described in the literature. More specifically, Kapur and Dunkley (1984) postulated two types of lateralizations in CA patients. In the first, both verbal and visuospatial skills are located in the right hemisphere, and in the second, verbal skills are in the right hemisphere and nonverbal abilities in the left. However, neither author accounted for intra-hemispheric organization variables nor for cases in which specific subsystems of language or visuospatial skills would be lateralized to different hemispheres. For example, in some of the "potential CA" cases (left-hemisphere lesions with typical right-hemisphere signs and without aphasia) just cited, the reversed laterality was not quite complete. In four cases, ideomotor apraxia and/or apraxic agraphia remained the responsibility of the left hemisphere (Alexander & Annett, 1996, cases 1 & 2; Cambier et al., 1985; Junqué et al., 1986), and in another case, subtle syntactic difficulties persisted (Taylor & Solomon, 1979).

The fact that the lateralization of skills should be examined microscopically rather than macroscopically is reflected in these cases where some typical right-hemisphere sign can coexist with left-hemisphere characteristics. For example, Haaland and Miranda (1982) observed both right- and left-hemisphere types of errors in their CA patient's block design task. Two important areas where right- and left-hemisphere signs can co-occur are constructional apraxia and writing.

In their review of 66 CA cases from the literature, Castro-Caldas et al. (1987) found constructional apraxia in 76% of the subjects. Alexander et al. (1989) reported that 75% of the 34 CA patients they reviewed had constructional apraxia. Castro-Caldas et al. (1987) concluded that these numbers were significantly higher than those reported for UCA (45%). However, Joanette et al. (1982) reported a frequency of 50% of constructional apraxia in their sample of 10 CA patients. Also, in the present sample of 114 patients with vascular etiology (Appendix A), constructional apraxia was present in 26 patients out of 89 cases (29.2%) in which apraxia in general was investigated. The discrepancy between these results probably reflects the lack of systematic reporting of constructional apraxia, but also the difficulty in distinguishing between the double nature of constructional apraxia in. Indeed, constructional apraxia can be diagnosed following a lesion in either hemisphere, and thus, the symptoms may or may not reflect visuospatial diffuculties. In the CA literature, this distinction is rarely reported, which renders a detailed analysis of constructional apraxia in CA currently impossible.

A few authors have reported typical right-hemisphere characteristics in the written production of CA patients (Assal et al., 1981; Demeurisse et al., 1986; Haaland & Miranda, 1982; Rétif et al., 1987, case 1). These authors noticed some stroke and letter reduplications in their CA patients. It could be that these typical right-hemisphere writing signs are only noticeable when agraphia is not so severe as to obscure them. However, Aboo-Baker and Labauge (1987) presented a patient with severe alexia–agraphia without aphasia as a consequence of a posterior right-hemisphere tumor. Although there is no doubt that the syndrome was partly linguistic, many errors in reading were based on visual perception. The patient confused "p" for "q," "b" for "d," "G" for "C," "W" for "M," "U" for "V," and so on. The patient missed lines of a text, and made paralexias based on the form of the words (e.g., *mireur* for *monsieur*). The authors qualified the disorders as an "apperceptive alexia due to impaired spatial perception" (p. 297, our translation). In conclusion, the fact that certain specific characteristics of CA could include linguistic and visuospatial components underscores the importance of a careful analysis of the symptomatology.

Neglect

Left-sided neglect appears to be frequent in CA (Cappa et al., 1993, case 1; Giovagnoli, 1993; Rey et al., 1994; Trojano et al., 1994). Castro-Caldas et al. (1987) found left-sided neglect in 82% of their 66 CA cases, about twice the reported frequency following right-hemisphere lesions in patients with typical left-hemisphere language lateralization. Alexander et al. (1989) reported that 59% of their 34 CA cases showed left neglect. Although there is little doubt that left-sided neglect is frequently associated with CA, the very high percentage computed by Castro-Caldas et al. (1987) may simply be due to an overestimation. For example, in 22 of their 66 CA cases, left-sided neglect was not investigated. If we assume that neglect would have been noted if present in these cases, the percentage of occurrence falls to 54.5% for Castro-Caldas et al. (1987) and to 47.1% for Alexander et al. (1989). In the present review (114 CA patients with vascular etiology), neglect was present in 65.2% of the cases in which it was reported, and in 37.7% of the total sample. It seems that neglect is somewhat more frequently observed in CA than after a right-hemisphere lesion in right-handed patients, a result that has been interpreted as meaning that CA patients have attentional skills more lateralized to the right hemisphere than patients with a left-hemisphere language lateralization pattern (Castro-Caldas et al., 1987). This strong conclusion, however, is in need of more substantiation.

Emotions and Affective Prosody

Berndt et al. (1991) and Donoso et al. (1980, case 2) reported CA patients with emotional lability typical of right-hemisphere involvement. Rey et al. (1994) described a crossed Broca's aphasia patient who displayed anosodiaphora. He lacked the typical "catastrophic reaction" and instead showed indifference toward his expressive difficulties. He joked about his unsuccessful attempts at communicating instead of displaying the typical frustration behaviors associated with failure in Broca's aphasic patients. Other authors also reported anosodiaphora or euphoria in their CA patients (Alexander et al., 1989, case 1; Henderson, 1983, case 2; Pillon et al., 1979, case 1). Interestingly, three CA patients (Fournet et al., 1987; Ihori et al., 1994; Nagaraja et al., 1989) displayed anosognosia for their written production only. This latter characteristic is unusual and remains unexplained.

Conversely, Trojano et al. (1994) reported their CA patient to be depressed and concerned. Assal et al. (1981), Berthier and Starkstein (1994), and Puel et al. (1982) reported CA patients who experienced catastrophic reactions. This type of reaction is characteristic of left-hemisphere anterior aphasia. Berthier and Starkstein (1994) concluded that CA can also involve the reversal of the lateralization of affect. These studies, indeed, suggest that a discrepancy between language abilities and associated affect is possible.

The Rey et al. (1994) CA patient had no trouble recognizing or expressing affective emotions. Similarly, several other CA patients (Alexander & Annett, 1996, cases 5, 6, & 8; Cohen et al., 1991; Giovagnoli, 1993; Henderson, 1983, cases 1, 2, & 3; Ihori et al., 1994; Walker-Batson et al., 1988) were able to produce and recognize emotional prosody features. Also, Alexander and Annett (1996, cases 1 & 2) and Ross, Anderson, and Morgan-Fisher (1989) reported a total of four cases of right-handed patients who displayed aprosodia without aphasia following left-hemisphere damage. In contradistinction, CA patients with associated affective aprosodia were also reported (Alexander & Annett, 1996, case 4; Coppens & Robey, 1992, case 1; Starkstein, Berthier, & Leiguarda, 1988). Taken together, these results indicate that affective prosody can also be lateralized independently of language skills.

CONCLUSIONS

Certain patterns of symptoms emerge from a broad view of these available cases of CA. It is, however, difficult to draw strong conclusions from this compilation of cases because of inconsistencies in the testing and the reporting of symptoms. For example, some investigators will observe and report the presence or absence of neglect or apraxia, whereas others will not. A more standardized approach to the study of each CA patient would undoubtedly yield much more information, when CA patients are then compared to other reported cases. Such an approach should include not only thorough, standardized language testing, but also examinations of oral and limb praxis, neglect, and receptive and expressive affective intonation. Investigators also need to be aware of the possible combination of right- and left-hemisphere signs in constructional apraxia and writing. Furthermore, less subjective measures of the superiority of written versus oral language should be devised and executed. Of course, patient characteristics such as familial sinistrality and multilingualism should be systematically reported in order to identify potential subgroups, or to dispel the existence of spurious subgroups, based on these characteristics. Conversely, strict criteria for acceptance of CA cases will reduce the number and perhaps the variability of CA cases, thereby obscuring possible subgroups. The use of strict criteria to define CA was attempted (Joanette et al., 1982) and appeared unsatisfactory. For example, CA patients with a positive history of familial sinistrality have been excluded from the reviews. However, our analysis revealed that there may not be any difference in symptomatology between CA patients with and without familial sinistrality.

The symptomatology of CA is certainly variable. However, it appears that some subsystems tend to cluster together, such as, for example, language and oral praxis, or handedness and ideomotor praxis. These characteristics can nevertheless be lateralized independently in some cases. The variability in the symptomatology does not preclude the fact that subgroups are almost certainly present. There appears to be a majority of mirror-image CA and a minority of anomalous CA. However, the presence of anomalous symptomatologies is not necessarily a feature of CA, because similar anomalous anatomopathological correlations have been described in UCA. In addition to mirror-image and anomalous CA, subgroups could also be identified on the basis of the presence or absence of typical right-hemisphere signs, even if there are data to suggest that the lateralization of visuospatial skills is independent from the lateralization of language abilities.

The anomalous CA cases can reflect both inter- and/or intrahemispheric language organization differences. However, there is a tendency to interpret anomalous CA cases only in interhemispheric terms, a logic that investigators are more reluctant to apply to UCA. On the one hand, each case of CA needs to be studied in view of other known cases. Broad generalizations about CA should not be made on the basis of one patient alone. On the other hand, the CA population should be compared to the UCA population. Therefore, future research needs to focus on comparing the nature and the frequency of the symptoms if we want to understand the difference between CA and UCA. For example, we need to determine the frequency of the discrepancy between oral and written language in UCA before we can draw any conclusions based on that feature in CA. Also, it could be argued that we need to divide the UCA population on the basis of familial sinistrality for a better comparison with the CA population. So far, no specific feature or combination of characteristics appears to make CA different from UCA.

REFERENCES

Aboo-Baker, F., & Labauge, R. (1987). Alexie et agraphie par lésion de l'hémisphère droit chez un droitier non aphasique. *Revue Neurologique, 143,* 294–297.

Alajouanine, T., Thurel, R., & Courchet, J. L. (1945). Hémiplégie gauche avec aphasie chez une droitière. *Revue Neurologique, 77,* 95–97.

Alexander, M. P., & Annett, M. (1996). Crossed aphasia and related anomalies of cerebral organization: Case reports and a genetic hypothesis. *Brain and Language, 55,* 213–239.

Alexander, M. P., Fischette, M. R., & Fischer, R. S. (1989). Crossed aphasias can be mirror image or anomalous. *Brain, 112,* 953–973.

Anastasopoulos, G., & Kokkini, D. (1962). Cerebral dominance and localisation of the language functions. *Psychiatria Neurologica, 143,* 6–19.

Angelergues, R., Hécaen, H., Djindjian, R., & Jarrié-Hazan, N. (1962). Un cas d'aphasie croisée. *Revue Neurologique, 107,* 543–545.

April, R. S. (1979). Concepts actuels sur l'organization cérébrale du language a partir de quelques cas d'aphasie croisée chez les orientaux bilingues. *Revue Neurologique, 135*(4), 375–378.

April, R. S., & Han, M. (1980). Crossed aphasia in a right-handed bilingual Chinese man. *Archives of Neurology, 37,* 342–346.

April, R. S., & Tse, P. C. (1977). Crossed aphasia in a Chinese bilingual dextral. *Archives of Neurology, 34,* 766–770.

Ardin-Delteil, Levi-Valensi, & Derrieu. (1923). Deux cas d'aphasie. *Revue Neurologique, 30,* 14–21.

Assal, G. (1982). Etude neuropsychologique d'une aphasie croisée avec jargonagraphie. *Revue Neurologique, 138,* 507–515.

Assal, G. (1987). Aphasie croisée chez un enfant. *Revue Neurologique, 143,* 532–535.

Assal, G., & Deonna, T. (1977). Aphasie par thrombose de la carotide interne droite, chez un enfant droitier. *Oto-Neuro-Ophtalmologia, 49,* 321–326.

Assal, G., Perentes, E., & Deruaz, J.-P. (1981). Crossed aphasia in a right-handed patient. *Archives of Neurology, 38,* 455–458.

Bakar, M., Kirshner, H. S., &Wertz, R. T. (1996). Crossed aphasia. Functional brain imaging with PET or SPECT. *Archives of Neurology, 53,* 1026–1032.

Barraquer-Bordas, L. (1965). Sobre las afasias cruzadas de los manidextros. *Revista Española de Oto-neuro-oftalmologia y Neurocirurgia, 107,* 123–124.

Barraquer-Bordas, L., Mendilaharsu, C., Peres-Serra, J., Acevedo de Mendilaharsu, S., & Grau-Veciana, J. M. (1963). Estudio de dos casos de cruzada en pacientes manidextros. *Acta Neurologica Latinomerica, 9,* 140–148.

Barroche, G., Marchal, J. C., Ascaillas, J. P., Rivail, J., & Lepoire, J. (1981). Aphasie par lésion hémisphérique droite chez une droitière. *Revue Otoneuroophtalmologique, 53,* 389–399.

Barroche, G., Presles, O., Ramel, P., Weber, M., & Arnould, G. (1979). L'aphasie croisée chez le droitier. *Revue Otoneuroophtalmologique, 51,* 251–262.

Bary. (1897). Ein fall linksseitiger Hemiplegie mit Aphasie [Review of the article by Moltschanow]. *Zentralblatt für Nervenheilkunde,* 206–207.

Basso, A., Capitani, E., Laiacona, M., & Zanobio, M. E. (1985). Crossed aphasia: One or more syndromes? *Cortex, 21,* 25–45.

Basso, A., Lecours, A. R., Moraschini, S., & Vanier, M. (1985). Anatomoclinical correlations of the aphasias as defined through computerized tomography: Exceptions. *Brain and Language, 26,* 201–229.

Basso, A., Taborelli, A., & Vignolo, L. A. (1978). Dissociated disorders of speaking and writing in aphasia. *Journal of Neurology, Neurosurgery, and Psychiatry, 41,* 556–563.

Berndt, R., Mitchum, C. C., & Price, T. R. (1991). Short-term memory and sentence comprehension. *Brain, 114,* 263–280.

Berthier, M. L., & Starkstein, S. E. (1994). Catastrophic reaction in crossed aphasia. *Aphasiology, 8,* 89–95.

Bishop, D. V. M. (1980). Measuring familial sinistrality. *Cortex, 16,* 311–313.

Bishop, D. V. M. (1990). On the futility of using familial sinistrality to subclassify handedness groups. *Cortex, 26,* 153–155.

Boller, F. (1973). Destruction of Wernicke's area without language disturbance. *Neuropsychologia, 11,* 243–246.

Borod, J. C., Carper, M., Naeser, M., & Goodglass, H. (1985). Left-handed and right-handed aphasic with left hemisphere lesions compared on nonverbal performance measures. *Cortex, 21,* 81–90.

Botez, M. I., & Wertheim, N. (1959). Expressive aphasia and amusia following right frontal lesion in a right-handed man. *Brain, 82,* 186–202.

Bramwell, B. (1899). On "crossed" aphasia. *Lancet,* June 3, 1473–1479.

Broca, P. (1865). Du siège de la faculté du langage articulé. *Bulletin de la Société d'Anthropologie, 6,* 377–393.

Brown, J. W. (1976). The neural organization of language: Aphasia and lateralization. *Brain and Language, 3,* 482–494.

Brown, J. W., & Chobor, K. L. (1987). Absence of aphasia in a dextral with a left hemisphere lesion: A case report. *Aphasiology, 1,* 425–441.

Brown, J. W., & Hécaen, H. (1976). Lateralization and language representation. *Neurology, 26,* 183–189.

Brown, J. W., & Wilson, F. R. (1973). Crossed aphasia in a dextral. *Neurology, 23,* 907–911.

Brust, J. C. M., Plank, C., Burke, A., Guobadia, M. I., & Healton, E. B. (1982). Language disorder in a right-hander after occlusion of the right anterior cerebral artery. *Neurology, 32,* 492–497.

Bub, D., & Kertesz, A. (1982). Evidence for lexicographic processing in a patient with preserved written over oral single word naming. *Brain, 105,* 697–717.

Burd, L., Gascon, G., Swenson, R., & Hankey, R. (1990). Crossed aphasia in early childhood. *Developmental Medicine and Child Neurology, 32,* 528–546.

Cambier, J., Masson, M., Guillot, M., & Robine, R. (1985). Négligence droite avec hémiasomatognosie, confusion mentale, apraxie et agraphie sans aphasie. *Revue Neurologique, 141,* 802–806.

Cameron, R. F., Currier, R. D., & Haerer, A. F. (1971). Aphasia and literacy. *British Journal of Disorders of Communication, 6,* 161–163.

Cappa, S. F., Perani, D., Bressi, S., Paulesu, E., Franceschi, M., & Fazio, F. (1993). Crossed aphasia: A PET follow up study of two cases. *Journal of Neurology, Neurosurgery, and Psychiatry, 56,* 665–671.

Carr, M. S., Jacobson, T., & Boller F. (1981). Crossed aphasia: Analysis of four cases. *Brain and Language, 14,* 190–202.

Castro-Caldas, A. (1991). Crossed aphasia as a model of atypical specialization. In I. P. Martins, A. Castro-Caldas, H. R. van Dongen, & A. van Hout (Eds.), *Acquired aphasia in children* (pp. 83–93). Dordrecht, The Netherlands: Kluwer.

Castro-Caldas, A., & Confraria, A. (1984). Age and type of CA in dextrals due to stroke. *Brain and Language, 23,* 126–133.

Castro-Caldas, A., Confraria, A., & Poppe, P. (1987). Non-verbal disturbances in crossed aphasia. *Aphasiology, 1,* 403–414.

Clarke, B., & Zangwill, O. L. (1965). A case of "crossed aphasia" in a dextral. *Neuropsychologia, 3,* 81–86.

Claude, H., & Schaeffer, H. (1921). Un nouveau cas d'hémiplégie gauche avec aphasie chez un droitier. *Revue Neurologique, 27,* 170–175.

Cohen, L., Gény, C., Hermine, O., Gray, F., & Degos, J.-D. (1993). Crossed aphasia with visceral situs inversus. *Annals of Neurology, 33,* 215–218.

Cohen, L., Rémy, P., Leroy, A., Gény, C., & Degos, C. (1991). Minor hemisphere syndrome following left hemisphere lesion in a right handed patient. *Journal of Neurology, Neurosurgery, and Psychiatry, 54,* 842–843.

Coppens, P., & Robey, R. R. (1992). Crossed aphasia: New perspectives. *Aphasiology, 6,* 585–596.

Cosman, A. (1923). *Les aphasies croisées*. Unpublished thesis, University of Algiers, Algeria.

Davous, P., & Boller, F. (1994). Transcortical alexia with agraphia following a right temporo-occipital hematoma in a right-handed patient. *Neuropsychologia, 32*(10), 1263–1272.

Deleni, F. (1917). Aphémie par tumeur l'hémisphère droit chez un droitier [Summary of a case study by Raggi, U.]. *Revue Neurologique, 21*, 178.

Delreux, V., de Partz, M. P., Kevers, L., & Callewaert, A. (1989). Aphasie croisée chez un droitier. *Revue Neurologique, 145*, 725–728.

Demeurisse, G., Coekaerts, M.-J., & Hublet, C. (1984). Agraphie, anarthrie corticale et troubles de la programmation par lésion hémispherique droite chez un droitier manuel. *Acta Neurologica Belgica, 84*, 119–130.

Demeurisse, G., Hublet, C., Coekaerts, M.-J., Derouck, M., & Capon, A. (1986). Assessment of hemispheric dominance for language in CA by two atraumatic methods. *Cortex, 22*, 305–311.

Denes, G., & Caviezel, F. (1981). Dichotic listening in crossed aphasia. *Archives of Neurology, 38*, 182–185.

Dobkin, J. A., Levine, R. L., Lagreze, H. L., Dulli, D. A., Nickles, R. J., & Rowe, B. R. (1989). Evidence for transhemispheric diaschisis in unilateral stroke. *Archives of Neurology, 46*, 1333–1336.

Donoso, A. (1984). Crossed aphasia in dextrals. In A. Ardila & F. Ostrosky-Solis (Eds.), *The right hemisphere: Neurology and neuropsychology* (pp. 125–143). New York: Gordon and Breach.

Donoso, A., Vergara, E., & Santander, M. (1980). Las afasias cruzadas en los diestros. *Acta Neurologica Latinoamerica, 26*, 238–257.

Ettlinger, G., Jackson, C. V., & Zangwill, O. L. (1955). Dysphasia following right temporal lobectomy in a right-handed man. *Journal of Neurology, Neurosurgery, and Psychiatry, 18*, 214–217.

Faglia, L., Rottoli, M. R., & Vignolo, L. A. (1990). Aphasia due to lesions confined to the right hemisphere in right handed patients: A review of the literature including the Italian cases. *Italian Journal of Neurological Sciences, 11*, 131–144.

Faglia, L., & Vignolo, L. A. (1990). A case of "crossed aphasia" in which the integrity of the left hemisphere is assessed by MRI. *Italian Journal of Neurological Sciences, 11*, 51–55.

Farge, E. (1877). Hémiplégie gauche avec aphasie, observation suivie de quelques réflexions sur la gaucherie cérébrale. *Gazette Hebdomadaire de Médecine et de Chirurgie, 31*, 488–490.

Fernández-Martín, F., Martínez-Lage, J. M., Madoz, P., & Maraví, E. (1968). La afasia cruzada. *Journal of the Neurological Sciences, 7*, 565–570.

Fischer, R., Alexander, M., Gabriel, C., Gould, E., & Milione, J. (1991). Reversed lateralization of cognitive functions in right handers. *Brain, 114*, 245–261.

Foroglou, G., Assal, G., & Zander, E. (1975). Une nouvelle observation d'aphasie croisée chez un droitier. *Schweizer Archiv für Neurologie, Neurochirurgie und Psychiatrie, 117*, 205–210.

Fournet, F., Virat-Brassaud, M. E., Guard, O., Dumas, R., Auplat, P., & Marchal, G. (1987). Alexie-agraphie croisée chez un droitier. *Revue Neurologique, 143*, 214–219.

Fujii, T., Yamadori, A., Fukatsu, R., Ogawa, T., & Suzuki, K. (1997). Crossed mixed transcortical aphasia with hypernomia. *European Neurology, 37*, 193–194.

Giovagnoli, A. R. (1993). Crossed aphasia. Report of a rare case in glioblastoma patient. *Italian Journal of Neurological Sciences, 14*, 329–332.

Gloning, I., Gloning G., Haub, G., & Quatember, R. (1969). Comparison of verbal behavior in right-handed and non right-handed patients with anatomically verified lesion of one hemisphere. *Cortex, 5*, 43–52.

Goldstein, B., Vaillant, C., Laplanche, A., & Pépin, B. (1979). Aphasie croisée chez les droitiers. *Concours Médical, 101*, 549–555.

Gomez-Tortosa, E., Martin, E. M., Sychra, J. J., & Dujovny, M. (1994). Language-activated single-photon emission tomography imaging in the evaluation of language lateralization—Evidence from a case of crossed aphasia. Case report. *Neurosurgery, 35*, 515–520.

Gonzalez Rothi, L. J., Roeltgen, D. P., & Kooistra, C. A. (1987). Isolated lexical agraphia in a right-handed patient with a posterior lesion of the right cerebral hemisphere. *Brain and Language, 30*, 181–190.

Gonzalo Barrio, M., Pareja Grande, J., Romero López, J., & Pérez García, P. (1986). Afasia cruzada: Controversias a propósito do un caso. *Revista Clínica Española, 178*, 462–463.

Guard, O., Fournet, F., Sautreaux, J. L., & Dumas, R. (1983). Troubles du langage au cours d'une lésion frontale droite chez un droitier. Incohérence du discours et paraphasies "extravagantes." *Revue Neurologique, 139*, 45–53.

Haaland, K. Y., & Miranda, F. (1982). Psychometric and CT scan measurements in a case of CA in a dextral. *Brain and Language, 17*, 240–260.

Habib, M., Joanette, Y., Ali-Cherif, A., & Poncet, M. (1983). Crossed aphasia in dextrals: A case report with special reference to site of lesion. *Neuropsychologia, 21*, 413–418.

Hadar, U., Ticehurst, S., & Wade, J. P. (1991). Crossed anomic aphasia: Mild naming deficits following right brain damage in a dextral patient. *Cortex, 27*, 459–468.

Hamasaki, T., Suzuki, K., Hirakawa, K., Imahori, Y., & Nakajima, S. (1987). Un cas japonais d'aphasie croisée chez un droitier. *Revue Neurologique, 143*, 47–54.

Han, M., & Foo, S.-H. (1983). Negative evidence for language capacity in the right hemisphere: Revised lateralization of cerebral function. In E. Perecman (Ed.), *Cognitive processing in the right hemisphere* (pp. 193–211). New York: Academic Press.

Hécaen, H., Mazars, G., Ramier, A. M., Goldblum, M. C., & Mérienne, L. (1971). Aphasie croisée chez un sujet droitier bilingue (vietnamien-français). *Sociéte Française de Neurologie, 124*, 319–323.

Heilman, K. M., Gonyea, E. F., & Geschwind, N. (1974). Apraxia and agraphia in a right-hander. *Cortex, 10*, 284–288.

Henderson, V. (1983). Speech fluency in crossed aphasia. *Brain, 106*, 837–857.

Henderson, V., Naeser, M. A., & Chui, H. C. (1983). Cerebral asymmetries evaluated by computed tomography in crossed aphasia. *Neurology, 33* [suppl. 2], 104.

Hier, D. B., & Mohr, J. P. (1977). Incongruous oral and written naming. *Brain and Language, 4*, 115–126.

Hindson, D. A., Westmoreland, D. E., Carroll, W. A., & Bodmer, B. A. (1984). Persistent Broca's aphasia after right cerebral infarction in a right-hander. *Neurology, 34*, 387–389.

Holmes, J. E., & Sadoff, R. L. (1966). Aphasia due to a right hemisphere tumor in a right-handed man. *Neurology, 16*, 392–397.

Hu, Y., Qiou, Y., & Zhong, G. (1990). Crossed aphasia in Chinese: A clinical survey. *Brain and Language, 39*, 347–356.

Hyodo, A., Maki, Y., Nakagawa, K., Enomoto, T., & Akimoto, H. (1979). Computed tomography in crossed aphasia. *No Shinkei Geka* [English abstract], 7, 791–796.

Ihori, N., Kashiwagi, T., Kashiwagi, A., & Tanabe, H. (1994). Jargonagraphia in Kanji and Kana in a Japanese crossed Wernicke's aphasic. *Brain and Language, 47*, 197–213.

Jackson, H. J. (1880). On aphasia, with left hemiplegia. *Lancet*, April 24, 637–638.

Joanette, Y., Puel, M., Nespoulous, J.-L., Rascol, A., & Lecours, A. R. (1982). Aphasie croisée chez les droitiers. *Revue Neurologique, 138*, 575–586.

Job, R., & Sartori, G. (1984). Morphological decomposition: Evidence from crossed phonological dyslexia. *Quarterly Journal of Experimental Psychology, 36A*, 435–458.

Joffroy, M. A. (1903). Sur un cas d'aphasie sensorielle avec lésion temporo-pariétale droite. *Revue Neurologique, 16*, 112–115.

Judd, T. (1989). Crossed "right hemisphere syndrome" with limb apraxia: A case study. *Neuro-psychology, 3*, 159–173.

Junqué, C., Litvan, I., & Vendrell, P. (1986). Does reversed laterality really exist in dextrals? A case study. *Neuropsychologia, 24*, 241–254.

Kapur, N., & Dunkley, B. (1984). Neuropsychological analysis of a case of crossed dysphasia verified at postmortem. *Brain and Language, 23*, 134–147.

Karanth, P., & Rangamani, G. N. (1988). Crossed aphasia in multilinguals. *Brain and Language, 34*, 169–180.

Kellar, L. A., & Levick, S. E. (1985). Reversed hemispheric lateralization of cerebral function: A case study. *Cortex, 21*, 469–476.

Kennedy, F. (1916). Stock-brainedness, the causative factor in the so-called "crossed aphasias." *American Journal of the Medical Sciences, 152,* 849–859.

Kinsbourne, M., & Durham, N. C. (1971). The minor cerebral hemisphere as a source of aphasic speech. *Archives of Neurology, 25,* 302–306.

Kitayama, I., Yamazaki, K., Shibahara, K., & Nomura, J. (1990). Pure word deafness with possible transfer of language dominance. *Japanese Journal of Psychiatry and Neurology, 44,* 577–584.

Klonoff, P. S., Prigatano, G. P., Hodak, J. A., & Shepard, D. L. (1987). A case report of crossed aphasia. *Barrow Neurological Institute Quarterly, 3,* 22–27.

Kramer, J. H., Delis, D. C., & Nakada, T. (1985). Buccofacial apraxia without aphasia due to a right parietal lesion. *Annals of Neurology, 18,* 512–514.

Kreindler, A., Fradis, A., & Sevastopol, N. (1966). La répartition des dominances hémisphériques. *Neuropsychologia, 4,* 143–149.

Kurthen, M., Helmstaedter, C., Linke, D. B., Hufnagel, A., Elger, C. E., & Schramm, J. (1994). Quantitative and qualitative evaluation of patterns of cerebral language dominance. *Brain and Language, 46,* 536–564.

Lanoë, Y., Fabry, B., Lanoë, A., Pedetti, L., Fahed, M., & Benoît, T. (1992). Aphasie croisée chez us adulte: Représentation du langage dans les deux hémisphères. *Revue de Neuropsychologie, 2,* 373–392.

Larrabee, G. J., Kane, R. L., & Rodgers, J. A. (1982). Neuropsychological analysis of a case of crossed aphasia: Implications for reversed laterality. *Journal of Clinical Neuropsychology, 4,* 131–142.

Lecours, A. R., & Lhermitte, F. (1979). *L'aphasie.* Paris: Flammarion.

Lewandowsky, M. (1911). Rechtshirnigkeit bei einem Rechtshander. *Zeitschrift für die Gesamte Neurologie und Psychiatrie, 4,* 211–216.

Lhermitte, F., & Derouesné, J. (1974). Paraphasies et jargonaphasie dans le langage oral avec conservation du langage écrit. *Revue Neurologique, 130,* 21–38.

Loring, D. W., Meador, K. J., Lee, G. P., Flanigin, H. F., King, D. W., & Smith, J. R. (1990). Crossed aphasia in a patient with complex partial seizures: Evidence from intracarotid amobarbital testing, functional cortical mapping, and neuropsychological assessment. *Journal of Clinical and Experimental Neuropsychology, 12,* 340–354.

Mani, R. B., & Levine, D. N. (1988). Crossed buccofacial apraxia. *Archives of Neurology, 45,* 581–584.

Marchetti, C., & Della Sala, S. (1997). On crossed apraxia. Description of a right-handed apraxic patient with right supplementary motor area damage. *Cortex, 33,* 341–354.

Marinesco, G., Grigoresco, D., & Axente, S. (1932). Aphasie croisée. Aphasie de Wernicke avec hémiplégie et hémianopsie homonyme latérale gauches chez un droitier. *Revue Belge de Science Médicale, 4,* 123–130.

Marinesco, G., Grigoresco, D., & Axente, S. (1938). Considérations sur l'aphasie croisée. *L'encéphale, 33,* 27–46.

Martins, I. P., Ferro, J., & Trindale, A. (1987). Acquired crossed aphasia in a child. *Developmental Medicine and Child Neurology, 29,* 96–109.

Mastronardi, L., Ferrante, L., Maleci, A., Puzzilli, F., Lunardi, P., & Schettini, G. (1994). Crossed aphasia. An update. *Neurosurgery Review, 17,* 299–304.

Mendel, K. (1912). Uber Rechtshrinigkeit bei Rechtshandern. *Neurologische Zentralblatt, 31,* 156–165.

Mendel, K. (1914). Uber Rechtshirnigkeit bei Rechtshandern. *Neurologische Zentralblatt, 33,* 291–293.

Mendez, M. F., & Benson, F. (1985). Atypical conduction aphasia. *Archives of Neurology, 42,* 886–891.

Mohr, J. P. (1973). Rapid amelioration of motor aphasia. *Archives of Neurology, 28,* 77–82.

Mohr, J. P., Weiss, G. H., Caveness, W. F., Dillon, J. D., Kistler, J. P., Meirowsky, A. M., & Rish, B. L. (1980). Language and motor disorders after penetrating head injury in Viet Nam. *Neurology, 30,* 1273–1279.

Nagaraja, D., Taly, A. B., Herlekar, G., Rangamani, G. N., Shivashankar, N., & Mukundan, C. R. (1989). Crossed aphasia in a dextral. *Clinical Neurology and Neurosurgery, 91–92,* 153–156.

Nass, R., & Myerson, R. (1985). Bilateral language: Is the left hemisphere still dominant? *Brain and Language, 25,* 342–356.

Nedelec-Ciceri, C., Anguenot, A., Rosier, M.-P., Joseph, P.-A., Vincent, D., Branchu, C., Pointreau, A., & Latinville, D. (1996). Aphasie croisée révélée par un trouble central de l'audition. *Revue Neurologique, 152,* 700–703.

Ochipa, C., & Gonzalez Rothi, L. J. (1989). Recovery and evolution of a subtype of crossed aphasia. *Aphasiology, 3,* 465–472.

Ogden, J. A. (1984). Dyslexia in a right-handed patient with a posterior lesion of the right cerebral hemisphere. *Neuropsychologia, 22,* 265–280.

Oppenheim, H. (1889). Zur Pathologie der Grosshirngeschwülste. *Archiv für Psychiatrie, 21,* 719–722.

Paradis, M., & Goldblum, M.-C. (1989). Selective CA in a trilingual aphasic patient followed by reciprocal antagonism. *Brain and Language, 36,* 62–75.

Perani, D., Papagno, C., Cappa, S., Gerundini, P., & Fazio, F. (1988). Crossed aphasia: Functional studies with single photon emission computerized tomography. *Cortex, 24,* 171–178.

Pillon, B., Desi, M., & Lhermitte, F. (1979). Deux cas d'aphasie croisée avec jargonagraphie chez des droitiers. *Revue Neurologique, 135,* 15–30.

Preobrashenski, P. A. (1893). Zur Pathologie des Gehirns. *Neurologisches Zentralblatt, 6,* 759–760.

Primavera, A., & Bandini, F. (1993). Crossed aphasia: Analysis of a case with special reference to the nature of the lesion. *European Neurology, 33,* 30–33.

Puel, M., Joanette, Y., Levrat, M., Nespoulous, J.-L. Viala, M.-F., Roch Lecours, A., & Rascol, A. (1982). Aphasie croisée chez les droitiers. *Revue Neurologique, 138,* 587–600.

Rapcsak, S. Z., Gonzalez Rothi, L., & Heilman, K. M. (1987). Apraxia in a patient with atypical cerebral dominance. *Brain and Cognition, 6,* 450–463.

Reinvang, I. (1987). Crossed aphasia and apraxia in an artist. *Aphasiology, 1,* 423–434.

Rétif, J., Lebrun, Y., Leleux, C., Coppens, P., & Dachy, B. (1987). L'aphasie croisée. A propos de deux observations. *Extraits des Comptes Rendus du Congrès de Psychiatrie et de Neurologie de Langue Française, LXXXV Session,* 429–442.

Rey, G. J., Levin, B. E., Rodas, R., Bowen, B. C., & Nedd, K. (1994). A longitudinal examination of crossed aphasia. *Archives of Neurology, 51,* 95–100.

Roberts, L. (1969). Aphasia, apraxia and agnosia in abnormal states of cerebral dominance. In P. J. Vinken & G. W. Bruyn (Eds.), *Handbook of clinical neurology* (Vol. 4, pp. 312–326). Amsterdam: North-Holland.

Roeltgen, D. P., & Heilman, K. M. (1983). Apractic agraphia in a patient with normal praxis. *Brain and Language, 18,* 35–46.

Ross, E. D., Anderson, B., & Morgan-Fisher, A. (1989). Crossed aprosodia in strongly dextral patients. *Archives of Neurology, 46,* 206–209.

Rothschild, K. (1931). The relation of Broca's center to lefthandedness. *American Journal of Medical Science, 182,* 116–118.

Sadasivam, P. B., & Jaganathan, V. (1977). Crossed aphasia in a dextral. *Journal of the Association of Physicians of India, 25,* 167–170.

Sakurai, Y., Kurisaki, H., Takeda, K., Iwata, M., Bandoh, M., Watanabe, T., & Momose, T. (1992). Japanese crossed Wernicke's aphasia. *Neurology, 42,* 144–148.

Sapir, S., Kokmen, E., & Rogers, P. J. (1986). Subcortical crossed aphasia: A case report. *Journal of Speech and Hearing Disorders, 51,* 169–172.

Sartori, G., Bruno, S., Serena, M., & Bardin, P. (1984). Deep dyslexia in a patient with crossed aphasia. *European Neurology, 23,* 95–99.

Sass, K. J., Novelly, R. A., Spencer, D. D., & Spencer, S. S. (1990). Postcallosotomy language impairments in patients with crossed cerebral dominance. *Journal of Neurosurgery, 72,* 85–90.

Schachter, M. (1977). L'aphasie croisée des droitiers. *Revue Médicale de Liège, 32,* 176–180.

Schweiger, A., Wechsler, A. F., & Mazziotta, J. C. (1987). Metabolic correlates of linguistic functions in a patient with crossed aphasia. *Aphasiology, 1,* 415–422.

Selnes, O. A., Rubens, A. B., Risse, G. L., & Levy, R. S. (1982). Transient aphasia with persistent apraxia. *Archives of Neurology, 39,* 122–126.

Selnes, O. A., Pestronk, A., Hart, J., & Gordon, H. (1991). Limb apraxia without aphasia from left-sided lesion in a right handed patient. *Journal of Neurology, Neurosurgery, and Psychiatry, 54,* 734–737.

Senator, H. (1904). Aphasie mit linksseitiger Hemiplegie bei Rechtshandigkeit. *Charité Annalen, 28,* 150–158.

Sollberg, G. (1963). Aphasie, Apraxie und Agraphie bei rechtshirniger Läsion und Rechtshändigkeit. *Deutsche Zeitschrift für Nervenheilkunde, 184,* 537–549.

Souques, M. A. (1910). Aphasie avec hémiplegie gauche chez un droitier. *Revue Neurologique, 20,* 547–549.

Starkstein, S. E., Berthier, M. L., Leiguarda, R. (1988). Disconnection syndrome in a right-handed patient with right hemispheric speech dominance. *European Neurology, 28,* 187–190.

Stone, L. (1934). Paradoxical symptoms in right temporal lobe tumor. *Journal of Nervous and Mental Disease, 79,* 1–13.

Subirana, A. (1952). La droiterie. *Archives Suisses de Neurologie et Psychiatrie, 69,* 321–359.

Sweet, E. W. S., Panis, W., & Levine, D. N. (1984). Crossed Wernicke's aphasia. *Neurology, 34,* 475–479.

Taylor, H. G., & Solomon, J. R. (1979). Reversed laterality: A case study. *Journal of Clinical Neuropsychology, 1,* 311–322.

Trojano, L., Balbi, P., & Russo, G. (1994). Patterns of recovery and change in verbal and nonverbal functions in a case of crossed aphasia: Implications for models of functional brain lateralization and localization. *Brain and Language, 46,* 637–661.

Trojanowski, J. Q., Green, R. C., & Levine D. N. (1980). Crossed aphasia in a dextral: A clinicopathological study. *Neurology, 30,* 709–713.

Urbain, E., Seron, X., Remits, A., Cobben, A., Van der Linden, M., & Mouchette, R. (1978). Aphasie croisée chez une droitière. *Revue Neurologique, 134,* 751–759.

Walker-Batson, D., Wendt, J. S., Devous, M. D., Sr., Barton, M. M., & Bonte, F. J. (1988). A long-term follow-up case study of CA assessed by single-photon emission tomography (SPECT), language, and neuropsychological testing. *Brain and Language, 33,* 311–322.

Wechsler, A. F. (1976). Crossed aphasia in a illiterate dextral. *Brain and Language, 3,* 164–172.

Weisenburg, T., & McBride, K. (1964). *Aphasia: A clinical and psychological study.* New York: Hafner.

Wertz, R. T. (1982, June). *Response to treatment in a case of crossed aphasia.* Paper presented at the meeting of the Clinical Aphasiology Conference, Oshkosh, WI.

Winterling, C. A. (1978). Crossed aphasia in Chinese dextral [Letter to the editor]. *Archives of Neurology, 35,* 694.

Woods, B. T., & Teuber, H.-L. (1978). Changing patterns of childhood aphasia. *Annals of Neurology, 3,* 273–280.

Yamada, M., Nakamura, Y., & Kobayashi, S. (1977). Hemisphere dominance in aphasia— "Crossed aphasia." *Bulletin of the Yamaguchi Medical School, 24,* 113–122.

Yarnell, P. R. (1981). Crossed dextral aphasia: A clinical radiological correlation. *Brain and Language, 12,* 128–139.

Zangwill, O. L. (1960). *Cerebral dominance and its relation to psychological function.* Edinburgh: Oliver and Boyd.

Zangwill, O. L. (1979). Two cases of CA in dextrals. *Neuropsychologia, 17,* 167–172.

Adult CA Patients With Vascular Etiology

Authors	Age	Sex	Lesion	Aphasia Diagnosis	Familial Sinistr.	Mirror Image	Oral vs. Written	Apraxia	Neglect
Farge (1877)	71	M	perisylvian	fluent	?	yes	=	?	?
Preobrashenski (1893)	?	?	Fr-T & deep	motor	?	?	?	?	?
Moltschanow (in Bary, 1897)	60	M	F3 & F1	mixed	?	?	?	?	?
Joffroy (1903)	77	M	T1-T2 & deep	sensory	?	yes	=	?	?
Senator (1904)	38	F	Perisylvian	global	?	yes	=	?	?
Souques (1910)	42	M	?	global	?	?	=	?	?
Mendel (1912; 1914)	42	F	Fr-T & insula	motor	no	yes	oral worse	none	?
Kennedy (1916)	36	F	?	sensorimotor	yes	?	?	?	?
Claude & Schaeffer (1921)	28	F	?	motor	?	?	written worse	?	?
Ardin-Delteil, Levi-Valensi, & Derrieu (1923)	59	F	deep	Broca's	?	?	=	?	?
Rothschild (1931)	?	M	?	?	?	?	=	?	?
Marinesco, Grigoresco, & Axente (1932; 1938)	60	M	Fr-P & corpus callosum	Wernicke's	no	?	=	none	?
Alajouanine, Thurel, & Courchet (1945)	30	F	P	motor	?	?	=	none	?

(Continued)

APPENDIX A
(Continued)

Adult CA Patients With Vascular Etiology

Authors	Age	Sex	Lesion	Aphasia Diagnosis	Familial Sinistr.	Mirror Image	Oral vs. Written	Apraxia	Neglect
Angelergues et al. (1962)	61	F	perisylvian	motor	no	no	written worse	none	?
Barraquer-Bordas et al. (1963) Case 1	46	F	T-O	mixed, predom. express.	no	?	=	none	yes
Case 2	21	F	P	express.	no	no	=	?	?
Weisenburg & McBride (1964, Case 20)	50	M	P-T-O	predom. express.	?	?	=	?	?
Kreindler et al. (1966) Case 3	40	M	(internal carotid)	global	?	?	=	ideomotor	yes
Case 4	64	F	?	predom. recept.	?	?	?	?	yes
Case 5	63	M	?	recept.	?	?	?	dressing	yes
Clarke & Zangwill (1965)	30	F	Fr-T-P	Broca's	no	?	=	construct.	yes
Hécaen et al. (1971)	28	M	P-Fr-T	global --> cond.	no	yes	=	none	?
Brown & Wilson (1973)	42	F	Fr-P	global --> Broca's	?	?	oral worse	oral	?
Wechsler (1976)	83	F	post. Fr	Broca's	no	yes	N/A	oral	?
April & Tse (1977)	54	M	Fr-T-P	Broca's	no	no	written worse	oral & construct.	?
Sadasivam & Jaganathan (1977)	50	M	?	global	no	?	?	none	?
Yamada et al. (1977)	42	M	P-T & deep	Broca's	no	?	=	none	?

Urbain et al. (1978)	37	F	Sylvian & deep	conduction	no	yes	=	oral & possibly apraxia of speech	?
April (1979)	72	M	F-T	Broca's	no	?	=	oral	?
Barroche et al. (1979)	72	M	perisylvian	global	yes	yes	oral worse	oral, ideomotor, construct., & possible apraxia of speech	?
Goldstein et al. (1979) Case 1	62	F	P-rol. & deep	Broca's	yes	yes	=	none	yes
Case 2	55	M	T & rol.	Broca's	no	no	=	construct.	?
Hyodo et al. (1979)	47	M	Fr-P	Broca's	?	yes	?	?	?
Pillon et al. (1979) Case 1	65	M	deep	?	yes	?	written worse	none	?
Case 2	70	M	(carotid)	nonfluent	yes	no	written worse	oral	?
Zangwill (1979) Case 1	59	M	?	Broca's	no	?	oral worse	none	yes
Case 2	54	M	Fr-T	Broca's	yes	?	=	?	?
April & Han (1980)	74	M	Fr-T	Broca's	no	yes	=	?	?
Donoso et al. (1980, Case 2)	36	M	Fr-T & deep	Broca's	no	no	=	none	yes
Trojanowski et al. (1980)	70	M	precentral supramarg.	Broca's	no	yes	=	oral	yes
Assal et al. (1981)	54	M	perisylvian	global	yes	yes	written worse	oral, ideomotor, & construct.	yes

(Continued)

APPENDIX A
(Continued)

Adult CA Patients With Vascular Etiology

Authors		Age	Sex	Lesion	Aphasia Diagnosis	Familial Sinistr.	Mirror Image	Oral vs. Written	Apraxia	Neglect
Carr et al. (1981)										
	Case 2	61	M	Fr-T	global	no	yes	oral worse	?	?
	Case 3	80	M	T-P & deep	Transcort. sensory	no	no	written worse	?	yes
	Case 4	50	F	?	Broca's	no	?	oral worse	?	yes
Denes & Caviezel (1981)		35	M	Fr-P & deep	Broca's	no	yes	?	oral	no
Yarnell (1981)	Case 1	61	M	T-P	Wernicke's	?	yes	=	apraxia of speech	no
	Case 2	68	M	Fr-T-P	conduction	?	no	=	oral	yes
	Case 3	66	M	P	Wernicke's	?	yes	=	none	yes
Assal (1982)		60	M	perisylvian	conduction	no	no	written worse	oral, & construct.	no
Haaland & Miranda (1982)		67	F	deep P	conduction	no	yes	=	none	?
Puel et al. (1982)		55	M	perisylvian & deep	Broca's --> conduction	no	no	written worse	oral	yes
Wertz (1982)		50	M	Fr-P	Broca's	?	yes	?	apraxia of speech	?
Habib et al. (1983)		61	M	subcort.	Wernicke's type III	no	yes	written worse	?	yes
Henderson (1983)	Case 1	51	M	P & deep	conduction	yes	yes	=	construct.	yes

Study	Age	Sex	Lesion	Aphasia type				Apraxia	
Case 2	60	F	T-P-O	Wernicke's	no	yes	=	ideomotor	yes
Case 3	61	M	P-T	Wernicke's	no	yes	=	ideomotor	yes
Roeltgen & Heilman (1983)	75	M	P	Transcort. sensory	no	?	written worse	none	yes
Demeurisse et al. (1984)	68	M	Fr	Apraxia of speech	yes	no	=	oral, construct.	yes
Hindson, Westmoreland, Carroll, & Bodmer (1984)	51	M	T	Broca's	no	no	=	construct.	?
Job & Sartori (1984)	33	M	Fr-T	Broca's	no	?	?	?	?
Kapur & Dunkley (1984)	57	M	Fr-P-O & deep	Transcort. motor	no	no	=	none	yes
Sartori et al. (1984)	33	M	T-P & deep	Broca's	no	?	=	construct.	?
Sweet et al. (1984)	72	M	T-P	Wernicke's	yes	yes	=	none	yes
Basso, Capitani, Laiacona, & Zanobio (1985) Case 1	64	F	Fr & deep	Broca's	no	yes	written worse	construct. & apraxia of speech	?
Case 2	53	F	Fr-T	Wernicke's	no	no	=	oral	?
Case 3	55	M	(Post.cereb. artery)	Wernicke's	no	yes	?	ideomotor & construct.	yes
Case 4	63	F	T-P	Wernicke's	no	yes	=	oral & construct.	?
Case 5	49	F	Fr-T-P	mild anomia	no	no	written worse	oral, ideomotor, & construct.	yes
Case 6	56	M	subcort.	Wernicke's	no	?	written worse	apraxia of speech	?

(Continued)

253

APPENDIX A
(Continued)
Adult CA Patients With Vascular Etiology

Authors	Age	Sex	Lesion	Aphasia Diagnosis	Familial Sinistr.	Mirror Image	Oral vs. Written	Apraxia	Neglect
Case 7	64	F	Fr-T	Broca's	no	yes	=	construct.	yes
Mendez & Benson (1985)	58	M	P-T	conduction	no	yes	=	none	yes
Demeurisse et al. (1986)	65	M	sylvian	? Wernicke's or conduction	no	?	written worse	none	no
Gonzalo Barrio et al. (1986)	72	F	O	Wernicke's	no	?	=	construct.	?
Sapir et al. (1986)	74	F	P subcort.	Anomic	no	?	written worse	apraxia of speech	?
Castro-Caldas et al. (1987) Case 1	34	M	Fr-P	Broca's	?	?	?	construct.	no
Case 2	66	M	perisylvian	global	?	yes	=	oral & construct.	yes
Case 3	40	M	prerolandic	Transcort. motor	?	yes	=	construct.	yes
Case 4	30	M	Rolandic	Anomic	?	?	=	construct.	yes
Fournet et al. (1987)	58	M	perisylvian & deep	Wernicke's type III	no	no	written worse	construct.	yes
Hamasaki et al. (1987)	64	M	subcort.	Broca's	yes	?	oral worse	oral	yes
Klonoff, Prigatano, Hodak, & Shepard (1987)	67	F	T-P-O	Wernicke's	?	yes	=	?	?
Reinvang (1987)	56	M	perisylvian	? Wernicke's or TS	no	yes	?	ideomotor, ideational, & oral	yes

Rétif et al. (1987, Case 2)	73	M	P-T	?	yes	no	oral worse	oral	yes
Gonzalez Rothi, Roeltgen, & Kooistra (1987)	54	M	P-O	agraphia	?	yes	N/A	none	no
Schweiger et al. (1987)	59	M	P-O	conduction	no	?	?	?	?
Perani et al. (1988, Case 2)	64	M	subcort.	Mixed transcort.	no	yes	?	oral, construct., & ideomotor	no
Walker-Batson et al. (1988)	55	M	perisylvian & deep	global	no	yes	=	oral	no
Alexander et al. (1989, Case 1)	54	M	Fr & deep	Wernicke's	yes	no	=	none	no
Delreux et al. (1989)	74	M	T-P	Broca's	no	no	=	oral	?
Nagaraja et al. (1989)	32	M	supramarg.	anomic	no	yes	?	none	no
Faglia & Vignolo (1990)	65	F	Fr-T-P & deep	global --> Broca's	no	yes	=	oral, ideomotor, & construct.	yes
Berndt et al. (1991)	56	F	T-P	conduction	no	yes	oral worse	none	no
Lanoë et al. (1992)	63	M	T-P	Wernicke's	no	no	=	none	no
Coppens & Robey (1992) Case 1	72	F	T-P	anomic	?	yes	written worse	none	no
Case 2	73	M	perisylvian	global	?	yes	=	construct.	yes
Sakurai et al. (1992)	55	M	perisylvian	Wernicke's	no	?	?	none	no
Cappa et al. (1993) Case 1	79	F	subcort.	Mixed transcort.	no	?	=	oral & ideomotor	yes
Case 2	56	M	subcort.	fluent	no	?	oral worse	none	no

(Continued)

APPENDIX A
(Continued)

Adult CA Patients With Vascular Etiology

Authors	Age	Sex	Lesion	Aphasia Diagnosis	Familial Sinistr.	Mirror Image	Oral vs. Written	Apraxia	Neglect
Cohen, Gény, Hermine, Gray, & Degas (1993)	72	F	T-P	?	no	?	=	oral & ideomotor	no
Davous & Boller (1994)	51	M	T-P	Mixed transcort.	no	no	written worse	none	no
Berthier & Starkstein (1994)	70	M	T-P-O	global	no	no	=	oral, ideomotor, & ideational	yes
Ihori et al. (1994)	68	M	T-P & deep	Wernicke's	no	yes	written worse	oral	no
Rey et al. (1994)	34	M	Fr-P & deep	Broca's	no	yes	=	none	yes
Trojano et al. (1994)	55	M	T-P-O & deep	Wernicke's	?	yes	written worse	oral, & ideomotor	no

Gomez-Tortosa et al. (1994)	38	F	P	conduction	no	yes	oral worse	none	no
Alexander & Annett (1996)									
Case 4	66	M	Fr & insula	fluent	no	no	=	none	no
Case 5	70	M	perisylvian	Mixed transcort.	yes	no	?	ideomotor	yes
Case 6	49	M	Basal ganglia	Broca's	?	no	=	none	no
Case 7	69	M	T-P & deep	global	no	yes	oral worse	none	yes
Case 8	75	F	T-P	conduction	no	?	=	none	yes
Bakar et al. (1996)									
Case 1	78	F	Fr-T-P	global --> Broca's	no	yes	=	?	?
Case 2	71	F	?	global	no	?	=	?	?
Nedelec-Ciceri et al. (1996)	80	F	T-P	TS	no	yes	=	construct.	no
Fujii et al. (1977)	75	F	large perisylvian	Mixed transcort.	no	no	=	construct.	yes

Note. Cereb = cerebral; Cond = conduction; Construct = constructional; Express = expressive; F = female; Fr = frontal; M = male; O = occipital; P = parietal; Post = posterior; Predom = predominantly; Recept = receptive; Rol = rolandic; Subcort = subcortical; Supramarg = supramarginal; T = temporal; Transcort = transcortical; TS = transcortical sensory.

APPENDIX B

Adult CA Patients With Tumor Etiology

Authors		Age	Sex	Lesion	Aphasia Diagnosis	Familial Sinistr.	Mirror Image	Oral vs. Written	Apraxia	Neglect
Oppenheim (1889)		19	M	?	fluent	?	?	?	?	?
Lewandowsky (1911)		55	M	posterior	sensory	?	yes	=	ideomotor	?
Kennedy (1916)		?	M	T deep	"complete"	yes	?	?	?	?
Raggi (1915, in Deleni, 1917)		?	?	F2 & F3	?	?	?	?	?	?
Stone (1934)		52	M	T deep	Wernicke's	no	yes	?	?	?
Kreindler et al. (1966)	Case 1	30	F	P	"receptive"	yes	?	?	none	no
	Case 2	53	M	Fr-P	predom. recept.	?	?	?	none	yes
Holmes & Sadoff (1966)		65	M	subcort.	nonfluent	no	?	=	?	yes

Study	Age	Sex							
Fernández-Martín et al. (1968)	61	M	inf. Fr	Broca's	no	yes	=	ideational, construct.	?
Foroglou et al. (1975)	23	M	ant. T	conduction	no	?	=	none	no
Larrabee et al. (1982)	60	M	T	acoustic-mnestic	no	yes	=	none	no
Ogden (1984)	44	M	P-T	pure alexia	no	no	written worse	?	no
Aboo-Baker & Labauge (1987)	63	M	T-P-O	alexia with agraphia	no	?	written worse	construct.	yes
Martins et al. (1987)	15	M	T-P-O	TS	no	yes	=	none	yes
Rétif et al. (1987, Case 1)	61	F	P	TM	yes	no	written worse	none	no
Paradis & Goldblum (1989)	25	M	Fr	Broca's	no	yes	N/A	apraxia of speech	?
Giovagnoli (1993)	50	F	T	Wernicke's	no	yes	=	construct.	yes
Primavera & Bandini (1993)	63	F	P-O	global --> Wernicke's	no	yes	=	construct.	?
Mastronardi et al. (1994) Case 1	69	M	T-P	"expressive"	no	?	?	?	?
Case 2	45	F	T	"mixed"	no	?	?	?	?

Note. Ant = anterior; Construct = constructional; F = female; Fr = frontal; Inf = inferior; M = male; O = occipital; P = perietal; Predom = predominantly; Recept = receptive; Subcort = subcortical; T = temporal; TM = transcortical motor; TS = transcortical sensory.

APPENDIX C

Crossed Aphasia in Children

Authors	Age	Sex	Lesion (Etiology)	Aphasia Diagnosis	Familial Sinistr.	Mirror Image	Oral vs. Written	Apraxia	Neglect
Assal & Deonna (1977)	5	M	perisylvian (CVA)	Broca's	yes	yes	= (3 years p.o.)	oral, & ideomotor	?
Burd et al. (1990)	4	M'	Fr-P (CVA)	nonfluent	no	yes	N/A	none	yes

Note. CVA = cerebrovascular accident; FR = frontal; M = male; P = parietal.

CHAPTER EIGHT

Aphasia in Users of Signed Languages

David Corina
University of Washington, Seattle

The possibility of a sign language aphasia has long fascinated researchers of the mind. In 1878 Hughlings Jackson wrote, "No doubt by disease of some part of his brain the deaf-mute might lose his natural system of signs" (p. 304). Since this time, numerous case studies have provided evidence to support this claim. Cross-modality comparisons of human language provide some of the strongest evidence to date for biological determination of human language. These studies provide keen insight into the determination of hemispheric specialization, neural plasticity, and the contribution of symbolic, motoric, and linguistic processes in human language. Investigations of sign language aphasia require an understanding of deafness, of the structure of sign languages, and of language competence in hearing-impaired individuals. This chapter provides an overview of these issues and explores the theoretical implications of some recent studies. The aim of this chapter is to document the current status of the field and to foreshadow issues that are likely to be of interest in future studies. Where possible, results from signing individuals are compared to neuropsychological results from nondeaf patients. Previous reviews can also be found in Kimura (1981), Poizner, Klima, and Bellugi (1987), and Poizner and Kegl (1992).

HEARING LOSS, ASL, AND THE DEAF COMMUNITY

According to recent estimates there are approximately 1.8 million deaf individuals in the United States (Schein & Delk, 1974). The prevalence rate of deafness in the United States is 2 per 1,000 (Schein & Delk, 1974). Deaf

261

individuals are subject to the same maladies that affect the normal population. However, as is the case with many linguistic/cultural minorities, inadequate education and lack of access to health care may adversely affect physical well-being. In the U.S. population every year roughly 80,000 persons suffer an acquired aphasia (Brody, 1992). Some small percentage of these cases involves deaf individuals whose primary means of communication is a visual-manual language; in the United States, this is likely to be American Sign Language (ASL).

Hearing loss occurs when there is an interference of the transfer of sound waves to the temporal lobe. In conductive hearing loss, the conduction of sound waves via the external and middle ear is impaired. In sensorineural hearing loss there is impairment in the transformation of motion to neural impulses. Sensorineural hearing loss may occur in the cochlea or the auditory nerve. Hearing impairment may also arise from injury to or failure of the central nervous system (CNS) directly. Finally, hearing loss may be of mixed or indeterminate etiology. Hearing loss is often not absolute, ranging from mild (20–40 dB loss, difficulty discriminating some sounds in normal conversation) to profound (greater than 90 dB loss, extreme difficulty in conversation, unlikely to understand speech to a useful degree). Hearing impairment may be congenital or adventitious, and may occur prior to acquisition of spoken language (*prelingual* deafness) or following spoken language acquisition (*postlingual* deafness).

American Sign Language is the language used by most of the deaf community in North America. ASL is a natural language, autonomous from English. ASL is only one of the many autonomous sign languages of the world, but it is the one that has been the most extensively studied. Under ideal circumstances, ASL is acquired as a native language by deaf children from deaf signing parents. Young children learning a sign language proceed through a similar developmental time course as children learning spoken languages (Battison, 1978; Boyes, 1973; Brentari, 1990; McIntire, 1977; Meier, 1991; Newport & Meier, 1985).

It is often assumed that all deaf people can sign and that all deaf people can read lips fluently. In reality, deaf people's language skills vary considerably. Fewer than 10% of deaf children have deaf parents and are socialized into the signing community from birth. ASL-signing deaf people constitute an unusual speech community embedded in a larger, normally hearing, and essentially monolingual society. The term *Deaf Community* has been used to describe this sociolinguistic entity, which plays a crucial role in a deaf person's exposure to and acceptance of sign language (Padden & Humphries, 1988). Factors that contribute to sign language skills in the deaf include parental input, age of acquisition, schooling, and affiliation with other deaf signing individuals (Meadows, 1980; Ramsey, 1989).

A signed language, although it may be the primary language used by deaf people, is unlikely to be the only language they know. In order to communicate with the hearing world, deaf signers must be able to use, at least to some extent, the language of the majority culture in which they live (Grosjean, 1982; Kettrick & Hatfield, 1986). Most deaf individuals have some competence in the use of English; however, deaf individuals vary greatly in their ability to use lip reading and intelligible spoken English. Writing and reading skills are often well below grade level, reflecting the unusual experience the deaf have with attempting to acquire English without full reference to the sound forms of the English language.

For deaf individuals, the choice of language used in a specific situation often varies. ASL is generally used for in-group functions such as casual communication among other deaf signing individuals. More English-like sign varieties may be used for interactions with hearing people (Markowicz & Woodward, 1978). This is an important sociolinguistic phenomenon that may affect language assessment in deaf patients. In a medical setting, even with a skilled interpreter present, there is often strong pressure for a deaf signer to produce more English-oriented varieties of communication, including overt mouthing or vocalizations of English words. Language assessment under these conditions may reflect a deaf person's competence in coping with nonsigning hearing individuals rather than demonstrating competence in ASL.

LINGUISTIC STRUCTURE
OF AMERICAN SIGN LANGUAGE

Within the last 10 years there has been a monumental increase in our knowledge of signed languages. Analysis of the structure of sign languages cast within formal linguistic models provides a basis of comparison for cross-language and cross-modality studies. All human languages exhibit levels of structures that govern the formation and composition of word forms in the lexicon and specify how words may, in turn, be combined into sentences. ASL is subject to both language-specific and language-universal constraints.

These advances in sign language linguistics come at an opportune time. Within the aphasia literature there is growing awareness that profiles of neurolinguistic impairment must be characterized against a backdrop of language-specific variation (see, e.g., Bates & Wulfeck, 1989). In this chapter, generalizations concerning linguistic breakdown in sign language are derived almost solely from studies of users of American Sign Language. Although general principles of breakdown will likely be similar across different sign languages, sign language-specific differences are to be expected.

Sign Phonology

Both signed and spoken languages have a level of phonological organization governing the structure of lexical units. In this context, *phonological organization* refers to the patterning of the formational units of the expression system of a natural language (Coulter & Anderson, 1993; see Corina & Sandler, 1993 for a recent overview). The phonological structure of sign language consists of subsegmental and suprasegmental units of organization. ASL signs are constructed from a limited set of formational elements drawn from four main articulatory parameters: movement, location, handshape, and orientation (Stokoe, Casterline, & Corneberg, 1965). These parameters are formally analogous to the analysis of speech sounds along parameters of place, manner, and so on. Each parameter encompasses a finite set of possible specifications. Figure 8.1 illustrates three places of articulation within the parameter of location that serve to distinguish the signs SUMMER, UGLY, and DRY. The signs CANDY, APPLE, and JEALOUS illustrate that small but discrete changes within the parameter of handshape serve to differentiate between lexical items. Recognition of a syllabic unit of organization in ASL

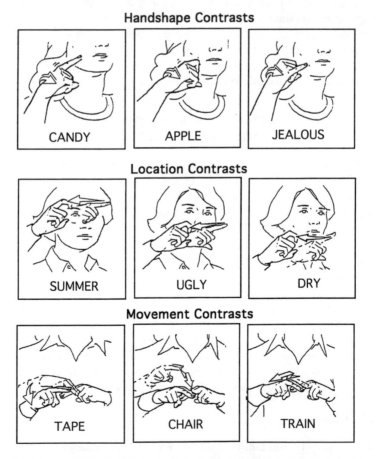

FIG. 8.1. ASL phonology. Copyright, Dr. Ursula Bellugi, The Salk Institute, La Jolla, CA.

phonology has given rise to the identification of "consonantal" and "vocalic" components of sign forms (Perlmutter, 1993). In simple terms, movement components of a sign may be considered analogous to a "vowel" in a spoken language syllable, whereas static handshapes and places of sign articulation are more "consonantal." Phonological structure is important in understanding formational paraphasias, prevalent in some aphasic signers.

Sign Morphology

ASL has both complex lexical and grammatical morphology. ASL lexical morphology permits creation of new sign forms, whereas grammatical morphology serves to modulate aspects of meaning, and permutes the shape of signs in accordance with syntactic requirements.

Grammatical morphological markings in ASL are unusual, as they are expressed as dynamic movement patterns imposed on a more basic sign form. For example, ASL has many verbal inflections that convey temporal information about a verb. Figure 8.2 shows how different movement patterns overlaid on a sign stem in a given plane modulate the meaning of the basic sign. The prevalence of nested morphological forms in sign languages, in contrast to the linear suffixation common in spoken languages, is considered an influence of modality on the realization of linguistic structure (Emmorey, 1996; Emmorey, Corina, & Bellugi, 1995; Klima & Bellugi, 1979).

One example of complex lexical morphology in ASL is illustrated by the classifier system. In many languages (spoken and signed), object and action descriptions require use of obligatory grammatical morphemes that specify salient semantic or visual properties of noun and verb referents. For example, in Chinese, a word describing a flat object like "paper" or "desk" requires the noun classifier *zhawg* to precede the noun, while words describing objects that are slender and long like "thread" or "road" require the classifier *tiao* (Tzeng, Chen, & Hung, 1991). In ASL, classifiers mark semantic categories such as human, animal, and vehicle, and visual properties like flat, thin, and round. Classifiers in ASL function as verbs of motion and location, specifying the path and the direction of the movement of their noun referent (Newport & Supalla, 1980; Supalla, 1982, 1986). Figure 8.3 illustrates the use of classifier handshapes, combined with movement morphemes, to designate complex location and motion predicates involving one or more objects. The system of classifiers is unusual in its conflation of language and object properties. The ASL classifier system is one of the most difficult aspects of ASL grammar, and poses particular problems for nonnative users of ASL. As discussed later, recent investigations suggest that a right-hemisphere lesion may selectively impair use of this unusual morphological system.

Another unusual aspect of ASL morphology concerns the class of linguistic facial expressions. In addition to the manual channel of grammatical ex-

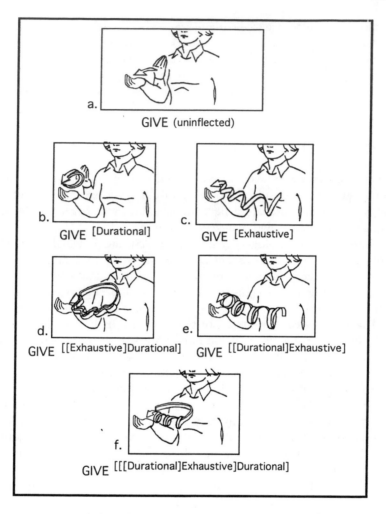

FIG. 8.2. Morphological contrasts. Copyright, Dr. Ursula Bellugi, The Salk Institute, La Jolla, CA.

pression (i.e., the arms and hands), facial expressions serve grammatical functions in ASL (Baker & Padden, 1978; Baker-Shenk, 1983; Liddell, 1980). In ASL, certain syntactic constructions (e.g., topics, conditionals, relative clauses, questions) are marked by specific and obligatory facial expressions. A second class of facial expressions signals adverbial markings, co-occurring with and modifying verb phrases, either with lexical signs or with signs inflected for grammatical aspect. Linguistic facial expressions are distinct markers that differ significantly in appearance and execution from universal affective facial expressions, such as those identified by Ekman and Friesen (1978).

"A small animal (right hand classifier) approaches and climbs an upright object (left hand classifier)."

"Vehicle (right hand classifier) moves to a stop, 'driver' looks left then right, vehicle turns right "

FIG. 8.3. ASL classifiers. Copyright, David P. Corina, all rights reserved.

ASL Syntax

American Sign Language makes use of two main strategies for distinguishing grammatical relations: word order (which is SVO in the majority of cases), and inflectional morphology. A prominent feature of ASL syntax is the use of signing space as a staging ground for the depiction of grammatical relations. At the syntactic level, nominals introduced into the discourse are assigned arbitrary reference points in a horizontal plane of signing space. Signs with pronominal function are directed toward these points, and verb signs obligatorily move between such points in specifying grammatical relations (subject of, object of) (see Lillo-Martin, 1991, Lillo-Martin & Klima, 1990, and Padden, 1983, for discussions). Various levels of syntactic embedding may be realized (see Fig. 8.4), and entire clauses may be embedded within signing spaces, with subsequent reference to this embedded space signaling contrastive events. Thus, grammatical functions served in many spoken languages by case marking or by linear ordering of words is fulfilled in ASL by spatial mechanisms (Klima & Bellugi, 1979). This same system of spatial reference is also used in the service of discourse relations. Consistency in cross-sentential spatial indexing serves as a means of discourse cohesion. The theoretical status of spatial location used in ASL syntax is not well understood. A fundamental question is whether physical spatial locations that serve co-referential and anaphoric function should be treated as part of the linguistic representation, or are merely deictic in nature (Emmorey et

MOTHER INDEX$_a$ $_a$FORCE$_b$ $_b$GIVE$_c$ BOX

"Mother$_i$ forced him$_j$ to give him$_k$ the box."

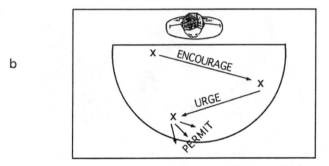

JOHN ENCOURAGE$_a$ $_a$URGE$_b$ $_b$PERMIT$_c$[Exhaustive] TAKE-UP CLASS

"John encouraged him$_i$ to urge her$_j$ to permit each of them$_k$ to take up the class."

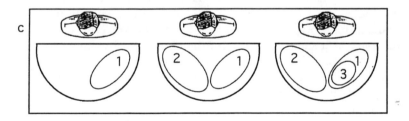

FIG. 8.4. Spatial mechanisms of ASL syntax. Copyright, Dr. Ursula Bellugi, The Salk Institute, La Jolla, CA.

al., 1995; Liddell, 1990, 1995). As discussed later, this seemingly esoteric distinction has implications for the interpretation of syntactic deficits observed in signers who have incurred brain damage.

Fingerspelling

In addition to American Sign Language, there exists the American manual alphabet. In this system, the letters of English words are represented by 26 distinct configurations of the hand, and meaningful units (the English words represented by their letters) are conveyed by sequences of these configu-rations. Fingerspelling provides one avenue for borrowing new English vo-cabulary into ASL (Klima & Bellugi, 1979). Proficient fingerspellers sequence letters into movement "envelopes," producing a seemingly continuous signal. Nevertheless, fingerspelling differs from signing in the degree of sequentiality of articulation used to convey information. The system of fingerspelling not only differs from signing in articulatory status, but fingerspelling incorporates processes involved in spelling and reading (Wilcox, 1992). Several finger-spelling systems exist. For example, the American manual alphabet utilizes a single hand, whereas the British fingerspelling system requires use of both hands to depict the same 26 letters (Sutton-Spence, Woll, & Allsop, 1990).

SIGN LANGUAGE APHASIA FROM PAST TO PRESENT

Sixteen cases of deaf or signing individuals who have incurred left-hemi-sphere brain damage and five cases of right-hemisphere-damaged signers are summarized in Table 8.1. These case studies vary greatly in their expli-cation of the underlying brain processes involved in signing. Many of the early case studies were hampered by lack of understanding of the relation ships among systems of communication used by deaf individuals. For ex-ample, several of the early studies compared disruptions of fingerspelling and only briefly mentioned or assessed sign language use. Studies seldom established premorbid language histories, and thus included reports of congenitally and adventitiously deaf individuals, native and nonnative sign-ers, right-handed and left-handed signers. Anatomical localization of lesions was often lacking or confounded by the existence of multiple infarcts, and rarely were audiological reports presented. Nevertheless, with careful read-ing general patterns do emerge. More recently, well-documented studies have started to provide a cleaner picture of the neural systems involved in language processing in users of sign languages. Technical discussions will be largely based on this later series of subjects.

Historical review of case studies of signers reveals gradual development in the field of aphasiology, in understanding deafness, and in the recognition of and status of sign languages. Early studies (roughly those from the late 1880s to the early-mid 1900s) reflected an emphasis on localization of func-tion. The studies by Grasset (1896), Burr (1905), and Critchley (1938) re-flected attempts to document manual impairments in deaf individuals with left-hemisphere damage. However, only Burr's study examined sign lan-guage use rather than fingerspelling. The studies by Leischner (1943), Tureen, Smolik, and Tritt (1951), and Douglass and Richardson (1959) provided more extensive language testing in a variety of modalities, but were limited by a lack of systematic sign language production and comprehension tests. In

TABLE 8.1
Summary of Case Studies of Signers With Left- and Right-Hemisphere Damage

Case No.	Reference	Hand-edness	Subject (age, sex)	Age of Deafness	Neurological Signs	Etiology	Anatomy	Premorbid Language/ Language Environment	Clinical Language Assessment	Comments
1	Grasset (1896)	n/a	n/a, male	n/a	Right arm weakness	Stroke	Possible cortico-spinal motor system (see Kimura, 1981, for some discussion)	n/a	Impaired right-handed finger-spelling; loss of right handed motor power and coordination	Case reported in Critchley (1938)
2	Burr (1905)	n/a	56, female	Early childhood	Right paralysis, right homonymous hemianopsia	Tumor	Posterior frontal lobe with extension into basal ganglia	Sign, reading, and writing	Global sign language aphasia	Repeated strokes, briefly documented
3	Critchley (1938)	Right	42, male	14 years	Right paralysis	Stroke	n/a	Sign, finger-spelling, and lip reading	Impaired finger-spelling produc-tion and compre-hension, intact sign language, speech dysarthria	British two-handed finger-spelling
4	Leischner (1943)	Right	64, male	Congenital	Right arm and right leg weakness	Stroke	Left frontal and parietal region (supramarginal gyrus and angular gyrus)	Native signer, Czech and German bilingual, signing and reading and writing	Fluent aphasia, neologistic output	Reported in Kimura (1981); autopsy reveals both left & right hemi-sphere damage

#	Reference	Handedness	Age, sex	Onset	Symptoms	Etiology	Lesion	Abilities	Impairment	Notes
5	Tureen, Smolik, & Tritt (1951)	Right	43, male	Congenital	Partial right paralysis	Tumor & hemorrhage	Second and third frontal convolutions (posterior), anterior tip of the internal capsule	Sign, fingerspelling and lip reading	Impaired fingerspelling comprehension and production; preserved reading ability; intermittent sign comprehension problems	Praxic function retained in left hand except for communication
6	Douglass & Richardson (1959)	Right	21, female	Congenital	Right paralysis, right sided facial weakness	Stroke	Probable frontal and rolandic lesion with possible parietal involvement	Sign, fingerspelling, and writing, limited reading	Impaired production and comprehension of signing and fingerspelling; sign and fingerspelling paraphasias	Detailed study for its time, no apraxia
7	Sarno, Swisher, & Sarno (1969)	Right	69, male	Congenital	Right central facial weakness, moderate right hemiplegia	Stroke	Probable left fronto-parietal lesion	Learned sign at age 7, fingerspelling, lip reading, writing, and reading	Good sign comprehension with mild impairment in production, impaired fingerspelling production and comprehension	Detailed study, no apraxia
8	Meckler, Mack, & Bennet (1979)	Left	19, male	Hearing	Right hemiparesis	Closed-head injury	Traumatic cerebral contusion	Speech, sign, and fingerspelling	Global aphasia for speech, initially sign language less impaired	English-ASL bilingual, left-handed
9	Underwood & Paulson (1981)	Left	57, male	Congenital	Right hemiplegia	Stroke	n/a	Learned sign at age 7, fingerspelling, lip reading, and functional writing abilities	Production problems in both sign and fingerspelling, jargon and paraphasias are noted, also seen in writing	Left-handed signer

(Continued)

TABLE 8.1
(Continued)

Case No.	Reference	Hand-edness	Subject (age, sex)	Age of Deafness	Neurological Signs	Etiology	Anatomy	Premorbid Language/ Language Environment	Clinical Language Assessment	Comments
10	Chiarello, Knight, & Mandel (1982)	Right	65, female, L.K.	6 months	Moderate right-sided weakness of arm, leg, and face	Stroke	Left inferior parietal lobule, with left frontal subcortical extent undercutting Broadman areas 4, 3, 1, and 2	Learned sign at age 5 years, fingerspelling and some functional writing ability	Severe anomia and comprehension loss for both sign and fingerspelling and writing; sign paraphasia and gesturing noted	See also Poizner et al. (1987), case K.L.
11	Poizner, Klima, & Bellugi (1987)	Right	81, male, P.D.	5 years	Right hemiparesis	Stroke	Subcortical lesion with anterior focus deep to Broca's area, including basal ganglia, posteriorly, white matter of the parietal lobe	Spoken and sign language abilities	Aphasic-paragrammatic, fluent production, syntactic and morphological errors	See also Kimura et al. (1976)
12	Poizner, Klima, & Bellugi (1987)	Right	38, female, G.D.	Congenital	Right hemiparesis	Stroke	Left frontal lobe, including Broca's area & anterior portions of the superior and middle temporal gyri	Signing, fingerspelling, reading and writing	Broca-like signing, impaired production with preserved sign comprehension	
13	Poizner & Kegl (1992)	Right	48, male, N.S.	Congenital	Partial right hemiparesis	Compound skull fracture	Left parietal lesion	Deaf sibling, residential school	Sign comprehension deficit, mild production problems, pyramidal deficit	No apraxia reported

#	Study	Handedness	Age/Sex	Onset	Symptoms	Etiology	Lesion location	Modalities	Language deficit	Notes
14	Brentari, Poizner, & Kegl (1995)	Right	81, female, E.N.	Congenital	n/a	Stroke	Distribution of left posterior cerebral artery, posterior limb of the internal capsule, posterior thalamus and left-mesial occipital cortex	Native signer	Motorically fluent sign production with sublexical and semantic paraphasias	Possible case of subcortical sign aphasia
15	Hickok et al. (1995)	Right	62, female	18 months	Right homonymous hemianopia, spastic right hemiparesis	Stroke	Left posterior cerebral artery stroke, medial temporal and occipital lobes, left occipital pole, & splenium of the corpus callosum	Signing, fingerspelling, reading, and writing	Severe sign language comprehension deficit (esp. sentence level); inability to read words; preserved sign production	Disconnection syndrome
16	Corina, Poizner, Feinberg, Dowd, & O'Grady (1992)	Right	76, male, W.L.	Congenital	Right-sided weakness	Stroke	Fronto-temporo-parietal lesion, including Broadman area 44 and 45 and white matter tracts, white matter deep to the inferior parietal lobule	Signing, fingerspelling, reading, and writing	Severe sign language production and comprehension problems; semantic and phonological paraphasia	
17	Poizner, Klima, & Bellugi (1987)	Right	71, female, S.M.	Congenital	Paralysis of left arm and leg	Stroke	Distribution of the middle cerebral artery	Signing, fingerspelling, reading, and writing	Severe visuospatial disruption, no aphasia	Sparing of nonlinguistic pantomime ability

(Continued)

273

TABLE 8.1
(Continued)

Case No.	Reference	Hand-edness	Subject (age, sex)	Age of Deafness	Neurological Signs	Etiology	Anatomy	Premorbid Language/ Language Environment	Clinical Language Assessment	Comments
18	Poizner, Klima, & Bellugi (1987)	Right	75, male, B.I.	Congenital	Dense left arm paralysis	Stroke	Distribution of right middle cerebral artery	Signing, fingerspelling, reading, and writing	Severe visuospatial disruption, no aphasia	
19	Poizner, Klima, & Bellugi (1987)	Right	81, male, G.G.	5 years	Lower left facial weakness, abnormal left-sided reflex	Stroke	Temporal-parietal lesion, cortex and underlying white matter in the superior temporal gyrus, lower inferior parietal lobule	Signing, fingerspelling, reading, and writing	Severe visuospatial disruption, no aphasia	
20	Corina, Krichevsky, & Bellugi (1996)	Right	61, male, J.H.	Congenital	Dense left hemiparesis	Stroke	Central portions of the frontal, parietal, and temporal lobes, associated deep white matter and basal ganglia structures	Signing, fingerspelling, reading, and writing	Severe visuospatial disruption, no aphasia, profound left neglect	Extinction for objects but not for sign language
21	Corina et al. (1990); Kegl & Poizner (1991); Poizner & Kegl (1992)	Right	35, female, D.N.	Hearing	Lower left quadrant visual field cut	AVM & stroke	Upper portion of the occipital lobe (medial) and superior lobule, whitematter involvement	Early sign language exposure, interpreter for the deaf	Deficits in sign language discourse and use of ASL classifier morphology; subtle visuospatial disruption	Unusual lesion site

Note. n/a = not available. Ages are given in years.

addition, these studies continued to erroneously regard signed language as "universal" and/or "primitive." However, these studies began to provide better anatomical lesion localization.

A trend observed in these early studies is the desire to provide taxonomic classification of language impairment in deaf patients. In some cases, sign deficits were traced to problems of motor impairment. For example, Critchley (1938) described his patient as suffering from "dactylological apraxia." Others suggested the impairments were manifestations of visual language problems. Douglass and Richardson (1959) reported their patient as suffering from "dactylological dyslexia." Others attempted to classify impairments as symbolic-based deficits. Tureen et al. (1951), using a classification based on Nielsen (1946), used the term "agnosia of finger movements in dactylology" to describe their patient. It was not until Sarno, Swisher, and Sarno's (1969) case study that the term *aphasia* was used with conviction in describing sign language impairments. No doubt the seminal work of Stokoe et al., who published the first linguistically sophisticated dictionary of American Sign Language in 1965, provided the impetus to evaluate sign language deficits in a fashion similar to spoken language breakdown. Two studies of left-handed signers subsequently appeared: Meckler, Mack, and Bennet (1979) reported on a hearing, left-handed, ASL–English bilingual, and Underwood and Paulson (1981) provided a case study of a left-handed deaf signer.

By the early 1980s, efforts to characterize sign language disturbances in relation to the linguistic properties of sign language began to appear. Chiarello, Knight, and Mandel's (1982) case served as a turning point, providing careful documentation of signing errors accompanied by good anatomical localization. During this time, Drs. Bellugi, Klima, Poizner and colleagues launched a research program to investigate sign language breakdown following brain damage. Building on their linguistic characterizations of sign languages and knowledge of acquisition processes of sign language (Klima & Bellugi, 1979), they described three left-hemisphere-damaged and three right-hemisphere-damaged deaf individuals. This important work culminated with the publication of the book *What the Hands Reveal About the Brain* (Poizner et al., 1987). This work was marked by the desire to evaluate the complementary specialization of the two hemispheres in deaf signing individuals. During this time other studies of right-hemisphere-damaged signers began to appear. In addition to reaffirming the left hemisphere's role in processing ASL, a major contribution of this work was the careful documentation of subtypes of sign language aphasia, and the surprising discovery that right-hemisphere damage did not severely disrupt sign language production. Additional studies reported by Kimura, Battison, and Lubert (1976) furthered the discussions of the relationships between signing deficits and motoric impairment. Recent works growing out of the Bellugi,

Klima, and Poizner research program have included several new case studies (Brentari, Poizner, & Kegl, 1995; Corina, Kritchevsky, & Bellugi, 1992; Corina, Kritchevsky, & Bellugi, 1996; Corina, Poizner, Feinberg, Dowd, & O'Grady, 1992; Hickok, Klima, Kritchevsky, & Bellugi, 1995; Kegl & Poizner, 1991; Poizner & Kegl, 1992). These reports signify a transition period in the study of sign language aphasia. With the modal pattern established, this new literature seeks to more carefully assess the neural systems involved in sign processing and confront the complexities of the subprocesses involved.

Cerebral Dominance in Deaf Signers

Since the 1800s, when Jackson broached the issue of neural control for sign language, researchers have looked to case studies of deaf signing individuals to answer the two basic questions: first, whether left-hemisphere structures mediate the sign languages of the deaf, and second, whether deaf individuals show complementary hemispheric specialization for language and nonlanguage visuospatial skills. With respect to this first question, if there is one conclusion that can be drawn from the sign aphasia literature it is that right-handed deaf signers, like hearing persons, exhibit language disturbances when critical left-hemisphere areas are damaged. Of the 16 left-hemisphere cases reviewed, 12 provide sufficient detail to implicate left-hemisphere structures in sign language disturbances (cases 2, 4, 5, 6, 7, 10, 11, 12, 13, 14, 15, 16) (see Table 8.1). Five of these cases provide neuroradiological or autopsy reports to confirm left-hemisphere involvement, and provide compelling language assessment to implicate aphasic language disturbance (cases 2, 5, 10, 12, 16). Cases that have been excluded from this tally include reports of left-handed and/or hearing individuals (cases 8 and 9), those without sign language impairment (cases 1 and 3), cases of multiple lesions or primarily subcortical lesions (cases 4 and 14), and nonaphasic cases or cases of mixed etiology of language disturbance (cases 11, 13, 15).

Five cases of right-hemisphere-damaged signers provide an opportunity to assess questions of hemispheric specialization (cases 17, 18, 19, 20, 21). All five of these signers showed moderate to severe degrees of visuospatial impairment following right-hemisphere damage. In contrast, none of the left-hemisphere-damaged signers tested on visuospatial tests were shown to have significant impairment. Taken together, these findings suggest that deaf signers show complementary specialization for language and nonlanguage skills. Damage to critical left-hemisphere structures produces sign language aphasia in deaf signers. Right- but not left-hemisphere lesions produce visuospatial impairments in deaf signers. These studies demonstrate that development of hemispheric specialization is not dependent on exposure to oral/aural language.

Language Comprehension and Production

In hearing individuals, severe language comprehension deficits are associated with left-hemisphere posterior lesions, especially posterior temporal lesions. Similar patterns have been observed in users of signed languages. For example, W.L. (case 16) and K.L. (case 10b), who had damage to posterior temporal structures, evidenced marked comprehension deficits (see Appendix). W.L. showed a gradation of impairment across tasks, with some difficulty in single sign recognition, moderate impairment in following commands, and severe problems with complex ideational material. Subject K.L. showed severe comprehension problems, especially with multipart commands. In each of these cases, comprehension deficits were accompanied by impaired sign production. In contrast, Hickok et al. (1995) have recently reported a case of a signer with severely impaired sign comprehension but well-preserved language production. This subject had a left-hemisphere lesion involving the medial temporal and occipital lobes, the left occipital pole, and the white matter tracks that give rise to the splenium of the corpus callosum. Sign comprehension at sentence level was severely impaired, whereas single sign comprehension was reasonably intact, with occasional semantic field errors in confrontation naming. Hickok et al. argued for a comprehension deficit based on a disconnection syndrome, in which visual information from the intact right visual field was unable to project to the language region of the left-hemisphere (like alexia without agraphia in users of spoken languages).

In users of spoken languages, language production impairment is associated with left-hemisphere anterior lesions. Execution of speech movements, for example, involves the cortical zone encompassing the lower posterior portion of the left frontal lobe (Goodglass, 1995). Left-frontal anterior regions are also implicated in sign language production impairment. Cases 5, 6, and 12 provide support for this claim. A representative case is that of the Poizner et al. (1987) subject G.D. (case 12), who experienced damage to areas 44 and 45 of the left frontal lobe. This subject's signing was effortful and dysfluent, and reduced largely to single-sign utterances.

In summary, evidence from lesion studies of deaf signers indicates left-hemisphere dominance for sign language processing, and the familiar patterns of comprehension and production deficits following posterior and anterior damage, respectively. In addition, the dissociation syndrome described by Hickok et al. (1995) illustrates the intimate relationships between neural systems involved in visual processing and sign language processing, not unlike those posited for auditory and spoken language processing (Geschwind, 1965). Finally, there is good evidence for hemispheric specialization for both language and nonlanguage functions in deaf signers. We now turn to a more thorough description of sign language aphasia and will then return to a more detailed discussion of neuroanatomical specialization for sign language.

NEUROLINGUISTICS OF SIGN LANGUAGE APHASIA

Language breakdown following left-hemisphere damage is not haphazard, but affects independently motivated linguistic categories. This observation provides support for a treatment of aphasia as a unique cognitive entity rather than as a subtype of a more general motor or symbolic deficit. In the sign language aphasia literature there is now ample evidence that sign language breaks down in a linguistically significant fashion. The best documented work concerns impairments in sign production. We focus on the description of phonemic paraphasias and lexical and inflectional morphology.

Phonemic Paraphasias in American Sign Language

Spoken language phonemic paraphasias arise from the substitution or omission of sublexical phonological components (Blumstein, 1973). In ASL, sublexical structure refers to the formational elements that comprise a sign form: handshape, location, movement, and orientation. In signed languages, paraphasic errors result from substitutions within these parameters. For example, the Poizner et al. (1987) subject K.L. (case 10b) produced paraphasic signing errors in which substitutions were found in all four major parameters. For example, the sign ENJOY, which requires a circular movement of the hand, was articulated with an incorrect up and down movement, indicating a substitution in the formational parameter of movement. Substitutions in the parameters of orientation, handshape, and location were also reported.

In principle, selectional errors could occur among any of the four sublexical parameters (and they do). However, the most frequently reported errors are those affecting the handshape parameter. Corina, Poizner, Feinberg, Dowd, and O'Grady (1992) described in some detail the phonemic errors produced by W.L. (case 16), which almost entirely affected handshape specifications. For example, W.L. produced the sign TOOTHBRUSH with the Y handshape rather than the required G handshape, and produced the sign SCREWDRIVER with an A handshape rather than the required H handshape (see Fig. 8.5). Based on a linguistic analysis of these types of errors, Corina, Poizner, Feinberg, Dowd, and O'Grady (1992) have presented evidence that these handshape substitutions are phonemic in nature, rather than simply phonetic misarticulations. The preponderance of handshape errors is interesting, as recent linguistic analyses of ASL have suggested that handshape specifications (and perhaps static articulatory locations) may be more consonantal in nature whereas movement components of ASL may be analogous to vowels (see Corina & Sandler, 1993, for some discussion). One of the most striking asymmetries in spoken language phonemic paraphasias is that errors overwhelmingly favor consonant distortions. Whether the vulnerability of consonants relative to vowels across language modality reflects

"FINE"

"SCREWDRIVER"

"WHITE"

"TOOTHBRUSH"

FIG. 8.5. W.L.'s handshape paraphasias (correct form is shown in inset). Copyright, Dr. Ursula Bellugi, The Salk Institute, La Jolla, CA.

a neural difference in representations or is owed to the statistical differences in inventory or articulatory/acoustic/visual variables (e.g., degree of freedom before misarticulating a consonant or a vowel is detected as an error) is not well understood.

Finally, phonological paraphasias in sign aphasia do not compromise the syllabic integrity of a sign (Brentari et al., 1995). For example, we observe substitutions of movements rather than omissions (the latter would violate syllable well-formedness in ASL).

Morphological and Syntax Errors

A common error pattern in spoken language aphasia is the substitution and omission of bound and free morphemes. Languages differ in the degree to which they use morphology to mark obligatory grammatical distinctions (e.g., case and gender, subject and object agreement, etc.); thus, patterns of impairment may be more striking in some languages than in others (Bates, Wulfeck, & MacWhinney, 1991; Menn & Obler, 1990). ASL is a highly inflected language; morphosyntactic agreement distinguishing grammatical subject and object requires directional movement trajectories in certain classes of ASL verbs. In the absence of grammatical movement trajectories, a verb sign will be produced in a uninflected "citation" form. Poizner et al. (1987) investigated their patients particularly well in this morphosyntactic realm. Poizner's patient G.D. (case 12) consistently omitted required inflectional morphemes in her spontaneous signing, and instead produced uninflected citation verb forms. Poizner's patient P.D. (case 11) produced both omissions in inflectional morphology, and inconsistent verb agreement substitutions. That is, P.D. failed to maintain consistent verb movement trajectories to spatial locations, as is required by syntactic and discourse conventions. G.D. had a large left-hemisphere lesion that involved most of the convexity of the left frontal lobe, including Broca's area. P.D. had a subcortical lesion in the left hemisphere, with anterior focus deep to Broca's area and posterior extension into the white matter in the left parietal lobe. The general pattern of omissions versus substitutions in signers G.D. and P.D., respectively, is consistent with profiles of agrammatic and paragrammatic impairment reported for users of spoken language.

In addition to morphosyntactic processes, ASL makes rich use of morphological devices to express distributional aspect (e.g., "give-to-each-one-of-them" vs. "give-to-all-of-them") and temporal aspect (e.g., continuous action vs. iterative action). The use of morphological inflections is vulnerable under conditions of brain damage. For example, G.D. omitted morphologically complex forms across the board, including morphosyntactic inflections and temporal and distributional inflections. Poizner et al. (1987) reported in detail unusual aspect-morphology errors in signer P.D. These errors involved semantically inappropriate inflections on a variety of lexical forms that do not subcategorize for these inflections. For example, they reported the ASL sign BRILLIANT, semantically an adjective with inherent quality, as being inflected for predispositional aspect, which only applies to adjectives with transitory quality. An example of a semantic subcategorization error in English might be inflecting an absolute adjective for comparisons (e.g., *invisible r/st, *absent er/est). In English, only relative adjectives inflect for comparison (e.g., red er/est, tall er/est). Paragrammatic speech errors often result in the substitution of morphological inflections, and, in contrast to agrammatic aphasia, the paragrammatic substitutions are more variable (Bates et al., 1991). However, to my knowledge, constructions of morphological neologistic forms which violate subcategorization have not been reported, even in languages like Hungarian (MacWhinney & Osman-Sagi, 1991) or Turkish (Slobin, 1991) with highly complex morphology systems. Whether these ASL errors reflect differences in the patterning of morphological impairment in signed versus spoken languages or represent nonaphasic symptoms in this older subject is not well understood.

The use of facial morphology following left-hemisphere lesion has been recently investigated. Recall that facial expressions serve a dual function in ASL: to convey affective information and to convey linguistic information. Separate classes of facial expressions participate in these two distinct functions. Differential impairment in these two classes of facial expression has been reported (Zein, Say, Bellugi, Corina, & Reilly, 1993). Recent recognition and production studies of facial expression of normal deaf signers indicate bilateral mediation of facial expressions, which contrasts with the strong right-hemisphere advantage shown by hearing persons, for whom facial expressions serve only affect purposes (Corina, 1989). In summary, production of sign language morphology, in its many guises, is vulnerable following left-hemisphere damage in deaf signers.

Taken together, these results demonstrate that language abilities in deaf signers break down in linguistically significant ways. These findings provide evidence that language impairments following stroke in deaf signers are aphasic in nature and do not reflect a general problem in symbolic conceptualization or motor behavior.

INTRAHEMISPHERIC LOCALIZATION

As discussed, patterns of hemispheric specialization in deaf signers broadly mirror those found in hearing individuals. Damage to critical left-hemisphere areas leads to discrete sign language aphasias, but leaves visuospatial abilities intact. Right-hemisphere damage disrupts visuospatial abilities but does not disrupt core language abilities in deaf signers. A more challenging question concerns the extent to which the neuroanatomical systems responsible for mediating auditory languages participate in visual sign languages. This question has important theoretical implications. On the one hand, if common anatomical areas are found to mediate both signed and spoken languages, then this would provide evidence for a modality-neutral system underlying human language processing. The existence of a modality-neutral language system has been taken by some to argue for the validity of a biologically determined and cognitively encapsulated language faculty (Bellugi, Bihrle, & Corina, 1991; Fromkin, 1991). On the other hand, if differences in language representation are found, then this would suggest that human language systems exhibit some degree of plasticity. Given the undeniable evidence that signed languages are true human languages, significant anatomical differences in language representation may indicate that there are multiple ways to realize functional human language in the brain. Behavioral evidence to date suggests a role for both biologically determined mechanisms and influences of environmental constraints in the development of signed and spoken languages (Neville, 1990).

Few cases of sign language aphasia are sufficiently well detailed in behavioral or anatomical description to definitively assess the fit between classical descriptions of spoken language symptom-complexes and sign language breakdown. Moreover, even the standard of comparison (for example, the Wernicke–Lichtheim–Geschwind classificatory system) has been questioned on explanatory-functional adequacy. Despite these limitations, some tentative observations can be made. Restricting our discussion to general characterizations of production problems in nonfluent aphasia and comprehension problems in fluent aphasia provides useful points of comparison.

Nonfluent Aphasia

It is generally accepted that lasting Broca's aphasia in a hearing person requires a lesion encompassing the cortical Broca's area (pars opercularis and pars triangularis) of the left frontal lobe, often extending posteriorly to include the lower portion of the motor strip. The lesion must extend in depth to the periventricular white matter, because a purely cortical or shallow lesion produces only a transient disorder (Mohr et al., 1978; Goodglass, 1993). One question that arises in the study of Broca-like signing and Broca-like speech is the degree to which there is overlap in the premotor regions. Levine and Sweet (1982) provided data based on spoken language users that suggest that pure cases of Broca's aphasia without associated agraphia may be limited to inferior regions of the precentral gyrus, whereas more extensive lesions extending dorsally may result in a Broca's aphasia with associated agraphia. This suggests that agraphia may result from involvement of arm and hand representations of the sensorimotor cortex. Thus, it may be possible to use agraphia as a metric for determining degree of overlap between signing and spoken language aphasia. That is, is it the case that all nonfluent Broca-like signers also have associated agraphia, or are the linguistic representations underlying writing and signing functionally distinct and dissociable? Two cases in the literature provide sufficient detail to make some tentative observations.

Tureen et al. (1951) (case 5) described production problems in a congenitally deaf patient following hemorrhage of a tumor in the left frontal lobe affecting the second and third frontal convolution and the tip of the internal capsule. Importantly, this subject was unable to use his nonaffected left hand for signing, fingerspelling, or writing. The Poizner et al. (1987) subject G.D. presented with Broca-like signing and had damage to areas 44 and 45 of the left frontal lobe. G.D. evidenced both agrammatic signing and agrammatic written language output following her stroke. In addition, G.D. showed considerable problems with fingerspelling. Finally, Douglass and Richardson's (1959) subject (case 6) is more speculative. This patient showed impairment of sign production and was described as dysgraphic. In addition, fingerspelling was impaired. It is interesting to note that across all of these modalities the subject is reported to present with perseverative errors and substitutions. Unfortunately, neuroanatomical localization is only inferred from behavioral deficits in this patient. Thus, in three cases in which there are well-described productive sign language impairments, we find associated disturbances in both writing and fingerspelling. The similarities of the disturbances in the nonaffected hand across modalities of manual expression are suggestive of a common disturbance. These three studies suggest that nonfluent signing aphasias require involvement of classic Broca's area and encroachment on cortical and subcortical motor areas of the precentral gyrus involved in hand and arm representations.

Fluent Aphasia

Fluent spoken language aphasias are associated with lesions to posterior temporal-parietal regions. Wernicke's aphasia, for example, is typically mapped onto the posterior region of the left superior temporal gyrus. However, it is not uncommon for lesions associated with Wernicke's aphasia to extend onto the lower second temporal gyrus and into the nearby parietal region (Damasio, 1991). Dronkers, Refern, and Ludy (1995) have recently reported that a lesion of the posterior half of the middle temporal gyrus is associated with chronic Wernicke symptoms. Two prominent features of Wernicke's aphasia are impaired comprehension, and fluent, but often paraphasic, output (semantic and phonemic). Persistent neologistic output sometimes occurring with severe Wernicke's aphasia is associated with lesions extending to the supramarginal gyrus (Kertesz, 1993).

Three cases of sign language aphasia discuss posterior lesions in sufficient detail to permit some tentative comparisons. Leischner (1943) (case 4) presented anatomical data based on autopsy, and reported a lesion in the left posterior region involving cortex and white matter extending to the angular and supramarginal gyri. Interestingly, this patient produced the closest approximation of jargon aphasia currently in the literature. The patient produced a great deal of signing, most of it erroneous or nonsensical, with frequent perseverations and meaningless signs. Unfortunately, comprehension skills were not reported in this case description. As noted, supramarginal lesions in hearing individuals may lead to severe jargon output. The case of K.L. (Chiarello et al., 1982; Poizner et al., 1987) and the case of W.L. (Corina, Poizner, Feinberg, Dowd, & O'Grady, 1992) are significant as these cases presented with severe comprehension difficulties but relatively fluent paraphasic output. Interestingly, neither subject's lesions occurred in cortical Wernicke's area, but rather involved more frontal and inferior parietal areas. In both cases, lesions extended posteriorly to the supramarginal gyrus. Lesions associated with the supramarginal gyrus alone do not typically result in severe comprehension loss in users of spoken language. These two cases suggest that sign language comprehension may be more dependent on inferior parietal areas in the left hemisphere. This difference may reflect within-hemisphere reorganization for cortical areas involved in sign comprehension (Leischner, 1943; Poizner et al., 1987; Chiarello et al., 1982). However, this observation must be qualified, given the variability in comprehension deficits observed in hearing individuals following lesions in left posterior temporal and adjoining parietal structures.

In summary, these observations show that the anterior/posterior and nonfluent/fluent dichotomies hold for sign language. However, there are some indications that within-hemisphere reorganization may be present in the deaf. Frontal lesions resulting in Broca-like sign production impairments may encroach on cortical association areas involved in hand and arm representation. Sign comprehension deficits were common in patients with lesions involving the supramarginal gyrus. In two patients, cortical Wernicke's area was not involved. These data suggest possible subtle differences in cortical organization of sign and speech that must be further validated with both lesion studies and functional in vivo imaging studies. The mapping of critical areas important in sign language mediation is hampered by the bias of positive cases in the literature. Equally interesting would be cases of left-hemisphere-damaged signers with lesions in classic language areas who do not demonstrate sign impairment.

RIGHT HEMISPHERE AND LANGUAGE

In discussing anatomical differences between users of signed and spoken language, it is worthwhile to reconsider the evidence for right-hemisphere contributions to sign language processing. Five right-hemisphere-damaged signers showed frank disruptions in nonlanguage visuospatial processing. Typically, these subjects were reported as having well-preserved language skills. Poizner et al. (1987) stated:

> There are several lines of evidence that sign language is intact in right-lesioned signers. The first (and most powerful) line of evidence lies in the fact that their signing is flawless and without aphasic symptoms and is in contrast to the signing of deaf patients after left-hemisphere damage where clear and marked disruption is found. (p. 153)

However, more recent studies suggest that this picture may be changing. We focus on three types of language-related issues in right-hemisphere-damaged signers. First, right-hemisphere damage in signers may, as is the case in hearing persons, disrupt the meta-control of language use as evidenced by disruptions of discourse abilities (Brownell, Simpson, Bihrle, & Potter, 1990; Kaplan, Brownell, Jacobs, & Gardner, 1990; Rehak et al., 1992). Second, there is new evidence that right-hemisphere structures may be important in using the ASL classifier system. Third, we examine the contribution of the right hemisphere in comprehension of spatialized syntax.

Impaired Discourse Abilities

There is growing evidence that the right hemisphere plays a crucial role in the discourse abilities of deaf signers. Analysis of language use in right-hemi-sphere-lesioned subject J.H. (case 20) (Corina, Kritchevsky, & Bellugi, 1992; Corina et al., 1996) revealed occasional non sequitur and abnormal attention to details, which are characteristics of the discourse of hearing patients with right-hemisphere lesions (Delis, Wapner, Gardner, & Moses, 1983). For example, in a description of the Cookie Theft picture, subject J.H. used full, grammatically complex ASL sentences. However, J.H. mentioned details neither inferable from nor particularly relevant to the Cookie Theft picture (e.g., stated "it's cold outside," showed inordinate interest in the drapes). Subject D.N. (case 21), reported in Poizner and Kegl (1992), showed another pattern of discourse disruption. Although D.N. was successful at spatial indexing within a given sentence, several researchers noted that she was inconsistent across sentences (Emmorey et al., 1995; Poizner & Kegl, 1992). That is, she did not consistently use the same index point from sentence to sentence. In order to salvage intelligibility, D.N. used a compensatory strategy in which she restated the noun phase in each sentence, resulting in an overly repetitive discourse style. An English equivalent could involve noun repetitions such as: "Tom went to the store, Tom looked for eggs. Tom paid for eggs. Tom went home," versus "Tom went to the store, he looked for eggs. He paid for them and then he went home." The cases of J.H. and D.N. suggest that right-hemisphere lesions in signers can differentially disrupt discourse content (as in the case of J.H.) and discourse cohesion (as in the case of D.N.). Lesion site differs significantly in these two patients; J.H.'s stroke involved central portions of the frontal, parietal, and temporal lobes, while D.N.'s lesion was predominantly medial and involved the upper part of the occipital lobe and superior parietal lobule. Whether similar lesions in hearing individuals would result in differential discourse patterns awaits further study.

Impaired Classifier Production

Recent investigation of the use of the ASL classifier system by a right-hemi-sphere-damaged signer (D.N.) has revealed systematic impairment. The classifier system contains morphologically complex forms that convey salient visual properties of the objects they signify. In the classifier system, classifier handshapes (handshapes that designate semantic classes of objects, analogous to classifiers in spoken languages) are combined with movement morphemes, to designate complex location and motion predicates involving one or more objects (Newport & Supalla, 1980). This system of classifiers is unique in its conflation of language and visuospatial properties.

In the case of D.N., we find interesting errors in the use of the classifier system. In a classifier elicitation task, the subject views short vignettes of animals and objects moving about and interacting and is asked to describe them. Descriptions of these vignettes require the use of ASL classifiers to depict the semantic category of the objects, as well as the use of a limited set of movement trajectories to faithfully depict interactions of the objects. D.N. showed significant problems with this task. At jeopardy were D.N.'s depictions of movement direction, object relations, and object orientations. For example, D.N. depicted a small barrel hopping down a platform as hopping up an incorrectly inclined plank. However, the manner of movement (small hopping movements) was correct. Another type of error involves relational errors in sentences in which the left and right hands each depict an independent object (e.g., a description of two cars in a head-on collision). In cases in which two-hand articulations were required, D.N. displayed great hesitancy, and often had to make multiple attempts at getting the two hands to correctly represent the spatial relationship of the objects. Importantly, D.N. showed no motor weakness which would explain these errors. Another common error is the simplification of classifier handshapes. Many ASL classifier handshapes encode inherent orientation. For example, in the handshape for a "vehicle" classifier (see Fig. 8.3 bottom), the tips of the middle and index finger are considered the "front" of the vehicle. Other classifier handshapes are more generic, such as the "upright-object" classifier (see Fig. 8.3 top), and do not encode orientation to the same degree. In simple descriptions with only one object present, D.N. used correct classifiers. However, in classifier descriptions requiring precise orientation of an object, and especially in multiple object relations, D.N. often used unmarked "generic" object classifiers. Her performance suggests that she was aware of the correct classifier handshape (she could use these occasionally), but she had developed a strategy of substitution to avoid the spatial demands imposed by the system of ASL classifiers.

In the cases of impaired discourse production and classifier use, it is reasonable to suppose that right-hemisphere cognitive deficits manifest themselves in aspects of language use. For example, an attentional deficit could manifest itself as a perseveration of topic of conversation, or a spatial memory impairment could result in an inability to keep track of references across stretches of discourse. For users of ASL these types of deficits may manifest themselves as impairments in language continuity and spatial reference. Similarly, D.N.'s problems with classifier forms may stem from a more general problem with encoding external spatial relations into body-centered manual representations, especially when two articulators must be used. It seems reasonable, then, to entertain the possibility that right-hemisphere damage does not disrupt linguistic function per se, but may impair the execution and processing of linguistic information in sign language, in which spatial information plays a particularly salient role. However, the issues become more complicated when we consider the syntactic aspects of ASL.

ASL Syntax in Right- and Left-Hemisphere-Damaged Signers

Disturbances in syntactic processing in American Sign Language have been attested after both left-hemisphere and right-hemisphere damage. In the case of left-hemisphere damage, we find problems in production and comprehension of spatialized syntax. For example, patient G.D. revealed production problems such as omitting necessary inflections, whereas subject P.D. was inconsistent in his use of spatial referencing in the service of grammatical relations. Subjects P.D., W.L., and K.L. all demonstrated problems in the comprehension of syntactic relationships expressed via the spatial syntactic system. More surprising, however, is the finding that some signers with right-hemisphere damage also exhibited problems. Two of the right-hemisphere-damaged subjects, S.M. (case 17) and G.G. (case 19), tested by Poizner et al. (1987), showed performance well below controls on two tests of spatial syntax. Indeed, as pointed out in Poizner et al. (1987), "Right lesioned signers do not show comprehension deficits in any linguistic test, other than that of spatialized syntax."

A central question is whether these comprehension deficits are similar for left- and right-hemisphere-damaged signers. Unfortunately, from the current literature we cannot be certain at this time. One crucial question, as yet unanswered, is whether left- and right-hemisphere-damaged subjects show deficits in grammatical processing of ASL syntax when it is not expressed spatially. As mentioned, not all verbs are spatially inflecting. It is therefore possible to construct tests of grammatical-syntactic knowledge that rely less upon spatial processing. In this way, one could ascertain whether the comprehension deficits are limited to the spatial nature of the task. Poizner et al. (1987) speculated that the perceptual processing involved in the comprehension of spatialized syntax involves both left and right hemispheres; certain critical areas must be relatively intact for accurate performance. In any case, the deficits in syntactic comprehension in the right- and left-hemisphere-damaged subjects raise an interesting theoretical question: Should these deficits in comprehension be considered aphasic in nature, or should they be considered secondary impairments arising from a general cognitive deficit in spatial processing? The answer to this question, in part, depends on whether one treats the spatial locations of the verb system as part of the syntactic representation or rather treats these physical location as deictics. If one argues that these spatial locations are part of the linguistic representation, then the forced conclusion is that right-hemisphere damage in deaf adults leads to morphosyntactic impairment in language comprehension. Even if space does not itself serve a syntactic function, it does perform both a referential and locative function within the language (see Emmorey et al., 1995). How are the principles involved in processing referential and locative function different from syntactic processing? Further work is required to tease apart these complicated theoretical questions.

APRAXIA AND SIGN LANGUAGE

Apraxia is defined as an impairment of the execution of a learned movement in response to a stimulus that would normally elicit the movement, subject to the conditions that the afferent and efferent systems involved are intact, and that the difficulty is not due to inattentiveness or lack of cooperation (Geschwind & Damasio, 1985). The assessments of apraxia typically involve asking subjects to perform simple transitive and intransitive movements of the limbs and face, both in response to verbal commands and by imitation, and with objects both present and absent. Apraxia is a multifaceted construct with many subtypes of impairment; efforts to understand apraxia are hampered by lack of consistent definitions. Most researchers acknowledge two main categories of apraxia: ideomotor apraxia and ideational apraxia. Ideomotor apraxia refers to failure to carry out a requested movement properly. Ideational apraxia applies to impairments of limb movement and generally denotes an impairment in the ability to carry out a sequence of movements (Geschwind & Damasio, 1985). Traditionally the left inferior parietal lobe has been treated as an area responsible for representation of learned movement. Lesions associated with the left inferior parietal lobe result in an inability to perform and comprehend gestures, whereas damage more anterior to this region may result in production impairment with sparing of pantomime comprehension (Heilman, Rothi, & Valenstein, 1982; Rothi, Ochipas, & Heilman, 1991). There is limited evidence that this distinction holds for deaf signers as well. For example, subject G.D. with a large fronto-anterior lesion shows impaired ability to produce representational intransitive and transitive movements to command, but nevertheless shows normal performance on a pantomime recognition test (Poizner et al., 1987).

The relationship between impairments of language production and motor behavior is a complicated and, at times, contentious literature. When one considers impairments in sign language production, the issues become even more glaring, as the surface appearance of the disorder always suggests impaired motor control. There is great interest in studying deaf signers in reference to the distinction between aphasia and apraxia, in the hope that, as the manual articulators are directly observable, quantification of the deficits involved may be more objective (see, e.g., Brentari et al., 1995). Here we consider evidence for dissociation between two categories of limb movement and aphasia in deaf signers.

In the early reports of sign aphasia it is not uncommon to find statements that various subjects were not apraxic, or that they had intact praxic functions. However, in many of these early studies, correct use of common objects was considered sufficient to label the subjects nonapraxic. More convincing dissociations of sign language impairment with well-preserved conventionalized gesture and pantomimed object use are reported in Kimura et al. (1976), Sarno et al. (1969), Chiarello et al. (1982), Poizner et al. (1987) (cases P.D. and K.L.), Poizner and Kegl (1992) and Corina, Poizner, Feinberg, Dowd, and O'Grady (1992). Subject W.L. (case 16), for example, had a marked sign language aphasia affecting both production and comprehension of signs. Abundant phonemic and semantic paraphasic errors were noted. Sign comprehension was extremely limited. Interestingly, W.L. produced unencumbered pantomime, often involving stretches of multisequenced pantomime to communicate ideas for which a single lexical sign would have sufficed. Moreover, both comprehension and production of pantomime were found to be better preserved than was sign language. These cases reemphasize the fact that language impairments following left-hemisphere damage are not attributable to undifferentiated symbolic impairments. More importantly, these cases demonstrate convincingly that linguistic gesture (e.g., ASL) is not simply an elaborate pantomimic system.

A more controversial issue concerns differential impairment in meaningless manual movements and sign language ability. According to Kimura (1993), the left hemisphere appears to be essential for selecting most types of movement postures. Thus, Kimura treats language production impairments following left-hemisphere damage as secondary to an impairment in sequential movement programming. A diagnostic test developed by Kimura and Archibald (1974) requires experimenters to perform a series of meaningless unfamiliar hand and arm movements for immediate reproduction by patients. The movements include a variety of both hand and arm postures, with various orientations with respect to the body, and bear no resemblance to known gestures or learned movements (for users of spoken languages). Two left-hemisphere-damaged language-impaired signers showed impairment in imitating complex nonlinguistic movements (Kimura et al., 1976; Chiarello et al., 1982). These findings were taken as support for Kimura's position that signing disorders are manifestations of movement disorders. However, Poizner et al. (1987) retested P.D. (who was the subject of the original Kimura et al., 1976, study), and reported that nonlinguistic movements were intact at the time the testing; however, he still remained severely aphasic. More recently, a severely aphasic patient (W.L.) also performed within normal limits on an abbreviated version of the Kimura copying task (the same test used by Poizner et al., 1987), suggesting a dissociation between linguistic impairment and sequential movement disorders (Corina, Poizner, Feinberg, Dowd, & O'Grady, 1992).

The conflicting results raise questions about the validity of the measures used. Some of the items used in the Kimura and Archibald (1974) test, although meaningless to hearing individuals, bear a great deal of similarity to existing sign forms, and thus warrant exclusion. For example, some of the movement sequences may be considered ASL "nonwords." (It is known that impairments in word and nonword production may be similarly disrupted in spoken language aphasics—Caplan, Vanier, & Baker, 1986; Kolk & Blomert, 1985.) However, abbreviated measures may not be sufficiently rigorous.

There are theoretical reasons why we might expect a dissociation between sequential movement control and linguistic movement. The emphasis on impairments in the selection of sequentially based movements as an explanation of aphasic impairment misses a crucial distinction of linguistic systems. Languages (either signed or spoken) are not simply extreme cases of highly sequentialized movements. A unique characteristic of human language is that smaller, meaningless units are built up to form higher order, complex units. Hierarchical composition is a crucial element of language structure. Thus a model of motor production based solely on sequential movement will not successfully account for the complexities of language behavior.

In summary, there is good evidence in favor of a dissociation between ideomotor and ideational movements and signing. There is some evidence for dissociations between sequential movement disorders and sign language use; however, more rigorous testing is required to conclusively evaluate the extent of these dissociations.

NEUROIMAGING STUDIES OF SIGNERS

Recently, functional imaging techniques have been used to examine sign language representation in the brain. A series of studies by Soderfeldt (1994) and Soderfeldt, Ronnberg, and Risberg (1994) used regional cerebral blood flow (rCBF) and positron emission tomography (PET) to look at functional representation of sign. Studies of hearing bilingual speaker-signers reported bilateral posterior temporal activation for both spoken language comprehension and sign comprehension. In a separate study with native deaf signers, a similar bilateral pattern was found, but with increased right-hemisphere parietal-occipital activation. Soderfeldt (1994) suggested that this increased activity reflected the greater spatial processing required for perception of a signed language. However, no direct measures were taken to evaluate this claim. Moreover, differences in baseline activation for the comparison groups of deaf and bilingual speaker-signers raise questions concerning the subtraction involved in these studies. The relatively poor spatial and temporal resolution of the rCBF method is also a limiting factor in these studies.

Neville et al. (1995) used the high spatial resolution of functional magnetic resonance imaging (fMRI) to investigate ASL and English language processing in native deaf and native hearing signers. The ASL studies compared the processing of well-formed ASL sentences with that of formationally complex "pseudo-signing." Deaf subjects displayed significant activation of classical language areas within the left hemisphere, including frontal cortex (Broca's area, dorsolateral prefrontal cortex [DPLC], and inferior precentral sulcus) and posterior superior temporal sulcus (Wernicke's area). Processing of ASL sentences also resulted in robust and extensive activation of the right hemisphere in deaf subjects. The activated areas included the entire superior temporal sulcus, the temporal pole and angular gyrus, the prefrontal cortex, and frontal regions (homologue of Broca's area and DPLC). Results of hearing native signers also displayed left-hemisphere activation of the classical inferior frontal and posterior temporal language areas. In addition, like the deaf subjects, these subjects displayed strong and extensive activation within parietal regions of the right hemisphere.

Together these results demonstrate that although within the left hemisphere there is overlap in the areas that are active when native users process their native language, by contrast within the right hemisphere robust and extensive activation of parietal structures when hearing and deaf native signers process sentences in ASL but not when native speakers process English. These results imply that the co-occurrence of visuospatial and language information results in the recruitment or maintenance of these areas in the language system.

Hickok et al. (1995) reported on an fMRI production study of covert naming and word (sign) generation. Analogous tasks with spoken language have shown significant activation in Broca's and Wernicke's areas in hearing individuals. Two native deaf signers showed activation in Brodmann areas 44/45 (Broca's area) and posterior area 22 (Wernicke's area) predominantly on the left, although right-hemisphere homologues did show significant activation. Additional sites of activation included premotor areas, cerebellum, and prefrontal cortex. These authors concluded that the similarity of activation of left perisylvian language areas in deaf and hearing subjects indicate that neural organization for language processing is modality independent.

It is interesting to note that imaging studies reveal far greater bilateral activation for signing than would otherwise be expected from the lesion studies. Further work is needed to clarify the bilateral patterns of activation. It is likely that there are significant anatomical processing differences between the language processing in neurologically intact individuals and that reported in the aphasia literature population. Case studies of neurologically impaired signers illuminate the necessary and sufficient brain structures for sign processing, whereas functional imaging may provide an understanding of sign processing in the normal, nonchallenged brain. Together, these studies provide important new insights into the biological foundation of human languages and reveal degrees of neural plasticity in systems underlying functional human language.

CONCLUSION

The studies to date provide ample evidence for left-hemisphere mediation of sign language in the deaf. Sign language disturbances following left-hemisphere damage show a linguistically significant breakdown that is not attributable to more general problems in motor or symbolic processing. Deficits in signing are separable from general apraxic deficits; evidence for dissociation between gestural ability and linguistic sign language ability has been reported. Right-hemisphere damage results in visuospatial deficits in deaf signers. In addition, there is growing evidence for the role of the right hemisphere in ASL discourse and classifier use. Recent functional imaging studies in non-brain-damaged deaf signers have shown greater bilateral activation than would have otherwise been expected from the lesion studies alone. Whether these differences reflect the greater visuospatial processing demands thought to underlie ASL comprehension or are merely a result of processing differences between normal and disordered brains is not yet known. Future advances in our understanding of sign language structure and processing will provide new answers.

APPENDIX: SUMMARIES OF CASE STUDIES

An annotated appendix of sign language aphasia case studies follows. Unless otherwise noted, signers were all right-handed before their strokes.

Left-Hemisphere Cases

1. Grasset (1896). Described a deaf individual with a unilateral deficit in sign production following a cerebral vascular accident. The subject was able to produce normal fingerspelling with his left hand, but was unable to use his right hand. His right arm showed some loss of motor power and coordination, although this loss was insufficient in degree to account for failure to write or fingerspell. The subject had preserved comprehension of others' finger-talk (sic) and was able to read. Kimura (1981) speculated that this case may reflect a lesion of the lateral cortico-spinal motor systems, which would result in marked weakness of digits, with the proximal musculature of the same side somewhat less affected. This type of lesion would result in distal movements of the hand, such as those required for fingerspelling, showing impairment. No mention of manual signing was made.

2. Burr (1905). Briefly described a 56-year-old female who became deaf in early childhood. She suffered a series of four strokes over the course of 3 months, each with increasing right-sided motoric involvement and temporary loss of sign language ability. After a fourth stroke, the subject became globally impaired and unresponsive. Autopsy revealed a large vascular glioma in the posterior part of frontal lobe, which extended in depth to the basal ganglia. Burr concluded that "the area of disease was so great that the case is of no interest in localizing speech, except that it shows that the left hemisphere controls language by signs as it does all other forms of language" (p. 1107). Two aspects of this case were noteworthy. First, the testing of sign language ability, although grossly underreported, was conducted by another deaf individual. Second, Burr's observations regarding the role of the left hemisphere in mediating all forms of language were insightful.

3. Critchley (1938). Reported a case of an adventitiously deaf male who gradually lost his hearing between the ages of 7 and 14 years. He was taught fingerspelling and lip-reading at a school for the deaf in London. He was reported to have relied chiefly upon manual signs and finger-speech to communicate with others. Initially, the stroke resulted in a right-sided paralysis, and the subject was unable to use any speech. Over the course of the next 4 weeks his paralysis improved and some speech returned, although his speech was described as dysarthric and ungrammatical. Initially, he was unable to understand or produce fingerspelling. Gradually his comprehension ability returned; however, he remained unable to produce fingerspelling. The use of "natural sign language" (sic) was not impaired in this subject. Over the course of 2 years, little improvement was noted. Deficits reported in fingerspelling include misselection of vowels (i.e., pointing to the wrong "vowel"), telegrammatical and ungrammatical fingerspelling, and inability to perform automatic fingerspelling sequences (i.e., the manual alphabet). Note that the British system of fingerspelling is dependent on two hands (e.g., the five vowels are indicated by pointing to the five fingers on the nondominant hand). From the characterizations provided we cannot determine whether the subject's fingerspelling deficit is the result of an impairment of left-handed sequential movements, or of an inability to coordinate the two hands. This case is significant as it demonstrates that a left-sided cerebral lesion can interfere with the performance of fingerspelling, while leaving signing intact. However, it is doubtful that Critchley systematically tested sign language ability.

4. Leischner (1943) (as reported in Kimura, 1981). Described a 64-year-old congenitally deaf male from a deaf signing family highly regarded in the Deaf Community. The subject could read and write Czechoslovakian. His daughter served as an interpreter for the case history. Nine months prior to admission, acquaintances noted some communication problems. Two months before admission, the subject lost consciousness, and lost strength in his right arm and leg. In the hospital, he suffered another episode of right-sided weakness. The subject's daughter reported that her ability to understand her father had declined from the time of his first hemiparesis. The subject produced fluent but nonsensical signing. Perseverations were noted. He signed the days of the week in an incorrect order or interspersed with other signs. He misnamed objects, both with and without perseveration. He produced many neologistic signs. Thus, he showed many of the types of errors shown by fluent spoken language aphasics. Unfortunately, no report of sign language comprehension is mentioned. The subject showed preserved drawing ability, could assemble parts of an object to form a whole, and appeared oriented in space. He also used objects correctly. After several months of improvement, he had a sudden relapse and died within a few days. Autopsy revealed a fresh bleed in the left frontal region and into the ventricle. An older softening (related to the earlier stroke and consequent signing disorder) was present in the left posterior region, involving the cortex and white matter of the supramarginal and angular gyri. There was also old destruction of the anterior basal ganglia on the right. Injury to the left posterior hemisphere was suggested as the source of the signing disability. This case is significant as it provided the first case study of a native deaf signer and provided confirmatory evidence from autopsy regarding brain involvement.

5. Tureen, Smolik, and Tritt (1951). Described a 43-year-old congenitally deaf male who developed aphasia after hemorrhage into a left frontal tumor. Little premorbid signing information was given. The subject had a complicated medical history beginning with a fall that resulted in a linear fracture of left parietal bone. Over the course of a month he developed seizures and had several incidents of partial right-sided paralysis. One month postfall he became mentally clouded and developed a full right-sided paralysis. A left fronto-parietal craniotomy was performed, identifying a tumor with recent hemorrhage in the second frontal convolution. The glioblastoma was subcortical in extent, and involved the posterior halves of the second and third frontal convolutions. The anterior tip of the internal capsule was also invaded.

During the transient paralysis he was able to converse in sign and writing using his left hand. After the total right-sided paralysis, he lost all ability to use his left hand for signing, fingerspelling, or writing, and showed significant comprehension problems in all modalities as well. One week later some sign language production returned, but he still did not comprehend sign language. He was able to follow simple written commands and pick out objects from written cues. Fingerspelling production and comprehension were both impaired relative to reading and writing. Nine days postoperative the subject could communicate and converse in sign language and had no difficulty with fingerspelling comprehension (for the first time since the onset of the aphasia) but showed some difficulty in the production of finger-spelling. No apraxia was evident and no deficit in reading was found. Prior to release he made significant improvement in "finger speak" (sic) and speech. He was noted to have occasional memory problems for spelling.

This case is significant as it provided some documentation of the anatomy of the tumor and the surgical resection. Attempts were made to discuss loss of function in relation to specific neuroanatomical sites. However, it is unclear whether all behavioral symptoms are attributable to focal involvement or generalized pressure resultant from the tumor. For example, one might not have predicted that sign language comprehension would be severely impaired if only frontal sites were involved. The dissociation between reading and sign processing is noteworthy. However, the documentation of signing and fingerspelling impairment was sparse.

6. Douglas and Richardson (1959). Described a 21-year-old deaf female from a family with older deaf siblings. She suffered an intrapartum stroke leading to a cerebral vascular lesion with extensive damage to the left hemisphere. Initially, the subject suffered from severe right hemiplegia and right homonymous hemianopia. Six months poststroke she had regained some power of the right leg, although weakness in the right arm and hand persisted. She had a mild degree of astereognosis and impaired two-point discrimination in the right hand and full visual fields.

Immediately after the cerebrovascular accident (CVA) the subject was impaired in sign and fingerspelling production and comprehension. She made trial-and-error attempts and often made incorrect signs. She was aware of her mistakes and tried to self-correct problems. Her fingerspelling was reportedly more impaired than her signing; she exhibited perseverations and misarticulations of single letters in production. Several of the errors discussed appear to have been structurally well motivated, and would be classified today as phonemic paraphasias in fingerspelling (e.g., substituting an "F" handshape for a "D" handshape). The subject had some ability to read single words and short sentences from print, and showed no visual agnosia. She showed no constructional or motor apraxia. She was unable to name objects by written expression, or to produce spontaneous thought via writing. After 9 months there was considerable improvement in her writing, fingerspelling, and signing. In production, sign finding problems and occasional misspelling in fingerspelling were reported. Her comprehension of fingerspelling and writing were normal, but in sign comprehension she occasionally "missed" signs.

This case is significant as the subject was from a family with older deaf siblings. It is thus likely that this subject's sign language abilities were quite good, despite Douglass and Richardson's claims. Testing was rather extensive, although, typical of these early reports, fingerspelling was better documented than was sign language. Assessments of sign comprehension were completely missing. There were some tantalizing dissociations between sign/fingerspelling comprehension and reading, but this is difficult to substantiate. This case is consistent with a left-hemisphere frontal and rolandic lesion and possible parietal involvement, producing an initial global aphasia affecting all modalities and resolving to an anomic aphasia.

7. Sarno, Swisher, and Sarno (1969).

Presented a detailed case study of a 69-year-old male born with profound, bilateral, sensorineural hearing loss from a family with two deaf siblings. He attended a residential school for the deaf and was reported to have learned sign language at age 7. This subject suffered a left cerebral infarct, exact site undetermined, which resulted in right central facial weakness, moderate paresis of the right arm, and mild weakness of the right leg. He was tested three times, at 8 weeks, 11 weeks, and 23 weeks poststroke. The subject was not severely impaired in ordinary conversational signing, but showed difficulty on structured tasks. The subject showed more expressive than receptive problems.

This subject was described as an efficient communicator using a combination of signing, lip reading, reading, and writing. The subject was tested in a variety of communicative modalities. Sarno et al. (1969) reported a hierarchy of impairment in the subject; he performed the worst in speaking, somewhat better in writing and fingerspelling, and best in sign language. Although he showed no oral apraxia, the subject was unable to produce speech, often pointing to his mouth in frustration. In fingerspelling production and repetition, he exhibited perseverations and substitutions. He showed some limited ability to write and copy simple geometric forms and words, but could not spontaneously write. His signing ability was described as better than his fingerspelling, but less proficient than his prestroke signing. The subject was successful in performing ideomotor and ideational gestures, and had no difficulty in manipulating objects.

Sign language and fingerspelling comprehension were assessed via informal conversation. The subject was able to understand and correctly respond to signed questions. However, he was less responsive to fingerspelling than to signing. A modified Token Test (De Renzi & Vignolo, 1962) was administered to evaluate comprehension in a variety of modalities including lip-reading, reading, and "combined method" using sign language, finger-spelling, and speech. Unfortunately, the Token Test was not administered in sign language alone, thus limiting an important cross-modality comparison. The subject performed best in reading, less well in the combined method, and worst in lip-reading. Additional tests of reading indicated he showed a moderate impairment. Overall, sign language showed more improvement than fingerspelling. Some speech ability returned.

This case is significant as it provided the first thorough testing of a subject in various language modalities, and it provided good premorbid language history. It is one of the few cases that provided audiological assessment to document the degree of hearing loss. The subject's deaf wife assisted in the administration and assessment of testing. It is very unfortunate that lesion localization is not available in this case. The Sarno et al. interpretation of their case was somewhat confusing. They reported that the subject showed a hierarchy of communicative abilities, yet they concluded that the areas and processes in the dominant hemisphere that subserve communication functions in congenitally deaf persons are the same as those in hearing individuals. What this case may point to, however, are the subtle differences between the neural language representations of sign language, speech and fingerspelling. This line of reasoning unfortunately was not pursued.

8. Meckler, Mack, and Bennet (1979). Described a case of a 19-year-old, hearing, ASL–English bilingual, left-handed male. The subject learned both sign and speech concurrently in infancy. Following a closed-head injury from an auto accident, he presented with deep right hemiparesis, right dystonia, and right hemisensory deficits for all modalities. No visual field deficits were present, and he could move his tongue and swallow. The subject was able to use his left limb without apraxia, and showed no spatial deficits. He remained mute and globally aphasic, but initially appeared to have recovered sign language to a greater degree than spoken language (although both were highly deficient). In addition, he used signing more accurately than fingerspelling. Six months postaccident, he remained globally aphasic, with some improvements in motor functions. The subject showed little spontaneous use of spoken language, seemed frustrated when attempting to speak intelligibly, and could not construct a sentence of two to three words written on cards. The subject showed a common pattern of global aphasia evolving into a nonfluent aphasia, following improvement in comprehension. The subject eventually showed greatest recovery in spoken language comprehension, whereas expressive language, both spoken and signed, showed much less improvement.

Meckler et al. (1979) attributed the improvement in spoken language comprehension to practice and interpreted the commonality of expressive language as supporting commonality in sign and speech impairment following left-hemisphere damage. This case, like the case of Sarno et al. (case 7), was taken by the authors as evidence of a common deficit in spoken and signed aphasias. However, if identical brain systems are being used, one would have to expect sign language comprehension on a par with spoken language comprehension in the absence of any visuospatial impairment. Little detail of sign comprehension tests was given; thus it is difficult to assess the authors' claim.

9. Underwood and Paulson (1981). Described a 57-year-old, left-handed, profoundly deaf male. This subject learned sign language at age 7 years in a residential school for the deaf, and was married to a deaf woman. The subject was reported to have some lip-reading ability, functional writing abilities, and good math skills. He used sign language exclusively with his wife. He suffered a left cerebral artery thrombosis with possible ischemic infarct. Right flaccid hemiplegia and aphasia were noted. The subject had severe production problems in sign language, and inconsistently signed names of simple objects, with word-finding difficulties and word substitutions. Automatic signing was noted; he could count from 1 to 10 and sign the Lord's Prayer. He produced jargon fingerspelling, and perseverations were noted. Repetition was inconsistent for single signs and fingerspelled items. Jargon, word substitutions, and perseverations were noted in writing as well. He showed comprehension problems at the single-sign level, and was unable to read. Six months after the first incident, the subject suffered another stroke and died. No autopsy or neuroradiological reports were available. Underwood and Paulson reported that this subject showed a better ability to fingerspell than sign, although no detailed documentation of either skill was presented, and no report of any fingerspelling comprehension was mentioned. Underwood and Paulson suggested that this pattern of dissolution may have been due to the fact that fingerspelling is one handed while signing is often two handed. This explanation, however, can be firmly rejected. Deaf signers with one of the manual articulators temporarily (or permanently) occupied, like hearing persons talking with a cigar in the mouth, have systematic compensatory strategies (Battison, 1978). Hemiplegia is unlikely to result in a subject favoring fingerspelling over sign. There are some questions raised by the assessment of abilities in this subject. Formational problems were reported in fingerspelling, but no signed mistakes were noted. From the evidence presented, it is unclear whether fingerspelling was actually less impaired than signing.

10a. Chiarello, Knight, and Mandel (1982). Described L.K., a 65-year-old prelingually deaf woman fluent in ASL, who suffered a left-hemisphere stroke. L.K. was deafened at age 6 months and entered a residential school for the deaf at age 5 years, where she was instructed in oral techniques and fingerspelling. The report stated she learned ASL at age 7 or 8 years. A CT scan revealed a circumscribed cortical lesion in the region of the left inferior parietal lobule that extended subcortically into the left frontal lobe, undercutting Broadman's areas 4, 3, 1, and 2. Both traditional Broca's and Wernicke's areas were spared. Neurological examination revealed moderate weakness of arm, and slight right leg and facial weakness. She had marked right-sided sensory decrease to primary somatosensory modalities, with the arm most severely affected. No hemi-inattention was noted.

L.K. initially presented with severe anomia and comprehension loss in both ASL and fingerspelling. She produced neologistic output and perseverative responses. Two weeks postonset her sign output improved, although it was still impaired. Spontaneous expression included a great deal of gesturing rather than signing, and many sign misarticulations. Grammatical modulations were generally preserved. Marked anomia in ASL, fingerspelling, and written responses persisted. Signing resolved to relatively fluent output, with many literal paraphasias and moderate anomia. ASL comprehension was intact at the single-sign level but broke down with increasing complexity. Agraphia was apparent under all test conditions. Reading comprehension paralleled sign comprehension. Apraxia testing revealed a preserved ability to imitate single, nonrepresentational, intransitive or transitive gestures; however, performance on the Kimura et al. (1976) test of nonrepresentational sequences was impaired. Object use was fully intact, as was pantomime comprehension. Imitation of signs was limited to single- and two-sign phrases.

Chiarello et al. reported that this subject's symptoms resembled those of a hearing aphasic with posterior lesions: namely, fluent but paraphasic signing, anomia, impaired comprehension and repetition, alexia, with agraphia, and elements of neologist jargon. She had a pronounced sequential movement-copying disorder, reduced short-term memory, and acalculia. The authors thus concluded that most aphasia symptoms are not modality dependent, but rather reflect a disruption of linguistic processes common to all human languages. This case is significant as it provided careful examination of the signing deficit and had good anatomical localization. This case study indicates the importance of the left supramarginal and angular gyri in the comprehension of visual/gestural language.

10b. Poizner, Klima, and Bellugi (1987). Poizner et al. presented a more thorough investigation of the sign forms produced by L.K. than was originally given in Chiarello et al. (1982). In Poizner et al.'s studies, L.K. is referred to as K.L. This subject effortlessly produced long strings of signs, with a wide range of correctly employed morphological and syntactic forms. However, this signer showed impairment at the phonological (formational) level, making frequent errors in the selection of hand configurations, movements, and places of articulation.

11. Poizner, Klima, and Bellugi (1987). Subject P.D. lost his hearing at age 5 years. At age 71 years, he suffered a left middle cerebral artery occlusion with a subsequent hemiparesis on the right, and aphasia in spoken and signed language. A CT scan revealed a subcortical lesion in the left hemisphere with anterior focus deep to Broca's area, including major portions of the basal ganglia. The lesion extended posteriorly into the white matter in the left parietal lobe. P.D. had a fluent sign aphasia, with impaired morphology and syntax and preserved phonology. He made frequent selectional errors in ASL morphology. These errors involved substitutions of one inflectional form for another, as well as occasional inappropriate inflections or derivations of root forms. This signer was described as paragrammatic. His writing paralleled his sign output, with frequent lexical selection errors but largely preserved syntax. Initially, P.D. was described as apraxic (Kimura, Battison, & Lubert, 1976), but when tested nearly 10 years poststroke he was within normal limits of the Kimura and Archibald test (1974). This case is noteworthy for several reasons. First, the discrepancies between apraxia testing sessions amplified the theoretically different points of view held between Poizner et al. and Kimura et al. Second, the morphological impairments observed in this subject are very atypical and unusual within the context of aphasia. Though discounted by Poizner et al., the possibility that language performance may have reflected the effects of dementia has been raised (Helm-Estabrooks, 1984). Subtle impairments on certain visuospatial tasks add to this concern.

12. Poizner, Klima, and Bellugi (1987). Subject G.D. was a 38-year-old congenitally deaf signer with deaf siblings and a deaf family. G.D. suffered a left-hemisphere stroke 8 months prior to initial testing. A CT scan revealed a large left-hemisphere lesion that involved most of the convexity of the left frontal lobe, including Broca's area and the anterior portions of the superior and middle temporal gyri. This signer was grossly impaired in sign output. At the initial time of testing the subject's signing was dysfluent, reduced to single-sign utterances of largely referential signs, and lacking in any required syntactic or morphological markings of ASL. Her sign language comprehension skills were intact, however. Her language profile was like that of a hearing person classified as having Broca's aphasia. Her writing paralleled her signing (agrammatic). During testing, G.D. relied heavily on fingerspelling; however, she was observed making frequent fingerspelling transpositions and perseverations. In addition, she attempted to mouth English words despite bucco-facial apraxia. G.D. was aware of her problems and made frequent corrections. Poizner et al. reported that this subject had an ideomotor apraxia, based on a failure to perform transitive limb movements such as wash a bowl, write her name, and so forth. However, she scored within normal limits on the Kimura nonsymbolic sequential movement copying test. Corina (unpublished observation) analyzed facial expression data from G.D. based on testing conducted 2 years after the initial reports. By this time, G.D. showed moderate improvement, with increasing phrase length and moderate sign-finding problems. She showed impairment in her use of facial behaviors to mark linguistic distinctions required in ASL, but no deficit in use of facial behaviors to communicate affective information.

G.D.'s case was significant as her impairment most closely approximated a traditional Broca's aphasia profile, with impaired sign production but well-preserved comprehension. She was described as "agrammatic" in several publications based on her productive profile. Unfortunately, thorough testing of performance on a variety of ASL syntactic constructions was not reported.

13. Poizner and Kegl (1992).   Reported a case of a 48-year-old congenitally deaf signer referred to as N.S. He attended residential school for the deaf and had a deaf twin brother. At age 27 years, N.S. suffered a left parietal lesion resulting from a compound fracture to the left side of the skull and damage to underlying brain matter. Neurological examination revealed a partial right hemiparesis. His right arm had strength but was not well controlled. He had a substantial pyramidal deficit, as indicated by the fact that the fingers on his right hand could not function independently. He was not apraxic on ideomotor tests or on the Kimura gesture copying task. He was reported as having occasional ordering reversals of ASL compound signs and occasional lexical access errors. He showed both production and comprehension problems at the sentence level. The major complaint, however, was that N.S. had difficulty in processing rapidly presented signed material. Poizner and Kegel provided evidence that this deficit was limited to the rapid processing of linguistic, but not nonlinguistic, information.

14. Brentari, Poizner, and Kegl (1995).   Subject E.N. was briefly reported in a study comparing sign production in left-hemisphere-damaged and Parkinsonian signers. E.N. was an 81-year-old female from a deaf family with a primarily subcortical lesion. A CT scan revealed an infarction in the distribution of the left posterior cerebral artery, involving the posterior limb of the internal capsule, small portions of the posterior thalamus on the left, and left-medial occipital cortex. Tested 5 years postonset, she presented with motorically fluent sign production with sublexical and semantic paraphasias. Elements of her signing were similar to those observed in Parkinsonian signing; for example, she displayed reduced amplitude in sign production. This appeared to be a case of subcortical aphasia. No data on comprehension were given.

15. Hickok, Klima, Kritchevsky, and Bellugi (1995). Reported on a female signer, deaf from 18 months of age. She attended a residential school for the deaf and was an active member of the deaf community. She suffered an ischemic infarction involving the left posterior cerebral artery. The medial left temporal and occipital lobes, left occipital pole, and adjacent anterior white matter were affected. This subject had preserved sign production (with occasional paraphasias) but severely impaired sign comprehension. Sign comprehension at the sentence level was severely impaired, whereas single-sign production remained reasonably intact, with occasional semantic field errors in confrontation naming. Fingerspelling comprehension was impaired. Single-sign repetition was reasonably intact, but signed sentence repetition was severely impaired. Reading and writing were severely impaired. Hickok et al. argued that a disconnection syndrome, in which visual information from the intact right visual field was unable to project to the language region of the left hemisphere, explained her symptoms. However, the subject was able to understand single signs with only some semantic errors. This case is noteworthy as it indicates a possible right-hemisphere contribution to single-sign comprehension. Moreover, the observation of the differential degree of impairment for single signs (moderate impairment) versus single written words (near total inability to read single words) suggests that sign comprehension is not a manual encoding of written language comprehension (Hickok et al., 1995).

16. Corina, Poizner, Feinberg, Dowd, and O'Grady (1992). Reported the case of W.L., a 76-year-old congenitally deaf male with two deaf signing brothers. He was a skilled signer, as documented by a rare video interview obtained 6 months prior to his stroke. A CT scan revealed large fronto-tempo-parietal lesions, including Broadman's areas 44 and 45 and white matter tracts. Wernicke's area was undercut but not cortically involved. There was also considerable damage to the white matter deep into the inferior parietal lobule. The damage produced a marked sign language aphasia affecting both production and comprehension of signs. Formational problems in sign phonology were noted in addition to semantic blends. Sign comprehension was limited. Interestingly, W.L. showed little apraxia, and produced unencumbered pantomime. Both comprehension and production of pantomime were found to be better preserved than sign language.

Right-Hemisphere Cases

17. Poizner, Klima, and Bellugi (1987). Subject S.M. was a 71-year-old congenitally deaf female. S.M. entered a residential school for deaf children at age 11 years. She was a fluent signer and had a deaf spouse. She suffered a stroke 1 year prior to testing. Neurological examination revealed paralysis of her left arm and leg, and deficits in tactile stimulation in the entire left side. She exhibited saccaddic eye movement towards her left, but no visual field deficits. A CT scan confirmed a large lesion involving most of the territory of the right middle cerebral artery. S.M. showed no deficits in sign production. She used complex sentences exhibiting intact morphology and syntax and made no sublexical errors. S.M. showed appropriate use of spatial classifiers. Her writing ability was also well preserved. Her comprehension of phonological and morphological distinctions was unimpaired. However, on tests of comprehension of ASL syntax, S.M. performed worse than control subjects. In nonlanguage visuospatial tests, S.M. showed impaired performance on WAIS-R block design and drawings. She exhibited hemispatial neglect.

18. Poizner, Klima, and Bellugi (1987).   Subject B.I. was a 75-year-old congenitally deaf female. She suffered a stroke 3 years prior to testing. Neurological examination revealed a dense paralysis of the left arm. Infarct was suspected in the distribution of the right middle cerebral artery, but no CT scan was obtained. B.I.'s signing was fluent and grammatical; however, she did commit sublexical errors in production. These errors included problems in specifying the correct orientations of some signs, and in one instance error was attributed to hemispatial neglect, specifying only half a sign. Nonlanguage visuospatial tests revealed impaired performance on WAIS block design and drawing tasks, hemispatial neglect, and impaired face discrimination. B.I. was noteworthy because she exhibited distortions of signing space when conveying topographic relations, but retained intact signing space for distinguishing syntactic relationships.

19. Poizner, Klima, and Bellugi (1987).   Subject G.G. was an 81-year-old male deafened at age 5 due to spinal meningitis. G.G. suffered a CVA at age 78. He initially presented with left-sided weakness, which resolved to a slight limp and left-sided facial weakness. He had difficulty recognizing objects felt with the left hand. His visual fields were intact. A CT scan revealed a lesion in the temporal-parietal right hemisphere, involving cortex and underlying white matter in the superior temporal gyrus, and extending inferiorly to partially involve the middle temporal gyrus. Posteriorly, the lesion extended into lower portion of the inferior parietal lobule, involving mainly the angular gyrus and minimally the supramarginal gyrus. Language testing revealed no impairments in ASL language production or in written expression. In comprehension, G.G. showed no deficits in distinguishing phonological or morphological distinctions, but scored at ranges equivalent to left-hemisphere-damaged signers on tests of spatial syntax.

On non-language visuospatial abilities, G.G. was somewhat impaired. He showed preserved drawing abilities on WAIS block design and drawing tasks, and only slight distortions in copying the Rey–Osterreith Complex Figure. He was not impaired on facial recognition tasks, but showed great difficulty in judgments of line orientation.

20. Corina, Poizner, et al. (1992); Corina et al. (1996).   Subject J.H. was a 61-year-old congenitally deaf male who suffered a right-hemisphere infarct 13 years prior to testing. The right-hemisphere stroke involved central portions of the frontal, parietal, and temporal lobes, as well as associated deep white matter and basal ganglia structures. Born to normally hearing parents, J.H. entered a residential school for the deaf when he was 5 years old. He was a fluent signer and was an active member of the Deaf Community prior to his CVA.

J.H. showed no evidence of core language impairment in either production or comprehension. However, elements of his discourse production were impaired. J.H.'s performance on a variety of nonlanguage, visuospatial tests revealed frank disruptions. J.H. showed profound impairments in line orientation judgments (Benton et al., 1977), form perception (Delis et al., 1983), and visuo-constructive tasks. One persistent finding in the testing of J.H.'s visuospatial abilities was left-sided neglect and double simultaneous extinction in all sensory domains. Surprisingly, J.H.'s ability to process visual linguistic signs and sentences was not affected by extinction. In contrast, his processing of nonlinguistic objects was severely impaired.

21. Corina, Bellugi, Kritchevsky, O'Grady, Batch, and Norman (1990); Kegl and Poizner (1991); Poizner and Kegl (1992).   Subject D.N. was a 35-year-old hearing female who worked as an interpreter and instructor for the deaf. She was tested and reported as subject A.S. in publications of Poizner and colleagues. She had deaf grandparents and was exposed to signing from an early age; however, she reported not learning ASL formally until she was in college. D.N. suffered a right occipital hematoma and underwent subsequent resection of an occipital arteriovenous malformation. An MRI scan revealed an area of abnormal signal intensity involving the posterior right hemisphere. The lesion was predominantly medial and involved the upper part of the occipital lobe. It extended to involve the superior lobule but may have involved some of the deep white matter coming from this structure. There was an enlargement of the right lateral ventricle, particularly posteriorly in the region of this abnormal signal intensity. The lesion produced a lower left quadrant visual field cut.

Language testing revealed that she was nearly at ceiling on every language measure administered, both in English and in ASL. In her signing, D.N. showed full command of morphological devices, excellent use of aspectual and syntactic constructions, correct lexical choice, and intact phonology. Nonlanguage testing revealed only slight impairment on Benton's line orientation test and on the copying of the Rey Complex Figure. She was very slow but accurate in WAIS-R Block Design. Her nonlanguage visual memory was impaired, and D.N. showed problems in mental rotation (see Emmorey et al., 1995, for some discussion).

D.N. did show problems in using some spatial devices in ASL. She showed impairments in coreference and discourse cohesion. This was manifested as a lack of maintenance of spatial indexing for person agreement, pronominal reference, and locative indexing. Corina reported a hierarchy of impairment in D.N.'s mapping of spatial relations using linguistic devices, which was worse in ASL than in English. D.N. showed great problems with ASL descriptions of room layouts, which was not evident in her analogous spoken descriptions. D.N. revealed specific deficits in her use of ASL classifiers. Poizner and Kegl (1992) reported that D.N.'s use of signing space was asymmetrical, favoring right-sided locations.

ACKNOWLEDGMENTS

This work was supported in part from a grant from the University of Washington, RRF-13401, awarded to David Corina. I thank Drs. Coppens, Lebrun, and Basso, and Connie Schachtel for their editorial assistance.

REFERENCES

Baker, C., & Padden, C. (1978). Focusing on the nonmanual components of American Sign Language. In P. Siple (Ed.), *Understanding language through sign language research* (pp. 27–57). New York: Academic Press.

Baker-Shenk, C. (1983). *A micro analysis of the nonmanual components of questions in American Sign Language.* Unpublished doctoral dissertation, University of California, Berkeley.

Bates, E., & Wulfeck, B. (1989). Crosslinguistics studies of aphasia. In B. MacWhinney & E. Bates (Eds.), *The crosslinguistic study of sentence processing* (pp. 328–371). New York: Cambridge University Press.

Bates, E., Wulfeck, B., & MacWhinney, B. (1991). Cross-linguistic studies in aphasia: An overview. *Brain and Language, 41*(2), 123–148.

Battison, R. (1978). *Lexical borrowing in American Sign Language.* Silver Spring, MD: Linstok Press.

Bellugi, U., Bihrle, A., & Corina, D. (1991). Linguistic and spatial development: Dissociations between cognitive domains. In N. A. Krasnegor, D. M. Rumaugh, R. L. Schiefelbusch, & M. Studdert-Kennedy (Eds.), *Biological determinants of language development* (pp. 363–393). Hillsdale, NJ: Lawrence Erlbaum Associates.

Blumstein, S. E. (1973). *A phonological investigation of aphasic speech.* The Hague: Mouton.

Boyes, P. (1973). *Developmental phonology for ASL.* Unpublished manuscript, Salk Institute for Biological Studies at La Jolla, CA.

Brentari, D. (1990). *Theoretical foundations of American Sign Language phonology.* Unpublished doctoral dissertation, University of Chicago, Chicago.

Brentari, D., Poizner, H., & Kegl, J. (1995). Aphasic and Parkinsonian signing: Differences in phonological disruption. *Brain and Language, 48*(1), 69–105.

Brody, J. (1992, June 10). When brain damage disrupts speech. *New York Times,* p. C13.

Brownell, H. H., Simpson T. L., Bihrle, A. M., & Potter H. H. (1990). Appreciation of metaphoric alternative word meanings by left and right brain-damaged patients. *Neuropsychologia, 28*, 375–383.

Burr, C. (1905). Loss of sign language in a deaf mute from cerebral tumor and softening. *New York Medical Journal, 81*, 1106–1108.

Caplan, D., Vanier, M., & Baker, C. (1986). A case study of reproduction conduction aphasia: 1. Word production. *Cognitive Neuropsychology, 3*(1), 99–128.

Chiarello, C., Knight, R., & Mandel, M. (1982). Aphasia in a prelingually deaf woman. *Brain, 105*, 29–51.

Corina, D. P. (1989). Recognition of affective and noncanonical linguistic facial expressions in hearing and deaf subjects. *Brain and Cognition, 9*, 227–237.

Corina, D. P., Bellugi, U., Kritchevsky, M., O'Grady-Batch, L., & Norman, F. (1990, October). *Spatial relations in signed versus spoken language: Clues to right parietal functions.* Paper presented at the meeting of the Academy of Aphasia, Baltimore, MD.

Corina, D. P., Kritchevsky, M., & Bellugi, U. (1992). Linguistic permeability of unilateral neglect: Evidence from American Sign Language. *Proceedings of the 14th Annual Conference of the Cognitive Science Society,* (pp. 384–389). Hillsdale, NJ: Lawrence Erlbaum Associates.

Corina, D. P., Kritchevsky, M., & Bellugi, U. (1996). Visual language processing and unilateral neglect: Evidence from American Sign Language. *Cognitive Neuropsychology, 13*(3), 321–351.

Corina, D. P., Poizner, H. P., Feinberg, T., Dowd, D., & O'Grady, L. (1992). Dissociation between linguistic and non-linguistic gestural systems: A case for compositionality. *Brain and Language, 43*, 414–447.

Corina, D. P., & Sandler, W. (1993). On the nature of phonological structure in sign language. *Phonology, 10*(2), 165–207.

Coulter, G. R., & Anderson, S. R. (1993). Introduction. In G. Coulter (Ed.), *Phonetics and phonology* (pp. 1–16). San Diego: Academic Press.

Critchley, M. (1938). Aphasia in a partial deaf-mute. *Brain, 61*, 163–169.

Damasio, H. (1991). Neuroanatomical correlates of the aphasias. In M. T. Sarno (Ed.), *Acquired aphasia* (pp. 45–71). San Diego: Academic Press.

Delis, D. C., Wapner, W., Gardner, H., Moses, J. A. (1983). The contribution of the right hemisphere to the organization of paragraphs. *Cortex, 19*, 43–50.

De Renzi, E., & Vignolo, L. (1962). The Token Test: A sensitive test to detect receptive disturbances in aphasics. *Brain, 85*, 655–678.

Douglass, E., & Richardson, J. (1959). Aphasia in a congenital deaf-mute. *Brain, 82*, 68–80.

Dronkers, N. F., Redfern, B. B., & Ludy, C. A. (1995). Lesion localization in chronic Wernicke's aphasia. *Brain and Language, 51*, 62–65.

Ekman, P., & Friesen, W. V. (1978). *Facial action coding system.* Palo Alto, CA: Consulting Psychologist Press.

Emmorey, K. (1996). The confluence of space and language in signed languages. In P. Bloom, M. Peterson, L. Nadel, & M. Garrett (Eds.), *Language and space* (pp. 171–209). Cambridge: MIT Press.

Emmorey, K., Corina, D. P., & Bellugi, U. (1995). Differential processing of topographic and referential functions of space. In K. Emmorey & J. Reilly (Eds.), *Language, gesture and space* (pp. 43–62). Hillsdale, NJ: Lawrence Erlbaum Associates.

Fromkin, V. A. (1991). Language and brain: Redefining the goals and methodology of linguistics. In A. Kasher (Ed.), *The Chomskyan turn* (pp. 78–103). Cambridge: Blackwell.

Geschwind, N. (1965). Disconnection syndromes in animals and man. *Brain, 88*, 237–294, 585–644.

Geschwind, N., & Damasio, A. R. (1985). Apraxia. *Handbook of Clinical Neurology, 1*(45), 423–432.

Goodglass, H. (1993). *Understanding aphasia.* San Diego: Academic Press.

Grasset, J. (1896). Aphasie de la main droite chez un sourd-muet. *Le Progrès Medical, 4*, 169.

Grosjean, F. (1982). *Life with two languages: An introduction to bilingualism.* Cambridge, MA: Harvard University Press.

Hickok, G., Bellugi, U., & Klima, E. S. (1996). The neurobiology of sign language and its implications for the neural basis of language. *Nature, 381,* 699–702.

Hickok, G., Clark, K., Erhard, P., Helms-Tillery, K., Naeve-Velguth, S., Adriany, G., Hu, X., Tomaso, H., Bellugi, U., Strick, P. L., & Ugurbil, K. (1995). Effect of modality on the neural organization for language: An fMRI study of sign language production. *Society for Neuroscience Abstracts, 21*(1), 694.

Hickok, G., Klima, E., Kritchevsky, M., & Bellugi, U. (1995). A case of "sign blindness" following left occipital damage in a deaf signer. *Neuropsychologia, 33*(12), 1597–1606.

Heilman, K. M., Rothi, L. J., & Valenstein, E. (1982). Two forms of ideomotor apraxia. *Neurology, 32,* 342–346.

Helm-Estabrooks, N. (1984). A discussion of apraxia, aphasia and gestural language. *American Journal of Physiology, 46,* 884–887.

Jackson, J. H. (1878). On affections of speech from disease of the brain. *Brain, 1,* 64.

Jackson, J. H. (1932). *Selected writings of Hughlings Jackson,* Vol. 2, Ed. J. Taylor. London:

Kaplan, J. A., Brownell, H. H., Jacobs, J. R., & Gardner, H. (1990). The effects of right hemisphere damage on the pragmatic interpretation of conversational remarks. *Brain and Language, 38*(2), 315–333.

Kegl, J., & Poizner, H. (1991). The interplay between linguistic and spatial processing in a right-lesioned signer. *Journal of Clinical and Experimental Neuropsychology, 13,* 38–39.

Kertesz, A. (1993). Clinical forms of aphasia. *Acta Neurochirurgica Supplementum, 56,* 52–58.

Kettrick, K., & Hatfield, N. (1986). Bilingualism in a visuo-gestural mode. In J. Vaid (Ed.), *Language processing in bilinguals* (pp. 253–269). Hillsdale, NJ: Lawrence Erlbaum Associates.

Kimura, D. (1981). Neural mechanisms in manual signing. *Sign Language Studies, 33,* 291–312.

Kimura, D. (1993). *Neuromotor mechanisms in human communication.* Oxford: Oxford University Press.

Kimura, D., & Archibald, Y. (1974). Motor functions of the left hemisphere. *Brain, 97,* 337–350.

Kimura, D., Battison, R., & Lubert, B. (1976). Impairment of non-linguistic hand movements in a deaf aphasic. *Brain and Language, 3,* 566–571.

Klima, E., & Bellugi, U. (1979). *The signs of language.* Cambridge, MA: Harvard University Press.

Kolk, H. H., & Blomert, L. (1985). On the Bradley Hypothesis concerning agrammatism: The nonword-interference effect. *Brain and Language, 26*(1), 94–105.

Leischner, A. (1943). Die "Aphasie" der Taubstummen. *Archiv für Psychiatrie und Nervenkrankheiten, 115,* 469–548.

Levine, D. N., & Sweet, E. (1982). The neurological basis of Broca's aphasia and its implications for the cerebral control of speech. In M. Arbib, D. Caplan, & J. C. Marshall (Eds.), *Neural models of language processes* (pp. 299–325). San Diego: Academic Press.

Liddell, S. K. (1980). *American Sign Language syntax.* The Hague: Mouton.

Liddell, S. K. (1990). Four functions of a locus: Reexamining the structure of space in ASL. In C. Lucas (Ed.), *Sign language research: Theoretical issues* (pp. 176–198). Washington, DC: Gallaudet University Press.

Liddell, S. K. (1995). Real, surrogate and token space: Grammatical consequences in ASL. In K. Emmorey & J. Reilly (Eds.), *Language, gesture and space* (pp. 19–41). Mahwah, NJ: Lawrence Erlbaum Associates.

Lillo-Martin, D. C. (1991). *Universal grammar and American Sign Language: Setting the null argument parameters.* Dordrecht: Kluwer.

Lillo-Martin, D. C., & Klima, E. S. (1990). Pointing out differences: ASL pronouns in syntactic theory. In S. Fischer, D. Siple, P. DeCaro, & J. James (Eds.), *Theoretical issues in sign language research, I: Linguistics* (pp. 191–210). Chicago: University of Chicago Press.

MacWhinney, B., & Osman-Sagi, J. (1991). Inflectional marking in Hungarian aphasics. *Brain and Language, 41*(2), 165–183.

Markowicz, H., & Woodward, J. (1978). Language and the maintenance of ethnic boundaries in the deaf community. *Communication and Cognition, 2*, 29–38.

McIntire, M. (1977). The acquisition of American Sign Language hand configurations. *Sign Language Studies, 16*, 246–266.

Meadows, K. (1980). *Deafness and child development.* Berkeley: University of California Press.

Meckler, J., Mack, J., & Bennett, R. (1979). Sign language aphasia in a non-deaf-mute. *Neurology, 29*, 1037–1040.

Meier, R. P. (1991). Language acquisition by deaf children. *American Scientist, 79*, 60–70.

Menn, L., & Obler, L. K. (1990). *Agrammatic aphasia.* Amsterdam: Benjamins.

Mohr, J. P., Pessin, M. S., Finkelstein, S., Funkenstein, H. H., Duncan, G. W., & David, K. R. (1978). Broca's aphasia: Pathological and clinical. *Neurology, 28*, 311–324.

Neville, H. J. (1990). Intermodal competition and compensation in development: Evidence from studies of the visual system in congenitally deaf adults. *Annals of the New York Academy of Sciences, 608*, 71–87.

Neville, H., Corina, D., Bavelier, D., Clark, V. P., Jezzard, P., Prinster, A., Padmanhaban, S., Braun, A., Rauschecker, J., & Turner, R. (1995). Effects of early experience on cerebral organization for language: An fMRI study of sentence processing in English and ASL by hearing and deaf subjects. *Human Brain Mapping, Supplement 1*, 278.

Newport, E. L., & Meier, R. P. (1985). The acquisition of American Sign Language. In D. I. Slobin (Ed.), *The crosslinguistic study of language acquisition: Vol. 1. The data* (pp. 881–938). Hillsdale, NJ: Lawrence Erlbaum Associates.

Newport, E. L., & Supalla, T. (1980). Clues from the acquisition of signed and spoken language. In U. Bellugi & M. Studdert-Kennedy (Eds.), *Signed and spoken language: Biological constraints on linguistic form* (pp. 187–211). Weinheim/Deerfield Beach, FL: Verlag Chemie.

Nielsen, J. M. (1946). *Agnosia, apraxia and aphasia.* New York: Hoeber.

Padden, C. (1983). *Interaction of morphology and syntax in American Sign Language.* Unpublished doctoral dissertation, University of California, San Diego.

Padden, C., & Humphries, T. (1988). *Deaf in America: Voices from a culture.* Cambridge, MA: Havard University Press.

Perlmutter, D. (1993). Sonority and syllable structure in American Sign Language. In G. Coulter (Ed.), *Phonetics and phonology* (pp. 227–259). San Diego: Academic Press.

Poizner, H., & Kegl, J. (1992). Neural basis of language and motor behavior: Perspectives from American Sign Language. *Aphasiology, 6*(3), 219–256.

Poizner, H., Klima, E. S., & Bellugi, U. (1987). *What the hands reveal about the brain.* Cambridge, MA: MIT Press.

Ramsey, C. (1989). Language planning in deaf education. In U. C. Lucas (Ed.), *Sociolinguistics of the deaf community* (pp. 123–146). San Diego: Academic Press.

Rehak, A., Kaplan, J. A., Weylman, S. T., Kelly, B., Brownell, H. H., & Gardner, H. (1992). Story processing in right-hemisphere brain-damaged patients. *Brain and Language, 42*(3), 320–336.

Rothi, L. J. G., Ochipa, C., & Heilman, K. M. (1991). A cognitive neuropsychological model of limb praxis. *Cognitive Neuropsychology, 8*(6), 443–458.

Sarno, J., Swisher, L., & Sarno, M. (1969). Aphasia in a congenitally deaf man. *Cortex, 5*, 398–414.

Schein, J. D., & Delk, M. (1974). *The deaf population in the United States.* Silver Spring, MD: National Association for the Deaf.

Slobin, D. I. (1991). Aphasia in Turkish: Speech production in Broca's and Wernicke's patients. *Brain and Language, 41*(2), 149–164.

Soderfeldt, B. (1994). *Signing in the brain.* Unpublished doctoral dissertation, Acta Universitatius Upsaliensis, Uppsala, Sweden.

Soderfeldt, B., Ronnberg, J., & Risberg, J. (1994). Regional cerebral blood flow in sign language users. *Brain and Language, 46*, 59–68.

Stokoe, W., Casterline, D., & Corneberg. C. (1965). *A dictionary of American Sign Language on linguistic principles.* Silver Spring, MD: Linstok Press.

Supalla, T. (1982). *Acquisition of verbs of motion and location in American Sign Language.* Unpublished doctoral dissertation, University of California, San Diego.

Supalla, T. (1986). The classifier system in American Sign Language. In C. Craig (Ed.), *Noun classes and categorization* (pp. 181–214). Amsterdam: Benjamins.

Sutton-Spence, W. B., & Allsop, L. (1990). Variation and recent change in fingerspelling in British Sign Language. *Language Variation and Change, 2*(3), 313–330.

Tureen, L., Smolik, E., & Tritt, J. (1951). Aphasia in a deaf mute. *Neurology, 1*, 237–244.

Tzeng, O. J. L., Chen, S., & Hung, D. (1991). The classifier problem in Chinese aphasia. *Brain and Language, 41*, 184–202.

Underwood, J. K., & Paulson, C. J. (1981). Aphasia and congenital deafness: A case study. *Brain and Language, 12*, 285–291.

Wilcox, S. (1992). The phonetics of fingerspelling. In *Studies in speech pathology and clinical linguistics* (pp. 1–108). Amsterdam: Benjamins.

Zein, G., Say, K., Bellugi, U., Corina, D., & Reilly, J. S. (1993, October). *The role of the right hemisphere for extra-syntactic aspects of ASL.* Paper presented at the meeting of the Academy of Aphasia, Tucson, AZ.

CHAPTER NINE

How Atypical Are the Atypical Aphasias?

Patrick Coppens
Moorhead State University, Moorhead, Minnesota

Yvan Lebrun
Vrije Universiteit Brussel, Brussels, Belgium

Anna Basso
Institute of Clinical Neurology, Milan University

The preceding eight chapters each deal with a population that is considered atypical. Although the reason why a specific population is atypical is idiosyncratic, in each case the ultimate rationale involves the notion that somehow these individuals are at risk for developing unusual language lateralization or organization patterns. This final chapter is an attempt at deducing general tendencies across all the populations discussed based on the individual authors' conclusions.

Among the populations analyzed in this volume, only crossed aphasia patients and a significant percentage of left-handed aphasic patients clearly have a different language lateralization. This is in fact the defining characteristic for these "atypical" populations. Still, in a majority of the crossed aphasia patients cases, the assumed genetic aberration of a right-hemisphere language dominance in a right-handed individual causes language to be organized in the right hemisphere similarly as it would be in the left hemisphere. A significant number of exceptions have been reported, and a number of interesting features, such as a discrepancy between oral and written language, have been emphasized. However, such exceptions and symptoms have also been described in "typical" aphasia patients. Similarly, Basso and Rusconi conclude that, in the majority of left-handed patients who are left-hemisphere dominant, language organization is comparable to that in right-handed individuals. Moreover, the left-handed patients who become aphasic following a right-hemisphere lesion show a mirror-image language organization. The only difference Basso and Rusconi observed between left-handed right-hemisphere-damaged patients and right-handed left-hemisphere-damaged patient was based on overall severity at onset, but not on qualitative differences or even on recovery rate. These conclusions challenge the classical views associated with left-handedness and aphasia. Also, several authors agree that "typical" aphasia is not understood well enough to adequately define atypicalities (e.g., Basso & Rusconi; Coppens & Hungerford).

In the present volume, most authors conclude that the population they investigate does not evidence a different language lateralization or representation as compared to the "typical" aphasia population. Therefore, there is no compelling reason why what we know about language organization should not apply to a great majority of the world population. In other words, we can now address the concerns of Lecours and Goodglass (cited in the introduction to this volume): Language organization is much more universal than previously assumed. The current model can indeed apply to the "atypical" populations described in this volume.

The authors who have found some, albeit limited, differences between their "atypical" aphasic population and classic aphasia (e.g., Coppens, Parente, & Lecours; Corina) do not contend that language lateralization is different in the two populations. Rather, they report that their studied population may use different language strategies, given the idiosyncrasies of the particular linguistic system used. For example, Corina focuses on a very specific characteristic of American Sign Language that combines syntactic and spatial characteristics. Nevertheless, it appears that the visuospatial and the linguistic components are neatly integrated instead of the spatial contribution of the right hemisphere replacing a left-hemisphere-mediated linguistic component; otherwise, right-hemisphere lesions would give rise to purely linguistic symptoms, which is clearly not the case. Paradis argues that a greater right-hemisphere activity (e.g., in children or bilinguals) may represent a more pragmatic (i.e., more situational, more implicit) approach to language. In other words, the right hemisphere is recruited not because it plays a more important part in linguistic functions, but simply because right-hemisphere skills (inferential, contextual) come into play. Still, Paquier and van Dongen argue that even children have a much more "adult-like" language representation than previously thought. Interestingly, Paradis' rationale also fits what we know about illiterate individuals. Luria clearly showed that the illiterate population uses a more concrete approach to language, and Lecours et al. may have identified a limited right-hemisphere contribution to naming (Coppens et al.).

These differences can be explained in functional terms as extensions of the language variability that must be present between two speakers of the same language or within the same speaker at different times. Indeed, at a microlinguistic level, it is evident that two people will have different lexicons. One person may have a more extensive vocabulary than another, or in the case of speakers of two different languages, their phonological representations will be different. Similarly, Yamadori argues that Kana and Kanji are probably processed differently in the posterior areas of the left hemisphere. Also, Paradis compares bilingual speakers to monolingual speakers using different registers. Interpreting all these variations as different underlying language representations leads to the *reductio ad absurdum* argument that language organization is idiosyncratic. Instead, we argue that language organization is essentially universal, but that there are differences in strategies between and within language users. Incidentally, Gandour expresses the same conclusion in terms of "surface" differences using the same "underlying brain mechanisms."

Author Index

Subject Index